D0900137

LEARNING
AND MEMORY
OF KNOWLEDGE
AND SKILLS

LEARNING
MᴬⁿᴰEMORY
KᴼᶠNOWLEDGE
SᴬⁿᴰKILLS
DURABILITY AND SPECIFICITY

ALICE F. HEALY
LYLE E. BOURNE, JR.

SAGE Publications
International Educational and Professional Publisher
Thousand Oaks   London   New Delhi

For information address:

 SAGE Publications, Inc.
2455 Teller Road
Thousand Oaks, California 91320

SAGE Publications Ltd.
6 Bonhill Street
London EC2A 4PU
United Kingdom

SAGE Publications India Pvt. Ltd.
M-32 Market
Greater Kailash I
New Delhi 110 048 India

Printed in the United States of America

Library of Congress Cataloging-in-Publication Data

Main entry under title:

Learning and memory of knowledge and skills: durability and
   specificity / edited by Alice F. Healy, Lyle E. Bourne, Jr.
      p. cm.
   Includes bibliographical references and index.
   ISBN 0-8039-5758-0 (hard). — ISBN 0-8039-5759-9 (pbk.)
      1. Long-term memory. 2. Learning, Psychology of.   I. Healy,
   Alice F. II. Bourne, Lyle Eugene, 1932–   .
   BF378.L65L43   1995
   153.1—dc20   94-31046

95 96 97 98 99   10 9 8 7 6 5 4 3 2 1

Sage Project Editor: Susan McElroy

We dedicate this book to the memory of our fathers,
Stanley J. Fenvessy and Lyle E. Bourne

Contents

Preface

*Durability and Specificity of
Knowledge and Skills*

ALICE F. HEALY

LYLE E. BOURNE, JR.

In the mid-1980s we (the editors) discovered that we shared a common research interest with another colleague (Anders Ericsson) in the acquisition and long-term retention of knowledge and skills. With the support of a small contract from the Air Force Human Resources Laboratory (1985-1986), we undertook a review of the empirical and theoretical literature (Fendrich et al., 1988; Ericsson & Crutcher, 1988) and we developed some new methodologies for the study of skill memory (Healy et al., 1988). We were particularly inspired by the work of Harry Bahrick (e.g., 1984) and his concept of *permastore*. But Bahrick's research, focused on knowledge acquisition and retention, seemed to us to leave open some important analogous questions concerning the long-term retention of skills. Further, it was not clear from his work whether manipulations of training could promote entry of knowledge and skill into permastore. These questions prompted us to write a research proposal, which was funded by the Army Research Institute (ARI) for the period 1986-1993 (Contracts MDA903-86-K-0155 and MDA903-90-K-0066). The experiments outlined in our initial proposal focused on some intuitive hypotheses about entry into permastore that had some empirical support. For example, we argued that automaticity (Schneider & Shiffrin, 1977) might be one prerequisite for permastore. Further, we hypothesized that the popular generation effect that had been demonstrated for episodic memory over relatively short time intervals (Slamecka & Graf, 1978) could be extended to longer retention periods and to the learning and memory of skills.

Over the next 7 years we conducted an extensive series of experiments on long-term memory for knowledge and skills. These experiments used a wide variety of training tasks, including some that were predominantly perceptual, cognitive, or motoric. In early studies we were impressed with the remarkable durability we found in some tasks in contrast to the rapid forgetting evident in others. For example, we obtained highly durable retention in tasks involving target detection, mental arithmetic, and data entry. In contrast, we observed rapid forgetting in tasks involving episodic memory for numbers, vocabulary learning, and autobiographical memory. An examination of the tasks that produced durable memory suggested that their common feature (which was not shared by the tasks that produced rapid forgetting) was what we have since called *procedural reinstatement.* According to the principle of procedural reinstatement, which is consistent with the ideas of Kolers and Roediger (1984) and Morris, Bransford, and Franks (1977), durable retention results when the procedures, or operations, employed during acquisition are reinstated, or duplicated, at the time of the retention test. This principle has important implications for education and training in that durable memory can be promoted if learners can be induced to use during training those procedures that will be required at the time of retention testing.

Since our initial work, we have begun to discover that there is at least one significant limitation on this durability phenomenon. Our more recent work has revealed that durable retention is often, and possibly always, associated with limited generalizability. That is, whenever durability is observed it is highly specific to the particular facts and skills encountered during training. For example, we observed that the benefit from training on data entry persisted undiminished over long retention intervals only for the specific number sequences that were encountered during training. This finding can be understood by extending the notion of procedural reinstatement to the reinstatement of fact-procedure combinations.

Over the years our research program has benefited from the contributions of a long list of collaborators, some of them students or postdoctoral associates at the University of Colorado and some of them visitors from other universities. The visitors included Tom Cunningham, from St. Lawrence University; Robert Proctor, now at Purdue University; Paula Schwanenflugel, from University of Georgia; Murray Singer, from University of Manitoba; and Chuck Thompson, from Kansas State University. The postdoctoral fellows included Ike Chen, now at Chinese University of Hong Kong; Bob Frick, now at State University of New York at Stony Brook; Janet Proctor, now at Purdue University; and Sheldon Tetewsky, now at McGill University. The students included Debbie Clawson, now at Catholic University;

Robert Crutcher, now at University of Illinois at Chicago; David Fendrich, now at Widener University; Antoinette Gesi, now at University of California at Santa Cruz; Rajan Mahadevan (who is the subject of research reported in Chapter 12), now at Florida State University; Lori Meiskey, now at U.S. West Advanced Technologies; Tim Rickard, now at the National Institutes of Health in Bethesda; Michael Scheall, now with the U.S. Air Force; and Bill Wittman, now at Wright-Patterson Air Force Base in Ohio. The current members of our laboratory include Immanuel Barshi (graduate student), Cheri King (postdoctoral associate), Bill Marmie (graduate student), Danielle McNamara (postdoctoral associate), Julia Moravcsik (graduate student), Steve Romero (graduate student), Vicki Schneider (postdoctoral associate), Grant Sinclair (postdoctoral associate), and Liang Tao (postdoctoral associate). We have also benefited from several very stimulating short-term visits to our laboratory, usually lasting less than a week, by prominent researchers from other universities, including Harry Bahrick, Bob Bjork, Bill Estes, Walter Schneider, and Richard Shiffrin. Finally, we are deeply indebted to the ARI officers who have supported our research, especially Michael Kaplan, George Lawton, Judith Orasanu, Michael Drillings, and Bob Wisher. Each of these named individuals advanced our work and provided inspiration for some of our studies.

In the chapters that follow we report some of the most significant research completed under this project. The book begins with a chapter summarizing our most recent studies of skill retention and transfer. (It should be noted that we have also published two other chapters reviewing earlier accomplishments in this project; see Healy et al., 1992, 1993. Also, see Healy & Sinclair, in press, for a comprehensive review of research on long-term memory for training and instruction.) The subsequent chapters are largely ones from our own laboratory documenting the durability and specificity effects found in particular paradigms. Chapters 2 through 7 describe studies exploring conditions that produce highly durable knowledge and skills and provide tests of the procedural reinstatement principle of memory durability. Chapters 8 through 12 demonstrate that, under some circumstances, durable memory is limited by high specificity. We conclude this preface with a brief outline of the contents of each of these chapters.

Chapter 1 summarizes our research on the following topics: (a) memory for temporal, spatial, and item information; (b) the Stroop effect; (c) mental calculation; and (d) vocabulary retention. It provides an overview and theoretical framework for many of the subsequent chapters in this volume.

Chapter 2 reports three experiments that investigate the conditions of acquisition and long-term retention of the complex skill of tank gunnery. No forgetting of this highly proceduralized skill was observed across

2-week to 22-month delays between training and testing. At a 1-month retention test, subjects in a part-training condition responded to threats more quickly than did subjects trained on the whole task. It is concluded that observing a part-training advantage is possible when the whole task is composed of a sequence of partial tasks.

Chapter 3 reports two experiments investigating the effects of procedural reinstatement on implicit and explicit memory for a data entry skill. The results show that both motoric repetition and perceptual repetition improve implicit memory and that motoric repetition has a stronger influence than does perceptual repetition on explicit memory.

Chapter 4 explores contextual interference effects by comparing random and blocked practice schedules in the acquisition and retention of skill in the use of logical rules. The results underline the importance of retrieval from working memory as a factor contributing to both the advantage of blocked practice in skill acquisition and the advantage of random practice in skill retention.

Chapter 5 reports experiments extending the generation effect to skills and knowledge over multiple learning trials. Specifically, a generation advantage is demonstrated for performance on difficult multiplication problems and in learning to associate nonword vocabulary terms with common English nouns. The results are explained in terms of the procedural reinstatement principle.

Chapter 6 reports two experiments evaluating memory for various aspects of course schedules learned by college students. Memory for the instructor's name (who), the course title (what), the building location of the class (where), and the time the class was held (when) were compared in one experiment involving subjects' own previous schedules and in another experiment involving the learning of other students' course schedules. A superiority for retention of where the class was held was explained in terms of the procedural reinstatement principle.

Chapter 7 reports a diary study of autobiographical memory. Data are reported from subjects who attempt to remember the date of events occurring over the previous $2\frac{1}{2}$ years of their life. The results document patterns of accuracy and error in dating performance and suggest various memory processes that might account for these patterns.

Chapter 8 reports an experiment on the effects of practice on the classic Stroop color-word interference effect. Practice effects on the Stroop task were found to be specific to the particular colors and words used as stimuli, but not to the orthographic form of the words.

Chapter 9 summarizes the results of five experiments that support a new theory of mental arithmetic. The theory assumes that arithmetic knowledge is represented in separate and distinct chunks corresponding to arithmetic facts. The results support the model by showing that the effects of practice transfer if and only if the elements of a test problem correspond to those of a practiced problem.

Chapter 10 reviews the literature on the acquisition and retention of skilled letter detection. First, studies are summarized showing that extensive training in letter detection leads to automaticity. These studies provide mixed support for two different conceptions of automaticity, namely strength-based theories and instance-based theories. Second, studies are summarized showing that the word frequency disadvantage for letter detection in prose is reduced with practice. These studies provide clear support for instance-based theories.

Chapter 11 summarizes a series of investigations on the acquisition and transfer of response selection skill. Practice rapidly leads to improvements in the speed with which particular responses are associated with particular stimuli. Practice effects are durable over a period of at least 1 week.

Chapter 12 reports an investigation of Rajan Mahadevan, who demonstrates exceptional memory performance on numerical tasks that does not transfer to their verbal counterparts. Rajan's performance is both specific to the items learned and extremely durable over time. Characteristics of Rajan's performance are compared to those of memorists studied by others.

References

Bahrick, H. P. (1984). Semantic memory content in permastore: Fifty years of memory for Spanish learned in school. *Journal of Experimental Psychology: General, 113,* 1-29.

Ericsson, K. A., & Crutcher, R. J. (1988). *Long-term retention of sequentially organized information, knowledge, and skills: An empirical review* (Tech. Rep. No. 88-14). Boulder: University of Colorado, Institute of Cognitive Science.

Fendrich, D. W., Healy, A. F., Meiskey, L., Crutcher, R. J., Little, W., & Bourne, L. E., Jr. (1988). *Skill maintenance: Literature review and theoretical analysis* (AFHRL-TP-87-73). Brooks AFB, TX: Training Systems Division, Air Force Human Resources Laboratory.

Healy, A. F., Clawson, D. M., McNamara, D. S., Marmie, W. R., Schneider, V. I., Rickard, T. C., Crutcher, R. J., King, C. L., Ericsson, K. A., & Bourne, L. E., Jr. (1993). The long-term retention of knowledge and skills. In D. Medin (Ed.), *The psychology of learning and motivation* (Vol. 30, pp. 135-164). New York: Academic Press.

Healy, A. F., Fendrich, D. W., Crutcher, R. J., Wittman, W. T., Gesi, A. T., Ericsson, K. A., & Bourne, L. E., Jr. (1992). The long-term retention of skills. In A. F. Healy, S. M. Kosslyn, & R. M. Shiffrin (Eds.), *From learning processes to cognitive processes: Essays in honor of William K. Estes* (Vol. 2, pp. 87-118). Hillsdale, NJ: Lawrence Erlbaum.

Healy, A. F., Meiskey, L., Fendrich, D. W., Crutcher, R. J., Little, W., & Bourne, L. E., Jr. (1988). *Skill maintenance: Specific sample methodologies* (AFHRL-TP-87-72). Brooks AFB, TX: Training Systems Division, Air Force Human Resources Laboratory.

Healy, A. F., & Sinclair, G. P. (in press). The long-term retention of training and instruction. In E. L. Bjork & R. A. Bjork (Eds.), *Handbook of perception and cognition: Vol. 10. Memory*. New York: Academic Press.

Kolers, P. A., & Roediger, H. L. (1984). Procedures of mind. *Journal of Verbal Learning and Verbal Behavior, 23*, 425-449.

Morris, C. D., Bransford, J. D., & Franks, J. J. (1977). Levels of processing versus transfer appropriate processing. *Journal of Verbal Learning and Verbal Behavior, 16*, 519-533.

Schneider, W., & Shiffrin, R. M. (1977). Controlled and automatic human information processing: I. Detection, search, and attention. *Psychological Review, 84*, 127-190.

Slamecka, N. J., & Graf, P. (1978). The generation effect: Delineation of a phenomenon. *Journal of Experimental Psychology: Human Learning and Memory, 4*, 592-604.

1 Optimizing the Long-Term Retention of Skills

ALICE F. HEALY

CHERI L. KING

DEBORAH M. CLAWSON

GRANT P. SINCLAIR

TIMOTHY C. RICKARD

ROBERT J. CRUTCHER

K. ANDERS ERICSSON

LYLE E. BOURNE, JR.

Studies on learning and retention of color-word interference, schedule components, list components, mental arithmetic, and vocabulary acquisition suggest that optimal retention depends on conditions of training, conditions of retention testing, and use of appropriate learning strategies. Guidelines are proposed for optimizing the long-term retention of skills. Specifically, optimal retention will be found when retention requires the use of procedures employed during training, when trained information can be related to previous experience, when trained information is made distinctive, when trained information can be retrieved directly, and when refresher or practice opportunities are provided.

AUTHORS' NOTE: This research was supported by Army Research Institute Contract MDA903-90-K-0066 to the Institute of Cognitive Science at the University of Colorado. Robert J. Crutcher is now at the University of Illinois, Chicago; K. Anders Ericsson is now at Florida State University, Tallahassee; Deborah M. Clawson is now at Catholic University of America; and Timothy Rickard is now at the National Institutes of Health, Bethesda.

1

Our research program is aimed generally at understanding and improving the long-term retention of knowledge and skills. Our initial work led us to propose that a crucial determinant of memory concerns the extent to which cognitive procedures acquired during study can be reinstated at test (Healy et al., 1992)—that is, to demonstrate durable retention across a long delay interval, it is critical that the cognitive procedures used when acquiring the knowledge or skill are reinstated at the later time. Using this work as a foundation, we have tried to develop additional guidelines for promoting superior long-term retention.

Elsewhere we have described how the approach we have taken differs from that used in most earlier studies (Healy et al., 1993). To summarize, four features of our program are especially important in distinguishing it from earlier research. First, we have been explicitly concerned with optimizing performance after a delay interval rather than assuming retention will be superior given optimized performance during acquisition. Second, relative to most other experimenters, we have used longer retention intervals, usually including tests after at least a week, and in some cases including intervals up to 1 or 2 years. Third, we have conducted experiments over a wide range of different types of tasks, because we assumed that our theoretical conclusions may rely heavily on the specific nature of the tasks we studied and we hoped to capitalize on different processes crucial to memory that could be highlighted in different tasks. Fourth, in many of our studies, we have used nontraditional methods to assess retention, providing training for subjects beyond a fixed accuracy criterion, monitoring component response time measures, or collecting verbal protocols. This research led to the support or identification of several guidelines for improving memory for skills (Healy et al., 1993). Here we focus on three classes of guidelines: those that relate to optimizing the conditions of training, the learning strategy used, and the retention conditions.

In our earlier studies, we were impressed with the remarkable degree of long-term retention that subjects were able to achieve in a number of perceptual, cognitive, and motor tasks, including target detection (Healy, Fendrich, & Proctor, 1990), data entry (Fendrich, Healy, & Bourne, 1991), and mental arithmetic (Fendrich, Healy, & Bourne, 1993; Healy et al., 1992). Our more recent research has identified one important limitation on this durable retention phenomenon, namely the specificity, or lack of generalizability, of the attained improvements in performance (Rickard & Bourne, 1992; Rickard, Healy, & Bourne, in press). First, we present some new evidence for such specificity, and then we discuss our optimization guidelines.

Specificity of Training: Color-Word Interference

Our new evidence for specificity involves the Stroop effect (Stroop, 1935). In the Stroop color-word interference task, subjects are asked to name the color of the ink in which color words are displayed. The ink color and word do not correspond. For example, given the word *purple* printed in red ink, the appropriate response is "red." Our study (which is discussed in greater detail by Clawson, King, Healy, & Ericsson, this volume) involved training in two different color-naming situations: The patches training condition involved practice in simply naming color patches; the Stroop training condition involved practice in naming the colors of incongruent color words.

Specifically, the study provided four subjects with 12 sessions of training either on the Stroop task itself or on simple color-patch naming; two subjects in a control condition received no training. All six subjects were tested in a pretest prior to training as well as in a posttest after training and in a retention test after a month-long delay. Included in each test session was a set of four tests related to Stroop interference: one test each on word reading and on simple color-patch naming plus a Stroop test and a test with Stroop stimuli but requiring word-reading responses (which we call "reverse Stroop"). Two additional orthographic manipulation tests consisted of a Stroop test in which the letters of the color words were bracketed by asterisks (e.g., *p*u*r*p*l*e* in red letters) and one in which the letters were all uppercase (e.g., PURPLE in red letters) as opposed to the lowercase letters used in training. These orthographic manipulations provided an indication of specificity to the word form. Another index of specificity was provided by the use of two different color-word sets. Although the experimental subjects *trained* on only one color-word set (with the set counterbalanced across subjects), all subjects were *tested* on both sets.

If there was specificity of training, then there should have been less improvement on the orthographic manipulations than on the normal Stroop test and less improvement on the untrained color-word set than on the trained set. On the basis of our previous studies showing extremely good retention of procedural skills (Healy et al., 1992), we also predicted relatively little evidence of forgetting across the 1-month delay interval. Of greatest interest was whether any specificity effects persisted across this long retention interval.

The results, averaged across the three training conditions, are summarized in Figure 1.1 in log correct reaction times at the pretest, posttest, and retention test for the four Stroop interference tests. As in previous re-

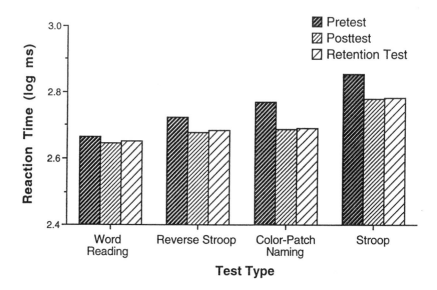

Figure 1.1. Results of the Experiment by Clawson, King, Healy, and Ericsson (this volume) for the Four Stroop Interference Tests. Mean Correct Log Reaction Time on the Pretest, Posttest, and Retention Test as a Function of Test Type.

search, reaction times were faster for the test types involving word reading than those involving color naming and were slower for the test types involving incongruous stimuli than for those that did not. Note that the test types in order of fastest to slowest were word reading, reverse Stroop, color-patch naming, and Stroop. The effects of training are evident by the fact that subjects were faster overall on the posttest than on the pretest. Note that, as in the previous studies of procedural skills (Healy et al., 1992), there was no significant forgetting evident from the posttest to the retention test.

The specificity of training is reflected by three related observations. First, reaction times decreased from the pretest to the posttest more for the color-word set on which subjects had trained (pretest $M = 2.765$, posttest $M = 2.698$) than for their untrained color-word set (pretest $M = 2.744$, posttest $M = 2.698$). Second, as shown in Figure 1.2, which presents data only from the Stroop-trained condition after training (i.e., on the posttest and retention test), subjects who were trained to name colors and ignore the words were faster on the trained set than on the untrained set when naming colors, that is, in the Stroop test and in the color-patch naming test; but not when reading words, that is, in the word-reading test and in the reverse Stroop test. For these last two tests, reaction times were

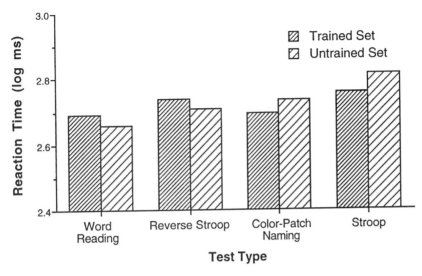

Figure 1.2. Results of the Experiment by Clawson, King, Healy, and Ericsson (this volume) for Only the Stroop-Trained Subjects on the Four Stroop Interference Tests, After Training. Mean Correct Log Reaction Time on the Trained and Untrained Color-Word Sets as a Function of Test Type.

actually faster for the untrained set. Third, this advantage for the trained set on color-naming responses and the advantage for the untrained set on word-reading responses were only found for subjects in the Stroop training condition, not for subjects in either the color-patch training or control conditions.

The results of the orthographic manipulation tests revealed no effect of orthographic test type, with reaction times nearly identical for the three orthographic test types (standard $M = 2.807$, asterisks $M = 2.810$, uppercase $M = 2.808$). Importantly, this finding suggests that the effects of training were not specific to the word form. In contrast, specificity of *color-word set* was again evident by two observations. First, as shown in Figure 1.3, the greatest decrease in reaction time from the pretest to the posttest occurred for the Stroop training condition with the trained color-word set. Second, as illustrated in Figure 1.4, after training (i.e., on the posttest and retention test), only the Stroop training condition yielded faster reaction times for the trained set than for the untrained set. Because the same pattern was found for all three orthographic test types, the results are consistent with the hypothesis that training is specific to the colors and words employed but *not* to the orthographic form of the color words.

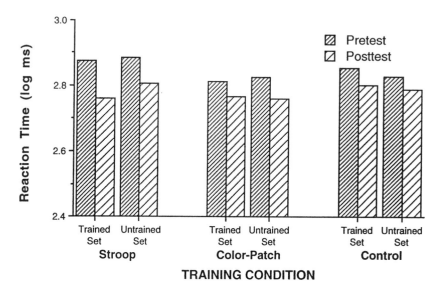

Figure 1.3. Results of the Experiment by Clawson, King, Healy, and Ericsson (this volume) for the Orthographic Stroop Tests. Mean Correct Log Reaction Time on the Trained and Untrained Color-Word Sets as a Function of Test Time and Training Condition.

In summary, we found clear evidence for lasting specificity of training effects in the Stroop task, suggesting that there are limits to the generalizability even of well-retained improvements in performance. We thus find cause for concern about training recommendations that limit learning to a subset of relevant materials.

Guidelines for Improving Long-Term Retention

We turn now to our research on the general optimization guidelines outlined earlier, starting with the class of guidelines regarding optimization of the conditions of training.

Retention of Components of Schedules

Researchers have described what we retain in memory as a composite of three qualitatively separate components based on spatial, temporal, and

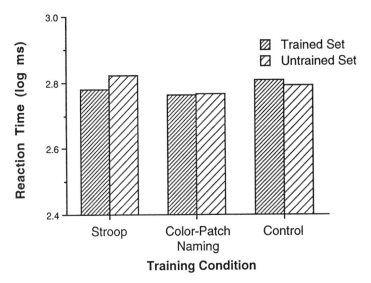

Figure 1.4. Results of the Experiment by Clawson, King, Healy, and Ericsson (this volume) for the Orthographic Stroop Tests, After Training. Mean Correct Log Reaction Time on the Trained and Untrained Color-Word Sets as a Function of Training Condition.

item information (e.g. Healy, 1974, 1975, 1982; Healy, Cunningham, Gesi, Till, & Bourne, 1991; Lee & Estes, 1981). More specifically, the spatial component involves knowledge about spatial relations, distances, and locations of physical objects in addition to knowledge about how to proceed through the environment. The temporal component includes knowledge of dates and times and the relative order of events. Memory for item information includes knowledge of specific facts and names.

Research has provided evidence that spatial, temporal, and item information are retrieved in different ways (King, 1992; Wittman & Healy, this volume). For example, Wittman and Healy (this volume) tested undergraduate students' recall of four different types of course schedule information: course times (temporal), the building in which the course was held (spatial), the title of the course (item), and the name of the course instructor (item). These four types of information can be referred to as *when, where, what,* and *who* information. In Wittman and Healy's (this volume) first experiment, during each of three tests separated by 6-month intervals, subjects were given a recall questionnaire using a cuing technique with a map to ask about their individual courses from a previous semester. As

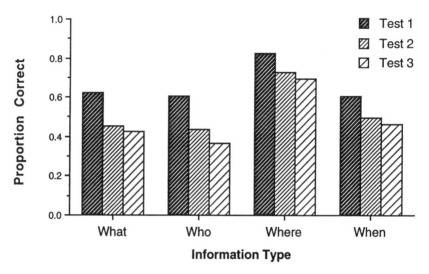

Figure 1.5. Results of Experiment 1 by Wittman and Healy (this volume). Mean Proportion of Correct Recall of *What, Who, Where,* and *When* Information as a Function of Test Time.

shown in Figure 1.5, Wittman and Healy (this volume) found a large degree of forgetting of course schedule information despite repeated exposure and natural learning. An important finding was the superiority of recall for spatial information (*where*) over item and temporal information (*who, what,* and *when*). Wittman and Healy (this volume) proposed that subjects learned *where* information by repeating the procedure of walking to the classroom for each class session. Conversely, the learning of course title, instructor name, and class time did not involve analogous procedures.

In a second experiment, Wittman and Healy (this volume) had subjects learn other individuals' course schedules in a laboratory setting. During the study phase, subjects were provided with both a campus map and a course schedule including the same four types of information as in the first experiment. Subjects received nine training trials in addition to two tests, the first test 1 week later and the second (retention) test after 5 additional weeks. The training trials consisted of studying the class schedule and map, followed by a recall task. Students were tested using the recall questionnaire as well as two new methods, a map test and a class listing test. In both of these new tests, subjects were required to provide the same type of item information (course title and instructor's name). However, the tests differed in the type of temporal and spatial information required. For the map test, subjects provided the temporal order of class occurrence during the school week, and as in the recall questionnaire, the building location of each class on the campus map. In contrast, for the class listing test, subjects provided the start time and the building name for each class. Thus, the map test was designed to resemble the natural procedures used in retrieving course locations, whereas the class listing test was designed to remove that procedural component from the recall of course locations.

As in the natural learning experiment, comparison of the 1-week test and 6-week retention test revealed an overall forgetting of course schedule information, as shown in Figure 1.6. Retrieval of *where* information was again superior; however, this superiority occurred only on the map tests. On the class listing tests, retention of *where* information was not superior on the 1-week test and showed significant loss on the 6-week retention test. These results support the notion that the superiority of spatial memory is due to the use of procedures during learning.

A further course schedule study by King (1992) separated procedural experience from the use of a map in order to explore the role of procedural knowledge in spatial memory superiority. To separate these two issues, subjects' memory for fictitious course schedules was tested in two separate situations: one in which subjects had previous procedural experience with the campus and one in which subjects lacked such experience. If the retention advantage of spatial information is due to procedural experience, then we would expect a retention advantage for spatial information only in the familiar condition, in which subjects had previous procedural experience.

Undergraduate students from the University of Colorado (CU) and Colorado State University (CSU) participated as subjects. All subjects were unfamiliar with the other campus. Four different fictitious course schedules were constructed, two using a CSU directory of classes, and two using a CU directory. Half of the students were assigned to the familiar condition in which schedules were from their own campus; the other half of the students, in the unfamiliar condition, were assigned to schedules from the other campus. The experiment used Wittman and Healy's (this volume) testing procedure with the three types of tests (recall questionnaires, class listing tests, and map tests).

The results of the recall questionnaire are summarized in Figure 1.7 as a function of test time and information type. There was a significant degree of forgetting across the approximately 1-month interval from the 1-week test to the retention test. Recall performance differed among the four types

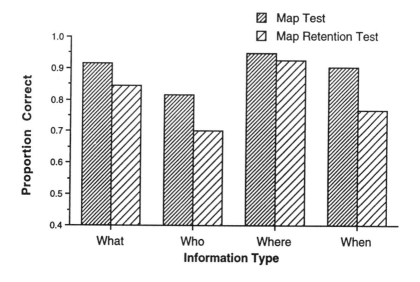

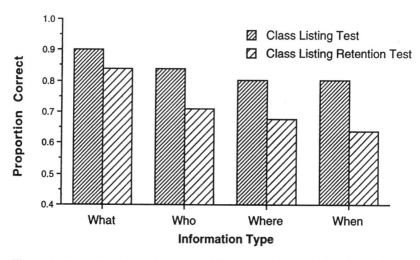

Figure 1.6. Results of Experiment 2 by Wittman and Healy (this volume) for the Map Test and the Class Listing Test. Mean Proportion of Correct Recall of *What, Who, Where,* and *When* Information as a Function of Test Time.

of information. This effect of information type was, however, modulated by familiarity, as shown in Figure 1.8. Performance was better for the

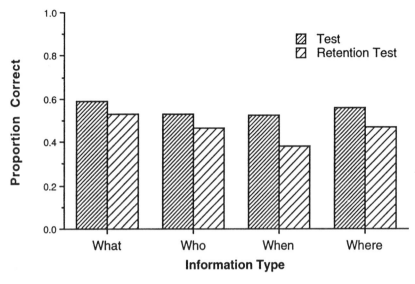

Figure 1.7. Results of the Experiment by King (1992) for the Recall Questionnaire Test. Mean Proportion of Correct Recall of *What, Who, When,* and *Where* Information as a Function of Test Time.

familiar condition than for the unfamiliar condition, but only on *where* information. These results also support the prediction that *where* information would be superior only for the familiar condition.

The results of the class listing test, in which the *where* information consisted of building names rather than locations, are summarized in Figure 1.9. Forgetting was evident. Performance on the 1-week test was superior to performance on the retention test. Performance varied across information types, with performance on *what* information highest and performance on *where* information lowest. Further, there was differential loss from the 1-week test to the retention test, with the greatest amount of loss for the *when* and *where* information. As shown in Figure 1.10, performance on *where* information was better for the familiar than for the unfamiliar condition, as in the recall questionnaire. Again, the effects of familiarity were not significant for the other types of information.

Figure 1.11 summarizes the results of the map test, in which, like the recall questionnaire, the *where* information consisted of building locations rather than building names. Again, forgetting was evident, but here there was a *where* advantage for both the 1-week test and the retention test.

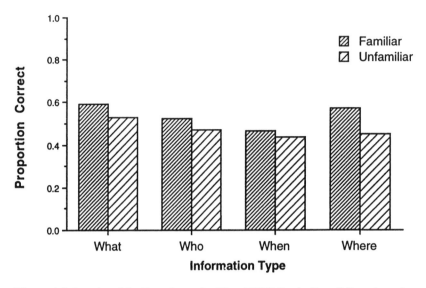

Figure 1.8. Results of the Experiment by King (1992) for the Recall Questionnaire Test. Mean Proportion of Correct Recall of *What, Who, When,* and *Where* Information as a Function of Familiarity of Campus.

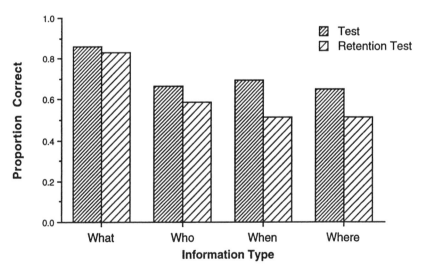

Figure 1.9. Results of the Experiment by King (1992) for the Class Listing Test. Mean Proportion of Correct Recall of *What, Who, When,* and *Where* Information as a Function of Test Time.

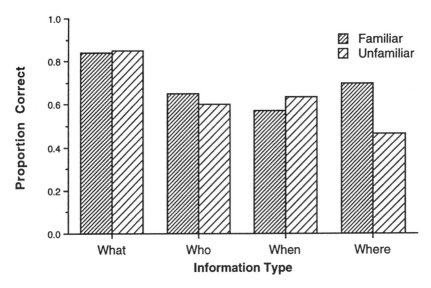

Figure 1.10. Results of the Experiment by King (1992) for the Class Listing Test. Mean Proportion of Correct Recall of *What, Who, When,* and *Where* Information as a Function of Familiarity of Campus.

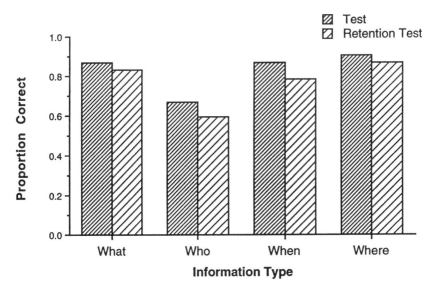

Figure 1.11. Results of the Experiment by King (1992) for the Map Test. Mean Proportion of Correct Recall of *What, Who, When,* and *Where* Information as a Function of Test Time.

In summary, on both the recall questionnaire and the class listing test, there was an effect of familiarity on *where* information but not on the other types of information. These results support our hypothesis that the spatial advantage was due to procedures, because procedural experience with the campus enhanced spatial recall.

For the class listing test, *what, who,* and *when* information was recalled better than *where* information. Thus, when the test required building names rather than locations, there was no spatial advantage over temporal and item information. Conversely, as expected, there was a spatial advantage on the map test, which required the building locations.

Answering questions about location affords an opportunity to relate information to previous experience and to use specific procedures engaged during learning and practice, leading to enhanced recall for location information and superior performance on location questions over other forms of course information.

Retention of Components of Lists

In the study of memory for course schedules, the *who, what, where,* and *when* questions necessarily differed from each other along a number of dimensions other than whether they involved temporal, spatial, or item information; for example, in the recall questionnaire and map tests used above, the *where* questions were a type of recognition test whereas the *who, what,* and *when* questions were recall tests. Two laboratory experiments by Sinclair, Healy, and Bourne (1994) controlled for those other dimensions. The objective was to determine whether a spatial advantage would occur under these more controlled conditions. Because there was no procedural component in these experiments, no spatial advantage was predicted.

In the first experiment, subjects learned a list of 20 common nouns, each beginning with a different consonant from the alphabet. The words were presented one at a time in a vertical array on a computer terminal, with each word occurring for 2 seconds in a different location within the array. At the termination of the list presentation, subjects recalled the words by writing them on a sheet of paper. A trial thus consisted of one presentation and one recall attempt.

Three groups of subjects recalled the words in an order determined by either the temporal, spatial, or item information in the list. The first group of subjects was required to recall the words according to the temporal sequence of presentation; for these subjects the spatial arrangement of the words was alphabetical. The second group of subjects was required to recall the words according to the words' spatial locations within the vertical field during presentation; for these subjects the temporal sequence of the words was alphabetical. For both of these groups, an alphabetical list of the words was constantly available to the subjects. The third group of subjects was required to choose the 20 words that had been presented from an alphabetically organized 210-word list including the critical words intermixed with similar distractor words. For this last group of subjects, both the temporal and spatial arrangements of the words were alphabetical. For all subjects, after each recall, another trial was started with the same words being presented in exactly the same sequence and locations. This process continued until the subject achieved a criterion of correct recall on three successive trials.

Subjects returned after a 1-week delay and were asked to recall the 20 words as they had during the first session. After this initial retention test, the presentation and recall trials were resumed as in the first session and continued until the criterion of correct recall on three successive trials was achieved again.

The initial retention test yielded the greatest proportion of correct responses for item information (.969) and substantially lower proportions for temporal (.769) and spatial (.750) information. The mean number of trials to criterion for each information type and session are summarized in Figure 1.12. Note that learning was most difficult in the spatial condition and least difficult in the item condition, and that first-session learning required more trials than did second-session relearning. Figure 1.12 illustrates the interaction between information type and session. Although initial learning proceeded more slowly in the spatial condition than in the temporal and item conditions, relearning of information in the spatial condition, once initial learning was achieved, was similar to that of the other conditions.

It is likely that the higher degree of learning difficulty observed in the spatial condition of Experiment 1 was due partially to the subjects' inability to discriminate effectively one spatial location from another. Central locations in the vertical array contained no unique information to distinguish them from neighboring locations. Hence, in the second experiment, a new array of 18 word locations arranged in two 3×3 matrices replaced the old vertical array of 20 word locations used in Experiment 1. Each spatial location was thus made unique and easily distinguishable from every other location within the new array. Half of the subjects had a retention period of 1 week and the others had a retention period of 6 weeks to elucidate the time course of forgetting from long-term memory.

Subjects showed substantially lower proportions of correct responses on the retention test after 6 weeks (temporal, .236; spatial, .347; item,

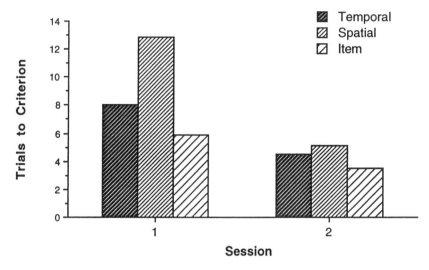

Figure 1.12. Results of Experiment 1 by Sinclair, Healy, and Bourne (1994). Mean Number of Trials to Criterion for Temporal, Spatial, and Item Information as a Function of Session.

.882) than after 1 week (temporal, .785; spatial, .875; item, .986). The mean number of trials to criterion for each information type and session are summarized in Figure 1.13. Most interesting is the observation that performance was better on the spatial than on the temporal information. Thus, the ordering of the temporal and spatial conditions was the reverse of that in Experiment 1, in which performance on temporal information was better than that on spatial information. As expected, simply changing the presentation array so that each of its component positions provided unique spatial information facilitated learning in the spatial condition. Also note that although initial learning proceeded at very different rates for the three types of information, their relearning was again similar; that is, the initial learning rates for the three types of information varied more than did their relearning rates.

The number of weeks intervening between original learning and second-session relearning affected recall greatly. The trials to criterion required for relearning in Session 2 were greater after a 6-week delay (Session 1 M = 5.54 trials, Session 2 M = 4.75 trials) than after a 1-week delay (Session 1 M = 5.71 trials, Session 2 M = 3.71 trials). It is clear, however, that even in the 6-week condition some information from the first session was

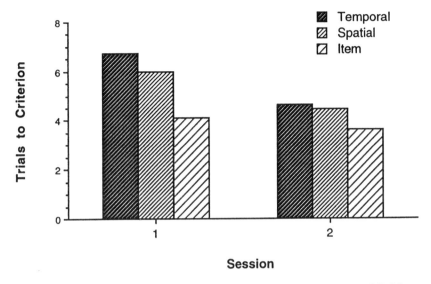

Figure 1.13. Results of Experiment 2 by Sinclair, Healy, and Bourne (1994). Mean Number of Trials to Criterion for Temporal, Spatial, and Item Information as a Function of Session.

retained because the number of trials required for *re*learning was less than that required for learning in the first session.

There are three conclusions that can be drawn from these findings. First, although there was considerable long-term retention evident for all three types of information, there was nonetheless significant forgetting for temporal and spatial information. This forgetting was already evident across the 1-week retention interval and was even greater across the 6-week retention interval. The forgetting observed for the declarative information studied here was generally consistent with that found in our study of course schedules but was in marked contrast to the substantial retention we found in our earlier studies examining the long-term retention of procedural skills (see Healy et al., 1992), such as the study of the Stroop task (see Clawson et al., this volume). Second, there were large differences in the *learning* of temporal sequence, spatial arrangement, and item identity, with smaller differences in the *relearning* of the three types of information. Third, learning spatial information was more difficult than learning temporal information when the spatial positions were hard to differentiate, but the opposite pattern of results was found when each spatial position was made distinctive. Thus, making the spatial information to be learned distinctive has a marked facilitative effect on learning.

Direct and Mediated Retrieval in Mental Arithmetic

Next we turn our attention to the guidelines regarding the optimization of learning strategies. The first study in this section concerns mental arithmetic, an area of our research that is further discussed by Rickard and Bourne (this volume).

Our previous work on mental arithmetic has uncovered several important facts about the acquisition, transfer, and retention of skill (Fendrich et al., 1993; Rickard et al., in press). First, in accordance with most other research on skill acquisition, speedup with practice on simple multiplication and division problems follows the power law of learning (Newell & Rosenbloom, 1981; Rickard et al., in press). Second, in accord with our work on the Stroop task, arithmetic skill is almost entirely specific to the problems practiced, suggesting that adult subjects store each problem separately in some form of fact memory (Ashcraft, 1992; Rickard et al., in press). Even complementary multiplication and division problems, such as 4×7 and $28 \div 7$, are represented by adults as independent facts. Third, we have shown that speedup from practice is maintained over retention intervals of a month or longer without significant decrement (Fendrich et al., 1993).

Although our research, as well as a substantial amount of other research in the literature (reviewed by Ashcraft, 1992), suggests that adult performance on simple arithmetic mostly reflects retrieval of facts from memory, it has been demonstrated by Siegler (1986, 1988) that children often rely on algorithms to calculate the solutions to arithmetic problems. To study similar processes in adults, we developed a novel mental arithmetic task that at least initially requires the application of a general algorithm (just as in the case of children beginning to learn arithmetic), but with sufficient practice should be performable by retrieving answers directly from memory (Rickard, 1994). This task allowed us to test the generalizability of our findings with simple arithmetic, for which practice simply strengthens access to already existing facts, to a task for which practice results in a transition from algorithm to retrieval.

Adult subjects were trained on two types of problems, based on a novel, arbitrary operation symbolized by the pound sign (#). On Type I problems, subjects were given two elements from a simple arithmetic progression and were required to generate the third (next) element. The generic progression that we used was one in which the third element is the second element plus the difference between the first and second elements, plus 1. For example, the answer to 7 # 15 = ___ is computed as 15 + (15 − 7) + 1 = 24. Type II problems were based on the reverse algorithm, the answer being the second element of the series (e.g., 7 # ___ = 24). Across five sessions subjects received 90 blocks of problems; a block consisted of a single presentation of each of 12 unique problems, 6 Type I problems and 6 Type II problems. At the end of the fifth session subjects were given a transfer test, on which they were retested on the practice problems (*no-change* problems) and were also tested on practice problems with the missing element changed (*type change* problems, e.g., a Type I problem became a Type II problem) and on unpracticed problems (*new* problems). Finally, subjects were given the same test 6 weeks later to measure retention.

During practice, subjects were probed on one third of the trials to determine whether they used the algorithm that they were taught, retrieved the answer directly from memory, or used some other, unspecified approach. During both the immediate and the delayed tests, subjects were probed after every trial. On probe trials, subjects signified "algorithm," "retrieve," or "other" by pressing labeled buttons on a response console.

The strategy probing results from practice are shown in Figure 1.14. Note that practice was successful in creating a transition from the algorithm to direct retrieval. By about Block 60, direct retrieval was the reported strategy on nearly all trials. The transition from algorithm to retrieval was virtually complete for all subjects. After Block 60, few if any problems required intermediate stages for solution.

Log reaction time averaged across subjects and across correctly solved problems is displayed in Figure 1.15, plotted as a function of log block. The average reaction time for Block 1 was about 13 seconds. By Block 90, the average reaction time was about 1 second. The line drawn through the data corresponds to the best-fitting power function. Note the clear deviation from linearity evident in the data. This pattern, combined with the evidence from the strategy probing data, suggested to us that the power law may actually be strategy specific and may not hold during the transition from algorithm to retrieval (cf. Logan, 1988).

To test this hypothesis, additional reaction time analyses were performed only for trials on which strategy probes were collected. Considering only algorithm trials, there should be power function speedup with practice; that is, the data should plot linearly in log-log coordinates. Similarly, when considering only retrieval trials, there should be power function speedup, and thus the data should plot linearly in log-log coordinates. However, the two power functions would be unlikely to share the same parameters. Figure 1.16 shows the log reaction time data for strategy

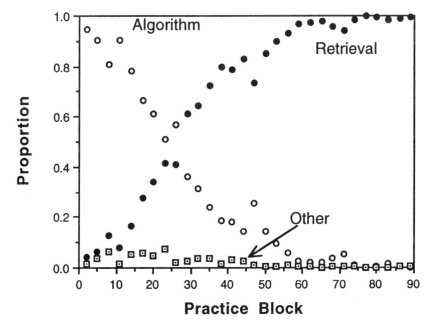

Figure 1.14. Results of an Experiment by Rickard (1994). Mean Proportion of Algorithm, Retrieval, and Other Strategy Reports as a Function of Practice Block.

probing trials overall, for algorithm responses only, and for retrieval responses only. As predicted by our hypothesis, when the data were separated by strategy, they conformed very nicely to two linear but different power functions.

The average reaction time results for the immediate and delayed tests are shown in Figure 1.17. On both tests, performance was much faster on no-change problems than on either new or type change problems. The strategy probing data help to explain this difference. Subjects reported using direct retrieval on nearly all no-change problems of the immediate test and on roughly half the no-change problems of the delayed test. In contrast, the algorithm was the reported strategy on nearly all new and type change problems on both tests. The additional finding of no reaction time difference between type change and new problems attests further to the extreme specificity of the skill that was acquired during practice.

Reaction times for no-change problems on the delayed test were about halfway between reaction times for no-change and new problems on the

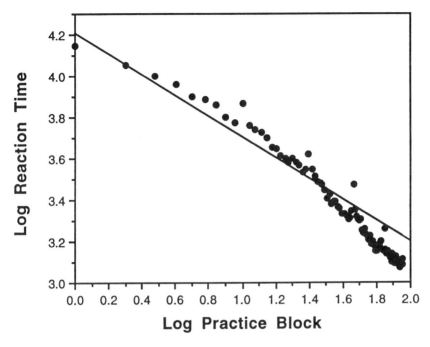

Figure 1.15. Results of an Experiment by Rickard (1994). Mean Correct Log Reaction Time as a Function of Log Practice Block.

immediate test, indicating some skill retention. Nevertheless, the substantial increase in reaction time for no-change problems on the delayed test indicated a much greater loss in skill across the retention interval than we had observed in our previous work on simple arithmetic (e.g., Fendrich et al., 1993; Rickard et al., in press). To investigate this finding further, we plotted the reaction times for no-change problems on the delayed test separately by strategy (algorithm or retrieval) as shown by the dotted lines in Figure 1.18. When retrieval was the reported strategy for no-change problems on the delayed test, the reaction times were almost exactly the same as for the no-change problems on the immediate test. When the algorithm was the reported strategy, the reaction times were nearly exactly the same as those for new and type change problems. This result suggests that the effects of the retention interval were primarily to decrease the probability with which the retrieval strategy was used, without changing the time required to execute that retrieval strategy when it was used. Thus,

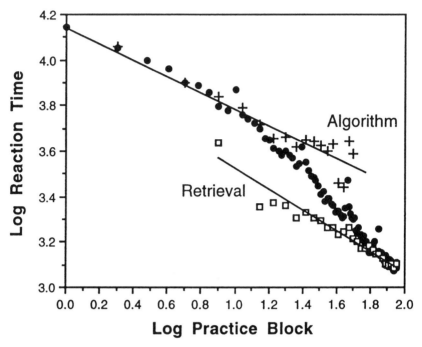

Figure 1.16. Results of an Experiment by Rickard (1994). Mean Correct Log Reaction Time for Algorithm Trials, Retrieval Trials, and Overall as a Function of Log Practice Block.

a training procedure that promotes the use of an optimal strategy for a given task appears to contribute to the maintenance of training levels of performance on later tests of retention.

Direct and Mediated Retrieval
in Vocabulary Acquisition

Retrieval strategies were also a focus of our studies concerning foreign vocabulary acquisition. Learning vocabulary items in a foreign language is in many ways an ideal everyday task for the study of retention under controlled conditions, due to the independent and often arbitrary nature of its required associations. In most of our earlier research (Crutcher, 1990; Crutcher & Ericsson, 1992), students unfamiliar with Spanish learned approximately 40 Spanish vocabulary items, after which their retention

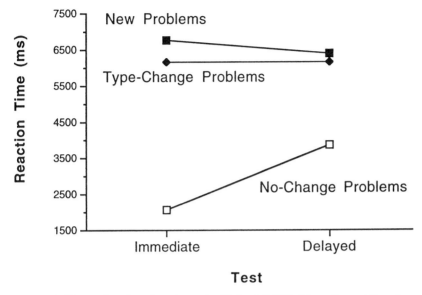

Figure 1.17. Results of an Experiment by Rickard (1994). Mean Correct Reaction Time (ms) for New Problems, Type Change Problems, and No-Change Problems as a Function of Test Time. (All means were calculated based on log reaction times and then transformed back to milliseconds by the antilog function.)

was tested 1 week, 1 month, and even 1 year later. The current set of studies extends our findings to significantly more practice. Before turning to these new findings, let us briefly review the procedures and general results of our previous work.

For the vocabulary items we used, the Spanish word was completely unrelated to its English translation (e.g., *doronico* and "leopard"). To facilitate learning we instructed subjects in the use of the keyword method. In the keyword method, the Spanish word is first related to a similar-sounding English word (the keyword) provided by the experimenter (e.g., *doronico* and "door"). The keyword is then associated to the English translation by forming an interactive image. This method of learning provided a great deal of control over the mediating processes, thus ensuring a very similar encoding structure across subjects. After subjects had acquired all vocabulary items, we examined their retrieval speed and accuracy in three ways: using the Spanish word as a cue to retrieve the English translation (vocabulary task), using the Spanish word as a cue to

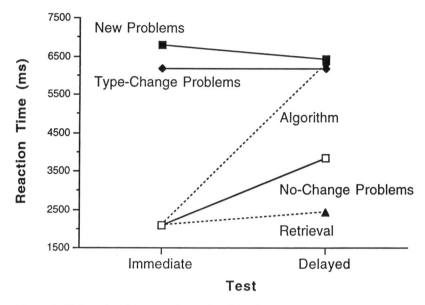

Figure 1.18. Results of an Experiment by Rickard (1994). Mean Correct Reaction Time (ms) for the Three Problem Types and Separately for Algorithm and Retrieval Trials of the No-Change Problems as a Function of Test Time. (All means were calculated based on log reaction times and then transformed back to milliseconds by the antilog function.)

retrieve the keyword (keyword subtask), and using the keyword as a cue to retrieve the English translation (English subtask).

The results from these tests immediately following acquisition showed that retrieval of the English translation when cued by the Spanish word involved access and mediation of the keyword (Crutcher, 1990). Retention testing at a 1-week or 1-month delay showed two further results. First, accuracy of retrieval was reduced (especially after a month) and inability to retrieve the English translation given the Spanish word was almost perfectly predicted by inability to retrieve the English translation given the keyword. Second, for a given item, retrieval speed on the first block of the retention test was considerably slower than on the immediate test after training, but on the second block of the retention test the speed was comparable to that on the immediate test—that is, after a memory trace was successfully accessed the *first time* at retention, its strength appeared to be completely recovered.

In more recent studies, subjects practiced retrieving the English translation for 80 training blocks (Crutcher, 1992; Crutcher & Ericsson, 1992). Half the items were consistently cued by only the Spanish word (the vocabulary task) and the other half of the items were cued by only the keyword (the English subtask). Subjects were then tested on both retrieval tasks for all items, first immediately after the extended practice and again 1 month later. On the immediate test, for items trained with the English subtask, the retrieval times on the vocabulary task were longer, consistent with sequential access mediated by the keyword. However, for items trained with the vocabulary task, the retrieval times on the English subtask were longer, implying the emergence of direct access. Retrospective reports provided convergent evidence for direct retrieval with extended practice on the vocabulary task.

In the experiment giving subjects extended practice (Crutcher, 1992), new analyses of retention after a 1-month delay showed a very interesting pattern. Although accuracy of retrieval was uniformly high on both retrieval tasks, there was a robust interaction of retrieval task and training condition. For items trained with the English subtask, recall proportion was reliably worse on the vocabulary task ($M = .90$) than on the English subtask ($M = .97$), which suggested a loss of the association between the keyword and the Spanish word. Training with the vocabulary task yielded worse performance for retrieval on the English subtask ($M = .95$) than on the vocabulary task ($M = .99$). For about 4% of the items, the English translation could be retrieved using the Spanish word as a cue without the subjects' being able to retrieve the English translation using the keyword as a cue. At the same time, the keywords remained effective cues for 95% of the items, although the keywords had hardly been presented since the original acquisition of the items.

Table 1.1 presents mean retrieval times for the immediate test after practice and for the retention test's Block 1 (the first encounter of an item) and Block 2 (the second encounter). For both blocks of the retention test, as well as for the immediate test, there was an interaction between training condition and retrieval task. Further, retrieval speed on the first block of the retention test was much slower than it had been 1 month earlier on the immediate test, but retrieval speed on the second block was virtually indistinguishable from that on the immediate test. Hence, this study with extensively practiced items replicated our earlier findings (Crutcher, 1990) with forgetting of responses due to loss of the connecting associations and a remarkable recovery of the entire pattern of retrieval times after the first exposure of the retrieval task after a long delay.

Table 1.1 Results of Experiment by Crutcher (1992). Mean Correct Retrieval Time in Milliseconds for Items Trained in the Vocabulary Task (V-Trained) and Items Trained in the English Subtask (E-Trained) as a Function of Test Type (Vocabulary, V, or English, E) and Test Time

| | Test Time and Test Type | | | | | |
| | Immediate | | Delayed, Block 1 | | Delayed, Block 2 | |
Item Type	V	E	V	E	V	E
V-trained items	830	963	1207	1332	883	952
E-trained items	1376	813	1636	1236	1146	888

NOTE: All means were calculated based on log reaction times and then transformed back to milliseconds by the antilog function.

The finding that the keyword remained accessible after delay even when only the direct connection between the Spanish word and its English translation had been practiced was consistent with other results obtained in our laboratory. For example, we found that after extended practice leading to apparent direct access of the English translation, it was still possible to interfere selectively with the speed of retrieval by requiring subjects to memorize new associates to the keywords (Crutcher, 1992). It would thus appear that the original encoding of an item during learning continues to influence retrieval after extended practice even when other evidence points to unmediated direct retrieval.

Summary and Conclusions

In closing, we will review three classes of guidelines, summarized in Table 1.2, for optimizing long-term retention. The first class of guidelines concerns conditions of training. We discussed three general guidelines in this class. First, superior memory results from the use of reinstatable procedures acquired during training. The procedural reinstatement framework accounts for the observed superiority of memory for spatial order found in our studies of the retention of course schedule information. Second, retention can be aided by prior familiarity with related information. Memory for spatial information of course schedules was improved when the information could be related to previous experience. Third, learning is facilitated by distinctiveness of individual items of information, as was evident in the acquisition of spatial information in our list learning study.

Table 1.2 Classes of Guidelines to Optimize Long-Term Retention

Guideline	Topic
(1) Optimize conditions of training:	
(a) Use procedures during learning.	Schedule components
(b) Relate information to previous experience.	Schedule components
(c) Make the to-be-learned information distinctive.	List components
(2) Optimize the learning strategy:	
Direct retrieval is best.	Mental arithmetic
(3) Optimize retention conditions:	
Provide refresher or practice tests.	Vocabulary acquisition

The second class of guidelines concerns learning strategies. We found in our study of mental arithmetic that the strategy used by the subject importantly influenced retention performance. A direct retrieval strategy led to faster responding than did a strategy based on a calculational algorithm. Our study of vocabulary acquisition demonstrated that a direct retrieval strategy is also usable in that domain, but mediating associations may still exert an influence even when retrieval appears to be direct.

The last class of guidelines concerns ways to optimize retention conditions. In our study of vocabulary acquisition we saw remarkable recovery of retrieval speed after the initial warm-up retrieval. Hence, it appears that the use of a refresher or practice trial *before* the critical test may have a profound impact on retention performance.

We began this chapter by summarizing some of our work demonstrating the specificity of improvement in performance. Stroop training on specific colors and words showed excellent retention across a month-long delay interval but limited transfer to new colors and words. Although our original goal in this research program had been limited to an examination of the optimization of long-term retention, we have learned that optimizing retention does not guarantee generalizability. There are conditions of training that lead to highly durable performance over time. Our basic interpretation of this result invokes the principle of procedural reinstatement, that is, retention performance will be best when the mental procedures required at test match those employed during training. Our more recent results have highlighted a limitation of this principle. Durable retention is associated with highly specific skill, that is, retention performance will be worse when the mental procedures required at test do not match *exactly* those employed during training. The relationship between durability and specificity in memory will be the focus of our future research.

References

Ashcraft, M. H. (1992). Cognitive arithmetic: A review of data and theory. *Cognition, 44,* 75-106.

Clawson, D. M., King, C. L., Healy, A. F., & Ericsson, K. A. (this volume). Training and retention of the classic Stroop task: Specificity of practice effects. In A. F. Healy & L. E. Bourne, Jr. (Eds.), *Learning and memory of knowledge and skills: Durability and specificity.* Thousand Oaks, CA: Sage.

Crutcher, R. J. (1990). *The role of mediation in knowledge acquisition and retention: Learning foreign vocabulary using the keyword method* (Tech. Rep. No. 90-10). Boulder: University of Colorado, Institute of Cognitive Science.

Crutcher, R. J. (1992). *The effects of practice on retrieval of foreign vocabulary using the keyword method.* Unpublished doctoral dissertation, University of Colorado, Boulder.

Crutcher, R. J., & Ericsson, K. A. (1992, November). *Mediation processes in memory retrieval before and after extended retrieval practice.* Poster presented at the 33rd Annual Meeting of the Psychonomic Society, St. Louis, MO.

Fendrich, D. W., Healy, A. F., & Bourne, L. E., Jr. (1991). Long-term repetition effects for motoric and perceptual procedures. *Journal of Experimental Psychology: Learning, Memory, and Cognition, 17,* 137-151.

Fendrich, D. W., Healy, A. F., & Bourne, L. E., Jr. (1993). Mental arithmetic: Training and retention of multiplication skill. In C. Izawa (Ed.), *Cognitive psychology applied* (pp. 111-133). Hillsdale, NJ: Lawrence Erlbaum.

Healy, A. F. (1974). Separating item from order information in short-term memory. *Journal of Verbal Learning and Verbal Behavior, 13,* 644-655.

Healy, A. F. (1975). Coding of temporal-spatial patterns in short-term memory. *Journal of Verbal Learning and Verbal Behavior, 14,* 481-495.

Healy, A. F. (1982). Short-term memory for order information. In G. H. Bower (Ed.), *The psychology of learning and motivation* (Vol. 16, pp. 191-238). New York: Academic Press.

Healy, A. F., Clawson, D. M., McNamara, D. S., Marmie, W. R., Schneider, V. I., Rickard, T. C., Crutcher, R. J., King, C. L., Ericsson, K. A., & Bourne, L. E., Jr. (1993). The long-term retention of knowledge and skills. In D. L. Medin (Ed.), *The psychology of learning and motivation* (Vol. 30, pp. 135-164). New York: Academic Press.

Healy, A. F., Cunningham, T. F., Gesi, A. T., Till, R. E., & Bourne, L. E., Jr. (1991). Comparing short-term recall of item, temporal, and spatial information in children and adults. In W. E. Hockley & S. Lewandowsky (Eds.), *Relating theory and data: Essays on human memory in honor of Bennet B. Murdock* (pp. 127-154). Hillsdale, NJ: Lawrence Erlbaum.

Healy, A. F., Fendrich, D. W., Crutcher, R. J., Wittman, W. T., Gesi, A. T., Ericsson, K. A., & Bourne, L. E., Jr. (1992). The long-term retention of skills. In A. F. Healy, S. M. Kosslyn, & R. M. Shiffrin (Eds.), *From learning processes to cognitive processes: Essays in honor of William K. Estes* (Vol. 2, pp. 87-118). Hillsdale, NJ: Lawrence Erlbaum.

Healy, A. F., Fendrich, D. W., & Proctor, J. D. (1990). Acquisition and retention of a letter-detection skill. *Journal of Experimental Psychology: Learning, Memory, and Cognition, 16,* 270-281.

King, C. L. (1992). *Familiarity effects on the retention of spatial, temporal, and item information in course schedules.* Unpublished doctoral dissertation, Colorado State University, Fort Collins, CO.

Lee, C. L., & Estes, W. K. (1981). Item and order information in short-term memory: Evidence for multilevel perturbation processes. *Journal of Experimental Psychology: Human Learning and Memory, 7,* 149-169.

Logan, G. D. (1988). Toward an instance theory of automatization. *Psychological Review, 95,* 492-527.

Newell, A., & Rosenbloom, P. S. (1981). Mechanisms of skill acquisition and the law of practice. In J. R. Anderson (Ed.), *Cognitive skills and their acquisition.* Hillsdale, NJ: Lawrence Erlbaum.

Rickard, T. C. (1994). *Bending the power law: The transition from algorithm-based to memory-based performance.* Unpublished doctoral dissertation, University of Colorado, Boulder.

Rickard, T. C., & Bourne, L. E., Jr. (1992, November). *Cross-operation transfer of mental arithmetic skill.* Paper presented at the 33rd Annual Meeting of the Psychonomic Society, St. Louis, MO.

Rickard, T. C., & Bourne, L. E., Jr. (this volume). An identical-elements model of basic arithmetic skills. In A. F. Healy & L. E. Bourne, Jr. (Eds.), *Learning and memory of knowledge and skills: Durability and specificity.* Thousand Oaks, CA: Sage.

Rickard, T. C., Healy, A. F., & Bourne, L. E., Jr. (in press). On the cognitive structure of basic arithmetic skills: Operation, order, and symbol transfer effects. *Journal of Experimental Psychology: Learning, Memory, and Cognition.*

Siegler, R. S. (1986). *Children's thinking.* Englewood Cliffs, NJ: Prentice-Hall.

Siegler, R. S. (1988). Strategy choice procedures and the development of multiplication skill. *Journal of Experimental Psychology: General, 117,* 258-275.

Sinclair, G. P., Healy, A. F., & Bourne, L. E., Jr. (1994). *The acquisition and long-term retention of temporal, spatial, and item information.* Manuscript in preparation.

Stroop, J. R. (1935). Studies of interference in serial verbal reactions. *Journal of Experimental Psychology, 18,* 643-662.

Wittman, W. T., & Healy, A. F. (this volume). A long-term retention advantage for spatial information learned naturally and in the laboratory. In A. F. Healy & L. E. Bourne, Jr. (Eds.), *Learning and memory of knowledge and skills: Durability and specificity.* Thousand Oaks, CA: Sage.

2 The Long-Term Retention of a Complex Skill

WILLIAM R. MARMIE

ALICE F. HEALY

Three experiments are reported that investigate the relationship between conditions of acquisition and the long-term retention of the complex skill of tank gunnery. The complexity of the tank gunner task puts it outside the scope of many current task classification systems. Experiment 1 showed no loss of this highly proceduralized skill across a 2-week retention interval and by one measure actual improvement across the delay. Experiment 2 showed very little forgetting of the tank gunner skill after 1-, 15-, and 22-month delays between training and testing. This durable skill retention is consistent with a procedural reinstatement account and poses challenges to current task classification systems. Experiment 3 demonstrated that at a 1-month retention test subjects in a part-training condition responded to threats more quickly than did subjects who were trained on the whole task. It is concluded that a part-training advantage occurs when the whole task is composed of sequential part tasks.

In earlier research, Healy et al. (1992) noted the remarkable durability of skill retention in three different domains: letter detection (Healy, Fendrich, & Proctor, 1990), data entry (Fendrich, Healy, & Bourne, 1991), and mental multiplication (Fendrich, Healy, & Bourne, 1993). The durability of those cognitive, perceptual, and motor skills was contrasted to the rapid forgetting found in studies of verbal learning, even over very short

AUTHORS' NOTE: The research reported here was supported by Army Research Institute Contract MDA903-90-K-0066. We wish to acknowledge the Army Research Institute division at Ft. Knox, Kentucky, for loan of the three TopGun tank simulators used in this research. We also wish to thank Lyle Bourne, Anders Ericsson, David Chiszar, and members of the skill retention research group at the University of Colorado for helpful discussions about this research. Thanks are also due to Andrew Bunin, Mark Gehman, Danielle McNamara, Gregory Rully, Vivian Schneider, and Liang Tao for help with testing subjects and tabulating data for these experiments.

retention intervals (see, e.g., Peterson & Peterson, 1959). Following Kolers and Roediger (1984), Healy et al. (1992) accounted for the high retention of skilled performance in terms of a theoretical framework centered around the hypothesis that "memory representations cannot be divorced from the procedures that were used to acquire them, and that the durability of memory depends critically on the extent to which the learning procedures are reinstated at test" (p. 103).

A goal of the present study was to determine whether this high-retention phenomenon and the procedural reinstatement account of it would generalize to a complex cognitive-motor task. The task involved the training of tank gunner skills using a TopGun tank simulator. Successful repeated performance of this task, by many standards, involves not only motor skills but also the acquisition and long-term retention of a complex set of cognitive skills. Given the predominantly procedural nature of the task, the procedural reinstatement account leads to the prediction of extremely good long-term retention of this skill despite the complexity of the task. In contrast, other theoretical frameworks lead to the contrary prediction of poor long-term retention.

One theoretical framework is suggested by Adams (1987), who in his historical review of the literature on the long-term retention of motor skills states that the most useful distinction emerging from studies of long-term retention is that of discrete and continuous motor responses (this distinction was originally discussed by Naylor & Briggs, 1961; see also Schendel, Shields, & Katz, 1978). In this framework continuous responses show superior memorability to discrete responses (see, e.g., Mengelkoch, Adams, & Gainer, 1971). In the TopGun task subjects are required, for example, to locate the target through a continuous tracking procedure that must be initiated by a discrete response (i.e., pressing and holding down a button). After locating the target, the subjects must execute another continuous procedure to sight the target, followed by another discrete response procedure (i.e., pressing a different button) to fire on the target. The fact that the TopGun task contains discrete as well as continuous procedures leads to the prediction that overall retention will be hindered because the discrete procedures will be forgotten.

Another general classification of skills was made by Driskell, Willis, and Copper (1992), who dichotomized skills into physical and cognitive components. They concluded that a longer retention interval more adversely impacted the cognitive components than the physical components of a task. In the TopGun tank gunner task, location of a target requires cognitive processing because the subject must obey verbal instructions from a simulated tank commander concerning the threat locations. Likewise, the sighting of the target requires cognitive processing because the subject must use numerical information spoken by the simulated commander to place the sight correctly. Further, firing on the target requires cognitive processing because the subject must fire when the commander issues the appropriate order. On the other hand, the location, sighting, and firing components all clearly also require physical processing because specific skilled motor movements must be made in each case. Because of the many cognitive procedures in the TopGun task, the prediction follows that overall retention will be hindered.

Thus, the TopGun simulator task contains *both* discrete and continuous motor responses as well as *both* physical and cognitive components. By either classification scheme, one should expect that some aspects of the TopGun task would be forgotten over a long interval.

This prediction of forgetting in the TopGun task, which follows from various skill classification theories, is also consistent with empirical studies. Recent investigations by Fisk and Hodge (1992) have supported findings by Healy and her colleagues of high retention of skilled performance in a visual search task, such as that used in letter detection (Healy et al., 1990). Fisk and Hodge (1992) also reported no decay over long retention intervals in a memory scan task. But in contrast, they found significant forgetting in a hybrid task that combined both visual search and memory scan components. They concluded, "Apparently an additional degree of complexity is present in the hybrid task but is absent in either of the individual tasks" (p. 162). Thus, Fisk and Hodge (1992) suggest the hypothesis that the degree of complexity of the hybrid task is largely responsible for its more rapid forgetting. In the present study, we provide a test for the Fisk and Hodge (1992) hypothesis by examining a skill that is clearly hybrid and thus appears to be complex by their definition. However, Fisk and Hodge (1992) do not provide a complete definition of task complexity. Such a definition is provided in the classic study by Naylor and Briggs (1963).

Naylor and Briggs (1963) in their investigations of part-whole training defined complexity as "the demands placed on [subjects'] information-processing and/or memory-storage capacities by each of the task dimensions independently" (p. 217). The factor of complexity was contrasted by Naylor and Briggs (1963) to that of task organization, which was defined by them as "the demands imposed on [a subject] due to the nature of the interrelationship existing among the several task dimensions" (p. 217). In their study, organization was manipulated by varying the predictability of one task dimension from another task dimension. For example, they presented a submarine, carrier, or airplane (i.e., the type dimension) in one of three locations on a screen (i.e., the location dimension). They considered the task highly organized when, for example, the location dimension was predictable from the type dimension.

In the TopGun task, each of the location, sighting, and firing components make many demands on subjects' information-processing and memory storage capacity. For example, a gunner must assess prior to firing whether ammunition is available. This information is provided by verbal instructions from a simulated loader, and these instructions can be given while the subject is performing any of the location, sighting, or firing components of the task. Thus, the classification of the TopGun task as complex is consistent with the more complete definition of task complexity used by Naylor and Briggs (1963). In the TopGun task, we may consider each of the location, sighting, and firing components as a separate dimension. Viewed in this way, the TopGun task we used was not only complex but also low in organization because the three dimensions were independent and therefore unpredictable.

It would seem that the TopGun task would be classified as complex by the definition of Naylor and Briggs (1963) as well as that of Fisk and Hodge (1992). Nevertheless, the TopGun task consists largely of procedures that can easily be reinstated. According to the hypothesis of Fisk and Hodge (1992), we should find significant forgetting over lengthy retention intervals of this skill, whereas according to the procedural reinstatement hypothesis of Healy et al. (1992), we should find minimal forgetting of the skill, despite its complexity, because the procedures used during acquisition are clearly reinstated at test.

More generally, we set out to examine the acquisition and long-term retention of a complex skill. Instead of selecting a fixed mastery criterion and training subjects only until they satisfy that criterion, as in the traditional approach (see Farr, 1987, for a discussion of this approach), we provided subjects with a fixed amount of training and provided response time as well as accuracy measures of performance (for further discussion of our approach see Healy et al., 1993).

A second goal of our investigation was to assess the advantages of part-task training in the TopGun task. Wightman and Lintern (1985), in attempting to establish a conceptual structure to guide research in part-task training, identified two specific features of studies that came under the purview of their framework. First, a study must involve a transfer-of-training design in which an experimental group initially trains on a segment of the whole task and is subsequently tested on the whole task. Second, a control group that experiences the whole task throughout training and testing must be part of the design. The design of our third experiment is consistent with these two features and thus provides us with a means for evaluating aspects of Wightman and Lintern's (1985) conceptual framework.

Wightman and Lintern (1985) classified the various ways parts of a task can be related to the whole task. According to their scheme, in a *segmented* task the part is either a temporal or spatial segment of the whole task. In a *fractionated* task the parts of a whole task are temporally concurrent. Finally, in a *simplified* task the part is a simplified version of the whole task. The TopGun tank gunner task is temporally segmented into searching and sighting/firing parts (or components).

The theoretical basis of Wightman and Lintern's (1985) framework rests on the observation that part-task training is most successful when a backward-chaining procedure is used in a segmented task; that is, when the terminal segment of a segmented task is practiced alone by an experimental group, performance on the whole task is superior to that of a control group practicing the whole task during training. Because the last action in many tasks converges to a point (e.g., landing an airplane, destroying a target), Wightman and Lintern (1985) argue that the superiority of the backward-chaining method occurs as a result of the development of a strong association between performance on the terminal task and the knowledge of results. They point to converging support provided by response-chaining paradigms in which the response closest to the reinforcer is the most strengthened. Their framework leads to the prediction that part-task training will be successful for the TopGun task when the terminal segment of the task (i.e., sighting/firing) is trained first.

EXPERIMENT 1

The purpose of this experiment was to assess retention in the complex and realistic tank gunners' task. We used 12 subjects, each of whom was given three sessions of training and returned 2 weeks later for a retention session. Each session included the presentation of 50 threat targets, each presented for 40 s. The primary measures of tank gunners' performance that we used were the proportion of threats destroyed, the proportion of threats destroyed on the first shot, the latency to locate a threat, and the latency to destroy the threat after it had been located. We expected to see improvement on all of these measures as a function of training. Importantly, on the basis of the procedural reinstatement hypothesis, we expected to see no deterioration in performance levels across the 2-week retention interval for these measures.

Method

Subjects

Twelve undergraduate students from the University of Colorado participated as subjects for experimental credit in an introductory psychology course. Data were discarded from one subject's second session due to an excessive number of penalties (a total of 40; see the section on stimulus and apparatus for the definition of a penalty). The empty data cells from the second session for that subject were filled in by averaging the corresponding cells from the first and third sessions.

Stimuli and Apparatus

Subjects were tested on TopGun tank simulators developed for the Army Research Institute by NKH Inc. The simulators utilized NEC Multisync Plus color monitors mounted in a sit-down, arcade-like unit. The unit was designed as a training machine for tank gunners, that is, soldiers who lay sights on and fire on threat targets. Subjects in our experiment controlled tank gun turret movements via hand controls. The hand controls and instrument panel switch options resembled those of an actual M-1 tank. Two digitized human voices played the roles of the commander and the loader. The voices told the "gunners" (i.e., the subjects) where to lay on their sight, when to fire, and when they had ammunition loaded and available for use.

Off-line software provided us with control over the presentation rate and duration of appearance of threats using uploadable programmed "scenarios." Subjects were tested on four different scenarios, counterbalanced, utilizing a Latin Square, over the four testing sessions. Each scenario presented the subject 50 sequential targets, one appearing every 40 s. The four scenarios used the same 50 threat targets, arranged in 5 blocks of 10 targets each, but in a different random order within blocks. A sample display of a target tank, as viewed by the subject looking at the simulator monitor, is presented in Figure 2.1.

Although it was possible to make targets move and to hide them behind hills in the computer-generated terrain, in our scenarios every target remained stationary and was visible to the subjects, with at most only a very small part hidden. Also, although it was possible for the simulator to allow enemy threats to destroy the gunner's tank, this feature was not enabled, so that a gunner's tank could not be destroyed. Subjects did hear, however, threat targets firing at them. The tank the subjects were in could

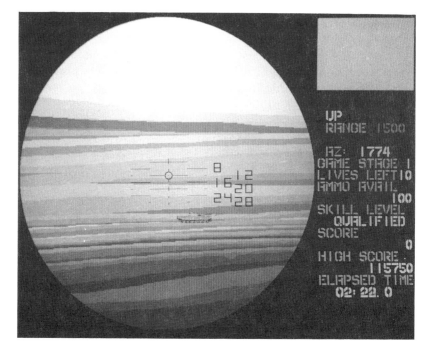

Figure 2.1. Typical View of the Simulation Environment as Seen by the Subject

not move. The hand controls that moved their sight allowed them 360-degree visibility from left to right (azimuth control for the horizontal plane) but a hardware limitation restricted the active playfield to 102 degrees. The hand controls were used by subjects primarily to position the fixed sight onto a threat target. Subjects also had visibility up and down (elevation control for the vertical plane), and threats ranged between 1,200 to 2,000 meters distance away in units of 100 meters. As illustrated in Figure 2.2, threat targets were able to be positioned at 10-degree location intervals; thus there were 10 location possibilities in the 102-degree active playfield area. Finally, although it was possible to manipulate the orientation of the threat target, the specific orientation covaried with the location of the tank in this experiment (i.e., each threat occurring at a given location interval was shown with the same orientation).

All 12 subjects were presented the same 50 threat targets in 5 blocks of 10 targets each. Each block included one target at each of the 10 different location possibilities. Four different scenarios were constructed, each

Threat placement possibilities

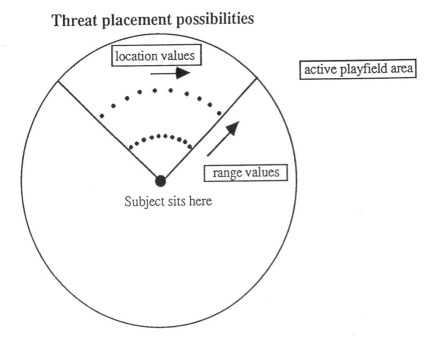

Figure 2.2. Overhead View of the Playfield. The Subject Is Seated in the Middle and Is Able to Look Around the Full 360 Degrees, But the Active Playfield Only Comprises 102 Degrees as Shown. The Potential Placement of Threats Is Indicated by the Black Dots (more placement possibilities exist than are shown). Location and Range Values Increase in the Direction of the Arrows.

utilizing the 50 threat targets, but in a different random order within blocks. Targets were randomized by the 10 location values within each block, and then range values were randomly assigned to the 5 distinct occurrences of a given location value within a session.

The range values, or distances of the threat targets, could not be precisely balanced due to the constraint provided by balancing the targets' location values, but we made certain that where a given range value was missing, a nearby range value was substituted for it. Note that our task organization, as defined by Naylor and Briggs (1963), was purposely low because the range values were independent of (and hence not predictable from) the location values. The range values were marked on the sight used by the subject to line up the target, as illustrated in Figure 2.3. Note that six range values, or distances from the subject, are indicated on the sight:

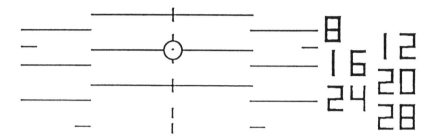

Figure 2.3. Fixed Sight Used by the Subject to Align Range Values on the Target

8 represents 800 meters; 12 represents 1,200 meters, and so forth. Also note that the range of 1,200 meters is indicated by a special circle marker, which might make it an important visual reference mark for the subject.

Subjects controlled the simulator by pressing buttons on the hand controls, one set of buttons for each hand. There were two types of buttons on the hand controls that were used by subjects in this experiment: palm buttons (which were grasped by the middle, ring, and little finger of each hand) and fire buttons (which were depressed by the index finger of each hand). A third type of button was not operational. To move the turret, it was necessary to hold down one or both of the palm buttons while turning the hand control device in the appropriate direction. To fire, it was necessary to hold down one or both of the palm buttons while depressing the fire button under either or both index fingers.

In this experiment, the size of the "kill window" (the window size within which a target threat would be destroyed) included every portion of the threat tank. A shot within this window was scored as a "kill"; a shot outside of it was scored as a "miss." If the subject failed to destroy the tank within the 40-s presentation period, the trial was scored as a "deactivation."

Subjects were given feedback from a constantly displayed game score (see the right-hand portion of Figure 2.1), but due to inconsistencies in the software, the feedback was not always precise. In general, scores were based on the following point system: 1,500 points were awarded for a kill with 0 misses preceding it, 1,000 points for a kill with 1 miss preceding it, 750 points for a kill with 2 misses preceding it, and 500 points for a kill with 3 or more misses preceding it. In addition, 100 points were deducted for a penalty assessed whenever subjects fired before the loader gave them the verbal signal "up." The word "penalty" was provided as feedback to the subjects on their status panel whenever this error occurred.

Procedure

Subjects participated in four sessions: The first three sessions were separated by 2 days each, and the third and fourth sessions were separated by 2 weeks. At the beginning of the first session subjects were told what to expect during the scenario: Enemy threats would appear, one every 40 s, and it was their job to destroy the enemy threats. Subjects were introduced to the hand controls; instructed in the responses necessary to search, sight, and fire; and given experience with these skills on five practice targets, one of which appeared every 50 s.

Results

Measures

The simulators, at the end of each session, provided a performance report for each subject that included kill record (i.e., number of tanks destroyed), time to identify (for successful kills), and time to fire (also for successful kills). Experiment 1 made use of four performance measures—two accuracy and two response time measures. The accuracy measures we tabulated were kills and first-round kills. First-round kills were kills made without a preceding miss (i.e., the kill was made with the first round fired). Kills and first-round kills were computed as a function of session, block, scenario, and location. In addition, first-round kills were computed as a function of range value. Neither kills nor first-round kills yielded significant main effects or interactions involving either scenario or location, so the analyses including those factors are not reported here. The response time measures we computed were time to identify and time to fire. These measures were computed as a function of session and block. Repeated-measures analyses of variance including the factors of session and block are reported for first-round kills, time to identify, and time to fire; a second analysis is reported for first-round kills including the factors of session, block, and range. In addition to the overall analysis of variance, planned comparisons of each pair of consecutive sessions were conducted for each of the three measures.

Accuracy

Kills. Kills were threats that were destroyed before they were deactivated. Of 2,400 total presentations of threats across all sessions and all subjects, only 12 were not killed by subjects before the 40-s interval was up. Thus, kills were not a useful measure in this experiment.

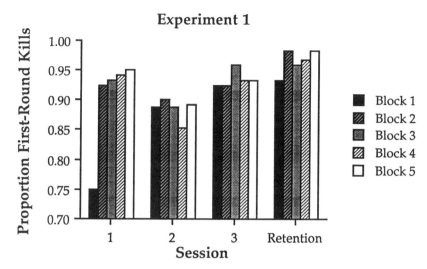

Figure 2.4. Proportion of First-Round Kills in Experiment 1 as a Function of Session and Block

First-Round Kills. Figure 2.4 presents the proportion of first-round kills as a function of session and block. There was a significant main effect of session for this measure, $F(3, 33) = 10.21$, $MS_e = .7700$, $p < .001$, with a significant *improvement* between the third (i.e., final acquisition) and fourth (i.e., retention) sessions being revealed in a planned analysis including only the last two sessions, $F(1, 11) = 6.06$, $MS_e = .0223$, $p < .05$. There was also a main effect of block, $F(4, 44) = 3.74$, $MS_e = .9287$, $p < .05$, which interacted with session, $F(12, 132) = 3.41$, $MS_e = .6032$, $p < .001$, reflecting the fact that the first block of the first session showed the worst performance of all.

To provide a picture of the pattern of errors as a function of the distance of the target from the subject's point of view, we analyzed first-round kills with range as a factor. Not all range values were equally difficult, as shown in Figure 2.5, which presents the proportion of first-round kills as a function of range value. Results for all sessions combined showed a main effect for both session, $F(3, 33) = 9.65$, $MS_e = .0140$, $p < .001$, and range value, $F(8, 88) = 3.47$, $MS_e = .0135$, $p < .01$, but no interaction. These results indicate that subjects' performance improved on any given range value over sessions, but the range values were consistently easy or difficult across sessions. Troublesome range values seemed to be 1,500, 1,800, and

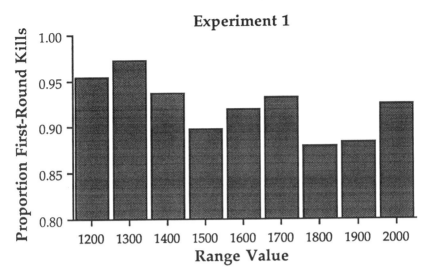

Figure 2.5. Proportion of First-Round Kills in Experiment 1 as a Function of Range Value

1,900 meters. This finding may be partly explained by the fact that the sight the subjects used to lay on targets only included the meter ranges 1,200, 1,600, and 2,000, thus making interpolation one aspect of subjects' cognitive tasks (see Figure 2.3).

Response Times

Time to Identify. A target was classified as "identified" when a subject was within firing range of it. This classification occurred automatically by the simulator when a target came within a subject's field of view. It was indicated to the subject by the commander's pronouncement of the verbal statement, "steady." The identification measure reflects the search component of the tank gunner's task. Table 2.1 presents the mean time to identify for targets that were successfully killed as a function of session. There was no effect of block, $F < 1$, but there was a significant main effect of session, $F(3, 33) = 3.76$, $MS_e = 3.1263$, $p < .05$. Planned analyses comparing each consecutive pair of sessions revealed that the only reliable improvement in this measure occurred between the first and second sessions of training, $F(1, 11) = 7.37$, $MS_e = 3.2700$, $p < .05$. Notably, as determined by a planned analysis including only the last two sessions,

Table 2.1 Mean Time (s) to Identify (TID) and to Fire (TF) as a Function of Session

Session	Experiment 1		Experiment 2	
	TID	TF	TID	TF
1	5.52	3.41	4.58	5.06
2	4.62	2.26	4.55	4.71
3	4.59	2.09	4.21	4.70
4	4.71	2.37	4.24	4.77
5			4.12	4.52
6			3.94	4.54
7			3.86	4.17
8			3.79	4.34
9			3.88	4.18
10			3.83	4.20
11			3.69	4.41
12			3.65	4.43
13			4.04	4.52
14			3.71	4.46
15			3.49	4.63

there was no significant increase in time to identify between the last session of training and the retention session two weeks later, $F < 1$.

Time to Fire. After an identification had been made, the time to fire was measured. This latency measure combined the components of sighting (or laying on the sights) and firing (or shooting at the target) as well as the time to make any unsuccessful firing attempts (i.e., misses). Table 2.1 presents the mean time to fire for targets that were successfully killed as a function of session. The main effect of session was significant, $F(3, 33) = 9.62$, $MS_e = 2.1989$, $p < .001$, as was the main effect of block, $F(4, 44) = 3.59$, $MS_e = 0.5673$, $p < .05$. According to planned analyses comparing each consecutive pair of sessions, there was a significant decrease in the time to fire across the first two sessions, $F(1, 11) = 30.58$, $MS_e = 1.2820$, $p < .001$, and no reliable difference across the 2-week retention interval separating the last two sessions, $F(1, 11) = 3.01$, $MS_e = 0.8865$, $p > .10$. In the overall analysis, there was also a significant interaction of session and block, $F(12, 132) = 2.07$, $MS_e = .9837$, $p < .05$ (see Figure 2.6). This interaction most likely results from the fact that time to fire was unusually high in the first two blocks of the first session. Note that for first-round kills (see Figure 2.4) only the first block, not the first two blocks, of the first session showed inferior performance. Thus, on average it appears that subjects become more accurate gunners prior to becoming faster gunners.

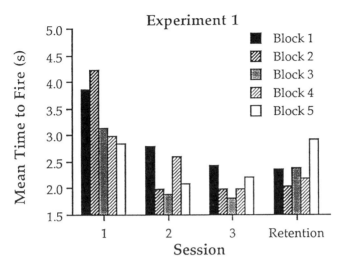

Figure 2.6. Mean Time (s) to Fire in Experiment 1 as a Function of Session and Block

Discussion

Experiment 1 is consistent with the procedural reinstatement framework of Healy et al. (1992) because it provided no evidence of forgetting across the retention interval. Experiment 1 did not entirely disconfirm the alternative theoretical frameworks considered in the introduction including the dichotomies of differential retention for continuous versus discrete components (Adams, 1987) or physical versus cognitive components (Driskell et al., 1992). However, Experiment 1 did serve to restrict effectively the application of these dichotomies. Neither theoretical framework includes assumptions for the forgetting rates in a hybrid task (combining both elements of the dichotomy), so that neither framework has a scope broad enough to deal with a complex task containing both components. Thus, our findings do not allow us to evaluate the usefulness of either of these dichotomies, but they do suggest that if either of them is correct, some mechanism for accounting for the interaction of components in a hybrid task is necessary.

In addition, the durable retention of skill found in Experiment 1 provided clear evidence for rejecting the idea that task complexity and forgetting are monotonically related (see Fisk & Hodge, 1992). Clearly, a task can be quite complex and retention can be quite high.

EXPERIMENT 2

The results of Experiment 1 suggested: (a) the task might have been too easy (performance on the kills measure was near the ceiling) and (b) a 2-week retention interval was not long enough to hamper improvement. In Experiment 2, therefore, we increased the first retention interval to 1 month and made the task more difficult to prevent ceiling effects both by decreasing the size of the kill window and by shrinking the time available to respond to a threat target. In addition, training time was increased fourfold and two additional retention sessions were added to the experiment after 6 and 22 months following the last training session. The longer retention intervals added to this experiment allow evaluation of the comment by Driskell et al. (1992), who in their review and meta-analysis of the advantages of overlearning as a function of retention interval suggested that for cognitive tasks, "any benefit provided by overlearning is likely to disappear after 5 to 6 weeks" (p. 620).

Method

Subjects

One undergraduate and five graduate students participated as paid subjects. The results from two sessions were lost due to simulator malfunction. The missing data cells for these two sessions were replaced with the average of the preceding and subsequent sessions' results. In addition, one subject mistakenly received a ½-hour exposure to an incorrect scenario that included moving targets at the first retention test. His results were discarded, but he was tested on the correct scenario the following day and the results from that test were included in the analysis. Finally, one subject was unable to return for the 22-month retention interval. In the analyses involving all 15 sessions, her 14th session data were repeated for the 15th session. In the planned comparison analysis, however, comparing the 14th session to the 15th session, her data were not used.

Stimuli and Apparatus

Several things were done to make the task more difficult than in Experiment 1. The kill window size was decreased by a factor of ten. Only shots within a small rectangle surrounding the target's center of mass were scored as kills. The engagement time given to search, sight, fire, and destroy threat targets was decreased from 40 s to 20 s. Finally, the number of threat targets was doubled (from 50 to 100) to keep the training time approximately 30 minutes per session.

Because threat target location was not an important variable in Experiment 1, instead of balancing the targets' location values, we balanced their range values. All six subjects were presented the same 100 threat targets in 10 blocks of 10 targets each. Each block included one target at each of the 10 possible range values. As in Experiment 1, four different scenarios were constructed, each utilizing the 100 threat targets, but in a different random order within blocks. Unlike Experiment 1, targets were randomized by the 10 *range* values within each block, and then *location* values were randomly assigned to the 10 distinct occurrences of a given range value within a session, in the same manner that range values were randomly assigned to location values in Experiment 1.

Procedure

Subjects were tested for 15 sessions. The first 12, which were designated as training sessions, occurred on Mondays, Wednesdays, and Fridays for four successive weeks. The 13th session occurred on a Friday 1 month after the last training session, the 14th approximately 6 months after the last session of training, and the 15th approximately 22 months after the final training session. As in Experiment 1, at the beginning of the first session subjects were told what to expect during the scenario: Enemy threats would appear, one every 20 s, and it was their job to destroy the enemy threats. Subjects were introduced to the hand controls; instructed in the responses necessary to search, sight, and fire; and given experience with these skills on five practice targets, which appeared one every 20 s. Four scenarios were constructed, as in Experiment 1, and scenario presentation order was counterbalanced across subjects using a Latin Square design for the 12 training sessions. For the three retention sessions, we used an incomplete Latin Square design.

Results

Measures

The modifications in this experiment concerning the reduction in both the size of the kill window and the time allowed to engage a threat target decreased the total number of successful kills for each subject in this experiment. We therefore report the kills measure instead of first-round kills. A repeated-measures analysis of variance is reported for the kills measure including the factors of session and block. Also, because of the reduction in the number of kills, we computed the two response time measures as a function of half session rather than block. A half session included 50 threat target presentations, encompassing five blocks. Repeated-measures analyses of variance are reported for the two response time measures including the factors of session and session half. In addition to the overall analysis of variance, planned comparisons comparing consecutive pairs of the last three sessions were conducted for the kills and response time measures.

Accuracy

Kills. As expected, a smaller overall proportion of kills ($M = .901$) was found in this experiment than in Experiment 1 ($M = .995$) because of the decrease in the size of the kill window. In general, the proportion of kills showed its largest increase in the first through the fifth session, with performance near the ceiling for the remainder of the training sessions and for the retention sessions ($M = .490, .745, .868, .877, .945, .962, .962, .957, .962, .971, .950, .977, .975, .952, .927$, Sessions 1-15, respectively). The main effect of session was significant, $F(14, 70) = 13.94$, $MS_e = 0.0716$, $p < .001$. Three planned tests were conducted to determine whether there was any forgetting across the last training session to the first retention session, the first retention session to the second, and the second retention session to the third. Only one of these tests was significant, with a reliable decrease in mean number of kills occurring in the retention interval separating the 1-month (.975) and 6-month (.952) retention tests, $F(1, 5) = 7.00$, $MS_e = 0.0233$, $p < .05$. In addition, the proportion of kills showed an overall increase across blocks ($M = .839, .876, .896, .914, .915, .907, .907, .921, .913, .924$, Blocks 1-10, respectively). The main effect of block was significant, $F(9, 45) = 8.16$, $MS_e = 0.0073$, $p < .001$. There was also a significant interaction of session and block, $F(126, 630) = 1.92$, $MS_e = 0.0063$, $p < .001$, as shown in Figure 2.7. This interaction presumably reflects three related observations: First, there is a dramatic improvement across the first five blocks of the first session. Second, there is a smaller, but still substantial, improvement across the first five blocks of the last retention session. Third, there is much less improvement evident in the intermediate sessions.

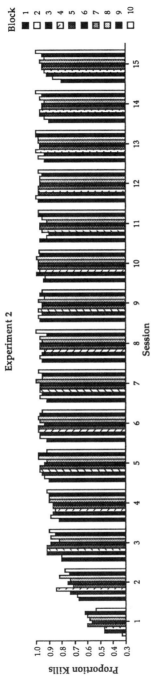

Figure 2.7. Proportion of Kills in Experiment 2 as a Function of Session and Block

47

Response Times

Time to Identify. Despite the fact that there was an apparent overall decrease in time to identify throughout the 12 training sessions (see Table 2.1), the analysis of variance on all 15 sessions failed to reveal a reliable effect of either session or session half, or their interaction, $F < 1$ in each case. This lack of statistical significance is presumably due to the smaller number of subjects and the smaller kill window in this experiment relative to those used in Experiment 1.

Time to Fire. As in the time to identify measure, there was an overall decrease in time to fire throughout the 12 training sessions (see Table 2.1), but the analysis of variance on all 15 sessions failed to reveal a reliable main effect of either session or session half, or a reliable interaction.

Discussion

Again, we found results consistent with the procedural reinstatement framework, with the only forgetting occurring between the 1-month and 6-month retention tests. Interestingly, although the interval between the 6-month and the 22-month retention tests was larger than the interval between the 1-month and 6-month retention tests (16 months vs. 5 months, respectively), there was no significant forgetting across the longer retention interval.

Although Experiment 2 is not a paradigmatic study on the effects of overlearning, because there is no control group trained only to a limited criterion for comparison, our findings still allow us to comment on some aspects of this phenomenon. Because our 6 subjects were destroying 94.5% of the threat targets by the fifth session, each training session beyond that could be considered overlearning. Driskell et al. (1992), in their meta-analysis of the effects of overlearning on retention, found differential effects of overlearning as a function of type of task. For physical tasks, oddly, as retention interval increased, the effect of overlearning also increased. They explained this finding by reference to "cheating"—that is, subjects may practice a balancing task, for example, during the retention interval. They were able to make a firmer prediction for cognitive tasks: that the benefits provided by overlearning were likely to disappear after 5 to 6 weeks. Driskell et al. (1992), however, provided no predictions for a complex task such as ours. The longest separation between sessions (between the 14th and 15th session) was 16 months or 64 weeks. Because we can rule out the "cheating" explanation, subjects should have entirely forgotten all of the cognitive aspects of the task (according to Driskell et al., 1992). There is, however, no evidence of such forgetting by any measure of performance. Perhaps a different method for analyzing a task into components is necessary to understand clearly the relationship of the parts of a task to the whole task. Experiment 3 explored this avenue.

Finally, we note that Weitz and Adler (1973) have cautioned against the use of overlearning in simulators because it may degrade performance on a more realistic transfer task. However, this caveat may not apply to the particular simulator employed in the present study, because earlier work by Hart, Hagman, and Bowne (1990) showed that training on TopGun tank simulators led to improved accuracy on distant targets in a more realistic unit-conduct-of-fire trainer; however, the improvement on close targets was negligible, and a subsequent study by Kraemer and Smith (1990) found no transfer from the TopGun simulator to the institutional-conduct-of-fire trainer. These issues are related to the discussion of specificity of training raised elsewhere in this volume.

EXPERIMENT 3

In Experiments 1 and 2, subjects participated in all aspects of the task throughout the entire course of training and testing. In a complex task such as this one, it may be beneficial to segment the whole task into trainable subtasks. In Experiment 3, we turned to the long-standing question of whether part training is superior to whole training (see, e.g., Adams, 1987).

In the TopGun task subjects were engaged in a realistic, goal-directed simulation exercise. The advantage of using this simulation exercise in part-whole training was threefold: First, it was a task that subjects generally found intrinsically motivating because of its similarity to an arcade video game. In contrast, for example, the important tests of part-whole training by Naylor and Briggs (1963) used training on a laboratory Markov prediction task, which seems less intrinsically motivating. Second, our division yielded clearly separable, meaningful, goal-directed subtasks (see Newell, Carlton, Fisher, & Rutter, 1989, who also recommended the use of natural subtasks). In contrast, for example, in a study of part-whole training with a video game environment, Mané, Adams, and Donchin (1989) found it necessary to use repetitive drills for subtasks. Third, and most important, the simulation exercises we used had separate dependent measures that allowed us to examine the specific decay of task components over a retention interval.

Thus, in Experiment 3 we examined the differences between part and whole training on the long-term retention of the skills involved in tank gunnery. In particular, initial training on subtasks was compared to training on the whole task. Specifically, the experiment included two groups of subjects, one group given part training and the other group given whole training. Both groups underwent three training sessions and a retention session 1 month later.

A special feature of the TopGun tank simulator programming environment enabled us to compare part and whole training. The simulator software allows for the commander to take over the search component of the task by means of a function called *autoslew*. When the autoslew function is enabled, the subject does not perform the search component of the task; rather, it is performed automatically by the simulated commander. The autoslew function was enabled only for the first two sessions in the part-training condition. Thus, the part-training group received initial training on only the sighting and firing subtasks, whereas the whole-training group received initial training on all three subtasks, including the search subtask. As in Experiment 2, on every trial each subject was given 20 s to find and destroy a target. Because the simulated commander performed the search subtask much more efficiently than untrained subjects could, during the initial sessions the part-training group presumably had more time to devote to sighting and firing on each target than did the whole-training group. Thus, part training had the net effect of giving the subjects additional training on the sighting and firing subtasks. There are three questions of interest: First, would overall performance, as measured by success in destroying targets (i.e., the proportion of kills), be better or worse as a function of initial training in either the part- or the whole-training condition? Second, at the retention test, would the part-training subjects' performance on the sighting and firing subtasks, relative to that of the whole-training subjects, benefit (i.e., would the time to fire be shorter) from the extra training in the initial sessions? Finally, again at the retention test, would the part-training subjects' performance on the search subtask suffer (i.e., would the time to identify be longer), relative to that of the whole-training subjects, from the lack of initial practice on this subtask?

In addition, we bear the Wightman and Lintern (1985) framework in mind in considering the effectiveness of part-task training of the terminal segment (sighting/firing) of the TopGun gunnery task. According to their conceptual framework, performance for our part-task training group should be superior to that for the whole-task training group because a backward-chaining procedure is used in a segmented task.

Method

Subjects

Twenty-four undergraduate students from the University of Colorado participated as subjects for experimental credit in an introductory psychology course. Subjects were assigned to the two conditions (part training and whole training) on the basis of their initial time of arrival for testing. Data were discarded from two subjects, one (in the whole-training condition) due to an excessive number of penalties in the first session (greater than 40), and the second (in the part-training condition) due to a simulator malfunction during the third session. Thus, all analyses were conducted on the data from 22 subjects.

Stimuli and Apparatus

The same apparatus and stimuli were used as had been employed in Experiment 2. The first four subjects (two in each training condition) were tested without any breaks during a scenario, as in Experiment 2. For the remaining subjects, however, a short break was interposed between the two halves of the scenario, at which time the computer copied the data to a floppy disk. This break enabled us to avoid storage capacity problems with the computer that were experienced with pilot subjects.

As in Experiment 2, in the whole-training condition and in the last two sessions of the part-training condition, subjects used the hand controls to move their sight to the general location of the threat targets. In contrast, in the first two sessions of the part-training condition, subjects experienced being moved to the general location of the threat targets, but that movement was not under their control (rather, it was under the control of the simulated commander). The visual stimuli associated with the movement were the same in the two conditions, although the movement was probably more rapid in the latter condition. Importantly, the subjects saw the same terrain rush past them in the two conditions as they moved from one location to another.

Procedure

The procedure was the same as in Experiment 2 except in the following respects. Subjects were tested for four sessions. The first three occurred on a Monday, Wednesday, and Friday of a single week. The fourth session occurred on a Friday 1 month after the last day of training. Subjects in the part-training condition were told at the end of the practice trials (which involved the whole task for all subjects) that for the experimental trials in the first two sessions when a threat appeared the commander would override the subjects' control of their gun and point them toward the threat target. All other instructions were identical for subjects in the two conditions.

Results

Measures

We used the same measures as in Experiment 2 with the addition of a new set of measures. Some kills required more than one round for the target to be destroyed. Because the time to fire measure includes all the time that elapses after identification until a successful kill is made, for targets that required more than one round to be destroyed, the time to fire measure does not reflect a simple response time. Consequently, for Experiment 3, we performed an analysis of the time to fire for first-round kills only because that measure does reflect a simple response time.

Mixed analyses of variance are reported for both the kills and first-round kills measures including the between-subjects factor of training condition and the within-subjects factors of session and block. Similar analyses are reported for the three response time measures—time to identify, time to fire, and time to fire for first-round kills—with the exception that the factor of session half replaces the factor of block.

Accuracy

Kills. The overall proportion of kills in this experiment ($M = .796$) was somewhat lower than the overall proportions in Experiments 1 and 2, although it was somewhat higher than the comparable first four sessions in Experiment 2 ($M = .745$). The mean proportion of kills is shown in Figure 2.8 as a function of training condition and session. There was an overall increase in the proportion of kills as training progressed, and no apparent decrease in the proportion of kills across the month-long delay interval separating the third and fourth sessions; there was a main effect of session, $F(3, 60) = 56.67$, $MS_e = 0.0448$, $p < .001$. During the first two sessions there was a large advantage for the part-training condition relative to the whole-training condition (presumably because the part-training subjects had more time to devote to sighting and firing), but in the final two sessions, there was no difference between the two training groups.

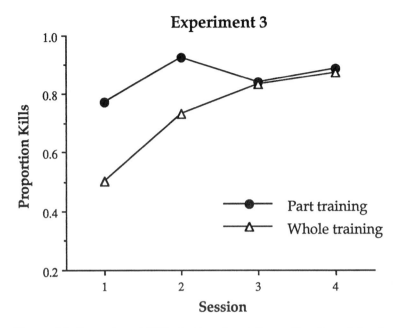

Figure 2.8. Proportion of Kills in Experiment 3 as a Function of Session and Training Condition

The main effect of training condition was only marginally significant, $F(1, 20) = 4.02$, $MS_e = 0.7909$, $p = .056$, but importantly, the interaction of training condition and session was significant, $F(3, 60) = 20.78$, $MS_e = 0.0448$, $p < .001$.

As in Experiment 2, there was an overall increase in the proportion of kills as a function of block within a session; there was a significant main effect of block, $F(9, 180) = 26.75$, $MS_e = 0.0152$, $p < .001$. Also as in Experiment 2, this increase in the proportion of kills across blocks was largely restricted to the first session; that is, there was a significant interaction of session and block, $F(27, 540) = 5.09$, $MS_e = 0.0149$, $p < .001$ (see Figure 2.9).

First-Round Kills. In general, the pattern of results for first-round kills was the same as that for kills, but this coincidence is because 84% of all kills were first-round kills. First-round kills increased significantly as a function of session, $F(3, 60) = 43.69$, $MS_e = .9901$, $p < .001$. As with kills, the part-training condition performed better than did the whole-training

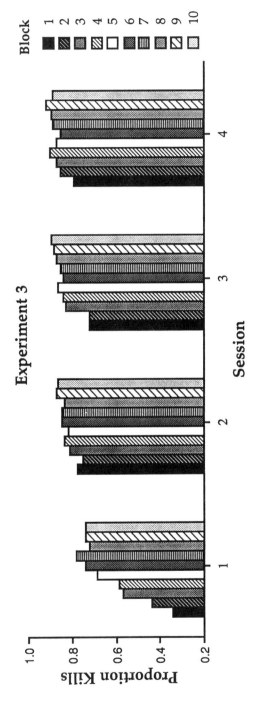

Figure 2.9. Proportion of Kills in Experiment 3 as a Function of Session and Block

54

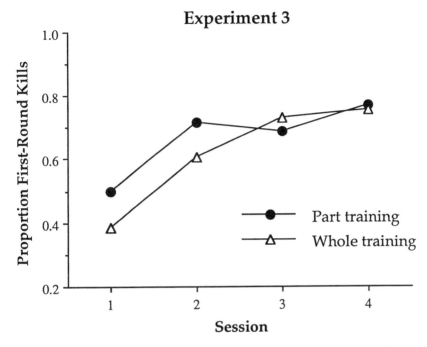

Figure 2.10. Proportion of First-Round Kills in Experiment 3 as a Function of Training Condition and Session

condition on the first two sessions and showed no difference on the third and retention sessions. Thus, as for kills, there was an interaction of session and training condition, $F(3, 60) = 3.25$, $MS_e = .9901$, $p < .05$. The mean proportion of first-round kills is shown in Figure 2.10 as a function of training condition and session.

There was an overall main effect of block, with more first-round kills being made as each session progressed from beginning to end, $F(9, 180) = 14.41$, $MS_e = .2423$, $p < .001$. This effect, however, did depend on session $F(27, 540) = 2.72$, $MS_e = .2120$, $p < .001$ (see Figure 2.11), with the effect most pronounced for the first session.

Response Times

Time to Identify. Because of the autoslew function, the first two sessions for the part-training condition reflected the simulated commander's perfor-

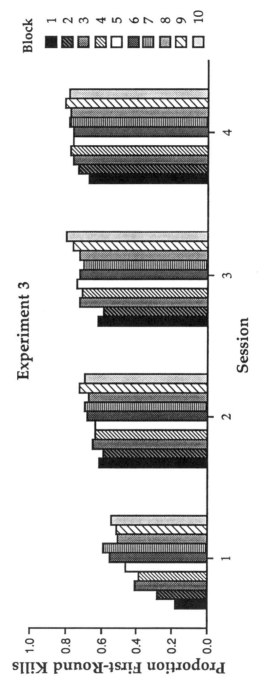

Figure 2.11. Proportion of First-Round Kills in Experiment 3 as a Function of Session and Block

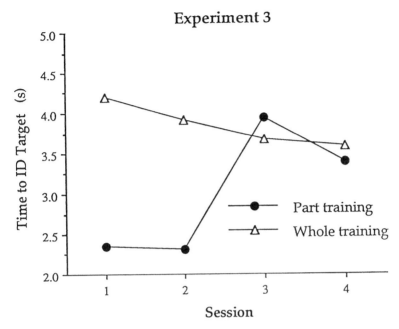

Figure 2.12. Mean Time (s) to Identify (ID) in Experiment 3 as a Function of Training Condition and Session

mance rather than that of the subjects, who had no practice during those sessions with the search (or time to identify) component of the task. Nevertheless, the part-training subjects' performance was indistinguishable from that of the whole-training subjects in the last two sessions (when all subjects performed the whole task, including the search component). Figure 2.12 presents the mean time to identify as a function of training condition and session. There were significant main effects of training condition, $F(1, 20) = 10.29$, $MS_e = 3.0429$, $p < .005$, and session, $F(3, 60) = 13.22$, $MS_e = 0.2984$, $p < .001$, as well as, importantly, a significant interaction of training condition and session, $F(3, 60) = 39.60$, $MS_e = 0.2984$, $p < .001$.

Overall, subjects made an identification more slowly in the first half of the session ($M = 3.551$ s) than in the second half of the session ($M = 3.278$ s); there was a significant main effect of session half, $F(1, 20) = 23.91$, $MS_e = 0.1371$, $p < .001$. This advantage for the second half of the session may reflect warm-up and practice.

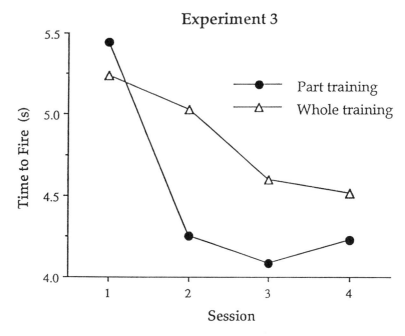

Figure 2.13. Mean Time (s) to Fire on All Kills in Experiment 3 as a Function of Training Condition and Session

Time to Fire for Kills. Because of the autoslew function, in the first two sessions for the part-training condition the subjects were required to perform only the sighting and firing components of the task (the search component was performed by the simulated commander). The commander completed the search component more rapidly than the subjects could complete it on their own (see Figure 2.12); thus, the subjects in the part-training condition were afforded more time during the first two sessions to devote to the sighting and firing components of the task. As a result of this extra time, subjects given part training showed a large advantage in time to fire in the second session of training, and that advantage was maintained not only in the third session 2 days later but also in the retention session 1 month later. Figure 2.13 presents the mean time to fire as a function of training condition and session. There was not a significant main effect of training condition, $F(1, 20) = 1.12$, $MS_e = 4.5975, p > .10$, but there was a significant main effect of session, $F(3, 60) = 13.50$, $MS_e = 0.7089$, $p < .001$, as well as, importantly, a marginally significant interaction of training condition and session, $F(3, 60) = 2.67$, $MS_e = 0.7089, p = .054$.

Experiment 3

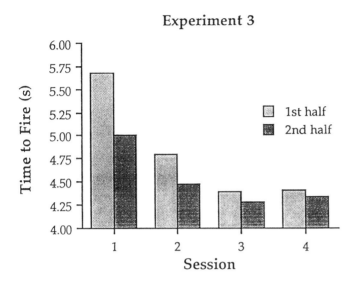

Figure 2.14. Mean Time (s) to Fire on All Kills in Experiment 3 as a Function of Session and Session Half

Subjects fired more slowly in the first half of the session ($M = 4.817$ s) than in the second half of the session ($M = 4.524$ s)—that is, there was a significant main effect of session half, $F(1, 20) = 10.14$, $MS_e = 0.3748$, $p < .005$. This effect may also reflect warm-up and practice. This difference between session halves, however, depended to some extent on the session; there was a significant interaction of session and session half, $F(3, 60) = 3.38$, $MS_e = 0.2532$, $p < .05$. As shown in Figure 2.14, the advantage for the second session half was greatest for the first session.

Time to Fire for First-Round Kills. Overall, across sessions, response time was faster for the part-training condition ($M = 3.172$ s) than for the whole-training condition ($M = 4.055$ s), $F(1, 20) = 6.02$, $MS_e = 5.7088$, $p < .05$. Within a session, the first half of the targets yielded slower responses ($M = 3.693$ s) than did the second half ($M = 3.534$ s), $F(1, 20) = 6.47$, $MS_e = 0.1732$, $p < .05$. There was a trend for a smaller advantage for the part-training condition in the last two sessions; however, the interaction of session and training condition was not significant, $F(3, 60) = 2.24$, $MS_e = 1.0735$, $p = .091$ (see Figure 2.15). Importantly, even in the third and fourth sessions the part-training condition was faster than the whole-training condition.

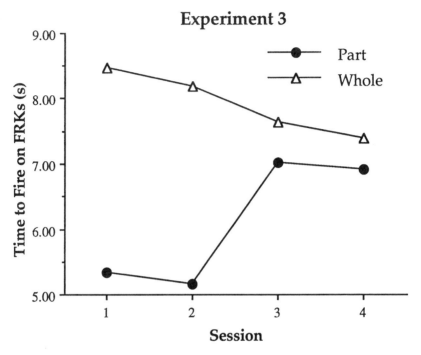

Figure 2.15. Mean Time (s) to Fire on First-Round Kills (FRKs) in Experiment 3 as a Function of Training Condition and Session

Discussion

Our finding of superior performance for the part-task training condition relative to the whole-task training condition is consistent with previous findings using segmented, backward-chained tasks (see Wightman & Lintern, 1985, for a review). Notably, we found that response time latency was shorter on the sighting and firing task segment for the part-task trained group. In addition, consistent with our procedural reinstatement framework, the durability of the part-training group's advantage was shown to extend over (at least) a 1-month retention interval.

A visual discrimination study (Pellegrino, Doane, Fischer, & Alderton, 1991) found that initial training on a difficult subset of stimuli was beneficial relative to initial training on an easy subset of the stimuli when tested on the full set of stimuli. This finding suggests that segment difficulty as well as segment position in the sequence must be considered when designing a part-task training method. Wightman and Lintern (1985) acknowledge that in "aircraft landing instruction . . . the final approach, flare and touchdown are the segments that are the most difficult to learn" (p. 270). Because these are the terminal segments in the whole task, segment position and segment difficulty are necessarily confounded for this task. Thus, the question remains open as to whether segment difficulty or segment position is responsible for the high efficiency of backward-chaining training procedures.

General Discussion

Retention of a Complex Task

In all three experiments of the present series, we found that retention on the TopGun task was amazingly good, with minimal forgetting and even some improvement occurring across retention intervals ranging from 2 weeks to 22 months. These results were expected on the basis of the procedural reinstatement framework of Healy et al. (1992), which led us to make the prediction of superior long-term retention for the TopGun task because of the fact that it largely comprised procedures that were readily reinstated at the retention test. The TopGun task is clearly a complex task, however, and consists of both discrete and continuous motor responses as well as of both cognitive and physical components. For these reasons, three other theoretical frameworks (Adams, 1987; Driskell et al., 1992; Fisk & Hodge, 1992) led to the opposite prediction that long-term retention for the TopGun task would be poor.

The procedural reinstatement framework may seem like a simple restatement of the generally accepted empirical fact of stimulus generalization—that is, like stimulus generalization, procedural reinstatement is a framework for explaining a general match between conditions of training and conditions during testing. But it would be inappropriate to view procedural reinstatement in this limited way, because such a view would lead to the neglect of the procedural reinstatement's more subtle predictions about performance in complex tasks, especially those involving cognitive procedures.

The procedural reinstatement framework is broad enough to accommodate the dichotomous distinctions that have been made to date in characterizing simple tasks. For example, it can accommodate the cognitive-physical, discrete-continuous, and individual task-hybrid task distinctions made by previous investigators. In accommodating these distinctions, however, it is not necessary to assume that each distinction is equally important or useful. For example, the individual task-hybrid task distinction proposed by Fisk and Hodge (1992) may be better understood in terms of task-sequencing variables (discussed later). Clearly, the identification and classification of relevant variables still remain top priorities of human factors psychology (see Stammers & Patrick, 1975, for a fuller discussion).

Although Adams's (1987) prediction of inferior retention of discrete procedures relative to continuous procedures does not appear to be supported by our general findings, there is some anecdotal evidence in support of it. Some subjects reported at the retention tests that they initially forgot the discrete motor response of pressing the palm button to initiate the continuous motor responses involved in the searching and sighting components. On the whole, our findings suggest, however, that the classification of tasks into discrete and continuous motor components may have limited value as a means to predict differential retention.

A classification of tasks based on their organization may have more value in predicting differential retention. However, Fisk and Hodge's (1992) prediction of inferior retention for hybrid tasks relative to simple tasks was not supported by our general findings of no forgetting of the TopGun task. Our gunner task was composed of two different simple components (i.e., searching, and sighting/firing) so it would appear to be hybrid. However, the hybrid task used by Fisk and Hodge (1992) was composed of simple tasks that were performed simultaneously. In our gunner task the simple tasks were performed sequentially. Thus, Fisk and Hodge's (1992) prediction may hold only for hybrid tasks that contain simple parts performed simultaneously. The more general conclusion follows that for predicting retention it may be important to consider not only the fact that parts are combined but also the manner in which they are combined.

Part-Whole Training

Throughout the history of research on part-whole transfer of training there have been proponents of the advantage of part training over whole training (e.g., Annett & Kay, 1956), but more recently, in his review of research on the learning, retention, and transfer of human motor skills, Adams (1987) summarized the state of the field as follows: "Positive transfer is easily found for part-task training, and sometimes part-task training is as good as whole-task training . . . but usually whole-task training is better. . . . The hope that a regimen of part-task training could be better than whole-task training was not realized, then or now" (p. 52).

Our findings (along with those summarized by Wightman & Lintern, 1985) have suggested that Adams's (1987) conclusion was premature.

On the basis of our most global measure of performance, that of proportion of kills, we would have reached the conclusion that part and whole training were essentially equivalent. In this respect, we would have agreed with Adams's (1987) conclusion that "sometimes part-task training is as good as whole-task training" (p. 52). However, on the basis of our more sensitive response-time measures of performance, in particular the measure of time to fire on first-round kills, we conclude that under certain conditions part training is *more* effective than whole training. For this conclusion to be valid, we must accept the response times as crucial aspects of successful performance. Certainly, in the tank gunner situation, a quicker response time is crucial because a rapid-fire response, even when it does not result in a kill, may have important impact as a deterrent. The conditions for part-training superiority appear to be a function of both the organization of the subtasks and the amount of time spent on the subtasks.

As summarized above, Wightman and Lintern (1985) introduced terminology for the description of the organization of subtasks. A *segmented* task contains sequentially arranged parts, whereas a *fractionated* task contains simultaneously performed parts. This distinction is useful because it enables us to contrast our task, which exhibited part-training superiority, from the task used by Adams and Hufford (1962), which exhibited whole-training superiority and formed an important basis for Adams's (1987) conclusion. Our tank gunner task is segmented, containing a search component followed by a sighting/firing component, whereas the task used by Adams and Hufford (1962) was clearly fractionated, the two parts being performed in a time-sharing fashion. In the study by Adams and Hufford (1962), learning only one procedure followed by the time-shared whole procedure initially disrupted performance on the whole procedure, whereas in our task, the learning of only one procedure (i.e., sighting and firing) did not hamper the subsequent learning of the whole procedure by any measure of performance, global or specific.

We propose a simple mechanism to account for the difference observed in the advantage of part training for a segmented versus a fractionated task. This mechanism is consistent with the procedural reinstatement framework. In both training routines, during acquisition (part-training phase), independent procedural representations are constructed for each part of the whole task. In a segmented task, when transfer to the whole task occurs, only a single interruption occurs between the two parts so that the procedural representations can remain intact and independent. But in a fractionated task, when transfer to the whole tasks occurs, multiple interruptions occur between the two tasks. What procedural representation is used in this case? We propose that a new procedural representation is probably established, one that represents the integration of the two parts, because the two parts are performed as an interlocked unit.

Additional anecdotal observations from the present experiments are consistent with the procedural reinstatement framework. According to that framework, procedural aspects of a task (i.e., knowledge of how to perform the cognitive and motoric operations of the task) are well retained, whereas declarative aspects of a task (i.e., knowledge of facts and rules) are lost more rapidly. In our experiments we observed that although there was little decline in performance evident across the retention interval, subjects often explicitly mentioned that upon returning for the retention session, they initially forgot two declarative rules about the TopGun task: (a) that the palm button must be held when turning the hand controls to move the turret, and (b) that a penalty would be assessed for firing before the loader gave the verbal signal "up."

References

Adams, J. A. (1987). Historical review and appraisal of research on the learning, retention, and transfer of human motor skills. *Psychological Bulletin, 101,* 41-74.

Adams, J. A., & Hufford, L. E. (1962). Contributions of a part-task trainer to the learning and relearning of a time-shared flight maneuver. *Human Factors, 4,* 159-170.

Annett, J., & Kay, H. (1956). Skilled performance. *Occupational Psychology, 30,* 112-117.

Driskell, J. E.,Willis, R. P., & Copper, C. (1992). Effect of overlearning on retention. *Journal of Applied Psychology, 77,* 615-622.

Farr, M. J. (1987). *The long-term retention of knowledge and skills.* New York: Springer-Verlag.

Fendrich, D. W., Healy, A. F., & Bourne, L. E., Jr. (1991). Long-term repetition effects for motoric and perceptual procedures. *Journal of Experimental Psychology: Learning, Memory, and Cognition, 17,* 137-151.

Fendrich, D. W., Healy, A. F., & Bourne, L. E., Jr. (1993). Mental arithmetic: Training and retention of multiplication skill. In C. Izawa (Ed.), *Cognitive psychology applied* (pp. 111-133). Hillsdale, NJ: Lawrence Erlbaum.

Fisk, A. D., & Hodge, K. A. (1992). Retention of trained performance in consistent mapping search after extended delay. *Human Factors, 34,* 147-164.

Hart, R. J., Hagman, J. D., & Bowne, D. S. (1990). *Tank gunnery: Transfer of training from TopGun to the Conduct-of-Fire trainer* (Research Report 1560). Alexandria, VA: U.S. Army Research Institute for the Behavioral and Social Sciences.

Healy, A. F., Clawson, D. M., McNamara, D. S., Marmie, W. R., Schneider, V. I., Rickard, T. C., Crutcher, R. J., King, C., Ericsson, K. A., & Bourne, L. E., Jr. (1993). The long-term retention of knowledge and skills. In D. Medin (Ed.), *The psychology of learning and motivation* (Vol. 30, pp. 135-164). New York: Academic Press.

Healy, A. F., Fendrich, D. W., Crutcher, R. J., Wittman, W. T., Gesi, A. T., Ericsson, K. A., & Bourne, L. E., Jr. (1992). The long-term retention of skills. In A. F. Healy, S. M. Kosslyn, & R. M. Shiffrin (Eds.), *From learning processes to cognitive processes: Essays in honor of William K. Estes* (pp. 87-118). Hillsdale, NJ: Lawrence Erlbaum.

Healy, A. F., Fendrich, D. W., & Proctor, J. D. (1990). Acquisition and retention of a letter-detection skill. *Journal of Experimental Psychology: Learning, Memory, and Cognition, 16,* 270-281.

Kolers, P. A., & Roediger, H. L., III (1984). Procedures of mind. *Journal of Verbal Learning and Verbal Behavior, 23,* 425-449.

Kraemer, R. E., & Smith, S. E. (1990). *Soldier performance using a part-task gunnery device (TOPGUN) and its effects on institutional-conduct-of-fire trainer (I-COFT) proficiency* (Research Report No. 1570). Alexandria, VA: U.S. Army Research Institute for the Behavioral and Social Sciences.

Mané, A. M., Adams, J. A., & Donchin, E. (1989). Adaptive and part-whole training in the acquisition of a complex perceptual-motor skill. *Acta Psychologica, 71,* 179-196.

Mengelkoch, R. F., Adams, J. A., & Gainer, C. A. (1971). The forgetting of instrument flying skills. *Human Factors, 13,* 397-405.

Naylor, J. C., & Briggs, G. E. (1961). *Long-term retention of learned skills: A review of the literature* (ASD-TR-61-390). Wright-Patterson AFB, OH: Advanced Systems Division.

Naylor, J. C., & Briggs, G. E. (1963). Effects of task complexity and task organization on the relative efficiency of part and whole training methods. *Journal of Experimental Psychology, 65,* 217-232.

Newell, K. M., Carlton, M. J., Fisher, A. T., & Rutter, B. G. (1989). Whole-part training strategies for learning the response dynamics of microprocessor driven simulators. *Acta Psychologica, 71,* 197-216.

Pellegrino, J. W., Doane, S. M., Fischer, S. C., & Alderton, D. (1991). Stimulus complexity effects in visual comparisons: The effects of practice and learning context. *Journal of Experimental Psychology: Human Perception and Performance, 17,* 781-791.

Peterson, L. R., & Peterson, M. J. (1959). Short-term retention of individual verbal items. *Journal of Experimental Psychology, 58,* 193-198.

Schendel, J. D., Shields, J. L., & Katz, M. S. (1978). *Retention of motor skills: Review* (Tech. Paper No. 313). Alexandria, VA: U.S. Army Research Institute for the Behavioral and Social Sciences.

Stammers, R., & Patrick, J. (1975). *The psychology of training.* London: Methuen.

Weitz, J., & Adler, S. (1973). The optimal use of simulation. *Journal of Applied Psychology, 58,* 219-224.

Wightman, D., & Lintern, G. (1985). Part-task training for tracking and manual control. *Human Factors, 27,* 267-283.

3 The Contribution of Procedural Reinstatement to Implicit and Explicit Memory Effects in a Motor Task

DAVID W. FENDRICH

ANTOINETTE T. GESI

ALICE F. HEALY

LYLE E. BOURNE, JR.

In this chapter, we report on two experiments that investigate the role of reinstating motoric and perceptual procedures on memory. In the first experiment, subjects responded to digit sequences in one of three ways during a study session. Subjects sat in front of a computer and entered digit sequences with the numeric keypad or the keyboard row, or they simply read the digits. At the test session 1 week later, subjects entered old and new digit sequences with either the keypad or the row and made explicit recognition judgments after typing each sequence. Old items were entered significantly faster at test than were new items (implicit memory measure). Recognition of old items (explicit memory measure) was better when the same entry mode was employed at study and at test than when the two modes differed. Experiment 2 showed that compared to typing, the reading condition produced an equivalent level of implicit memory but a weaker level of recognition memory. The results of these experiments show that motoric repetition can improve recognition memory and that perceptual repetition can enhance performance with a procedural task.

AUTHORS' NOTE: Experiment 1 formed the basis of an undergraduate honors thesis by Antoinette T. Gesi and was supported in part by the U.S. Army Research Institute Contract Numbers MDA903-86-K-0155 and MDA903-90-K-0066 to the Institute of Cognitive Science at the University of Colorado.

We would like to thank Michael Wertheimer for his helpful comments on an earlier version of this manuscript, Steve Elliot for his extensive and valuable help writing the data analysis computer program, Mike Kos for his help with computer programming, and Bill Marmie for helping us compose the figures.

The effect of prior experience on present behavior is of central interest in psychology. An actor recalling the lines of a play, a student answering examination questions, a gymnast executing a tumbling routine, and a pilot landing an airplane all depend critically on the precise retention of previous experience. What is the best way to characterize the mental processes responsible for retention in each of these cases? Does the retention of lines by the actor or of facts by the student involve memory processes that are different from the retention of skill by the gymnast and the pilot? Or is there a general theory of memory that can account for all forms of retention?

A great deal of recent research in memory has been centered on identifying different forms of memory and understanding the relationships among them. Graf and Schacter (1985) proposed a distinction between explicit memory, which involves a successful conscious attempt to remember a previous experience, and implicit memory, which is the influence of previous experience in performance without conscious remembering. Explicit memory is reflected primarily in memory tasks that require recall or recognition, whereas implicit memory refers to the role of prior experiences in such "nonmemory" tasks as lexical decision and perceptual identification. Implicit memory effects are sometimes referred to as direct priming, or repetition effects (Salasoo, Shiffrin, & Feustel, 1985).

In recent years, many investigators have focused on the distinction between implicit and explicit memory (see Hintzman, 1990; Schacter, 1987; Richardson-Klavehn & Bjork, 1988, for reviews). In particular, many studies have shown dissociations between implicit and explicit memory tasks. For example, implicit and explicit measures of memory have different decay rates (e.g., Tulving, Schacter, & Stark, 1982), are not subject to the same experimental manipulations (e.g., Jacoby & Dallas, 1981), and are sometimes stochastically independent (e.g., Light, Singh, & Capps, 1986; Tulving et al., 1982). Much of the theorizing done in conjunction with these experiments has been devoted to specifying the underlying mechanism that produces these dissociations.

Tulving and Schacter (Tulving, 1985; Tulving & Schacter, 1990) have proposed that dissociations between implicit and explicit memory arise from the use of different memory systems for these two classes of tasks. More recently, Schacter (1992) has argued that direct priming effects involve a perceptual representation system that operates independently of memory structures responsible for explicit memory.

Other researchers (e.g., Jacoby, 1983; Roediger, Weldon, & Challis, 1989) have proposed that the difference between implicit and explicit memory tasks can best be understood by their different processing require-

67

ments. Jacoby (1983) proposed that the study of a list of items involves two types of processing, data driven and conceptually driven. Data-driven processing involves lower-level perceptual operations; conceptually driven processing involves higher-level semantic operations. According to Jacoby (1983), the demands of the memory task determine which type of study processing will be employed. Many of the dissociations between implicit and explicit memory tasks have been explained by the notion that implicit memory tasks rely primarily on data-driven processing and explicit memory tasks rely primarily on conceptually driven processing. For example, in a perceptual identification task, previously read words are identified more often than new words because the same data-driven operations used during study are repeated at test. In contrast, a recall task invokes conceptually driven processing as subjects consciously try to recollect the previously studied items.

More recently, this basic notion has been qualified and expanded. Jacoby (1991) argued that memory tests are not "process pure" but contain a mixture of data- and conceptually driven processing. For example, Jacoby (1991) argued that data-driven processing at study can also aid explicit recognition memory through the process of perceptual fluency— subjects are aware at test not only of the semantic processing of the previously studied words but also of the ease with which they perceive the words. Fluently perceived words might be judged by the subject as words that must have been presented during the study phase, thereby influencing recognition judgments (e.g., Jacoby, Woloshyn, & Kelley, 1989; Kelley, Jacoby, & Hollingshead, 1989). Further, implicit memory tasks, such as answering general knowledge questions (Blaxton, 1989) and category production (Rappold & Hashtroudi, 1991), can be conceptually driven.

Roediger, Srinivas, and Weldon (1989) have shown dissociations between different implicit memory tasks. In one experiment, subjects viewed words and pictures during a study phase and were then given word and picture fragment completion tasks in a retention phase. Facilitation in fragment completion was maximal when the same format was maintained across the two phases (i.e., word-word or picture-picture). Roediger et al. (1989) interpreted these findings within the framework of transfer-appropriate processing (Bransford, Franks, Morris, & Stein, 1979; Morris, Bransford, & Franks, 1977). Simply put, what is important in producing explicit or implicit memory effects is not whether the retention test taps data-driven or conceptually driven processing, but whether there is a good match in the specific type of processing from study to test (Roediger et al., 1989). In stronger language, Kolers and Roediger (1984) stated that memory for previous events is actually embedded in the processing task in which that information was acquired. Retention, then, will depend critically on the degree to which the cognitive procedures employed during acquisition are reinstated at test. We have referred to this relationship as *procedural reinstatement* (Fendrich, Healy, & Bourne, 1991; Healy et al., 1992; Healy, Fendrich, & Proctor, 1990) and have shown its importance in long-term retention.

The majority of implicit memory tasks studied to date rely to a great extent on the repetition of perceptual operations. Although the implicit memory tasks are often conceptual (e.g., fragment completion, lexical decision) rather than perceptual (e.g., perceptual identification) the study task usually involves only perceptual processing of items. Thus, perceptual repetition is the primary source of facilitation. However, the effect of different conceptual orientation tasks on implicit memory performance has recently been investigated. Hamann (1990) showed that semantic processing was superior to physical processing in producing implicit memory on general knowledge question answering and category production. Hamann (1990) argued that this levels-of-processing effect occurred with the conceptual implicit tasks because the semantic study task provided for more of an overlap in processing than did the physical task. Previous studies have failed to find a levels-of-processing effect on implicit tasks with a larger data-driven component, such as lexical decision and perceptual identification, because these tasks do not benefit from the reinstatement of semantic processing. Thus, the findings with implicit tasks are consistent with the findings with explicit tasks; the memorial consequence of a given level of processing depends on whether that level of processing is reinstated at test (Bransford et al., 1979).

Also relevant to our theory of procedural reinstatement are studies of procedural learning. These studies examine the effect of repetition on the enhancement of motoric responding, an implicit measure of memory. Nissen and Bullemer (1987) have developed a serial reaction time task that has been used in a number of studies to examine procedural learning (e.g., Howard, Mutter, & Howard, 1992; Nissen & Bullemer, 1987; Perruchet & Amorim, 1992; Stadler, 1992; Willingham, Nissen, & Bullemer, 1989). In the standard task, a light appears on a computer screen above one of four buttons on a computer keyboard and the subject's task is to press the button below the light as quickly as possible. After each button press the light moves to a new location and a continuous series of trials is formed. Nissen and Bullemer (1987) found that when a series of 10 trials was repeatedly presented, reaction time (RT) to the button presses decreased relative to when the series was random. Subjects were said to have obtained procedural knowledge of the repeated series. Note that procedural knowledge defined in this manner could be considered an implicit measure of memory because it involves performance enhancement without requiring explicit remembering.

Using a different procedural task, Fendrich et al. (1991) have shown that the repetition of specific motoric operations can produce a facilitating effect. In one experiment, subjects typed long lists of digit sequences on the keypad of a computer keyboard and were retested after a 1-month retention interval. At the retention test, subjects typed old digit lists faster than new digit lists. The entry speed advantage for old relative to new digit lists at retention was taken as an implicit measure of memory for the lists presented during acquisition.

Recognition memory for the digit lists was also obtained during the retention test. In the first experiment, half of the subjects made their recognition judgment immediately after they entered each list of digits, whereas the remaining subjects made their recognition judgment before each list was typed. Recognition for the old lists was significantly better when the recognition test was given after typing the digits rather than before. We tentatively interpreted this result as suggesting that explicit memory was enhanced by retyping the lists relative to simply perceiving them visually. However, because recognition judgments were based on long lists of digit sequences, it is possible that when typing responses preceded recognition judgments, the typing task forced subjects to encode fully all of the sequences in a list, whereas when recognition judgments were made before the digit strings were typed, the subjects may have only encoded a portion of the sequences in a list. Thus, the advantage in recognition produced by entering the digits first may be due to perceptual factors rather than to motoric ones. In this chapter, we report on a new experiment that clarifies this issue.

Similar to the perceptual fluency mechanism proposed by Jacoby and Dallas (1981), Fendrich et al. (1991) suggested that relative motoric fluency was used as a cue for recognition, that is, the ease with which the motoric operations were performed was used as a source of evidence in making recognition judgments. Evidence for a motoric fluency mechanism was provided by a comparison of digit typing times for correctly and incorrectly recognized lists. Fendrich et al. (1991) found that old lists were typed faster than new lists, but only when those lists were correctly recognized, suggesting that subjects were to some extent basing recognition judgments on the speed of digit typing. This finding is in contrast to the many results of stochastic independence obtained in the implicit memory literature (e.g., Kolers, 1976; Light et al., 1986; Tulving, 1985).

Based on the framework of Jacoby (1983), Fendrich et al. (1991) argued that the data entry task differs from most other study tasks in that it involves a large degree of data-driven processing and little or no conceptually driven processing. In the absence of conceptually driven processing at study, subjects must base their recognition decisions largely on the fluency of performing the data entry task. Because the data entry task and recognition memory were both based on the same data-driven processing, a dependency between the two measures should be expected. Similarly, other investigators have found stochastic dependence between recognition and perceptual identification of pseudowords (Jacoby & Witherspoon, 1982; Johnson, Dark, & Jacoby, 1985), presumably because recognition of pseudowords, like digit lists, relies primarily on fluency of processing.

A second experiment was conducted by Fendrich et al. (1991) to ensure that their long-term repetition effect was due to the repetition of motoric operations and not simply to the repetition of the perceptual operations involved in encoding the digit lists. This experiment made use of two different keypad configurations, a calculator pad and a touch-tone telephone pad. Subjects entered digit lists during an acquisition phase and returned 1 week later for a retention phase. At the retention test, subjects either typed digits using the same keypad configuration used during the acquisition phase (same group) or the alternative configuration (switch group). Three types of lists were presented to subjects in the switch group. One type (old digit) consisted of the same digit stimuli but required a different pattern of motor responses because of the keypad switch. The second type (old motor) consisted of new digit sequences that matched the motor patterns of lists presented during acquisition. The third type (new) consisted of new digit sequences that required new motor patterns. The results showed that both old digit and old motor lists were typed faster than new lists, thereby indicating separate motoric and perceptual contributions to the repetition effect.

In a related study, Howard et al. (1992) employed the Nissen and Bullemer (1987) task to determine if procedural learning *requires* a response component or can occur by observation alone. In this study, subjects either observed and responded to the stimulus (response group) or they observed it and responded to it on only 10% of the patterns (observation group, Experiment 1) or not until after 30 presentations of the pattern (observation group, Experiment 2). In either case, the RT pattern was the same in the response and observation groups, indicating that observation without responding can produce procedural learning. This result is consistent with the repetition effect observed by Fendrich et al.

(1991) in which repetition of the perceptual processing with a new pattern of key presses was associated with a reduction of RT.

In this chapter we report on two new experiments that expand upon the results of Fendrich et al. (1991). Fendrich et al. (1991) showed separate motoric and perceptual components of the repetition effect with the data entry task. In the experiments reported here we are concerned with how the combination of these components influences memory. Specifically, the theory of procedural reinstatement leads to the prediction that the repetition of motoric procedures should enhance recognition only if the motoric operations are reinstated at test. To test this prediction we employed three conditions: a "same" condition, in which items were read and typed in the same manner at study and at test; a "different" condition, in which items were read in the same manner at study and test, but the typing operations differed; and a new "read" condition, in which items were read in the same manner at study and test, but only typed at test. The read condition is closest to the observation condition employed by Howard et al. (1992) in that it involves no specific motoric responding at study. At the testing situation these three types of items were intermixed with new items and subjects made recognition judgments after typing each digit string.

The theory of procedural reinstatement makes two predictions concerning recognition memory in these three conditions. First, recognition will be best for the same condition, because it involves the repetition of perceptual and motoric operations whereas the other conditions involve only perceptual repetition. If this prediction is confirmed, it will corroborate the suggestive evidence from the Fendrich et al. (1991) study that motoric repetition can serve as a source of evidence for recognition judgments. Second, procedural reinstatement leads to the prediction that recognition will be no better in the different condition than in the read condition. Although items in the different condition receive additional motoric processing at study, that processing should provide no memorial benefit because it is not reinstated at test. This prediction is interesting because it is in contrast with the view that a greater amount of study processing will produce stronger retention. This experiment provides a good test of whether memory depends more upon the match of processing or the amount of processing.

What predictions are made concerning the implicit entry time measure of memory? First, we expect to find that the RTs at test will be shorter for the items presented during study than for the new items. Second, we expect to find parallel findings for recognition and entry speed with respect to the three study conditions. Specifically, we expect to find the largest repetition effect for items in the same condition because they receive both perceptual and motoric repetition. A smaller repetition effect is also predicted for the different and read conditions, because they both involve perceptual repetition. Repeating perceptual operations has been shown to reduce RTs in procedural tasks (Fendrich et al., 1991; Howard et al., 1992). Third, this experiment should replicate the findings of Fendrich et al. (1991) in showing a dependency between recognition response and entry RT. This dependency is expected because, as discussed previously, the implicit and explicit measures of memory are both based largely on the same data-driven processing.

In a study phase of our first experiment, subjects viewed a random list of four-digit sequences one at a time and were asked simply to read them and press the space bar once for each digit or to read and enter them on a keyboard. Unlike the Fendrich et al. (1991) study, in which lists of digit strings were presented, the present study involved individual digit strings to more carefully control the perceptual processing of the items. A digit sequence was entered with one of two different spatial key configurations, a 1 × 9 "row" configuration or a 3 × 3 "keypad" configuration. Items were presented once or repeated three times during the study phase. During a test phase 1 week later, subjects were presented with old items that had been presented in the first session, randomly intermixed with new items that had not previously been shown to the subjects. Each digit sequence in the second session was entered with one of the two key configurations. Items that were read but not entered during the study phase will be referred to as "read" items. These are items that received only perceptual processing during study. Items that were entered with the same key configuration at study and at test will be referred to as "same" items. These are items that received the same perceptual and motoric processing at study and at test. Items that were entered with different key configurations at study and at test will be referred to as "different" items. These are items that received perceptual and motoric processing at study, but because of the different key placement at test, received only perceptual repetition. Following the entry response for each item at test, subjects were asked to make a recognition judgment for that item as to whether it had been presented during the first session.

EXPERIMENT 1

Method

Design. The order of the tasks during the study session (keypad, row, read), assignment of items to old or new, assignment of items to repeating or nonrepeating, and the order of the tasks during the test session (keypad, row) were counterbalanced across subjects. The within-subjects factors for the items shown at test were type of test task (keypad, row), type of test items (old, new), and nested within the old test items, type of study item (nonrepeating, repeating). For the analyses assessing procedural reinstatement, only old study items were included and there was a factor reflecting the relation between the study and test tasks (read, same, different).

Subjects. Forty-eight students who were enrolled in an introductory psychology course at the University of Colorado at Boulder participated in this experiment to fulfill a course requirement. The experiment was restricted to right-handed subjects. Subjects were assigned to counterbalancing groups according to a fixed rotation on the basis of their time of arrival for testing.

Apparatus and Materials. Each subject worked at a Visual 200 terminal that was connected to a VAX-11/780 computer. The four-digit sequences were randomly generated with the following two constraints: (a) the digit zero was excluded, and (b) three of the four digits had to be located on different rows of the keypad with only two of the four digits occurring on the same row as each other.

Procedure. Each block of the experiment began with five practice trials to familiarize the subjects with the task for that block (keypad, row, read). The subject was informed when the practice trials were completed and the experimental trials began. For each trial, a stimulus item appeared in the center of the screen and remained on the screen until the subject had completed the appropriate task. Then, after a delay of 0.5 s, the next item appeared in the same location. Subjects were instructed to enter the items as quickly and as accurately as possible, using their right hand only.

Each item was a four-digit sequence centered horizontally on the screen. The sequences appeared in this same location one at a time for 240 trials, with a break after every block of 80 trials. The duration of the break was the time it took to read the next instructions to the subject and begin the task for that block (approximately 5 minutes). All subjects served in two sessions. The first session was a study session, and the second was a test session.

During the study session, each subject served in three different task conditions, keypad, row, and read, with the tasks blocked and the order of the tasks counterbalanced across subjects. During the keypad task, the subject read each four-digit sequence silently while entering it into the computer using the keypad to the right of the letter keys on the keyboard. During the row task, the subject read the four-digit sequence silently while entering it into the computer using the row of number keys above the letter keys on the keyboard. During the read condition, the subject read the four-digit sequence silently while pressing the space bar once for each digit (i.e., four times). When the last digit of the four-digit sequence was entered, the response time was recorded. Each of the three tasks included 40 different items, totaling 120 different four-digit sequences across the three tasks. Twenty of the items in each task were presented only one time, whereas the remaining 20 items were repeated three times with the same task. The order of the items was pseudorandom with the constraint that in every eight of the 80 consecutive sequences for a given task, there were two nonrepeating items and six repeating items. The first presentation of every repeating item occurred within the first 26 consecutive sequences; the second presentation occurred within the second 26 consecutive sequences; and the third presentation occurred within the final 28 consecutive sequences. The instructions for each task were the same with one modification, namely the description of the response keys that the subject was to use to enter the four-digit sequences into the computer.

The subjects returned 1 week after their first session for the second (test) session. At that time each subject served in two different tasks, keypad and row, with the tasks blocked and the order counterbalanced across subjects. The stimuli for the test session consisted of the 120 different old items from the study session intermixed with 120 new items that had not been presented during the study session. Thus, the test session, like the study session, included 240 stimulus items. An equal number of items from the different conditions of the study session occurred in each of the two tasks of the test session. In addition to performing the appropriate task during the test session, the subject was also asked to make a binary recognition response, indicating whether each item had been presented during the study session (i.e., whether it was old or new) by typing the letter O for an old item or the letter N for a new item. All subjects made their recognition response for each string immediately after typing the string.

Results

The data were analyzed for all items that were correctly entered. Because some items were presented only once during study, response times for items ever incorrectly entered either at study or at test (or on both occasions) were not included in the means. The percentage of test items deleted from the analyses because of entry errors was 7.6. An alpha value of .05 was chosen as the significance criterion for all statistical tests. Because the factor of type of study item (repeating, nonrepeating) did not enter into any significant effects in the examination of the test session data, it was not included in the analyses reported here.

Response Time. The first analysis included two factors, type of test items (old, new) and type of test task (keypad, row). Of primary concern is whether subjects exhibited implicit memory for the digit sequences after the 1-week retention interval. Indeed, response times were faster for the old sequences shown previously during the study phase ($M = 3.002$ s) than for the new sequences ($M = 3.029$ s), $F(1, 47) = 7.76$, $MS_e = 0.0045$. This analysis also revealed a significant effect of test task, $F(1, 47) = 344.44$, $MS_e = 0.0385$; subjects were faster at entering the sequences with the keypad ($M = 2.753$ s) than with the row ($M = 3.279$ s). The interaction of type of test items and type of test task was not reliable, $F(1, 47) < 1$.

A second analysis of the response times was limited to the old items to examine the effect of procedural reinstatement. This analysis included two factors: type of test task (keypad and row) and procedural reinstatement (the relationship between the study and test tasks). There were three levels of procedural reinstatement: The first level (read) occurred whenever the study task was the read task; the second level (same) occurred whenever the study task matched the test task (i.e., keypad at study and at test or row at study and at test); and the third level (different) occurred whenever the study task differed from the test task but both involved motor responses (i.e., keypad at study and row at test or row at study and keypad at test). Figure 3.1 presents the mean RT for the same, different, and read conditions. As in the previous analysis, this analysis yielded a significant effect of type of test task, $F(1, 47) = 262.26$, $MS_e = 0.0750$. Most crucial, the effect of procedural reinstatement was also significant, $F(2, 94) = 3.46$, $MS_e = 0.0145$, as shown in Figure 3.1. However, a planned analysis excluding the read study task yielded only a marginally significant effect of procedural reinstatement (same, different), $F(1, 47) = 3.06$, $MS_e = 0.0159$, $p = .083$. That is, RT for the old items was only marginally faster in the same condition than in the different condition.

A third analysis of the RT data was conducted to determine if perceptual study processing alone produced a reduction in entry RT at test. Collapsing across test task, there was no significant difference in RT at test between items read during study ($M = 3.020$ s) and new items ($M = 3.030$ s), $t(47) < 1$. Simply reading digit strings as a study task did not significantly increase the speed with which they were entered on a subsequent test phase.

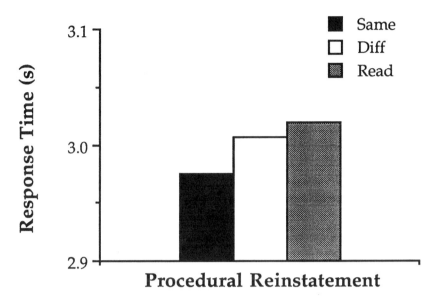

Figure 3.1. Mean Response Times for Test Items as a Function of Procedural Reinstatement. ("Same" represents those responses that employed the same motor task at study and at test; "Diff" represents those responses that employed a motor task at study and a different motor task at test; "Read" represents those responses that employed the read task during study and a motor task at test.)

Recognition. A second set of analyses was concerned with the explicit recognition data. We computed d' scores for each subject in each condition. Of most interest in these analyses is the effect of procedural reinstatement. Figure 3.2 shows the mean d', averaged over test task, for the same condition, different condition, and the read condition. Each of these means was reliably greater than chance performance, $ts(47) > 2.17$, indicating that subjects did have explicit, as well as implicit, memory for the digit sequences. Although there was only a marginal effect of procedural reinstatement on typing times, it did have the expected strong effect on recognition memory. An analysis of variance on the d' scores included the factors of type of test task (keypad, row) and procedural reinstatement (same, different, read). Only the main effect of procedural reinstatement was reliable, $F(2, 94) = 3.93$, $MS_e = 0.1014$. As shown in Figure 3.2, subjects showed highest d' scores for the sequences entered the same way at study and at test. A planned analysis excluding the read study task also yielded a significant effect of procedural reinstatement (same, different),

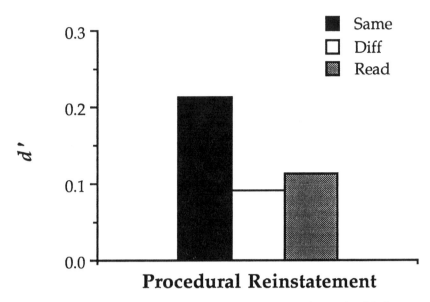

Figure 3.2. d' Scores for Recognition Test as a Function of Procedural Reinstatement. ("Same" represents those responses that employed the same motor task at study and at test; "Diff" represents those responses that employed a motor task at study and a different motor task at test; "Read" represents those responses that employed the read task during study and a motor task at test.)

$F(1, 47) = 5.90$, $MS_e = 0.1188$. Interestingly, a second planned analysis excluding the same condition indicated that when sequences were entered with a different response at study and at test, subjects' recognition memory was no better than when they simply read the sequences at study, $F(1, 47)$ < 1. Thus, entering the sequence at study only aided explicit recognition if the sequence was entered in the same way on the retention test. Therefore, the facilitation due to adding a procedural memory component can be seen as limited to the situation when the procedures employed at study are reinstated at test.

Response Time Conditional on Recognition. A third analysis was concerned with the contingency between recognition and response time, or between explicit and implicit memory. As in the study by Fendrich et al. (1991), the response time data were broken down by the subjects' recognition responses. For each subject and each type of test item, the mean of the correct entry RTs was computed separately for the "old" recognition

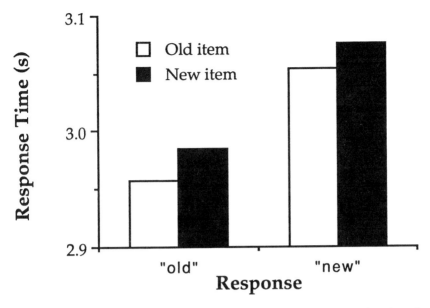

Figure 3.3. Mean Response Times for Old and New Test Items as a Function of Recognition Response

responses and the "new" recognition responses. Because subjects did not necessarily make the same number of "old" and "new" recognition responses for a given type of test item, these subject means were usually based on an unequal number of observations. Thus, the main effect of type of test item in these conditional analyses is somewhat distorted from that obtained in the previous analyses in which all RTs for correctly entered items are given equal weight.

The analysis conducted on these data included the factors of recognition response ("old," "new"), type of test items (old, new), and type of test task (keypad, row). Figure 3.3 presents the mean RT as a function of recognition response and type of test item, collapsed over type of test task. As in previous analyses, both the type of test task, $F(1, 47) = 324.92$, $MS_e = 0.0827$, and the type of test items, $F(1, 47) = 5.74$, $MS_e = 0.0099$, had significant effects. Most interesting was the fact that there was also a significant effect of recognition response, $F(1, 47) = 27.01$, $MS_e = 0.0309$. As shown in Figure 3.3, items responded to as "old" were entered faster than those responded to as "new," regardless of their actual "old"/"new" status. In other words, there was a dependency between the time to type the digit strings and the decision to respond "old" or "new."

Discussion

Experiment 1 replicated and extended the findings from the study by Fendrich et al. (1991) in several ways. First, long-term memory was evident in both an implicit test (facilitation in the typing times for previously entered digit sequences relative to new ones) and an explicit test (discrimination by recognition between old and new items).

Second, explicit recognition judgments were more accurate when items were entered in the same manner at study and test than when the entry methods differed. This result provides a clear demonstration that the repetition of motoric procedures from study to test enhances recognition memory.

Third, our prediction that recognition would depend more on the match between study and test processing than the amount of study processing was confirmed. Relative to the read control condition, adding motoric processing to the study task only improved recognition when that processing was reinstated at test. Recognition was no better in the different condition than in the read condition. This result supports the theory of procedural reinstatement and is at odds with a theory that considers only the amount of study processing as a determinant of retention.

Fourth, the results of the implicit entry RT measure of memory generally paralleled recognition results. It was predicted that RTs would be faster in the same condition, in which both perceptual and motoric procedures were repeated, than in the different and read conditions, in which only perceptual procedures were repeated. This result was obtained although the difference between the same and different conditions was only marginally significant. As was true of the recognition data, the RTs for the different and read conditions did not differ.

Fifth, the implicit and explicit measures of memory were found to be dependent: Fast RTs were associated with "old" recognition responses and slow RTs were associated with "new" recognition responses, regardless of the actual old/new status of the items. This finding replicated that of Fendrich et al. (1991) and suggests that to some extent a common type of processing contributes to performance on the two memory measures. One possibility for such common processing is a motoric fluency mechanism similar to the perceptual fluency mechanism proposed by Jacoby and Dallas (1981). The dependency result is consistent with the hypothesis that explicit recognition judgments are based at least in part on the ease or skill with which the digit sequences are typed and entered on the keypad. Given our assumption that an increase in digit typing speed in the different condition is produced purely by perceptual repetition, it is unclear why a repetition effect for the new read condition was not evident— the repetition of the perceptual operations of reading the digit sequences at study in the read condition should have produced a facilitation of RTs at test. Howard et al. (1992) showed that simply watching a repeated temporal sequence of spatial positions produced a reduction in later RTs for key presses in response to that sequence.

There are two possible explanations of the difference in typing RTs between the different and read study conditions of the present study. First, the act of producing a differentiated motoric response at study, even if it is unlike that performed at test, may be necessary to yield a repetition effect with the data entry task. Second, subjects might not have encoded the digit sequences as well in the read condition as in the typing conditions. Because the read condition only required pressing the space bar, there was no guarantee that subjects encoded the digits to the extent required by the typing conditions. The fact that subjects did not expect a retention test in Experiment 1 further reduces the likelihood that they fully encoded the digit sequences in the read condition. Experiment 2 was conducted to correct for any differences in encoding processes so that the true effect of perceptual repetition on data entry performance could be examined.

EXPERIMENT 2

The main purpose of Experiment 2 was to compare the implicit and explicit measures of retention of digit sequences that were typed or simply read within a procedure that ensured equivalent perceptual operations. Rather than blocking the read and type trials as in Experiment 1, they were mixed in Experiment 2. In each condition a digit sequence remained on the screen for a fixed period of time and was replaced with a message either to type the sequence on the keypad or to press the + key. Subjects were unaware of which task they had to perform when each digit sequence was on the screen, so that the perceptual processing should be equivalent for both types of trials. Retention tests were administered immediately following this study phase. Previously typed, previously read, and new digit sequences were displayed one at a time, and subjects had to type each sequence on the keypad and then make an "old"/"new" recognition response.

Method

Design and Subjects. The assignment of items to study task (read, enter, new) was counterbalanced across subjects. Twenty-four undergraduates enrolled in an introductory psychology course at Widener University participated in this experiment as partial fulfillment of a course requirement. Subjects were assigned to counterbalancing groups according to a fixed rotation schedule.

Apparatus and Materials. Each subject worked at an IBM/PS2 computer. The four-digit sequences were randomly generated with the following two constraints: (a) the digit zero was excluded, and (b) no digit was repeated within a sequence.

Procedure. The study phase of the experiment began with four practice trials (two read and two enter) to familiarize the subjects with the two tasks. For each trial, a digit sequence was displayed in the center of the screen for 2 s. The item was then erased from the screen and after a 0.5 s delay one of two messages was displayed at random. In the enter condition the message "Type digits" was displayed. In this condition the subject was instructed to type the item as quickly and accurately as possible on the numeric keypad of the keyboard. In the read condition the message "Press + key" was displayed. The subject was instructed to press the + key on the numeric keypad four times as quickly and accurately as possible. In both conditions the message was erased from the screen after the fourth keystroke, and after a 0.5 s delay the next item was displayed. If the subject performed the wrong task on a trial the computer "beeped" and displayed the message "Wrong task!" for 2 s.

Immediately following the four practice study trials were 200 experimental study trials. The experimental trials consisted of 20 enter items repeated five times each intermixed with 20 read items repeated five times each. The order of trials was pseudorandom with the lag between item repetitions a random value between 21 and 59.

A 5-minute unfilled delay separated the study phase and the test phase. The test phase of the experiment began with four practice trials. For each trial of the test phase an item was displayed in the center of the screen with the message "Type digits" above it. For all trials of the test phase subjects were instructed to type the digit sequence on the numeric keypad as quickly and accurately as possible. Immediately following the fourth keystroke the message "Type digits" was replaced by the message "Old or New?" Subjects were instructed to press the O key on the keyboard if they

Table 3.1 Mean Correct Response Time in Seconds and Proportion of Errors at Test in Experiment 2 as a Function of Study Task and Keystroke

Study Task	Keystroke				Total	Proportion of Errors
	1	*2*	*3*	*4*		
Enter	1.501	.285	.355	.262	2.403	.054
Read	1.502	.289	.362	.260	2.414	.042
New	1.498	.292	.389	.288	2.468	.044

thought the digit sequence was displayed during the study phase (old) and to press the N key if they thought the digit sequence had not been previously displayed (new). A delay of 0.5 s separated the subject's recognition response and the display of the next item. Immediately following four practice test trials were 80 experimental test trials including the 20 items from the read study condition, the 20 items from the enter study condition, and 40 new items. The order of trials was pseudorandom with each type of item occurring at each serial position in the test list an equal number of times across subjects.

Results

The proportion of trials in which the wrong task was performed at study was low (.01); these trials were not included in the error or RT analyses. The mean proportion of entry errors at test as a function of study task is shown in Table 3.1. A one-way ANOVA showed no significant difference between the mean proportion of errors as a function of study task, $F(2, 46) < 1$.

Response Time. Whereas in Experiment 1 we recorded the RT to type the entire four-digit sequence, the apparatus used in Experiment 2 allowed for the recording of individual keystroke RTs. The mean correct response time at test as a function of keystroke and study task (read, enter, new) is shown in Table 3.1. A two-way ANOVA was performed on the RT data with the factors of study task and keystroke. Planned contrasts were performed to determine the specific differences among the means. RTs were significantly slower for the new items relative to the enter and read items, $F(1, 23) = 5.39$, $MS_e = .0026$. The RT difference between the enter and read items was not significant, $F(1, 23) < 1$. The mean RT for the first keystroke of each digit sequence was much longer than for the remaining keystrokes, $F(1, 23) = 317.70$, $MS_e = .2413$, as has been found previously (Fendrich et al., 1991). The long first keystroke time reflects the encoding and response preparation stages of processing that take place before the key pressing is initiated. The mean RT for the third keystroke was longer than for the second or fourth keystrokes, $F(1, 23) = 75.29$, $MS_e = .0051$. This effect also replicates one found by Fendrich et al. (1991) and suggests that some additional encoding or response preparation processing is performed between the second and third keystrokes. None of the keystroke differences significantly interacted with the study task effect. In the study by Fendrich et al. (1991) virtually all of the difference in RT between old and new items occurred at the first keystroke. As shown in Table 3.1, the old/new difference in RT is not present for the first keystroke of this experiment. The difference between the results of the present study and that in the earlier study is likely due to the frequency with which subjects alternated between entry and recognition responding. In the present study, subjects were switching between making a recognition response on one trial and entering a digit string on a subsequent trial with only a 0.5 s delay between trials. The rapid alternating between tasks probably added noise to the RT of the first keystroke of each sequence and obscured the repetition effect for this keystroke. In the Fendrich et al. (1991) study, subjects entered 10 digit strings before each recognition response. This procedure probably resulted in less noise in the entry RTs and provides a more accurate pattern of old/new differences across keystrokes.

Recognition. The recognition responses of items that were entered correctly' during the test phase of the experiment were converted into d' scores. Two d's were computed for each subject, one contrasting the new items with the items entered during the study phase and one contrasting the new items with the items read during the study phase. The mean d' for the enter items was .80 and the mean d' for the read items was .41. Both of these d's differed significantly from zero, $ts(23) > 3.56$, indicating greater than chance recognition for both types of items. The two mean d's also differed significantly from each other, $t(23) = 3.50$, indicating that recognition performance was better for the enter items than for the read items.

Response Time Conditional on Recognition. Table 3.2 shows the mean correct RT as a function of study task, keystroke, and recognition response. A three-way ANOVA was computed that included the factors of study task, keystroke, and recognition response. There was a significant effect of recognition response, $F(1, 23) = 5.16$, $MS_e = .0062$. Table 3.2 shows that items classified by subjects as old were entered faster than items classified as new. Although Table 3.2 shows a slight overall reversal

Table 3.2 Mean Correct Response Time in Seconds in Experiment 2 as a Function of Study Task, Keystroke, and Recognition Response

Study Task and Recognition Response	Keystroke				
	1	2	3	4	Total
Enter					
"Old"	1.517	.284	.341	.251	2.393
"New"	1.463	.287	.404	.287	2.440
Read					
"Old"	1.541	.273	.345	.252	2.412
"New"	1.457	.307	.375	.267	2.407
New					
"Old"	1.464	.280	.368	.280	2.392
"New"	1.526	.299	.404	.300	2.529

of this effect on test RTs for the read items, the interaction between study task and recognition response was not significant, $F(2, 46) = 1.77, MS_e = .0086$. In this analysis there were no differences among the study task means, $F(2, 46) < 1, MS_e = .0099$. The apparent loss of the study task effect in the conditional analyses is an artifact of the greater weight given to the entry RTs from the relatively small number of incorrect recognition responses. The interaction of keystroke and recognition response was significant, $F(3, 69) = 3.00, MS_e = .0099$. As shown in Table 3.2, the difference between the entry RTs for the old and new responses was larger for the third keystroke than for the other keystrokes.

Discussion

The results of Experiment 2 clarified two issues raised by the results of Experiment 1. First, the finding of no repetition effect on test RTs for the read study condition in Experiment 1 appears to be due to the inferior perceptual processing of read items in that experiment. When the perceptual processing during study of the read and enter conditions was made equivalent in Experiment 2, the repetition effect on entry RTs at test was equivalent for both study tasks. The finding that simply reading digit sequences as a study task produces a facilitation in the speed of later data entry suggests that performance on this motor task benefits from the reinstatement of perceptual procedures. This explanation is consistent with the results of Howard et al. (1992), who showed that observation produced as much procedural learning as responding.

One could argue that during the read trials of the study phase subjects were surreptitiously responding to the items and that this surreptitious responding enhanced RT at test. We consider this possibility to be unlikely for the following reasons. First, subjects were not informed that their memory for the digit sequences would be tested in a later phase of the experiment and so they had no motivation to process the items more than was necessary for the appropriate study task. Second, the pacing of the procedure was fast and left little room for extraneous activity. In both conditions, subjects were given 2 s to encode each four-digit sequence, followed by a 0.5 s delay, four rapid button presses, and a 0.5 s delay before the presentation of the next item. Because the actual enter responses required an average of approximately 2.4 s, it is unlikely that surreptitious responses could be executed during the read trials with our procedure.

Second, Experiment 2 showed that recognition memory was better for items entered at study than for items simply read at study, replicating Experiment 1. This effect cannot be explained by a bias in the perceptual processing between the read and enter conditions because subjects did not know whether or not an item was to be typed until after the item was displayed. Instead, we argue that recognition memory for the typed digit sequences is enhanced by the reinstatement of motoric procedures at test.

An alternative interpretation of this result is that the enter condition did not enhance recognition because of the repetition of specific motoric operations at test, but because the items in the enter condition simply received *more* processing at study than did the read items (i.e., processing during encoding and then processing while entering). We believe this interpretation to be false for the following reason. In Experiment 1, items that were entered in a different manner at study and at test were not better recognized than items that were simply read during study. Additional processing beyond encoding was only beneficial when that processing was reinstated at test.

General Discussion

This study was concerned with several interrelated issues following directly from results reported by Fendrich et al. (1991). In that study, subjects typed old sequences (repeats from a study phase) faster than new ones, which is evidence of implicit memory, and distinguished reliably old from new items in a recognition test, which is evidence of explicit memory. Similar effects were found in the present study with independent four-digit number stimuli in contrast to the lists of 10 three-digit numbers employed by Fendrich et al. (1991), which shows that the effect has a small grain size.

Explanations of the repetition effect in terms of the activation of preexisting memory representations, as have been made in previous studies employing familiar words as stimuli (see, e.g., Schacter, 1987), are less compelling when randomly composed unfamiliar digit strings, pseudowords (Feustel, Shiffrin, & Salasoo, 1983; Salasoo et al., 1985; Whitlow & Cebollero, 1989), or novel line drawings (Musen & Treisman, 1990) are the items to be remembered. We believe that the results of the present study, and other studies of implicit memory in general, are better accounted for by the theory of skill and procedural reinstatement. In line with Kolers and Roediger (1984), we argue that retention depends on the degree to which procedures executed, and thereby exercised, at study are reinstated at test.

Fendrich et al. (1991) have shown that there are separate contributions of perceptual and motoric operations in producing the repetition effect with the data entry task. The goal of the present study was to understand the role of these two types of operations in greater detail. We hypothesized that when both perceptual and motoric operations performed at study are repeated at test, memory should be greater than when either type of procedure is repeated alone. Thus, we predicted that when digit sequences were typed in the same manner at study and at test (perceptual and motoric repetition), responding would be faster than when the key configuration differed (perceptual repetition alone). This difference was in the right direction, but only marginally significant, providing weak support for our argument that the repetition of perceptual and motoric operations should have an additive effect on data entry performance. Our failure to find a clear difference in the RT measure might reflect a low "ceiling."[1] The RT enhancement with the data entry task may have reached a maximum value within the relatively short period of practice in these experiments. Consistent with this explanation is the finding from Experiment 1 of no difference in RTs at test between the repeating and the nonrepeating items that received a different number of study presentations.

The combined effect of perceptual and motoric repetition was, however, clearly evident on the explicit memory measure. Subjects were significantly more accurate on the recognition test when they entered the sequences in the same mode at test as at study than when they entered the sequences in a different manner. Thus, motoric repetition clearly can enhance recognition memory.

The enhancement of recognition memory through motoric repetition is specific to the exact operations performed. In Experiment 1, recognition of old items was improved when the same entry mode was employed at study and at test, but not when the two modes differed. The specificity of motoric repetition on the enhancement of recognition is similar to the test appropriateness effect obtained with the generation effect. Nairne and Widner (1987) compared recognition memory for words and nonwords that were either generated by transposing two letters or simply copied. For the nonwords, recognition was superior in the generation task relative to the copy task but only when the recognition test focused the subjects' attention on the transposed letters. Similarly, Glisky and Rabinowitz (1985) found that words presented as word fragments at study were better recognized when they were presented at test as the same fragments than if they were presented as different fragments or as complete words.

The baseline condition of reading without typing employed as a study task, the read condition, sheds additional light on the effects of combining perceptual and motoric operations. This condition provides a relatively pure source of perceptual repetition. Experiment 1 showed no repetition effect at test for items simply read during study. However, when the perceptual processes for read items were equated with those for typed items in Experiment 2, a repetition effect at test was obtained for previously read items. These data demonstrate, similar to those of previous studies (Cohen, Ivry, & Keele, 1990; Howard et al., 1992), that perceptual repetition plays a significant role in procedural task performance. Somewhat unexpectedly, but consistent with the findings of Howard et al. (1992), the repetition effect was as large for items previously read as it was for items previously typed. As in the comparison of same and different typing modes examined in Experiment 1, we expected but failed to find an advantage in typing speed when perceptual and motoric operations are repeated relative to when only perceptual operations are repeated. Again, a ceiling effect on RT improvement cannot be ruled out as an explanation of this null effect.

The contribution of perceptual repetition to procedural learning has also been addressed by Willingham et al. (1989). Using a variation of the Nissen and Bullemer (1987) task, Willingham et al. (1989, Experiment 3) found that when perceptual and response components were independently repeated from an acquisition task to a transfer task, neither condition showed an RT advantage over a control group. Based on this finding, Willingham et al. (1989) concluded that perceptual and response learning are integrated and do not occur independently. This finding from the study of Willingham et al. (1989) appears to conflict with the results of Fendrich et al. (1991), Howard et al. (1992), and the present study in its failure to find a motoric benefit from perceptual repetition. As noted by Howard et al. (1992), the method of perceptual repetition used by Willingham et al.

(1989) may have been inadequate because it was based on a stimulus dimension irrelevant to the acquisition task. Specifically, subjects responded to the spatial location of the stimulus during the transfer task, which was repeated from the acquisition task, but responses were determined by the color of the stimulus during acquisition. In our experiments and those of Howard et al. (1992) the stimulus dimension that was repeated was always the one on which responses were based. The aggregate results of these studies support the conclusion that perceptual repetition can improve performance on a procedural task if responses are based on those perceptual attributes that are repeated.

Whereas we found that recognition memory was enhanced by repeating motoric operations relative to simply reading items at study, Howard et al. (1992) found the opposite result. Howard et al. (1992) compared observation and response groups in terms of their explicit knowledge of the repeating pattern with a generate task. The generate task was the same as the standard task except that subjects pressed a button to indicate the subsequent stimulus location rather than the current location. Results showed that accuracy of generation was higher for the observation group than for the response group. This result is contrary to what was found in the present study, that is, that explicit memory was better in the enter condition than in the read condition.

One explanation put forth by Howard et al. (1992) to account for their generation result is that the observation condition induces more declarative coding of the pattern than does the response condition and that the generation task relies on declarative memory. In a sense, the observation task is more conceptually driven, whereas the response condition is more data driven. Because the generation task is essentially a recall task, it is more likely to rely on conscious recollection than familiarity and thus it would benefit from the conceptually driven encoding promoted by the observation task. The observation condition may have prompted subjects to declaratively encode the sequence because no other task was required of them other than to watch the stimuli. In Experiment 2 of the present study we minimized the opportunity for subjects to devote conceptually driven processing to the read items by using a within-subjects design with randomized presentation of read and enter trials and postencoding cuing of tasks. Thus, in our experiment the recognition of previously entered and read items would both be based primarily on the repetition of data-driven processing, benefiting the enter condition, which reinstated more processing than did the read condition.

What is the mechanism by which repeating procedures improves recognition memory? Perceptual fluency has been implicated as a source of recognition memory in a number of studies (e.g., Johnson et al., 1985;

Johnson, Hawley, & Elliott, 1991; Kelley et al., 1989). Fendrich et al. (1991) hypothesized that motoric fluency can also be used as a recognition cue, that is, subjects tend to judge quickly entered digit strings as old and slowly entered strings as new (independent of their appearance in the study list). In both of the present experiments, as well as in the study by Fendrich et al. (1991), shorter typing times were associated with "old" recognition responses and longer typing times were associated with "new" recognition responses. Although these results are consistent with the fluency hypothesis, great care must be taken in inferring a causal relationship from contingency data (see Hintzman, 1980; Hintzman & Hartry, 1990), for it has been argued that a dependency between two measures of memory may arise not from fluency but from an item-selection artifact—items that are processed fluently are also items that subjects tend to give an "old" response to on a recognition test. Johnson et al. (1991) attempted to distinguish between fluency and item selection as explanations of a dependency between identification latency and recognition. A dependency was found between the two measures when the tasks were completed for each item contiguously but not when the tasks were separated into blocks. An item-selection effect should have produced a dependency in either case, whereas fluency would play a larger role when the tasks were contiguous. This result is consistent with the fluency hypothesis and inconsistent with the item-selection hypothesis. Although this issue has not been completely settled, the notion of fluency as a source of recognition evidence has gained some direct empirical support.

Given the assumption that motoric fluency is used as a recognition cue, our results suggest that some additional mechanism must also be operating. If fluency is defined solely in terms of the speed of entry responses, then fluency cannot account for the difference in recognition between items previously read and items previously entered. Because the read and enter items were equivalent in entry speed at test, a mechanism other than fluency of task performance must be responsible for the recognition advantage of the enter items.

An additional cue by which motoric repetition could influence recognition is the spatial pattern of key presses. For example, the sequence 7412 produces a distinctive L-shaped pattern when typed on the keypad. Subjects in these experiments often report that they base their recognition responses on the familiarity of the pattern of key presses. The spatial pattern produced by the key presses could potentially benefit recognition in the enter condition. Additional experiments are currently being conducted to test this hypothesis.

Summary and Conclusions

Our experiments with the data entry task show retention of specific digit sequences, both in terms of entry speed and recognition memory, over intervals as long as 1 month (Fendrich et al., 1991). This retention is rather remarkable in that the learning situation is incidental; subjects are not informed that their memory for the sequences will be tested; and the stimuli are unfamiliar, meaningless random digit strings. The present experiments have shed new light on the retention processes involved in the data entry task. First, we found that subjects showed reliable implicit and explicit memory for individual sequences of four digits that were presented a week previously. Thus, it is not essential for the subjects to type long, complex lists of digits, as they did in the study by Fendrich et al. (1991), in order to exhibit long-term memory for the digit sequences. Second, we found that motoric repetition can enhance recognition memory. Third, we found that motoric processing aided recognition memory only when that processing was reinstated at test. This finding supports the role of procedural reinstatement in showing that the match of processing was a better determinant of memory than the amount of processing. Fourth, the baseline study condition of digit reading showed that perceptual study processing in the absence of motoric responding can produce a repetition effect in a motoric task. This finding is in line with a growing body of evidence that perceptual processes play a large role in procedural tasks.

The theoretical framework we have chosen to interpret these findings is based on the position developed by Kolers and Roediger (1984). We propose that memory representations cannot be divorced from the procedures that were used to acquire them, and that the durability of memory depends critically on the extent to which learning procedures are reinstated at test. The question of whether a single theoretical framework can account for the many diverse forms of learning cannot be answered conclusively yet. Rather than fractionate memory into many different components, we believe that the notion of procedural reinstatement provides a common ground for interpreting retention found in both verbal and perceptual-motor tasks.

Note

1. We would like to thank Larry Jacoby for suggesting this explanation to us.

References

Blaxton, T. A. (1989). Investigating dissociations among memory measures: Support for a transfer-appropriate processing framework. *Journal of Experimental Psychology: Learning, Memory, and Cognition, 15,* 657-668.

Bransford, J. D., Franks, J. J., Morris, C. D., & Stein, B. S. (1979). Some general constraints on learning and memory research. In L. S. Cermak & F.I.M. Craik (Eds.), *Levels of processing in human memory* (pp. 331-354). Hillsdale, NJ: Lawrence Erlbaum.

Cohen, A., Ivry, R. I., & Keele, S. W. (1990). Attention and structure in sequence learning. *Journal of Experimental Psychology: Learning, Memory, and Cognition, 16,* 17-30.

Fendrich, D., Healy, A. F., & Bourne, L. E., Jr. (1991). Long-term repetition effects for motoric and perceptual procedures. *Journal of Experimental Psychology: Learning, Memory, and Cognition, 17,* 137-151.

Feustel, T. C., Shiffrin, R. M., & Salasoo, A. (1983). Episodic and lexical contributions to the repetition effect in word identification. *Journal of Experimental Psychology: General, 112,* 309-346.

Glisky, E. L., & Rabinowitz, J. C. (1985). Enhancing the generation effect through repetition of operations. *Journal of Experimental Psychology: Learning, Memory, and Cognition, 11,* 193-205.

Graf, P., & Schacter, D. L. (1985). Implicit and explicit memory for new associations in normal and amnesic subjects. *Journal of Experimental Psychology: Learning, Memory, and Cognition, 11,* 501-518.

Hamann, S. B. (1990). Level-of-processing effects in conceptually driven implicit tasks. *Journal of Experimental Psychology: Learning, Memory, and Cognition, 16,* 970-977.

Healy, A. F., Fendrich, D. W., Crutcher, R. J., Wittman, W. T., Gesi, A. T., Ericsson, K. A., & Bourne, L. E., Jr. (1992). The long-term retention of skills. In A. F. Healy, S. M. Kosslyn, & R. M. Shiffrin (Eds.), *From learning processes to cognitive processes: Essays in honor of William K. Estes* (Vol. 2, pp. 87-118). Hillsdale, NJ: Lawrence Erlbaum.

Healy, A. F., Fendrich D. W., & Proctor, J. D. (1990). Acquisition and retention of a letter detection skill. *Journal of Experimental Psychology: Learning, Memory, and Cognition, 16,* 270-281.

Hintzman, D. L. (1980). Simpson's paradox and the analysis of memory retrieval. *Psychological Review, 87,* 398-410.

Hintzman, D. L. (1990). Human learning and memory: Connections and dissociations. *Annual Review of Psychology, 41,* 109-139.

Hintzman, D. L., & Hartry, A. L. (1990). Item effects in recognition and fragment completion: Contingency relations vary for different subsets of items. *Journal of Experimental Psychology: Learning, Memory, and Cognition, 16,* 955-969.

Howard, J. H., Mutter, S. A., & Howard, D. V. (1992). Serial pattern learning by event observation. *Journal of Experimental Psychology: Learning, Memory, and Cognition, 18,* 1029-1039.

Jacoby, L. L. (1983). Remembering the data: Analyzing interactive processes in reading. *Journal of Verbal Learning and Verbal Behavior, 22,* 485-508.

Jacoby, L. L. (1991). A process dissociation framework: Separating automatic from intentional uses of memory. *Journal of Memory and Language, 30,* 513-541.

Jacoby, L. L., & Dallas, M. (1981). On the relation between autobiographical memory and perceptual learning. *Journal of Experimental Psychology: General, 110,* 306-340.

Jacoby, L. L., & Witherspoon, D. (1982). Remembering without awareness. *Canadian Journal of Psychology, 36,* 300-324.

Jacoby, L. L., Woloshyn, V., & Kelley, C. (1989). Becoming famous without being recognized: Unconscious influences of memory produced by dividing attention. *Journal of Experimental Psychology: General, 118,* 115-125.

Johnson, W. A., Dark, V. J., & Jacoby L. L. (1985). Perceptual fluency and recognition memory. *Journal of Experimental Psychology: Learning, Memory, and Cognition, 11,* 3-11.

Johnson, W. A., Hawley, K. J., & Elliott, J.M.G. (1991). Contribution of perceptual fluency to recognition memory. *Journal of Experimental Psychology: Learning, Memory, and Cognition, 17,* 210-223.

Kelley, C. M., Jacoby, L. L., & Hollingshead, A. (1989). Direct versus indirect tests of memory for source: Judgments of modality. *Journal of Experimental Psychology: Learning, Memory, and Cognition, 15,* 1101-1108.

Kolers, P. A. (1976). Reading a year later. *Journal of Experimental Psychology: Human Learning and Memory, 2,* 554-565.

Kolers, P. A., & Roediger, H. L. (1984). Procedures of mind. *Journal of Verbal Learning and Verbal Behavior, 23,* 425-449.

Light, L. L., Singh, A., & Capps, J. L. (1986). Dissociation of memory and awareness in young and older adults. *Journal of Clinical and Experimental Neuropsychology, 8,* 62-74.

Morris, C. D., Bransford, J. D., & Franks, J. J. (1977). Levels of processing versus transfer appropriate processing. *Journal of Verbal Learning and Verbal Behavior, 16,* 519-533.

Musen, G., & Treisman, A. (1990). Implicit and explicit memory for visual patterns. *Journal of Experimental Psychology: Learning, Memory, and Cognition, 16,* 127-137.

Nairne, J. S., & Widner, R. L., Jr. (1987). Generation effects with nonwords: The role of test appropriateness. *Journal of Experimental Psychology: Learning, Memory, and Cognition, 13,* 164-171.

Nissen, M. J., & Bullemer, P. (1987). Attentional requirements of learning: Evidence from performance measures. *Cognitive Psychology, 19,* 1-32.

Perruchet, P., & Amorim, M. (1992). Conscious knowledge and changes in sequence learning: Evidence against dissociation. *Journal of Experimental Psychology: Learning, Memory, and Cognition, 18,* 785-800.

Rappold, V. A., & Hashtroudi, S. (1991). Does organization improve priming? *Journal of Experimental Psychology: Learning, Memory, and Cognition, 17,* 103-114.

Richardson-Klavehn, A., & Bjork, R. A. (1988). Measures of memory. *Annual Review of Psychology, 39,* 475-543.

Roediger, H. L., Srinivas, K., & Weldon, M. S. (1989). Dissociations between implicit measures of memory. In S. Lewandowsky, J. C. Dunn, & K. Kirsner (Eds.), *Implicit memory: Theoretical issues* (pp. 67-84). Hillsdale, NJ: Lawrence Erlbaum.

Roediger, H. L., Weldon, M. S., & Challis, B. H. (1989). Explaining dissociations between implicit and explicit measures of retention: A processing account. In H. L. Roediger & F.I.M. Craik (Eds.), *Varieties of memory and consciousness: Essays in honor of Endel Tulving* (pp. 3-41). Hillsdale, NJ: Lawrence Erlbaum.

Salasoo, A., Shiffrin, R. M., & Feustel, T. C. (1985). Building permanent memory codes: Codification and repetition effects in word identification. *Journal of Experimental Psychology: General, 114,* 50-77.

Schacter, D. L. (1987). Implicit memory: History and current status. *Journal of Experimental Psychology: Learning, Memory, and Cognition, 13,* 501-518.

Schacter, D. L. (1992). Priming and multiple memory systems: Perceptual mechanisms of implicit memory. *Journal of Cognitive Neuroscience, 4,* 244-256.

Stadler, M. A. (1992). Statistical structure and implicit serial learning. *Journal of Experimental Psychology: Learning, Memory and Cognition, 18,* 318-327.

Tulving, E. (1985). How many memory systems are there? *American Psychologist, 40,* 385-398.

Tulving, E., & Schacter, D. L. (1990). Priming and human memory systems. *Science, 247,* 301-305.

Tulving, E., Schacter, D. L., & Stark, H. (1982). Priming effects in word fragment completion are independent of recognition memory. *Journal of Experimental Psychology: Learning, Memory, and Cognition, 8,* 336-342.

Whitlow, J. W., Jr., & Cebollero, A. (1989). The nature of word frequency effects on perceptual identification. *Journal of Experimental Psychology: Learning, Memory, and Cognition, 15,* 643-656.

Willingham, D. B., Nissen, M. J., & Bullemer, P. (1989). On the development of procedural knowledge. *Journal of Experimental Psychology: Learning, Memory, and Cognition, 15,* 1047-1060.

4 The Effects of Contextual Interference on the Acquisition and Retention of Logical Rules

VIVIAN I. SCHNEIDER

ALICE F. HEALY

K. ANDERS ERICSSON

LYLE E. BOURNE, JR.

In three experiments a cognitive task was used to explore contextual interference effects previously demonstrated in verbal and motor tasks. Subjects practiced a task involving logical rules in a random, blocked, or serial practice schedule. Subjects in the random group were significantly slower than those in the blocked group to respond during the acquisition phase. In subsequent tests given immediately after the practice phase or after a 1-week or 4-week delay, subjects in the random group responded faster than did subjects in the blocked group, especially on random trials. The serial group's response times were intermediate. Precues indicated which rule would be applicable on some trials. Response time was faster for those trials with a precue, and this advantage was greater for random than for blocked trials. These results support the hypothesis that contextual interference is due to the need to reload the rule into working memory on each trial.

AUTHORS' NOTE: This research was supported in part by Army Research Institute Contracts MDA 903-86-K-0155, MDA 903-90-K-0066, and MDA 903-93-K-0010 to the Institute of Cognitive Science at the University of Colorado. Experiments 1 and 2 were conducted by the first author in partial fulfillment of the requirements for the Ph.D. degree. Thanks are extended to Dr. John S. Werner and Dr. Verne Keenan for serving on the dissertation committee. Thanks are also due to Deborah Clawson for writing the computer programs for the on-line experiments, and to Bill Marmie and Cheri King for help with the preparation of the figures and the formatting of the manuscript.

K. Anders Ericsson is currently at Florida State University. Correspondence should be addressed to Vivian Schneider, Department of Psychology, University of Colorado, Campus Box 345, Boulder, CO 80309-0345.

High contextual interference slows learning but often produces superior long-term memory and greater intertask transfer (e.g., Battig, 1972, 1979). For example, increasing the similarity of items to be learned or varying the processing requirements from trial to trial interferes with acquisition but aids retention and transfer. According to Battig (1972, 1979), contextual interference must be overcome by deeper cognitive processing so that items thus affected will be learned more slowly. But if well learned initially, the same items are retained as well as, or better than, the low-interference items. This finding is of clear importance to the study of long-term skill retention because it implies that the methods used to optimize performance during training are not necessarily those that optimize performance during subsequent retention tests.

One of the methods of producing contextual interference is by using random, as opposed to blocked, practice schedules for acquisition. Practice in a task domain is often organized into blocks of trials, each block consisting of only one of several parts of the whole task—what we refer to as *blocked practice*. Practice in the task domain can also be organized in such a way that all the different parts of the whole task are randomly intermixed across trials. We refer to this condition as random practice. The hypothesis is that random schedules cause higher contextual interference by virtue of the intertrial shifts in the type of cognitive processing required, which make acquisition more difficult.

Shea and Morgan (1979) were the first to test this hypothesis in a motor skill task. The task involved knocking down barriers in three specified orders. The subjects who practiced the three orders randomly intermixed had considerably slower reaction times during the acquisition phase but better retention and transfer relative to those who practiced each order in blocked trials. More specifically, subjects who trained in the blocked condition did very poorly when tested on a random test at either a 10-minute delay or a 10-day delay. Differences on a blocked test were minimal at both the 10-minute and the 10-day retention test. The subjects were also given two transfer tasks, one of equivalent complexity to the acquisition tasks and the other of greater complexity. Random acquisition groups performed faster on both transfer tasks, with the difference being greater for the more complex task. These results support Battig's (1979) idea that practice under conditions of high contextual interference causes less dependence on memory reinstatement of contextual factors during acquisition.

Lee and Magill (1983) asked subjects to respond to a stimulus light as quickly as possible by knocking down a series of hinged barriers in an order specific to the color of the light. They pointed out that in this task random presentations could be considered a choice-reaction paradigm, because a selection among different responses had to be made by the subject, whereas blocked presentations would be a simple-reaction paradigm, because the subject always knew which response to give. By adding a cuing factor, a warning light that provided information about the nature of the trial to come, Lee and Magill (1983) were able to collect evidence on two variables—practice schedule (random and blocked) and type of reaction paradigm (choice or simple)—that had been confounded in the Shea and Morgan (1979) study.

Lee and Magill (1983) found that for the acquisition phase the main impact on reaction time was due to the reaction paradigm. However, they found that the differences for the retention phase came from the practice schedule. They proposed that the blocked and random difference could be due to the predictability of the trial sequence. To test this hypothesis in their second experiment they added a new, serial condition in which the three types of trials were intermixed, but given in a fixed predictable order. There was no difference found between the serial and random groups; therefore, unpredictability during acquisition did not seem to be the cause of the contextual interference effect observed in Experiment 1. Lee and Magill (1983) concluded that repetition of the "cognitive-motor" event was the crucial factor differentiating the blocked condition from the other conditions and that because blocked practice allowed the maintenance of the skill in consciousness from trial to trial, whereas random and serial practice required the reconstructing of the skill for each trial, differences in trial-to-trial processing requirements produced the difference in retention (see also Jacoby, 1978; Cuddy & Jacoby, 1982).

Most of the studies previously conducted on contextual interference consisted of verbal learning or motor skill tasks. The major exceptions are Hiew (1977), who used a conceptual rule learning and generalization task; Carlson and Schneider (1989), who examined judgments using causal rules; and Carlson and Yaure (1990), who investigated the learning of cognitive procedural skills used in problem solving.

Hiew (1977), the first to look for contextual interference effects in a primarily cognitive task, tested subjects on conceptual rule learning and generalization. Two conditions were included, one in which the rules were mixed in a series of problems and one in which they were presented in a systematic manner. The results supported the hypothesis that randomly presenting the rules aided in subsequent transfer.

Carlson and Schneider (1989) examined the effect of acquisition context on judgments using a causal rule. For their task they made use of five logic gates, each with an associated logical rule (inverter, *and, or, nand, nor*). The rules were shown to subjects during the instructional phase and subjects could ask for help any time during the trial. Randomizing the types of gates in a subsequent test interfered with performance as evidenced both by the subjects' objective performance and by their comments. Carlson and Schneider (1989) point out that this increase in difficulty with the random orders of gates indicates that discriminating between the symbols and accessing the appropriate rules were major sources of difficulty in early learning.

In two experiments, Carlson and Yaure (1990) compared blocked and random practice schedules to determine if the contextual interference effect could be extended to the learning of logical rules to be used in problem solving. They found that subjects in a practice condition blocked by rule did learn Boolean logic functions faster than those in a random practice condition, and that transferring from blocked to random was more difficult than transferring from random to blocked. Subjects in the random practice group had little trouble switching to blocked, but when the blocked practice group switched to random their speed fell to the initial level of the random groups. In a third experiment, Carlson and Yaure (1990) introduced intervening tasks between the trials of the blocked acquisition. The content of the intervening tasks was dissimilar to the logic functions and varied in the nature of the cognitive procedures required. Carlson and Yaure (1990) hypothesized that the intervening tasks that required active processing would produce benefits similar to those produced by random practice. They interpreted these results in terms of the "ability to coordinate representations and procedures in working memory" (Carlson & Yaure, 1990, p. 494)—that is, during the learning phase the subjects in the random practice schedule had to reload the procedure into working memory on each trial, whereas the blocked practice subjects already had the procedures in working memory from the preceding trial and did not need to reload (or reprocess). It is this extra processing that provided the benefit seen in random practice.

Two types of explanations have been offered for the contextual interference effect produced by random practice schedules. The first, favored by Jacoby (1978) and Lee and Magill (1983), relies on an intraitem processing mechanism and the second, favored by Shea and Zimny (1983, 1988), involves interitem processing. Intraitem processing emphasizes the cognitive procedures executed within each practice trial. For each trial in random practice, the subject must construct the item to be learned. In the blocked condition, the item can remain in working memory over a number of trials and need not be reconstructed each time.

Thus, the blocked condition allows learning to proceed rapidly but affords the subject little or no practice in trial preparation procedures. In random practice, more practice is given to reconstructing the item or component skill and thus procedures in accessing and using the component skills (as opposed to procedures for choosing which of several skills to use) become fluent. This explanation emphasizes the efficiency of processes in working memory rather than the structure of long-term memory. In contrast, an interitem processing hypothesis emphasizes the structure of the memory representation that is developed by practice. High contextual interference (or random practice) causes relational interitem processing and results in a richer set of retrieval cues that can better discriminate among the set of items, or component skills, to be learned. Random practice allows the subject to contrast the different items to be learned, whereas blocked practice limits the comparison.

Carlson and Yaure (1990) conclude that their results indicate that the transfer effect relies more on the intraitem processing mechanism than on the relational interitem processing mechanism. This conclusion is supported by the fact that random practice and an intervening task in the blocked condition share a characteristic that is sufficient for producing the transfer advantage. This characteristic is that the procedure for applying a particular rule is cleared from working memory and must be reloaded on each trial. However, Carlson and Yaure (1990) believe that both mechanisms are needed to account for their results—that is, differences in interitem processing might account for slower acquisition by the random practice group, but differences in intraitem processing might account for the better transfer performance of the random group. It seems unlikely that one explanation could account for both the large decrement in acquisition for the random practice group and for the facilitation of transfer for the same group. Their main point is that one locus of the contextual interference effect is the ability to load procedures efficiently into working memory, rather than the content of working memory.

Jacoby (1978) believes the cause of contextual interference to be "effortful" remembering as opposed to "effortless" remembering. Again, if an item remains in working memory, no effort is required to recall it and nothing is learned. If, however, effort is required to recall it, more learning takes place. Similarly, Cuddy and Jacoby (1982) refer to constructing the items in working memory as opposed to just holding the items in working memory. More is learned when reconstruction is required.

In summary, contextual interference refers to the fact that items learned under conditions of high interference are slower to be acquired but are retained better and show more positive transfer. Interference can be caused by the similarity of the items or by varying the processing requirement from trial to trial. It can also be caused by random practice schedules, rather than blocked; by spaced, rather than massed, presentations; or by generating rather than reading items (i.e., the generation effect; see Slamecka & Graf, 1978).

EXPERIMENT 1

The purposes of the first experiment were (a) to test for the contextual interference effects produced by different practice schedules in a cognitive procedural task and (b) to test the idea that a precue as to the applicable rule on each trial might make performance in the random and blocked conditions more similar—that is, will including a precue in the random condition allow the subjects to retrieve the applicable rule in advance and thus make their performance similar to that in the blocked condition with no precue? To this end we used a display meant to simulate a simplified aircraft instrument monitor consisting of four panels, only one of which was active on any trial. The subjects' task was to decide if the display in the active panel indicated an emergency or not. Each panel involved a different logical rule on which the decision was to be made. The four rules were *and, or, nand,* and *nor;* each was assigned to a particular panel throughout training and test. On half of the trials we gave a 1,000 ms precue denoting which panel would be relevant on that trial. The other half of the trials had the same cue denoting the relevant panel, but the cue occurred at the same time as the test stimulus itself.

All subjects received an acquisition phase and then immediately afterward two test trial blocks, one consisting of blocked rules and one of random rules, with the order of the test blocks counterbalanced across subjects. As in the acquisition phase, half of the trials in the test blocks included the 1,000 ms precue and half did not. We expected that the random practice group would be slower to respond in the acquisition phase of the task but faster in both test blocks, as found previously by Shea and Morgan (1979) in a motor skill task. Based on the results of Lee and Magill (1983), we expected the 1,000 ms cue to make more of a difference to the random group than to the blocked group and on the random test than on the blocked test because when trials were blocked the subjects would usually already know which panel they should attend to.

Method

Materials and Design. The experiment was conducted on an IBM PC programmed in Micro Experimental Laboratory (MEL; Schneider, 1988).

'AND'	'OR'	'NAND'	'NOR'
XXX XXX Yes	XXX XXX Yes	XXX XXX No	XXX XXX No
XXX OOO No	XXX OOO Yes	XXX OOO Yes	XXX OOO No
OOO XXX No	OOO XXX Yes	OOO XXX Yes	OOO XXX No
OOO OOO No	OOO OOO No	OOO OOO Yes	OOO OOO Yes

Figure 4.1. Rule Table

The four logical rules used were *and, or, nand,* and *nor.* They were exemplified in two rows of XXX or OOO, as shown in Figure 4.1. The acquisition phase consisted of eight blocks of 32 trials. There were 16 possible stimulus configurations (four for each of four rules), and in the random practice condition, each block had two presentations of each configuration. In the blocked condition, subjects saw two blocks of each rule, and within each block each stimulus configuration occurred eight times. For the random practice condition, a fixed order of presentation was constructed so that for the first 16 trials of a block each of the configurations occurred once in a fixed random order and then for the last 16 trials of a block each configuration occurred again in a different fixed random order. The random order was further constrained by allowing no more than two stimuli from the same rule to occur successively. All eight blocks were randomized separately. A second set of presentation orders was formed by reversing within each block the order of the first set. For the blocked practice condition, the four stimuli within each block were randomly ordered within each 16 trials, with the constraint that no more than two presentations of any stimulus configuration could occur successively. Again, a second set of presentation orders was made by reversing the order of the stimuli within each block. The order of rule presentation was the same for all subjects in the blocked condition, and the rule for each of the four panels was held constant in both conditions. The order of rules in the panels from left to right was always *and, or, nand, nor.* In the blocked condition the panels were always presented in order from left to right, followed by a repetition of the four blocks in the same order.

The two tests consisted of four blocks of 16 trials, with four occurrences of each pattern of XXX and OOO in each block. For both the random and the blocked tests the blocks were randomized the same way and with the same constraints as in the acquisition phase. Again, a second order of stimuli was formed for the two test blocks by reversing the presentation orders. The order of rules for the blocked test was the same for all subjects: *nand, or, and, nor.*

The cue conditions (0 ms and 1,000 ms) were assigned to the stimuli on a pseudorandom basis, so that for the acquisition phase in the random condition in each block each one of the 16 stimulus configurations had one presentation with a 1,000 ms cue and one with a 0 ms cue. For the blocked condition, each of the four configurations had four presentations with a 1,000 ms cue and four with a 0 ms cue. For the test, the same constraints held across pairs of 16-trial blocks. To counterbalance for the order of cues, a second set was formed by switching the cues on all stimuli.

The subjects studied a packet containing the instructions for the task, the verbal rules for each of the four panels, and a truth table version of the four rules (see Figure 4.1). Flash cards containing examples of all the 16 possible configurations as seen on the computer screen were used for testing the subjects before they began the task.

The design for the acquisition phase was a $2 \times 2 \times 2 \times 2 \times 8$ mixed factorial. Three factors were varied between subjects; practice schedule (blocked vs. random) was the factor of interest. The other two between-subjects factors, stimulus order (forward vs. reverse) and cue order (original vs. switched) were counterbalancing factors. Two factors, cue (0 ms vs. 1,000 ms) and block (Blocks 1-8) were varied within subjects.

The design for the test phase was the same as for the acquisition phase except that the factor of block was replaced by the factor of test type (blocked vs. random test) and a between-subjects factor of test order (blocked test first, random test first) was added.

Subjects. Sixteen Introductory Psychology students from the University of Colorado participated as subjects for class credit. Each subject was randomly assigned to one of the 16 counterbalancing conditions. Subjects were tested in individual rooms containing a computer. As many as four subjects were tested at the same time.

Procedure. After the subject had had enough time to read and study the instructions for the task, the experimenter described the task verbally and tested the subject, using the flash cards, to be sure that the task was fully understood. The subject was then left alone in the room to complete the experiment. Subjects were not informed about the different conditions of the experiment.

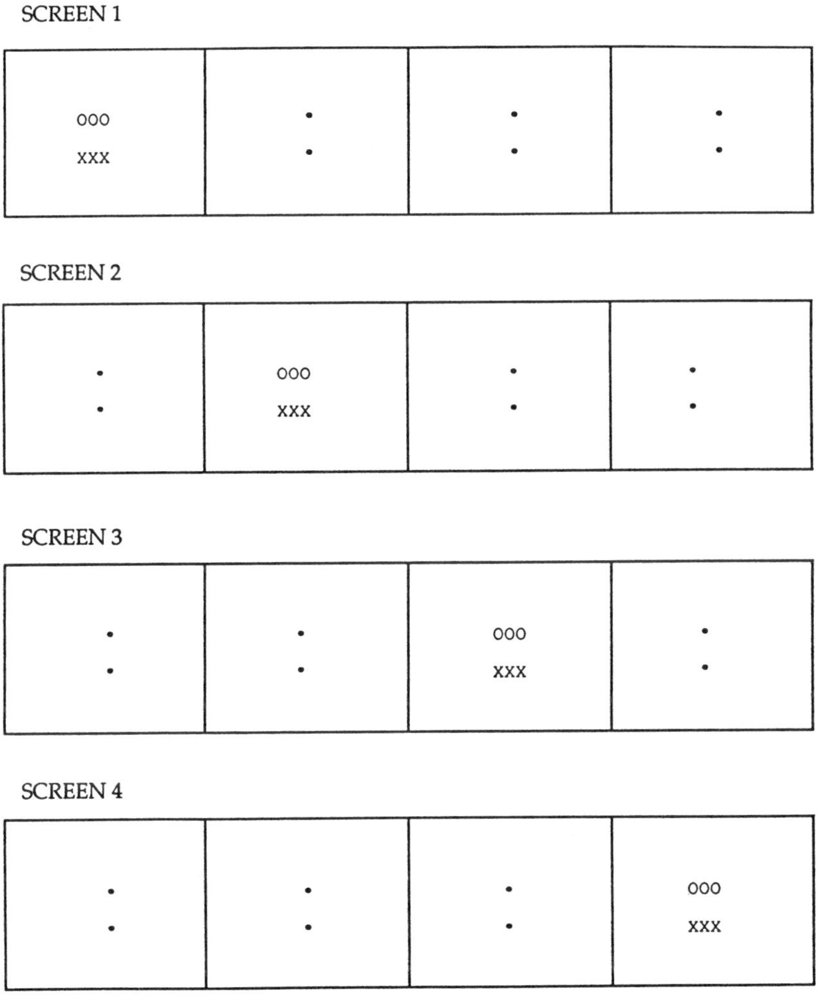

SCREEN 1

ooo xxx	• •	• •	• •

SCREEN 2

• •	ooo xxx	• •	• •

SCREEN 3

• •	• •	ooo xxx	• •

SCREEN 4

• •	• •	• •	ooo xxx

Figure 4.2. Sample Screens

On the computer terminal the subjects first saw a screen stating that they should press the space bar for the next trial (see Figure 4.2 for sample screens). The subject was to decide whether or not the stimulus configuration on each trial indicated an emergency. The subject was to press the key labeled "Y" for an emergency and the key labeled "N" for no emergency. This response was then followed by feedback indicating whether the subject was correct or incorrect. If correct, the reaction time was also given. After each stimulus configuration, the subject saw a screen that showed the truth table. The subject was allowed 32 s to look at this screen. If the subject did not wish to examine the rule table for the full 32 s, pressing the space bar brought up the next screen, which was again the screen requesting the subject to press the space bar for the next trial. This screen would also remain for 32 s if the subject did not press the space bar. The subjects were instructed to use this screen if they needed to stretch or rest and not to use the rule table screen for that purpose because the computer was keeping track of time used to look at the rules. The test trial sequence was arranged in the same way except that feedback for each response and the truth table were not available. If the blocked test was first, subjects were informed that several trials in a row would all appear in the same panel before going on to another panel; if the random test was first, they were told that the panels would appear in random order over the trials. In all, participation in the experiment took about 1 hour and 20 minutes.

Results

All reaction time data were transformed by taking the natural log of the reaction time minus 200 ms, that is, LN(RT − 200 ms). All analyses were conducted on these transformed data, but the means reported have been retransformed to milliseconds by taking the exponent of the log means and adding back the 200 ms.

An arcsine procedure for transforming the accuracy data was performed for each subject. The data were collapsed to obtain mean proportion correct for each cue length for each block. These means were then transformed by taking the arcsine of the square root of the means. Analyses of variance (ANOVAs) were then conducted on these transformed means. The reported means were retransformed by taking the sine of the arcsine means and squaring them.

Acquisition Phase. A mixed ANOVA was conducted on the reaction time data. There were no significant effects involving the counterbalancing factors, stimulus order and cue order, in a preliminary analysis, so they will not be considered further. The analysis yielded a significant main effect of practice schedule, $F(1, 14) = 11.68$, $MS_e = 2.8501$, $p < .01$, with the random group (RT = 1005) slower than the blocked group (RT = 592). There were also significant main effects for cue, $F(1, 14) = 109.28$, $MS_e = 0.1230$, $p < .001$, responses on 1,000 ms cue trials being faster (RT =

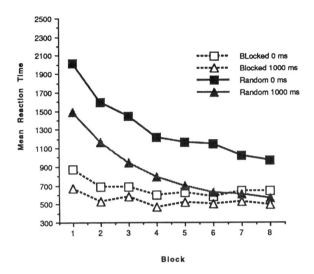

Figure 4.3. Experiment 1 Acquisition: Mean Reaction Time (ms) as a Function of Practice Schedule, Block, and Cue

646) than on 0 ms cue trials (RT = 906), and for block, $F(7, 98) = 28.39$, $MS_e = 0.0726$, $p < .001$, with responses becoming faster on successive blocks. There were significant interactions for practice schedule and cue, $F(1, 14) = 8.32$, $MS_e = 0.1230$, $p < .05$, with the 1,000 ms cue making more of a difference for the random group than for the blocked group; for practice schedule and block, $F(7, 98) = 7.30$, $MS_e = .0726$, $p < .001$, with more improvement across blocks for the random than for the blocked group; and for cue and block, $F(7, 98) = 2.51$, $MS_e = 0.0189$, $p < .05$, with more improvement across blocks for trials with a 1,000 ms cue than for those with a 0 ms cue. The analysis also yielded a three-way interaction of practice schedule, cue, and block, $F(7, 98) = 4.41$, $MS_e = 0.0189$, $p < .001$ (see Figure 4.3). Improvement across blocks for blocked subjects in the 1,000 ms and the 0 ms cue conditions was roughly parallel, whereas for the random subjects there was more improvement across trials with a 1,000 ms cue than for those with a 0 ms cue.

For accuracy, the only significant results were the interactions between practice schedule and block, $F(7, 98) = 3.10$, $MS_e = 0.0329$, $p < .01$, and practice schedule, block, and cue, $F(7, 98) = 2.75$, $MS_e = 0.0162$, $p < .05$ (see Figure 4.4). The first result indicated more improvement across trials for the random practice group than for the blocked group. In the first trials

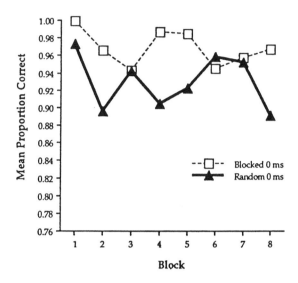

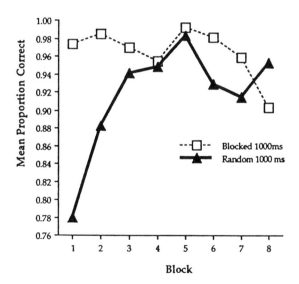

Figure 4.4. Experiment 1 Acquisition: Mean Proportion Correct as a Function of Practice Schedule, Block, and Cue

Table 4.1 Experiment 1 Test: Mean Reaction Time (ms) as a Function of Practice Schedule, Test Type, and Cue

	Practice Schedule		
	Blocked	Random	Mean
Blocked Test	689	631	659
0 ms	767	676	720
1,000 ms	622	591	606
Random Test	1371	917	1116
0 ms	1614	1165	1368
1,000 ms	1171	733	919
Mean	957	756	849

the blocked group was much higher in accuracy than the random group, but in the later trials the two groups were almost the same.

The three-way interaction reflects the fact that only the 1,000 ms precue trials for the random group showed improvement across blocks.

Test Phase. For reaction times, the main effect of practice schedule was not significant; however, the trend was in the direction opposite to that for the acquisition phase, with the random group now responding faster than the blocked group. The main effect of test type was significant, $F(1, 12)$ = 168.67, MS_e = 0.0452, $p < .001$, with subjects responding faster on the blocked than on the random test. The main effect of cue was also significant, $F(1, 12)$ = 45.87, MS_e = 0.0468, $p < .001$, with subjects responding faster with a 1,000 ms cue than with a 0 ms cue. The interaction between practice schedule and test type was significant, $F(1, 12)$ = 11.83, MS_e = 0.0452, $p < .01$, with greater difference between the two test types for the blocked group and a greater difference between the groups on the random test. Crucially, reaction times were longest for the blocked group on the random test. Also significant was the interaction between test type and cue, $F(1, 12)$ = 17.63, MS_e = 0.0130, $p < .01$, showing that the 1,000 ms cue made more of a difference far the random test than for the blocked test. The three-way interaction of practice schedule, test type, and cue was significant, $F(1, 12)$ = 7.85, MS_e = 0.0130, $p < .05$. This result shows that for the blocked test the difference between the reaction times for the 1,000 ms cue versus the 0 ms cue trials is larger for the blocked group than for the random group, whereas for the random test the difference between the 1,000 ms cue and the 0 ms cue trials is very similar for both groups (see Table 4.1).

Table 4.2 Experiment 1 Test: Mean Proportion Correct as a Function of Test
Type and Cue

	Test Type		
Cue	Blocked	Random	Mean
0 ms	.976	.926	.954
1,000 ms	.972	.951	.962
Mean	.974	.939	.958

For accuracy, the main effect of test type was significant, $F(1, 12) =$
7.28, $MS_e = 0.0171$, $p < .05$, with accuracy higher for the blocked than for
the random test. Also, the main effect of test order was significant, $F(1, 12)$
$= 4.80$, $MS_e = 0.0841$, $p < .05$, with accuracy higher when the blocked test
was first (blocked test first $M = .983$, random test first $M = .921$). There
was a significant interaction between test type and cue, $F(1, 12) = 5.07$,
$MS_e = 0.0013$, $p < .05$. The 1,000 ms cue increased the accuracy for the
random test, but it made no difference in the blocked test (see Table 4.2).

Discussion

The results are consistent with those of Carlson and Yaure (1990) and of
Hiew (1977), showing that contextual interference effects can be produced
in a cognitive task by using random versus blocked practice schedules. The
subjects in the random practice group were significantly slower on the
acquisition phase than were the blocked practice subjects. This advantage
for the blocked group tended to be reversed on later tests, especially the
random test. Both outcomes support the hypothesis that high interference
causes learned material to be more durable in memory over time.

The interaction between practice schedule and cue suggests that some
of the disadvantage in reaction time during acquisition for the random
practice schedule can be attributed to the time needed to access and load
the relevant rule into working memory. Another benefit of the cue must
be more simply that it provides information to the subjects about where
the stimulus will be displayed and hence where in the display they should
look. The blocked subjects may have been at a disadvantage on the tests,
especially on the random test, because they did not have as much practice
during training accessing the rules and loading them into working memory. The interaction between practice schedule and block, for both the
reaction time and accuracy data, reflects the fact that the random subjects
improved more in the acquisition phase than did the blocked subjects.

Note, however, that although overall the random subjects never achieved the performance level of the blocked subjects, in the last two blocks of trials the random subjects with a precue were actually somewhat faster than the blocked subjects without a precue (see Figure 4.3). The three-way interaction of practice schedule by cue by block for reaction time showed that for subjects in the random group, unlike those in the blocked group, the precue promoted improved performance across blocks. This finding suggests that subjects in the random group learned how to use the precue to access the required rule for a given trial.

Having a precue in the random test aided accuracy as well as reaction time, indicating that the rule may have already been accessed by the time the stimulus was presented and suggesting that the precue not only sped up the subjects' processing but also led to some change in the nature of the processes or representations used by the subjects, although the exact nature of that change is not clear.

The difference between the blocked and random training conditions might be due to the predictability of rules in the blocked conditions or to the necessity to reinstate the operative rule in the random condition. In Experiment 2 we attempted to differentiate between these alternative explanations by comparing blocked and random conditions to a serial condition in which the rule changed from trial to trial, but in a completely predictable sequence. Lee and Magill (1983) concluded that the lack of repetition of the "cognitive-motor" event was largely responsible for the equivalence of the serial and the random conditions, both of which per-formed better than did the blocked condition. However, in the present study the blocked group has in every block a fixed rule, but not a fixed response, so that there is no repetition of a "cognitive-motor" event in any condition—that is, subjects in the blocked group, like those in the serial and random groups, have to make a decision as to the correct response for each trial.

EXPERIMENT 2

In the serial condition the trials followed a set order of rules. This condition should yield similar results to those of the random condition if the contextual interference effect is due to nonrepetition of the rules and the need to access the operative rule on each trial. If, however, the predictability of the rule is the important factor, then the serial condition should yield similar results to those of the blocked condition.

In Experiment 1, the availability of a precue did improve the performance of the random subjects. In the present experiment we further explored this result by including a third precue presented 500 ms before the stimulus. The purpose of this additional cue condition is to determine whether the precue interval allows subjects to reinstate the appropriate rule into working memory or merely directs attention to the appropriate panel. If the latter, then no difference between the 500 ms and 1,000 ms precues would be expected. If it is found that 500 ms is not enough time to be of benefit to the subject, as indicated by no difference between the 0 ms cue and the 500 ms cue, then this finding would suggest that the benefit of the cue is to allow the subjects time to preload the rule into working memory. If it is found that the 500 ms cue is beneficial, but not as beneficial as the 1,000 ms cue, then this finding would suggest that 500 ms is at least long enough to allow subjects to focus their attention on the relevant panel and maybe to begin loading the rule, but that when given 1,000 ms, processing or loading is continued.

Because the difference for the two practice schedule groups was greater for the random test in Experiment 1, and because the random test is more ecologically valid, the present experiment included only a random test at the end of the acquisition phase. Experiment 2 also included a retention test consisting of the same random test. The retention intervals were 1 week and 1 month. It was expected that on the retention test the random and serial groups would perform similarly and would have faster reaction times and better accuracy than would the blocked group, based on the assumption that Lee and Magill's (1983) results for retention after a very short interpolated task (about 1 minute) generalize to a longer retention interval and a cognitive task.

Method

Materials and Design. The second experiment utilized the same equipment as did Experiment 1, and the same four logical rules were used. For this experiment the acquisition phase consisted of eight blocks of 48 trials, allowing for the occurrence of each of the 16 possible stimulus configurations with each of the three cue lengths in each block for the random and serial practice conditions. In the blocked condition subjects saw two blocks of each rule, and within each block each stimulus configuration occurred 12 times, 4 times with each of the cue lengths. For the blocked and random conditions the order of presentation of the stimulus configurations was pseudorandom in each block, as in Experiment 1, with the addition of 16 more trials and one more cue length. A similar pseudorandom order was used in the serial condition with the added constraint that the first trial occurred in Panel 1, the second in Panel 2, the third in Panel 3, the fourth in Panel 4, the fifth in Panel 1, and so on. This order continued throughout all the blocks. The order of the stimulus configurations was random within each panel, with each configuration occurring three times within each block, once with each cue length. For counterbalancing purposes three orders of cue lengths were formed. In all three sets the order of stimulus presentations was the same, but across the sets every stimulus presentation was associated with each of the three cue lengths. The order of rule presentations in the blocked condition and the rule for each panel were the same as in Experiment 1.

After the acquisition phase, only a random test was given to all subjects. It consisted of three blocks of 48 trials, with three occurrences of each stimulus in each block, one occurrence of each stimulus with each cue length. The blocks were ordered in the same pseudorandom manner with the same constraints as in the acquisition phase. The order of stimuli was the same for all subjects, but again three separate orders of cue length were used so that across orders each stimulus was used with each cue length. The same test was administered immediately after the acquisition phase and again when the subjects returned after the retention interval(s).

Before beginning, the subjects studied the same packet of instructions that was used in Experiment 1.

The design for the acquisition phase was a $3 \times 2 \times 3 \times 3 \times 8$ mixed factorial. Three factors were varied between subjects; two of these, practice schedule (blocked, serial, and random) and retention interval (1 week, 4 week) were the factors of interest. The other between-subjects factor, cue order (three orders), was a counterbalancing factor and not included in the analysis. Two factors, cue (0, 500, 1,000 ms) and block (Blocks 1-8), were varied within subjects.

The immediate test and the retention tests were combined in an analysis making the design a $2 \times 3 \times 2 \times 3 \times 3$ mixed factorial, with two factors, retention interval (1 week, 4 week) and practice schedule (blocked, random, serial) varied between subjects. The other three factors, test (immediate, delayed), block (1-3), and cue (0, 500, 1,000 ms), were varied within subjects.

Subjects. Thirty-six right-handed Introductory Psychology students from the University of Colorado participated as subjects for class credit. Each subject was randomly assigned to 1 of the 18 counterbalancing conditions. Thus, there were 12 subjects in each of the three practice conditions, with 6 of these in the 1-week retention group and 6 in the 4-week retention group, 2 in each of the three cue orders.

Procedure. The procedure for the first day was identical to that of the first experiment, with the exception that subjects were informed about the condition to which they were assigned, that is, whether the stimuli would occur in a blocked, serial, or random order.

Subjects returned for the retention test either 1 or 4 weeks later. Subjects who returned after 1 week were asked after the test to return again 3 weeks later. They were offered either more class credit or $10 for returning. All but two subjects returned and were retested. This procedure allowed us to compare the 4-week subjects with a group of subjects who were also tested at 4 weeks but had had a "refresher" test at 1 week.

When subjects returned for a retention test, they were first given the sheet containing a rule table without the names of the rules or the correct "yes" or "no" responses and they were asked to fill in as much as they could. If subjects could not complete the table with correct responses, they were given the complete rule table and allowed to look at it for several minutes. Six subjects were unable to fill in the responses correctly when they returned for their first retention test. Of the six, two were in the blocked practice group and four were in the serial practice group. One of the two subjects in the serial group who failed to fill in the responses correctly at 1 week was again unable to fill them in when returning at 4 weeks. Subjects who were able to complete the table correctly were also offered the opportunity to examine the rule table. Only four subjects, two from the random group and two from the serial group, were able to name the rules when returning for their first retention test. Subjects then received the same test that they had had in the first session. As mentioned earlier, the 1-week subjects were asked to return again after an additional 3 weeks. All said they would (although two failed to return). For those who returned the same procedure as just described was again followed.

Results

For significant effects involving the factors of practice schedule and cue, planned comparison analyses were conducted by using the Bonferroni method of multiple comparisons (see Judd & McClelland, 1989, p. 320). Using the Bonferroni adjustment, the probability level of .05 was divided by the number of analyses conducted on the data and the resulting probability compared to the probability obtained in the analysis.

Acquisition Phase. A mixed ANOVA was conducted on the reaction time data from the acquisition phase. The analysis yielded a significant main effect of practice schedule, $F(2, 33) = 10.05$, $MS_e = 4.7328$, $p < .001$,

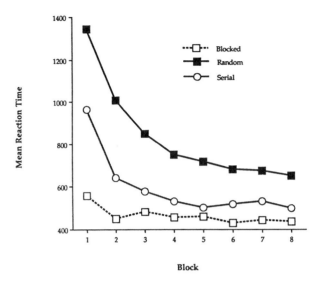

Figure 4.5. Experiment 2 Acquisition: Mean Reaction Time as a Function of Practice Schedule and Block

with the random group slowest, the blocked group fastest, and the serial group about halfway between the other two. The planned comparison analyses showed that only the difference between the blocked and random groups was significant. The main effect of block was also significant, $F(7, 231) = 57.01$, $MS_e = 0.1263$, $p < .001$, with subjects becoming faster across blocks. A significant interaction was obtained for practice schedule and block, $F(14, 231) = 3.45$, $MS_e = 0.1263$, $p < .001$, with more improvement over blocks for the random and serial groups than for the blocked group (see Figure 4.5). The planned comparison analyses indicated that the improvement for all three groups was significant. There were also significant main effects for cue, $F(2, 66) = 176.16$, $MS_e = 0.0699$, $p < .001$, with subjects' performance improving as cue length increased. Planned comparison analyses indicated that this difference was significant for all three comparisons. There was also a significant interaction of practice schedule and cue, $F(4, 66) = 4.61$, $MS_e = 0.0699$, $p < .005$, with the precues making more of a difference for the random group than for the other two groups, the difference for these two groups being essentially the same (see Table 4.3).

Accuracy was also analyzed, with a significant main effect of cue, $F(2, 66) = 5.87$, $MS_e = 0.0304$, $p < .005$. In the 0 ms precue condition subjects were significantly less accurate ($M = .940$) than in the other two cue

Table 4.3 Experiment 2 Acquisition: Mean Reaction Time (ms) as a Function of
Practice Schedule and Cue

	Practice Schedule			
Cue	Blocked	Random	Serial	Mean
0 ms	525	1014	651	692
500 ms	462	761	564	577
1,000 ms	427	680	524	528

conditions (500 ms $M = .959$; 1,000 ms $M = .958$). There was no difference
between the 500 ms and the 1,000 ms intervals. There was also a significant effect of block, $F(7, 231) = 2.36$, $MS_e = 0.0222$, $p < .05$, with subjects
improving in accuracy across blocks. A significant result was found for
the interaction of practice schedule by block, $F(14, 231) = 3.85$, $MS_e =
0.0222$, $p < .001$ (see Figure 4.6). This interaction results from the blocked
group becoming less accurate with practice, whereas the serial and random
groups both improved in accuracy. The most improvement was made by
the random group even though this group never achieved the same level of
performance as the other two groups. A planned comparison analysis indicated that the decrease for the blocked group across trials was not significant,
but the increase for both the random and serial groups was significant. A
planned comparison ANOVA on the last block found no significant differences between any of the groups.

Test and Retention. The immediate test and the first retention test for
all subjects were analyzed together. The random group responded faster
than did the blocked group on both the immediate test and the retention
test (see Table 4.4), but the main effect for practice schedule was not
significant. The main effect of cue was significant, $F(2, 60) = 130.88$, $MS_e
= 0.1270$, $p < .001$, with subjects responding fastest to those trials with a
1,000 ms precue, next to the 500 ms precue, and slowest to no precue.
Planned comparison analyses indicated that the differences were significant for all comparisons. No overall difference was found between the
immediate test and the retention tests, although subjects were somewhat
slower overall on the retention test than they had been on the immediate
test. The interaction between test and cue was significant $F(2, 60) = 6.00$,
$MS_e = 0.0148$, $p < .01$, with the cue helping more on the immediate test
than on the retention test (see Table 4.5). The post hoc analysis of this
interaction indicates that the difference between the immediate test and
the retention test is significant for both the 500 and the 1,000 ms cues but

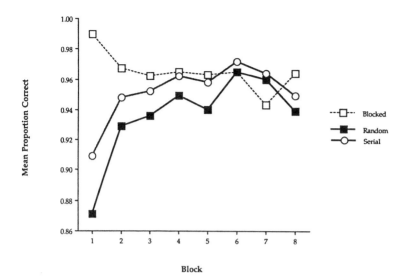

Figure 4.6. Experiment 2 Acquisition: Mean Proportion Correct as a Function of Practice Schedule and Block

Table 4.4 Experiment 2 Test and Retention: Mean Reaction Time (ms) as a Function of Practice Schedule and Test

| | Practice Schedule | | | |
Test	Blocked	Random	Serial	Mean
Immediate	868	695	782	778
Retention	857	750	837	812
Mean	861	722	809	794

Table 4.5 Experiment 2 Test and Retention: Mean Reaction Time (ms) as a Function of Test and Cue

| | Test | | |
Cue	Immediate	Retention	Mean
0 ms	1000	1012	1006
500 ms	740	772	756
1,000 ms	646	691	668
Mean	778	812	794

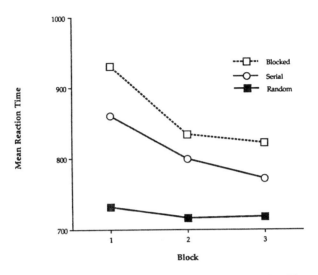

Figure 4.7. Experiment 2 Test and Retention: Mean Reaction Time as a Function of Practice Schedule and Block

not for the 0 ms cue. The main effect of block was also significant, $F(2, 60) = 16.59$, $MS_e = 0.0455$, $p < .001$, with improvement being made across the three test blocks (see Figure 4.7).

To see if we had replicated the effects of the first experiment for the blocked and random groups, an analysis was conducted on the test data for these two groups alone. The main effect of retention interval now reached a significant level, $F(1, 20) = 6.15$, $MS_e = 2.6223$, $p < .05$. The 4-week retention group was faster on both the immediate test and the retention test (1-week $M = 920$; 4-week $M = 686$). Because the difference occurred on both the immediate and the retention tests, this outcome probably can be attributed to uncontrolled factors in the assignment of subjects. As before, the main effect of block was significant, $F(2, 40) = 10.49$, $MS_e = 0.0377$, $p < .001$, as was the main effect of cue, $F(2, 40) = 87.97$, $MS_e = 0.1292$, $p < .001$. The interaction of practice schedule and block was significant, $F(2, 40) = 5.02$, $MS_e = 0.0377$, $p = .01$ (see Figure 4.7), with the blocked group improving over trials and the random group changing little. An interaction between test and cue was significant, $F(2, 40) = 10.24$, $MS_e = 0.0108$, $p < .001$, which was due to a greater effect of cue length on the immediate test than on the retention test. This same result was found for the analysis of all three practice schedules (see Table 4.5).

Table 4.6 Experiment 2 Test and Retention: Mean Proportion Correct as a Function of Practice Schedule and Test

| | Practice Schedule | | | |
Test	Blocked	Random	Serial	Mean
Immediate	.876	.977	.948	.940
Retention	.946	.984	.949	.962
Mean	.914	.981	.949	.952

An analysis including all three groups was also conducted on the accuracy data. The main effect of retention interval was significant, $F(1, 30) = 7.50$, $MS_e = 0.3022$, $p < .01$, with accuracy higher for the 1-week retention group (1-week interval, $M = .974$; 4-week interval $M = .923$). Again this difference must be due to uncontrolled factors in the assignment of subjects to conditions as the difference occurred on both the immediate and the retention tests. The main effect of practice schedule was significant, $F(2, 30) = 4.44$, $MS_e = 0.3022$, $p = .05$, with the random group the most accurate, serial next, and blocked the least accurate. The planned comparison indicated a significant difference only between the blocked and random groups. There was a significant effect of test, $F(1, 30) = 12.63$, $MS_e = 0.0340$, $p < .005$, with subjects overall more accurate notably on the retention test than on the immediate test. There was a significant interaction between practice schedule and test, $F(2, 30) = 6.84$, $MS_e = 0.0340$, $p < .005$. According to the planned comparison tests, the blocked practice group was significantly more accurate on the retention test than on the immediate test; the random group was slightly, but not significantly, more accurate on the retention test than on the immediate test; and the serial group was equally accurate on both (see Table 4.6). The planned comparisons yielded a significant difference between the blocked and random groups and between the random and serial groups on both tests, whereas the blocked and serial groups differed significantly only on the immediate test. The effect of block was significant $F(2, 60) = 7.88$, $MS_e = 0.0195$, $p < .01$ (Block 1 $M = .941$; Block 2 $M = .949$; Block 3 $M = .963$), indicating improvement with practice during the tests. The effect of cue was also significant, $F(2, 60) = 6.44$, $MS_e = 0.0028$, $p < .005$, indicating that the longer the cue length the more accurate the subjects were (0 ms cue $M = .943$; 500 ms cue $M = .948$; 1,000 ms cue $M = .964$). This finding is consistent with the finding of Experiment 1, showing that the cues aided accuracy as well as speed. Planned comparison analyses indicated that the only significant difference was between 0 ms and 1,000 ms. A significant

Table 4.7 Experiment 2 Test and Retention: Mean Proportion Correct as a Function of Retention Interval and Practice Schedule

	Practice Schedule			
Retention Interval	Block	Random	Serial	Mean
1 week	.950	.976	.989	.974
4 weeks	.870	.985	.883	.923

Table 4.8 Experiment 2 Test and Retention for Subjects Who Took Two Retention Tests: Mean Reaction Time (ms) as a Function of Cue and Test

	Cue			
Test	0 ms	500 ms	1,000 ms	Mean
Immediate	1067	834	727	838
Retention 1 (1 week)	1073	862	787	897
Retention 2 (4 weeks)	1009	830	771	862
Mean	1049	842	761	874

interaction was also obtained for practice schedule by retention interval, $F(2, 30) = 3.39$, $MS_e = 0.3022$, $p < .05$. This interaction is due to the fact that the serial group subjects in the 4-week retention condition were significantly less accurate than were subjects in the 1-week condition. The subjects in the 4-week blocked group were somewhat, but not significantly, less accurate than were those in the 1-week group, whereas the random subjects were the same at both retention intervals. This result led to a significant difference by the planned comparisons between the random and serial subjects and between the random and blocked subjects in the 4-week retention condition (see Table 4.7). No significant differences were found in the 1-week retention condition.

Additional Analyses. In an analysis of the reaction time data comparing the immediate test, 1-week retention test, and 4-week retention test for the 15 subjects who returned twice, test and cue yielded a significant interaction, $F(4, 48) = 5.22$, $MS_e = 0.0124$, $p < .005$. Improvement in response time as cue time increased was greatest for the immediate test and decreased across the two retention tests (see Table 4.8). In a parallel analysis of accuracy, only the interaction between Practice Schedule and Test was

Table 4.9 Experiment 2 Test and Retention for Subjects Who Took Two
Retention Tests: Mean Proportion Correct as a Function of Practice
Schedule and Test

| | Practice Schedule | | | |
Test	Blocked	Random	Serial	Mean
Immediate	.932	.968	.991	.968
Retention 1 (1 week)	.978	.970	.994	.982
Retention 2 (4 weeks)	.991	.959	.989	.982

Table 4.10 Experiment 2 4-Week Retention, Comparing Group With One
Retention Test and Group With Two Retention Tests: Mean
Reaction Time (ms) as a Function of Retention Test Number and Cue

| | Test Number | | |
Cue	One	Two	Mean
0 ms	927	1009	820
500 ms	668	830	780
1,000 ms	596	771	751
Mean	713	862	783

significant, $F(4, 24) = 2.93$, $MS_e = 0.0438$, $p < .05$, with subjects in the blocked condition least accurate on the immediate test but somewhat more accurate than the other two groups on the second retention test (see Table 4.9).

Another analysis was conducted on reaction times to compare the 4-week retention of the subjects who either had or did not have a prior retention test at 1 week. Although subjects with two retention tests tended to have longer reaction times than did those with only one test, the main effect was not significant, but there was a significant interaction of the number of retention tests (one or two) by cue, $F(2, 48) = 6.67$, $MS_e = 0.0599$, $p < .005$ (see Table 4.10). This result seems to indicate that the disadvantage for two retention tests was smallest for the 0 ms cue. The parallel analysis for accuracy revealed a significant main effect of number of tests, $F(1, 24) = 7.87$, $MS_e = 0.1610$, $p < .01$, subjects with two retention tests being more accurate than those with one retention test (see Table 4.11). This result taken with the reaction time result may indicate a speed/accuracy trade-off for the two groups, although the main effect of number of tests was significant only in the accuracy data, because the

Table 4.11 Experiment 2 4-Week Retention, Comparing Group With One Retention Test and Group With Two Retention Tests: Mean Proportion Correct as a Function of Practice Schedule and Test Number

	Practice Schedule			
Number of Tests	Blocked	Random	Serial	Mean
One	.895	.985	.873	.928
Two	.991	.959	.989	.982
Mean	.955	.974	.946	.959

subjects with one retention test were faster to respond but less accurate than the subjects with two retention tests. The interaction of practice schedule by number of tests was significant, $F(2, 24) = 5.02$, $MS_e = 0.1610$, $p < .05$. According to planned comparison analyses, the blocked and serial groups that had two retention tests were more accurate than the groups that had only one test, whereas there was no difference for the random group. For subjects who had two retention tests, there were no differences between groups; for subjects who had only one test, there were significant differences between the blocked and random groups, with the random group more accurate, and between the random and serial groups, with the random group more accurate.

Discussion

At acquisition, the random group was slower and less accurate than the serial group, which in turn was slower and less accurate than the blocked group, although only the reaction time difference between blocked and random groups was significant. The fact that the serial and random groups were not equivalent may be at least partly due to the fact that in this experiment the serial task was not a simple reaction time paradigm, as was the comparable condition in the study by Lee and Magill (1983). Although the subjects always knew which rule would be relevant, they did not know which answer would have to be made until the stimulus configuration appeared. Thus, in this experiment a choice still had to be made at the occurrence of the stimulus. However, for the serial group, but not for the random group, the rule for responding to any stimulus could be accessed and loaded in advance. Thus, the fact that the serial group was faster and more accurate than the random group during acquisition would seem to be attributable to its access to the rule operative on each trial. Availability of a precue helped the subjects in both speed and accuracy. As before, the cue was more beneficial to subjects in the random group, who otherwise were unable to access the rule in advance. The difference between the 0 and 500 ms cue lengths and between the 500 and 1,000 ms cue lengths were both significant, although the biggest difference was between the 0 and 500 ms cue lengths. This finding seems to suggest that whatever is being done by the subjects cannot be fully completed by the end of 500 ms. There are at least two possibilities for the benefit of the precue: (a) it indicates to the subjects which panel to attend to and/or (b) it gives the subject time to activate the appropriate rule. Because attending to the appropriate panel should require 500 ms or less, the results suggest that indicating the panel is one function of the precue, but activation of the operative rule is also a function of the precue.

The results for the immediate test and retention tests are consistent with the contextual interference hypothesis. Subjects in the random group tended to be faster and were more accurate on the tests than were those in the blocked group, with subjects in the serial group intermediate. Again, this result is not the same as that found by Lee and Magill (1983). The differences are that this is still a choice-reaction time task for all groups and that only the rules, not the stimuli, were repeated in the blocked group and were predictable in the serial group of the present experiment. The predictability of the rules in the serial group allowed the subjects to preload the rule into working memory. The blocked group could maintain the rule in memory for each trial, and the random group had to have all four rules available on any trial until the cue was displayed. These results indicate that during acquisition the random group had the most contextual interference, caused by needing all four rules available on all trials. The serial group also had some contextual interference because of having to reinstate a new rule for each trial, and the blocked group could retain the same rule from trial to trial. Thus, the predictability of the rule aided (at acquisition) in allowing only one rule to be loaded for each trial, and having to reload the rule gave some (although not significant) benefit over the blocked group at test. But it is only the random group that received the full help of contextual interference by having to have all four rules ready for all trials.

The fact that the blocked group improved significantly in accuracy from the immediate test to the retention test shows that this group continued to learn on the immediate random test. Note also that there was no sign of forgetting across the retention intervals, and improvement continued across the retention test blocks. The fact that we did not get much of a difference between the groups on the retention test may thus be due to the immediate random test, which forced the blocked group to practice accessing the rule for each trial (see Shea, Morgan, & Ho, 1981, for a similar finding in which subjects with any amount of random practice performed better on a retention and transfer test than did those with all blocked practice). Another experiment with some of the subjects having no immediate random test might very well show more of a retention difference for the groups.

EXPERIMENT 3

In Experiment 2 the blocked group was significantly more accurate on the retention test than on the immediate test. Tentatively, we attributed this result to the fact that the blocked group was forced to learn how to access the rule for each trial on the immediate random test, which then afforded an advantage to the delayed test. To test this hypothesis, one group of subjects in Experiment 3 was given the random test immediately following the acquisition phase, as in Experiment 2, whereas a second group was given no immediate test. Both groups were then given a retention test after a 1-week delay interval. This experiment included both blocked and random groups but no precues. No precues were used because in Experiments 1 and 2 the precues had aided the random group subjects and thus lessened the difference between the blocked and random groups. We wanted a purer test of the two conditions in Experiment 3.

Method

Materials and Design. Experiment 3 utilized the same materials and design as did Experiment 2 with four main changes: (a) no precue was used, (b) no serial condition was included, (c) only a 1-week retention interval was used, and (d) half of the subjects had no immediate test. The same four logical rules were used. The acquisition phase again consisted of eight blocks of 48 trials. The order of rule presentation, the rule for each panel, and the order of presentation of stimulus configurations were the same as in Experiment 2.

Only a random test was used. It consisted of three blocks of 48 trials, with three occurrences of each stimulus in each block. The blocks were randomized in the same way and with the same constraints as in the acquisition phase. The order of stimuli was the same for all subjects. The same test was administered to half of the subjects immediately after the acquisition phase and to all the subjects when they returned after the retention interval.

Before beginning, the subjects studied the same packet of instructions that was used in Experiments 1 and 2. The design for the acquisition phase was a 2×8 mixed factorial. The first factor, practice schedule (blocked, random), was varied between subjects. The other factor, block (Blocks 1-8), was varied within subjects. The design for the immediate test was a 2×3 mixed factorial. The first factor, practice schedule (blocked, random), was varied between subjects, whereas the second factor, block (Blocks 1-3), was varied within subjects. The design for the retention test was a $2 \times 2 \times 3$ mixed factorial, with the first two factors, practice schedule (blocked, random) and immediate test (present, not present), varied between subjects, and the last factor, block (Blocks 1-3), varied within subjects.

Subjects. Twenty-four right-handed Introductory Psychology students from the University of Colorado participated as subjects for class credit. Each subject was assigned by fixed rotation to one of the four counterbalancing conditions. Thus, there were 12 subjects in each of the two practice conditions, with 6 of these receiving an immediate test and 6 being given their first test after 1 week.

Procedure. The procedure for the first day was identical to that of Experiment 2, with the exception that half of the subjects were not given a test immediately following the acquisition phase. Subjects returned for the retention test 1 week later. When subjects returned for the retention test, they were first given the sheet containing the rule table without the names of the rules or the correct "yes" or "no" responses, and they were asked to fill in as much as they could. If subjects could not complete the table correctly they were given the complete rule table and allowed to look at it for several minutes. Five subjects were unable to fill in the responses correctly. Four of these subjects were in the blocked practice group and one was in the random practice group. Subjects who were able to complete the table correctly were also offered the opportunity to examine a rule table, but all said that they did not need to do so. Only four subjects (two from the blocked practice group and two from the random practice group) were able to name the rules. Subjects then received the same test that half of them had had in the first session.

Results

Acquisition Phase. A mixed ANOVA was conducted on the reaction time data. The analysis yielded a main effect for practice schedule, $F(1,$

22) = 60.59, MS_e = 0.6421, $p < .001$, with the random group slower than the blocked group. A main effect was also found for block, $F(7, 154)$ = 30.14, $MS_e = 0.0286$, $p < .001$, with subjects becoming faster across trials. The interaction of practice schedule by block was also significant, $F(7, 154) = 3.22$, $MS_e = 0.0286$, $p < .01$. This interaction is due to the random group improving more across the trials, even though on the last block of trials they were still not as fast as the blocked group was on the first block of trials (see Figure 4.8).

An ANOVA was conducted on the accuracy data. No main effects were significant, but the interaction of practice schedule by block yielded a significant outcome, $F(7, 154) = 3.87$, $MS_e = 0.0074$, $p < .001$. This interaction is due to the fact that the random group improved from the first to the last block, whereas the blocked group showed no improvement from the first to the last block of trials (see Figure 4.9).

Immediate Test. The ANOVA for the immediate test reaction time data yielded a significant main effect for practice schedule, $F(1, 10) = 12.81$, $MS_e = 0.2133$, $p < .01$, with the random practice subjects now faster ($M = 773$) than the blocked practice subjects ($M = 1194$). No other effects were significant.

An ANOVA for the accuracy data for the immediate test resulted in no significant effects although the trend was for better performance by the random practice subjects ($M = .946$) than for the blocked practice subjects ($M = .869$), showing that a speed/accuracy trade-off does not account for the difference between the two groups.

Retention Test. An ANOVA conducted on the retention test reaction time data yielded main effects of practice schedule, $F(1, 20) = 30.29$, $MS_e = 0.1767$, $p < .001$, and block, $F(2, 40) = 6.34$, $MS_e = 0.0085$, $p < .01$. Random practice subjects responded faster than did blocked practice subjects. The main effect of immediate test (present, not present) was not significant, $F < 1$, showing that having an immediate test did not make a difference to the subjects' performance on the retention test. Thus, there is also no evidence of forgetting from the immediate to the retention test. The interaction of practice schedule by block was significant, $F(2, 40)$ = 11.20, $MS_e = 0.0085$, $p < .001$. Blocked practice subjects, but not random practice subjects, showed improvement over the blocks of trials (see Figure 4.10).

The ANOVA for the accuracy data again yielded no significant results although the trend was for superior performance by the random group (M

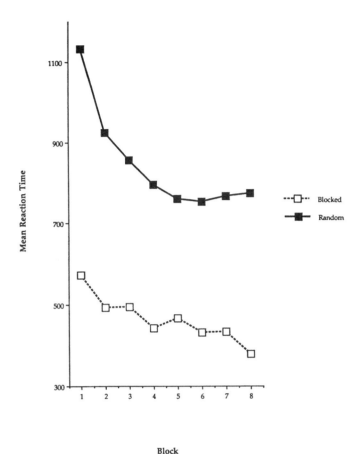

Figure 4.8. Experiment 3 Acquisition: Mean Reaction Time as a Function of Practice Schedule and Block

= .935) relative to the blocked group (M = .930), again ruling out a speed/accuracy trade-off.

Additional Analysis. An additional planned comparison was conducted yielding the following result: There was no difference between the two (immediate and retention) tests for the 12 subjects who had both.

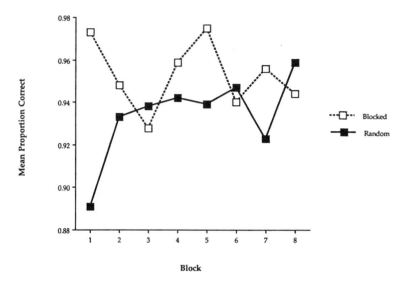

Figure 4.9. Experiment 3 Acquisition: Mean Proportion Correct as a Function of Practice Schedule and Block

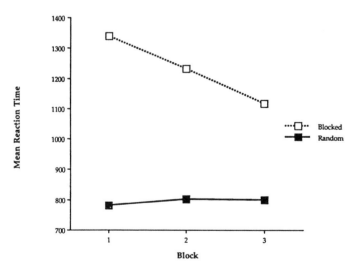

Figure 4.10. Experiment 3 Retention: Mean Reaction Time as a Function of Practice Schedule and Block

Discussion

Contextual interference caused by random practice schedules resulted in slower (and less accurate) performance at acquisition but faster (and more accurate) performance on immediate and retention testing. The finding that in this experiment (but not in the two previous experiments) we obtained significant reaction time results on both test phases and on the acquisition phase would seem to have occurred because we did not attenuate the effect of contextual interference by the presence of precues during either the acquisition phase or the test phase.

It is interesting that there was no difference between the performance on a delayed test of retention between subjects who did or did not have an immediate test. It was expected that there would be a difference for at least the blocked practice subjects because of the improvement of the blocked subjects from the immediate to the retention test in Experiment 2. That we did not find this improvement may indicate the necessity for the precue to be present for the blocked practice subjects to learn so rapidly on the immediate random test—that is, what the blocked subjects may be learning on the immediate test is how to make use more effectively of the precue to reinstate the appropriate rule in memory.

General Discussion

The results of all three experiments support Battig's (1979) contextual interference hypothesis. In the current experiments the random practice group (high interference) was slower to learn the task than was the blocked practice group (low interference) but retained better what it had learned. Thus, on the retention tests, the subjects in the random practice group were slightly faster and more accurate than were those in the blocked group, though not significantly so except for Experiment 2, in which the random group was significantly more accurate, and Experiment 3, in which the random groups were significantly faster on both an immediate test and a delayed retention test.

The results are also in accord with the procedural reinstatement framework previously described by Healy et al. (1992). According to the procedural reinstatement framework, retention is enhanced if during the training phase subjects engage in the mental procedures that will be required during the test phase. Because rule retrieval is required during the test in the present study, it should be practiced during training. Such practice occurs with the random, but not with the blocked, practice schedule.

The interaction in the test reaction time data between practice schedule and test type in Experiment 1 agrees with Carlson and Yaure's (1990) finding that it is harder for the subjects who started with a blocked practice schedule to switch to random testing than it is for the subjects who started with a random schedule to switch to blocked testing. This interaction cannot be explained simply by referring to the notion of test appropriateness (e.g., Morris, Bransford, & Franks, 1977) because the random practice group tended to perform better than did the blocked group even on the blocked test in Experiment 1. Further, on the immediate test in Experiment 2, the performance of the serial group tended to be better than that of the blocked group even though the test was not really any more similar to the practice in the serial condition than to that in the blocked condition. Thus, the differences among the three groups must be due to the different types of processing used, as is consistent with the contextual interference hypothesis.

Lee and Magill (1983), in a motor task, found that a serial group, for which rules varied from trial to trial, but in a predictable way, performed the same as the random group and better than the blocked group at test. The results reported here are different from Lee and Magill's (1983) but are straightforward to explain. In Lee and Magill's (1983) experiment knowing which trial was next also meant knowing which response was next. Here there is an extra step: Knowing the rule does not indicate a response. The subject needs also to know the stimulus configuration before the response can be determined. But subjects in the serial condition need only to load one rule and hold it in working memory to make the response decision. Subjects in the random group, in contrast, cannot load in a single rule and thus need to process more completely all the rules on each trial to be able to respond effectively. This outcome leads us to conclude that the need to load a rule into working memory on each trial (serial group) is more beneficial than is merely holding a rule in working memory from trial to trial (blocked group), but neither is as good as the need to load and engage in more elaborative processing (random group). The current results lead to the conclusion that greater elaborative processing facilitates longer-term retention. Thus, the requirements of the three different conditions led to three different sets of processing activities and these, in turn, led to three different patterns of results at test.

In Experiment 2 the precue facilitated performance at both precue intervals, with a greater benefit for the longer interval. These results indicate that the benefit of the cue includes the advantage of allowing the subjects time to attend to the appropriate panel but also includes additional advantages. The benefit of the 500 ms cue length could be solely for the purpose of focusing on the appropriate panel, but the 500 ms cue length could also allow time for some processing of the rules. More experiments with shorter cue lengths are needed to identify the minimal amount of time that would produce beneficial results. It seems clear, however, at least in terms of reaction times, that the additional time provided by the 1,000 ms cue length allowed for some kind of added beneficial processing of the rules.

In Experiment 2, we had expected that there would be a larger difference between the random practice group and the blocked practice group after the retention intervals, if random practice schedules lead to better retention as well as better performance on immediate testing. The fact that the blocked group performed as well as it did, and even improved from the immediate test to the retention test, seems to be due to the learning from the immediate random test. Indeed, Shea, Morgan, and Ho (1981) showed that random acquisition at any point in the training is beneficial to performance. However, this improvement in the blocked acquisition group from the immediate to the retention test was not found in Experiment 3, in which no precues were available to maximize the learning, although there was significant improvement for the blocked group across the three blocks of the retention test in Experiment 3.

The findings lead to the suggestion that an optimal learning condition for this type of task would be to provide blocked trials first to learn the rules more quickly and then to switch to a random practice condition to improve retention and transfer skills. Further research needs to be done to validate this suggestion.

The implications of this suggestion are clear for cognitive skill training procedures as found in aviation, military, medical, police, computer, and other fields requiring that certain procedures be retained for later, sudden recall. Especially in emergency situations, immediate and accurate recall is necessary. If a pilot has a sudden engine failure, only the proper procedure can save lives. If the initial training does not result in complete learning and complete retention, then it can be useless in stressful situations. Training regimens should be designed for such learning and retention capabilities.

In summary, the results of these experiments indicate that a random practice schedule leads to the best test performance and retention after initial acquisition, even though it hinders the initial learning. Blocked practice schedules allow for easier and quicker initial acquisition but worse performance at immediate and delayed tests. Thus, it is suggested that an optimal learning program should include a blocked practice schedule for enhancing rapid learning and a random practice schedule for improving the immediate test performance, ease of transfer, and long-term retention by the subjects.

References

Battig, W. F. (1972). Intratask interference as a source of facilitation in transfer and retention. In R. F. Thompson & J. F. Voss (Eds.), *Topics in learning and performance* (pp. 131-159). New York: Academic Press.

Battig, W. F. (1979). The flexibility of human memory. In L. S. Cermak & F.I.M. Craik (Eds.), *Levels of processing and human memory* (pp. 23-44). Hillsdale, NJ: Lawrence Erlbaum.

Carlson, R. A., & Schneider, W. (1989). Acquisition context and the use of causal rules. *Memory & Cognition, 17,* 240-248.

Carlson, R. A., & Yaure, R. G. (1990). Practice schedules and the use of component skills in problem solving. *Journal of Experimental Psychology: Learning, Memory, and Cognition, 16,* 484-496.

Cuddy, L. J., & Jacoby, L. L. (1982). When forgetting helps memory: An analysis of repetition effects. *Journal of Verbal Learning and Verbal Behavior, 21,* 451-467.

Healy, A. F., Fendrich, D. W., Crutcher, R. J., Wittman, W. T., Gesi, A. T., Ericsson, K. A., & Bourne, L. E., Jr. (1992). The long-term retention of skills. In A. F. Healy, S. M. Kosslyn, & R. M. Shiffrin (Eds.), *From learning processes to cognitive processes: Essays in honor of William K. Estes* (Vol. 2, pp. 87-118). Hillsdale, NJ: Lawrence Erlbaum.

Hiew, C. C. (1977). Sequence effects in rule learning and conceptual generalization. *American Journal of Psychology, 90,* 207-218.

Jacoby, L. L. (1978). On interpreting the effects of repetition: Solving a problem versus remembering a solution. *Journal of Verbal Learning and Verbal Behavior, 18,* 585-600.

Judd, C. M., & McClelland, G. H. (1989). *Data analysis: A model comparison approach.* San Diego, CA: Harcourt Brace Jovanovich.

Lee, T. D., & Magill, R. A. (1983). The locus of contextual interference in motor-skill acquisition. *Journal of Experimental Psychology: Learning, Memory, and Cognition, 9,* 730-746.

Morris, C. D., Bransford, J. D., & Franks J. J. (1977). Levels of processing versus transfer appropriate processing. *Journal of Verbal Learning and Verbal Behavior, 16,* 519-533.

Schneider, W. (1988). Micro-Experimental Laboratory: An integrated system for IBM PC compatibles. *Behavior Research Methods, Instruments, and Computers, 20,* 206-217.

Shea, J. B., & Morgan, R. L. (1979). Contextual interference effects on the acquisition, retention, and transfer of a motor skill. *Journal of Experimental Psychology: Human Learning and Memory, 5,* 179-187.

Shea, J. B., Morgan, R. L., & Ho, L. (1981). *Contextual interference revisited.* Paper presented at the Rocky Mountain Psychological Association Annual Convention, Denver, CO.

Shea, J. B., & Zimny, S. T. (1983). Context effects in memory and learning movement information. In R. A. Magill (Ed.), *Memory and control of action* (pp. 345-366). Amsterdam: North-Holland.

Shea, J. B., & Zimny, S. T. (1988). Knowledge incorporation in motor representation. In O. G. Meijer & K. Roth (Eds.), *Complex movement behavior: "The" motor-action controversy* (pp. 289-314). Amsterdam: North-Holland.

Slamecka, N. J., & Graf, P. (1978). The generation effect: Delineation of a phenomenon. *Journal of Experimental Psychology: Human Learning and Memory, 4,* 592-604.

5 A Generation Advantage for Multiplication Skill Training and Nonword Vocabulary Acquisition

DANIELLE S. MCNAMARA

ALICE F. HEALY

The generation effect is extended to tasks requiring the learning or enhancement of skills and knowledge over multiple learning trials or episodes. In two experiments subjects were trained in either a *read* or *generate* condition. In Experiment 1, subjects performed simple and difficult multiplication problems. A generation advantage occurred only for the difficult, less familiar problems. In Experiment 2, subjects learned to associate nonword vocabulary terms with common English nouns. A generation advantage occurred for this case in which new knowledge was acquired. We also found that subjects using mnemonic strategies showed superior performance and that items for which subjects used a mnemonic strategy were learned better and retained better over a weeklong interval. The results are explained in terms of a procedural account of the generation advantage, and the implications of this research are discussed for instructional applications.

The generation effect refers to the finding that people show better retention of learned material when it is self-produced, or generated, than when it is simply copied or read. Slamecka and Graf (1978) demonstrated that an advantage for generating held across a variety of production rules and retention tasks. They showed subjects word pairs following

AUTHORS' NOTE: This research was supported in part by Army Research Institute Contract MDA903-90-K-0066 to the Institute of Cognitive Science at the University of Colorado. We are indebted to David Fendrich for help designing the preliminary study that led to Experiment 1 of this series. We also acknowledge the assistance of Michael Kos in the computer programming of both experiments and the help of William Marmie and Gregory Rully in scoring the data from Experiment 2. In addition, we are grateful to Lyle Bourne, Peter Graf, Mark McDaniel, and Rose Zacks for helpful comments on earlier versions of this chapter.

explicit production rules, such as an antonym rule. Subjects in a read condition were shown both words, which they simply read aloud (e.g., hot and cold). In a generate condition, subjects were provided the stimulus word (hot) and the first letter of its pair word (cold). The word pairs were read aloud—the second word in the pair being generated by the subject. Slamecka and Graf's (1978) paradigm ensured that the overt responses in the read and generate tasks were equated.

Since that time, there have been some failures to obtain the generation effect (e.g., Begg & Snider, 1987; Slamecka & Katsaiti, 1987) and even some reversals of the generation effect (e.g., Jacoby, 1983; Schmidt & Cherry, 1989). Nevertheless, the generation effect has been replicated in numerous studies using a wide variety of retention measures and stimuli. Specifically, the generation effect has been found for recognition measures (e.g., Glisky & Rabinowitz, 1985; Jacoby, 1978), recall measures (e.g., Donaldson & Bass, 1980; McFarland, Frey, & Rhodes, 1980), confidence ratings (e.g., McElroy & Slamecka, 1982), and some implicit memory measures (e.g., Gardiner, 1988, 1989). It has been found both with single- and multitrial learning (e.g., Gardiner, Gregg, & Hampton, 1988; Graf, 1980), with incidental as well as intentional learning (e.g., Nairne, 1988; Watkins & Sechler, 1988), and has been found to sustain retention intervals of at least 1 week (e.g., Crutcher & Healy, 1989; Johnson, Raye, Foley, & Foley, 1981). Further, the generation effect has been obtained with words cued by related words (e.g., Slamecka & Fevreiski, 1983), words cued by meaningful sentences (e.g., Gollub & Healy, 1987; Graf, 1980), isolated words (e.g., Glisky & Rabinowitz, 1985; Nairne, Riegler, & Serra, 1991), nonwords (e.g., Johns & Swanson, 1988; Nairne & Widner, 1987; but see, e.g., McElroy & Slamecka, 1982; Payne, Neely, & Burns, 1986), cue words (e.g., Greenwald & Johnson, 1989; but see, e.g., Slamecka & Graf, 1978), meaningful noun compounds (e.g., Gardiner & Hampton, 1985), meaningful bigrams (e.g., Gardiner & Hampton, 1985), computer commands (Scapin, 1982), product names (Thompson & Barnett, 1981), answers to multiplication problems (e.g., Gardiner & Rowley, 1984), unitized numbers (e.g., Gardiner & Hampton, 1985), and pictures (Peynircioglu, 1989).

Despite the wide range of studies showing the generation effect, these investigations have been primarily limited to examinations of episodic memory or memory for events (e.g., memory for the occurrence of an item in a previously presented list). Little attention has been afforded to testing the generation effect with tasks requiring the learning or enhancement of skills and knowledge[1] over multiple learning trials or episodes. Some investigations have successfully used a generation procedure to train subjects in tasks involving skills and knowledge (see, e.g., Fendrich, Healy, & Bourne, 1993; Glisky, 1992), but those investigations did not compare a generation procedure to a read procedure. A notable exception is a recent study by Carroll and Nelson (1993), who, however, were unable to obtain a generation effect for the learning of new information. Thus, the primary goal of the experiments presented here is to examine how skill and knowledge acquisition may be differentially affected by generating or reading during training. The importance of extending the investigation of the generation effect in this way is highlighted in a comment by Tulving (1984) concerning the relationship between episodic memory and formal education: "Formal education is aimed at the acquisition, retention, and utilization of skills and knowledge that have to do with the world; episodic memory is irrelevant to the accomplishment of these aims. The general utility of semantic knowledge for an individual is greater than is the remembering of personal events" (p. 225). Whereas previous investigations of the generation effect, which have used tasks requiring episodic memory, have been of undeniable theoretical utility, the most apparent deficit in the literature lies in the question of just how applicable the generation effect is to real-world problems.

Extending the generation effect to tasks involving skill and knowledge acquisition prompts the question of whether it is still the *generation effect* that is being investigated. Crucial tests of previous explanations of the generation effect may not be provided with paradigms involving skill and knowledge acquisition such as those presented here. Indeed, the effects of generating in the more traditional paradigms examining episodic memory may involve entirely different processes and may require different theoretical explanations than the effects of generating on skill and knowledge acquisition. However, with the goal of parsimony in mind, it is useful to assume at the outset that the same theoretical explanations apply to both sets of data. The theoretical explanations proposed for the previous findings regarding the generation effect can thus be borrowed to make certain predictions about the possible generation advantage in tasks involving skill and knowledge acquisition. In the same vein, McDaniel, Riegler, and Waddill (1990) pointed out that "if the generation effect were restricted to one very particular paradigm, then its potential application (e.g., in educational situations) and illumination of learning and memory processes in general would be of questionable value" (p. 796). Thus, it is assumed here that theoretical explanations of the generation effect can be applied to this new paradigm involving the generation advantage for skill and knowledge acquisition. However, to avoid potential confusion, the benefits of generating when applied to tasks involving skill and knowledge acquisition will be referred to here as *generation advantages* rather than as *generation effects*.

Four classes of theoretical explanations of the generation effect (discussed in more detail in the General Discussion) have received the most attention in the literature: (a) those attributing the effect to the amount of effort or arousal (e.g., Griffith, 1976; Jacoby, 1978; McFarland et al., 1980), (b) those proposing the necessity of lexical or semantic activation (e.g., Graf, 1980; McElroy & Slamecka, 1982), (c) those emphasizing relational processes (e.g., Donaldson & Bass, 1980; Rabinowitz & Craik, 1986), and (d) those proposing that the generation effect is based on multiple factors (e.g., Hirshman & Bjork, 1988; McDaniel et al., 1990; McDaniel, Waddill, & Einstein, 1988). We favor instead an alternative account of the generation effect. According to this *procedural* account (Crutcher & Healy, 1989), the important factor is that the subjects engage in cognitive operations that serve to connect a question (i.e., stimulus context) to a target answer (i.e., required response) rather than that the subjects actually (or successfully; e.g., Slamecka & Fevreiski, 1983) generate, or produce, the target. It is also crucial that at the time of the memory test the subjects are able to reinstate the learning procedures, or cognitive operations, that were used at study. We define a cognitive procedure as the mental operation that links a cue, or question, to a target answer. For example, in the case of multiplication, it is the multiplication operation itself, which could be either a direct retrieval operation or an operation involving mediated retrieval. When this mental operation is reinstated at test, then subjects can rapidly derive the target answer given the stimulus context.

The important distinction between this account and the alternatives is that it is process oriented, as opposed to item oriented; that is, it focuses on the process of generating rather than on the nature of the items or the relationship between the items. Although the effort explanation also emphasizes the process of generating, it is concerned only with the difficulty of the processing, not with the nature of the cognitive operations employed or the correspondence between the cognitive operations performed at study and at test. Many researchers have recently emphasized the importance of turning to process-oriented cognitive principles (e.g., Jacoby, 1991; Kolers & Roediger, 1984; Roediger, 1990); and indeed, processing factors, in contrast to item-related factors, have been recognized increasingly as potentially crucial to the understanding of the generation effect (e.g., Begg, Vinski, Frankovich, & Holgate, 1991; McDaniel & Waddill, 1990; Nairne et al., 1991).

Our procedural account derives from several previous investigations. The importance of mental procedures was introduced by Kolers and Roediger (1984) as a general cognitive principle. Glisky and Rabinowitz (1985) demonstrated more specifically that the memorial benefits associated with generation were enhanced by the repetition of the crucial mental operations. Subsequently, Crutcher and Healy (1989) showed that the most important factor in obtaining the generation effect for the answers to simple multiplication problems was that the subjects themselves perform the necessary mental operations, or cognitive procedures, to derive the answers. More recently, Healy et al. (1992; see also Healy et al., 1993, this volume) extended the notion of procedural reinstatement to account for a variety of empirical findings in the domain of long-term skill retention.

The present study extends the procedural account to the generation advantage for the acquisition of skills and knowledge. In Experiment 1, we test certain predictions of this account with respect to the effects of generating simple versus difficult multiplication problems. In Experiment 2, we extend the generation paradigm to the learning of new facts. In addition, we explore one example of a mental procedure. As mentioned earlier, we have defined a mental procedure as a specific cognitive operation that links together a cue and a target (in contrast to a global cognitive strategy). One way to link items is via a mnemonic code. Thus, in Experiment 2, we examined mnemonics developed by subjects while learning foreign vocabulary items paired with English words.

In summary, the general aims of these experiments are twofold: (a) to extend the generation paradigm to the investigation of skill and knowledge acquisition, thereby investigating the advantages of generating for tasks more relevant to educational settings; and (b) to investigate more thoroughly the plausibility of a procedural account of the generation advantage and to provide concrete examples of what might constitute a cognitive procedure.

EXPERIMENT 1

The first experiment of the present investigation was prompted by three previous studies, which were conducted in our laboratory. First, Fendrich et al. (1993) showed college students simple single-digit multiplication problems, such as 3×5, to which they responded with the answer, in this case 15. Considerable decreases were found in the response time for this task as training progressed. Also, virtually no forgetting of this skill was found. (For a discussion of further research along these lines, see Rickard & Bourne, this volume.)

Second, Crutcher and Healy (1989) found a generation effect for the retention of the answers to simple multiplication problems. In this study, two of the conditions involved either reading or generating the answers. Afterward, subjects were asked to recall or recognize the specific answers that they had previously read or generated. Subjects recalled and recognized significantly more answers that had been generated than had only been read.

The third study was an unpublished preliminary investigation that led to the present experiment. Like the study done by Crutcher and Healy (1989), we were interested in examining the effects of generation with simple multiplication problems. However, this study evaluated acquisition and retention of the skill itself, rather than memory for the specific answers encountered. From the study by Fendrich et al. (1993), we already knew that repeatedly generating the answers to multiplication problems resulted in significant improvement in response times. However, we did not know whether we would find for this skill an advantage for generating relative to reading. In this preliminary investigation, we trained college students on simple single-digit multiplication problems for three separate 1-hour sessions. Subjects were given a pretest before training, a posttest on the last day of training, and then after a month interval, a retention test. Training for the group of subjects in the read condition involved reading and copying the problem and the answer; training for the group of subjects in the generate condition involved reading and copying the problem, but generating the answers. Training led to a significant improvement in response times across sessions, and this improvement in the multiplication skill was retained with very little forgetting across the 1-month delay interval. However, there were no differences between the read and generate conditions.

The failure to find a generation advantage in our preliminary study of multiplication skill acquisition is consistent with our procedural account if it is assumed that a critical factor leading to a generation advantage for skill acquisition is that cognitive procedures be developed during the learning process; that is, the assumption is made that for a skill to be acquired, new cognitive procedures must also be acquired, because procedures constitute the essence of a skill. In light of the important role of procedural reinstatement in this account, it is also crucial that the procedures developed be stable across different occasions on which the skill is exercised. Thus, the promotion of stable, as opposed to multiple or variable (e.g., encoding variability; see Melton, 1970), procedures is emphasized by this account. Multiplication is a skill for which most college students have already developed some stable cognitive procedures—that is, for simple multiplication problems, the cognitive procedures necessary to retrieve the answer (i.e., the mental links between the problems and the answers) already exist for most college students (see, e.g., Fendrich et al., 1993). The results of the preliminary study indicated that reading these simple equations was enough to make this skill more efficient (i.e., faster), but no new procedures would be necessary and little or no change would be expected in existing procedures as a function of training because they are extremely well entrenched. In fact, answer retrieval tends to be automatic for simple multiplication problems (Bourne & Rickard, 1991). In contrast, most college students have not developed well-established cognitive procedures for more difficult multiplication problems with operands greater than 12. Indeed, Ashcraft (1992) found that retrieval of the answers to more difficult multiplication problems is less direct and slower than is that for simple multiplication problems. Moreover, Bourne and Rickard (1991) found, by using a protocol methodology, that as multiplication problem difficulty increases, the likelihood of direct answer retrieval decreases. This observation led us to the prediction that a generation advantage would be found for more difficult problems because the generate condition would be more apt than the read condition to promote the formation of new cognitive procedures.

One example of a cognitive procedure that may be developed to solve multiplication problems is an anchor-and-adjust algorithm. For example, for the problem 14*9 = 126, the subject might obtain the answer by first multiplying 14*10 (the anchor) and then adjusting by subtracting 14 (i.e., 14*10 − 14 = 126). Note that by our account, cognitive procedures include both the algorithmic procedures and the direct retrieval discussed by Logan (1988). According to Logan's instance theory of automatization, practice leads to a transition from algorithm-based performance to memory-based performance, with no change in the algorithm itself. In contrast, according to our approach, with practice subjects may modify the algorithm they use to solve a problem, so that practice may lead either to a transition from algorithmic-based performance to memory-based performance or to a transition from one algorithm to another (presumably more efficient) one (e.g., a transition from a standard multiply-and-carry procedure to an anchor-and-adjust procedure).

In Experiment 1, we tested the prediction that a generation advantage would be found for more difficult (but not for easy) problems by comparing read and generate conditions for the training of both easy and difficult multiplication problems. The generate condition was expected to be better than the read condition only for the difficult problems (because new cognitive procedures would be developed only for the difficult problems).

Note that this prediction of a generation advantage for difficult but not for easy problems follows from the fact that our task involves skill and knowledge acquisition. The same prediction would *not* be made for an episodic memory task. Indeed, in Crutcher and Healy's (1989) episodic memory task, there was a generation effect for simple multiplication problems, and other researchers have found generation effects with seemingly trivial or effortless episodic memory tasks (see, e.g., Glisky & Rabinowitz, 1985).

Method

Subjects were given a pretest on 10 easy and 10 difficult multiplication problems. They were then provided with 10 blocks of either read or generate training on the 20 problems (i.e., training was varied between subjects). Read training involved copying both the problem and the answer; generate training involved copying the problem and typing in the answer that they generated themselves. Training was followed by a posttest on the 20 problems.

Subjects. Sixty-four undergraduate students taking a class in introductory psychology participated for course credit. Thirty-two subjects were assigned to each of two experimental conditions (*read* and *generate*) on the basis of their time of arrival for testing. Exactly half of the subjects in each condition were tested during the summer and the remaining half were tested during the subsequent fall.

Design. A 2 × 2 × 2 mixed factorial design was employed, with one between-subjects factor, training condition (read, generate), and two within-subjects factors, test (pretest, posttest) and problem type (easy, difficult). A pretest before training was included as well as a posttest after training to control for any differences between the subject groups that were not attributable to training per se.

Apparatus and Materials. Stimuli were presented with Zenith Data Systems or IBM/PC computers. The Zenith computers were equipped with Zenith monitors, and the IBM/PC computers had Amdek 310 or 410 monitors. Each keypad included a label over the minus sign with an equals sign, and the computers were programmed to interpret the minus sign as an equals sign.

Ten easy and 10 corresponding difficult multiplication problems were shown to the subjects. As shown in Table 5.1, both types of problems

Table 5.1 Multiplication Problems Used in Experiment 1

Easy Problems	Difficult Problems	Easy Problems	Difficult Problems
40 × 9 = 360	14 × 9 = 126	80 × 8 = 640	18 × 8 = 144
60 × 7 = 420	16 × 7 = 112	80 × 9 = 720	18 × 9 = 162
60 × 8 = 480	16 × 8 = 128	90 × 7 = 630	19 × 7 = 133
70 × 7 = 490	17 × 7 = 119	90 × 8 = 720	19 × 8 = 152
70 × 8 = 560	17 × 8 = 136	90 × 9 = 810	19 × 9 = 171

consisted of a two-digit multiplier followed by a one-digit multiplier. The products all consisted of three-digit answers. For the easy multiplication problems the second digit of the two-digit multiplier was always 0 (e.g., 40 × 9). For the difficult multiplication problems, the first digit was always 1 (e.g., 14 × 9). Thus, apart from the second digit of the easy problems and the first digit of the difficult problems, the multipliers remained constant for both sets of problems.

Two pseudorandom orders of the 20 problems were constructed for the pretest and the posttest with the constraints that no more than two problems with the same single-digit multiplier occurred consecutively. Each subject saw a different order on the two tests. The orders were counterbalanced across subjects in each condition so that the two orders were used equally often in both the pretest and the posttest. During training subjects were exposed to 10 blocks of problems, each block consisting of a random permutation of the 20 problems. The permutation for a given block of a given subject was created by the computer at the time of training.

Procedure. Subjects were tested and trained in small rooms with one or two computers. Each subject sat facing a computer monitor, which was at eye level. At the start of the session, subjects were given a verbal general introduction to the experiment including, for example, the fact that the experiment would include three parts, and that the instructions for each part would be given on the computer monitor. Subjects were told that they could not correct typing errors (e.g., by using the backspace key). However, they were encouraged to complete any response even after they noticed that they had made a typing error. They were also told that they should use only the keypad (not the number row) of the terminal for their responses, and they were shown the location of the keys representing the multiplication sign (the asterisk key) and the equals sign (the minus sign key was relabeled with an equals sign).

Instructions appeared on each subject's computer monitor at the beginning of each part of the experiment (i.e., pretest, training, and posttest).

All subjects were given the same instructions for the pretest and posttest. Specifically, subjects were told that they were going to take a short arithmetic test with multiplication problems; they were given as an example the problem 12*7= . They were instructed to type in the answer followed by the enter key as quickly and accurately as they could and that the computer would record both their answer and their response time.

For the pretest and posttest, each problem appeared in the middle of the screen with the signal "answer:" directly below it. The subject was to type a response, which appeared next to the colon, followed by the enter key. To ensure that subjects entered a response, pressing the enter key on its own was not sufficient. Two presses of the enter key alone, without a response, caused a tone to sound, which alerted the experimenter of the error. Each problem remained on the screen until the subject entered a response and pressed the enter key. After pressing the enter key, the subsequent problem appeared immediately on the screen. No feedback was provided during the tests.

Following the pretest subjects were given instructions for the training, with different instructions for the read and generate conditions. Subjects in the read condition were told they were going to read series of multiplication equations that would appear in the middle of the computer screen one at a time. They were told to type the problem and the answer exactly as written under each equation presented. They were again given the example 12*7=84. They were told further that as soon as they typed an answer, they should press the enter key, after which the computer would provide feedback. The subjects were also informed that they would be tested on the multiplication problems at the end of their session. The most important aspect of the read condition was that the subjects were shown the answer at the same time as the problem, thus ensuring that they could not generate the answer before it was presented. In contrast, subjects in the generate condition were told that they were going to read series of multiplication problems (i.e., not full equations) and they were to type the problem exactly as it was written and type the answer (which they generated themselves). Otherwise, the instructions for the generate condition were equivalent to those for the read condition. At the end of each of the 10 blocks of training, subjects were given the opportunity for a short break, with the instructions to press the enter key twice when they were ready to continue.

For the training phase of the experiment, each problem (or, in the read condition, each equation) remained on the screen until the subject entered a response and pressed the enter key. Feedback for incorrect responses included a 1,000 ms tone followed by a 2,500 ms display of the word

Table 5.2 Proportions of Correct Responses in Experiment 1 as a Function of Training Condition, Test, and Problem Type

| | Test | | | |
| | Pretest | | Posttest | |
Condition	Easy	Difficult	Easy	Difficult
Read	.881	.681	.925	.669
Generate	.866	.703	.928	.825

"incorrect" along with the correct equation; feedback for correct responses included simply a 750 ms display of the word "correct," and the correct answer remained on the screen.

Results and Discussion

Accuracy. The results are summarized in Table 5.2 in proportions of correct responses as a function of training condition (read, generate), problem type (easy, difficult), and test (pretest, posttest). An analysis of variance was conducted including the between-subjects factor of condition and the within-subjects factors of problem type and test. Because a generation advantage is only expected for difficult problems, not for easy problems, and is only expected on the posttest (i.e., after training), not on the pretest, we are predicting a three-way interaction of condition, problem type, and test.

There was an overall improvement in accuracy from the pretest (M = .783) to the posttest (M = .837), $F(1, 62) = 9.8$, $MS_e = 0.0189$, $p = .003$; and easy problems (M = .900) yielded higher accuracy overall than difficult problems (M = .720), $F(1, 62) = 70.9$, $MS_e = 0.0294$, $p < .001$. Most crucially, an advantage for generate training was only found on the difficult problems after training (i.e., in the posttest), that is, the expected three-way interaction of training condition, test, and problem type was significant, $F(1, 62) = 5.9$, $MS_e = 0.0090$, $p = .017$, as was the two-way interaction of training condition and test, $F(1, 62) = 5.0$, $MS_e = 0.0189$, $p = .028$, as well as the two-way interaction of training condition and problem type, $F(1, 62) = 4.9$, $MS_e = 0.0294$, $p = .028$.

The magnitude of the generation advantage can be indexed by computing the difference between mean proportions correct on the generate and read conditions. By that index, a generation advantage was not evident on the pretest for either the easy problems ($M = -.015$) or the difficult problems ($M = .022$), or on the posttest for the easy problems ($M = .003$).

Table 5.3 Mean Correct Response Latencies (log s) in Experiment 1 as a Function of Training Condition, Test, and Problem Type

	Test			
	Pretest		Posttest	
Condition	Easy	Difficult	Easy	Difficult
Read	.520	.887	.299	.737
Generate	.543	.898	.294	.646

In contrast, the generation advantage was sizable on the posttest for the difficult problems ($M = .156$).

Separate analyses of variance were conducted on the data from each problem type. For the easy problems, there was only a main effect of test, $F(1, 62) = 10.4$, $MS_e = 0.0087$, $p = .002$; the interaction of training condition and test was not significant, $F(1, 62) < 1$. In contrast, for the difficult problems, there was both a main effect of test, $F(1, 62) = 5.0$, $MS_e = 0.0193$, $p = .028$, and an interaction of training condition and test, $F(1, 62) = 7.5$, $MS_e = 0.0193$, $p = .008$.

The failure to find an interaction of training condition and test for the easy problems was expected on the basis of our preliminary study. It was also predicted on the basis of our procedural account, because college students already have well developed cognitive procedures for these problems. Alternatively, however, the failure to find this interaction for easy problems could be attributed to a ceiling effect on performance of those problems at the posttest. To eliminate this alternative explanation, response latencies are examined because ceiling effects are not obtained with that measure.

Response Latency. Correct response latencies in seconds, reflecting the time to press the first digit of the answer, were transformed by a log to the base 10 function in order to ensure that the latencies were normally distributed. An analysis of variance was conducted on the mean log response latency for each subject as a function of problem type and test. Three subjects were excluded from the analysis (two from the generate condition and one from the read condition) because they made no correct responses for the difficult problems on the pretest. The resulting mean response latencies (in log s) are summarized in Table 5.3 as a function of training condition, problem type, and test.

There was an overall decline in response latency from the pretest ($M = .712$ log s) to the posttest ($M = .495$ log s), $F(1, 59) = 338.0$, $MS_e = 0.0085$,

$p < .001$, and easy problems ($M = .414$ log s) yielded lower response latencies overall than did difficult problems ($M = .792$ log s), $F(1, 59) = 432.2$, $MS_e = 0.0201$, $p < .001$. In addition, there was an overall improvement due to generation training; that is, the interaction of training condition and test was significant, $F(1, 59) = 7.6$, $MS_e = 0.0085$, $p = .008$. Although the three-way interaction of training condition, test, and problem type did not reach standard levels of significance, $F(1, 59) = 2.8$, $MS_e = 0.0073$, $p = .100$, the generation advantage clearly appears larger for the difficult problems than for the easy problems.

Because an improvement in performance is reflected in decreased latencies, the magnitude of the generation advantage can be indexed by computing the difference between read and generate mean latencies. By that index, a generation advantage was not evident on the pretest for either the easy problems ($M = -.023$) or the difficult problems ($M = -.011$) or on the posttest for the easy problems ($M = .005$). In contrast, the generation advantage was sizable on the posttest for the difficult problems ($M = .091$).

Separate analyses of variance were conducted on the data from each problem type. For the easy problems, there was only a main effect of test, $F(1, 59) = 271.3$, $MS_e = 0.0062$, $p < .001$; the interaction of training condition and test was not significant, $F(1, 59) = 1.0$. In contrast, for the difficult problems, there was both a main effect of test, $F(1, 59) = 126.4$, $MS_e = 0.0097$, $p < .001$, and an interaction of training condition and test, $F(1, 59) = 8.2$, $MS_e = 0.0097$, $p = .006$.

Summary. We found overall higher accuracy and faster correct response times on the easy problems as compared with the difficult problems, demonstrating that our a priori classification of problems was appropriate. Most crucially, we found an advantage due to generate training for difficult multiplication problems, but not for easy problems, both for response accuracy and correct response latency.[2] According to our procedural account, the most important difference between easy and difficult problems is that before training the subjects already have well-established cognitive procedures for the easy problems, but not for the difficult problems (Ashcraft, 1992; Bourne & Rickard, 1991). Accordingly, the results of Experiment 1 are consistent with our hypothesis that generate training would be more apt than read training to promote the formation of the new cognitive procedures needed to solve the difficult problems.

Unlike most previous investigations of the generation effect, Experiment 1 showed a generation advantage for performance based on access to facts and procedures learned or enhanced over multiple learning trials. The facts studied in this experiment were already known by the subjects before training, although the subjects presumably developed new cognitive procedures for more efficient retrieval of those facts in the case of the difficult problems. We were also interested in the question of whether a generation advantage would be found for situations in which individuals are learning new facts. On the basis of our findings from Experiment 1, we predicted a positive answer to this question. Such a question has important educational implications because most work in the classroom involves teaching new material rather than improving the efficiency with which previously learned material is retrieved from memory. Therefore, one purpose of our second experiment was to extend our comparison of the read and generate training conditions to the learning of new facts. For this purpose, we used verbal material instead of arithmetic calculations.

EXPERIMENT 2

As mentioned earlier, our procedural account of learning led us to predict that the development of cognitive procedures would aid learning and retention. In Experiment 1, we proposed that subjects in the generate condition were more apt than those in the read condition to form new cognitive procedures (e.g., an anchor-and-adjust procedure) for the difficult multiplication problems. However, we did not directly examine any indices of the cognitive procedures involved. Hence, in the present experiment a more direct measure of cognitive procedures is examined by investigating mnemonic codes developed during the learning process. Further, to evaluate the long-term impact of generate training and to eliminate any ceiling effects evident at the immediate posttest, we also included a retention test after a 1-week delay.

We taught subjects word-nonword associations, under the cover story that they were learning foreign vocabulary items. We expected that subjects in the generate condition would be more likely to develop new cognitive procedures than would subjects in the read condition and therefore to show superior learning and retention of the word-nonword pairs. This result would be consistent with our assumption that generating during skill and knowledge acquisition promotes the development of cognitive procedures. One type (but not the only type) of cognitive procedures in this case might be the use of mnemonic codes to link the word and nonword components of each pair. Hence, we collected retrospective reports from subjects concerning whether they used mnemonic codes. We expected subjects who used mnemonics to show superior learning and retention of the word-nonword pairs. Further, we expected that subjects in the read condition who developed mnemonics would show a level of performance comparable to that of subjects in the generate condition. This result would imply that the crucial factor leading to enhanced performance is that cognitive procedures be developed during the learning process rather than that the information be generated by the subjects.

Our prediction of a generation advantage for the learning of word-nonword associations may at first seem misguided because many early studies with episodic memory tasks failed to find the generation effect for nonwords or other meaningless responses (see, e.g., Gardiner & Hampton, 1985; Graf, 1980; McElroy & Slamecka, 1982; Nairne, Pusen, & Widner, 1985; Payne et al., 1986). However, more recently, Nairne and Widner (1987) showed that a generation effect could be obtained with nonwords when the retention test provided a stimulus context appropriate to (i.e., consistent with) the training context. Further, Johns and Swanson (1988) demonstrated that a generation effect can be obtained with nonwords when the subjects are shown the entire nonword stimuli via feedback. Moreover, although Nairne et al. (1985) did not report a generation effect in their Experiment 1, which involved testing over five repeated trials, they did obtain a significant interaction of trials and the read/generate variable, consistent with the observation that a generation advantage was obtained by the last trial. Further, Nairne et al.(1985) interpolated test trials between repeated read and generate study trials. Hence, subjects in their read condition actually "generated" on every other trial, so that the differences between the read and generate conditions may have been depressed. In the present experiment we used an appropriate stimulus context at test, provided the entire nonwords via feedback, and examined the generation advantage at the end of a series of training trials. Hence, our prediction of a generation advantage under these conditions does not seem farfetched given that we utilized methods previously found in studies of episodic memory to be successful in obtaining a generation effect with nonwords.

Method

Subjects were given a 10-minute initial study period to become familiar with the 30 word-nonword pairs. They were next given a pretest, 14 blocks of either read or generate training, and then a posttest; 1 week later a retention test was administered. To assess the extent of mnemonic coding, after the retention test we administered a retrospective questionnaire asking the subjects to report their use of mnemonics for each word-nonword pair.

Subjects. Twenty-four men and women who were undergraduate students taking a class in introductory psychology participated for course credit. There were two experimental conditions (read and generate); subjects were assigned to conditions on the basis of their time of arrival for testing. Exactly half of the subjects in each condition were tested during the summer, and the remaining half were tested during the subsequent fall.

Design. A 2×3 mixed factorial design was employed, with one between-subjects factor, training condition (read, generate), and one within-subjects factor, test (pretest, posttest, retention test).

Apparatus and Materials. As in Experiment 1, stimuli were presented with Zenith Data Systems or IBM/PC computers. The Zenith computers were equipped with Zenith monitors, and the IBM/PC computers had Amdek 310 or 410 monitors.

Thirty word-nonword pairs were constructed. The English words were all single-syllable nouns three to six ($M = 4.47$) letters in length. The English words were all frequent according to the Kucera and Francis (1967) norms; the minimum frequency (out of approximately 1 million words of text) was 67, the maximum was 2,316, and the mean was 540. The corresponding nonwords were all pronounceable single syllables, beginning and ending with a consonant, three to five ($M = 4.17$) letters in length. The nonwords were paired with the words in such a way as to minimize obvious mnemonic links. The pairs are shown in Table 5.4.

Three random orders of the 30 English words were constructed. Each subject was shown a different one of these orders at each of the three tests (pretest, posttest, and retention test). Across subjects in each condition, each of the six permutations of the three orders was used twice.

Subjects were exposed to 14 blocks of training, 4 blocks on the first day and 10 blocks on the following day, each block consisting of a random permutation of the 30 English word-nonword pairs. The permutation for a given block of a given subject was created by the computer at the time of training.

Procedure. Subjects were tested in small rooms with one or two computers. At the start of the first session subjects were given a typewritten list of the 30 English word-nonword pairs to study. They were told that the nonword was from a foreign language with the equivalent meaning of its English word mate. They were also told that they would be learning these foreign words throughout the course of the study. They were given

Table 5.4 Word-Nonword Pairs Used in Experiment 2

Word	Nonword	Word	Nonword
box	shem	job	lerb
year	kril	home	skal
hand	bruk	mile	vlat
school	cron	day	swib
time	plic	view	dword
work	squiv	arm	trin
house	tralt	food	prug
child	wath	peace	blent
part	spem	fire	zwird
place	hirg	street	flirn
heart	dront	game	slif
field	vour	club	tob
month	grat	floor	cruf
light	yord	bed	gult
rate	baz	spring	raub

10 minutes to study the pairs any way they wished, but without using paper and pencil. It was suggested to the subjects that they begin by reading over all of the pairs at least once.

Following the 10-minute initial study period, subjects were given a pretest sheet of paper with each English word followed by a blank line. They were told to write down as many of the foreign words as they could remember next to their English word equivalents. They were also encouraged to guess and to try not to leave blanks, but they were allowed to do so if necessary. The same procedure and instructions were employed for the posttest following training and the retention test 1 week later.

During the training period each subject sat facing a computer monitor at eye level. They were given written instructions appropriate for their training condition (read or generate). They were also provided answer sheets with two or three blanks per line, depending on the condition. Subjects in the read condition were reminded that they had just learned a list of foreign words with their English equivalents and that the English words would be presented on the computer screen. They were instructed to write the English word on the answer sheet in the first blank after which they were to press the space bar, which caused the foreign word to be presented on the screen. The subjects were instructed to copy the foreign word in the second blank (i.e., next to the English word). After they had finished writing the foreign word down, they were instructed to press the space bar to begin the next word-nonword pair. After the complete list of

30 word-nonword pairs was presented, there was a short break, after which the subjects were to press the space bar twice, and then the next list of pairs was presented. The subjects were required to use the same hand to press the space bar as they used to write down the words. This requirement ensured that they wrote down the words only after they had seen them on the computer screen, as would be necessary for a read condition.

The generate condition was identical to the read condition apart from the instructions given to the subject. After writing down the English word, the subjects were instructed to write down the foreign word, which was not shown to them on the computer screen. The subjects were required to write something in the second slot whether they were certain or not. After writing both the English word and the foreign word, the subjects were to press the space bar. At that point the foreign word was displayed on the computer screen, and subjects were told to copy that word in the third blank only if they had not written it correctly on their first try (i.e., in the second blank).

Following the retention test the subjects were given a sheet of paper containing a brief questionnaire. The subjects were provided an explanation and an example of what constituted a mnemonic procedure for learning a word-nonword pair. Specifically, they were told: "Sometimes when people want to learn and remember something they use some kind of strategy, or mnemonic, to link what they are learning to something that they already know." As an example, for a hypothetical word-nonword pair "lion-dlim," they were given the mnemonic "the lion in the dlim." The word-nonword pairs were listed on a second sheet of paper in the same order shown to subjects during the initial study period. Subjects were told to indicate by writing "yes" or "no" beside each pair whether they had employed some strategy or mnemonic as a means to learn that pair. Whenever they wrote "yes," they were also to describe the mnemonic in detail. If they could not recall the mnemonic, but were sure that they had used one, they were told to write down that they did not remember the mnemonic. If they remembered using more than one mnemonic for a particular pair, they were to write them all down.

Subjects were observed during training to ensure that they complied with the instructions, that is, to ensure that subjects in the read condition wrote the nonword only *after* seeing it and subjects in the generate condition wrote the nonword only *before* seeing it. Nevertheless, after completing the experiment each subject was asked verbally a question that indicated the degree to which read or generate instructions were followed. Generate subjects were asked if they had ever gone ahead and pressed the space bar to see the foreign word without trying to recall it. Read subjects were asked if they had ever tried to think of the foreign word before seeing it on the screen (they were never explicitly instructed not to do so) and if so, how often on a scale of 10% to 100% of the time. This question gives an indication of how often the read condition is actually treated as an internal generate condition by the subject. Because of the internal nature of this process, this generation is something that could not be observed by the experimenter.

Results and Discussion

Subject Compliance. Confirming the experimenter's observations, none of the subjects in the generate condition reported ever pressing the space bar to see the foreign word without trying to recall it. In contrast, only two of the subjects in the read condition reported not ever trying to think of the foreign word before seeing it on the screen. Ten of the 12 subjects trained in the read condition reported that at some time during the training they attempted to recall the foreign word internally before seeing it—thus transforming the read training into internal generate training. On average, subjects in the read condition (n = 12) reported attempting to recall internally the foreign word 73% of the time.

Accuracy. A nonword was scored as correct on a test only if it was placed beside the appropriate English word. Misspellings were allowed if pronunciation of the nonword was preserved. Two separate scorers tabulated all the data; any discrepancies between the scorers were resolved after discussion. The results are summarized in Table 5.5 in terms of proportions of correct responses as a function of training condition (read, generate) and test (pretest, posttest, retention test). An analysis of variance was conducted including the between-subjects factor of condition and the within-subjects factor of test. A generation advantage is only expected after training, that is, on the posttest and retention test, but not on the pretest. Hence, an interaction of training condition and test is expected. Two orthogonal tests using contrast codes were conducted to examine the separate contributions of learning and forgetting to the effects involving the test factor. Specifically, one contrast, reflecting learning, was made between the pretest and both of the subsequent tests (i.e., the posttest and the retention test), and a second contrast, reflecting forgetting, was made between the posttest and the retention test. It was predicted that the interaction of training condition and test would be found for the contrast between the pretest and the subsequent tests.

Table 5.5 Proportions of Correct Responses in Experiment 2 as a Function of Training Condition and Test

Condition	Pretest	Test Posttest	Retention
Read	.353	.833	.658
Generate	.297	.956	.756

The magnitude of the generation advantage can be indexed by computing the difference between mean proportions correct on the generate and read conditions. By that index, a generation advantage was not evident on the pretest ($M = -.056$), but was sizable on both the posttest ($M = .123$) and the retention test ($M = .098$). In the overall analysis of variance, there was a main effect of test, $F(2, 44) = 118.3$, $MS_e = 0.0171$, $p < .001$, reflecting both an overall improvement in accuracy from the pretest ($M = .325$) to the posttest ($M = .894$) as well as forgetting from the posttest to the retention test ($M = .707$). Single-degree of freedom tests (i.e., using contrast codes) show that the difference between the pretest and both the subsequent tests, reflecting learning, is significant, $F(1, 22) = 155.7$, $p < .001$, as is the difference between the posttest and the retention test, reflecting forgetting, $F(1, 22) = 38.7$, $p < .001$. As expected, the generation effect was only evident after the pretest (indeed there was a slight nonsignificant trend in the opposite direction on the pretest); the interaction of training condition and test was significant, $F(2, 44) = 3.3$, $MS_e = 0.0171$, $p = .048$. Crucially, the single-degree of freedom tests showed that whereas there was an interaction of training condition and test, comparing the pretest and both subsequent tests, $F(1, 22) = 4.7$, $p = .041$, there was not an interaction of training condition and test, comparing the posttest and the retention test, $F(1, 22) < 1$. Thus, a generation advantage did occur for learning the nonwords—despite the finding that many of the read subjects attempted to recall the foreign word internally before seeing it.

Because accuracy was near the ceiling for the generate condition on the posttest, an analysis of variance was conducted including the same factors as in the previous analysis (training condition and test), but including only two levels (pretest and retention test) of the test factor. That analysis yielded, as in the previous analysis, a main effect of test, $F(2, 22) = 102.9$, $MS_e = 0.0170$, $p < .001$, reflecting overall improvement in accuracy from the pretest to the retention test. Again, the generation advantage was only evident after the pretest; the interaction of training condition and test was marginally significant, $F(2, 22) = 4.1$, $MS_e = 0.0170$, $p = .052$. Thus, the advantages of generating were retained even after a 1-week interval.

Table 5.6 Proportions of Correct Responses in Experiment 2 for the Read Condition as a Function of Internally Generating and Test

Internally Generate	Pretest	Test Posttest	Retention
High	.461	1.000	.789
Low	.244	.667	.527

A separate analysis was conducted to determine if there was a main effect of internally generating within the read condition. The percentage of time subjects internally generated was transformed into a categorical variable (high vs. low internally generate) by means of a median-split procedure. The six read subjects categorized as low reported internally generating an average of 49% of the time, and the six read subjects categorized as high reported an average of 97% of the time spent internally generating. The results of this analysis are summarized in Table 5.6 in terms of proportions of correct responses as a function of the internal generate category (high, low) and test.

There, again, was a main effect of test, $F(2, 20) = 27.8$, $MS_e = .0256$, $p < .001$, showing significant learning during training and forgetting during the retention interval for the subjects in the read condition. Most important, the main effect of internally generating approached standard levels of significance, $F(1, 10) = 4.6$, $MS_e = .1434$, $p = .058$, reflecting the overall difference between the high ($M = .750$) and low ($M = .480$) internal generate groups within the read condition. There was not, however, a significant interaction of test and internally generating, $F(2, 20) < 1$. This last finding may indicate that read subjects who often internally generated during training also may have used a more effective memorization strategy during the 10-minute study period prior to training than did those read subjects who internally generated less often during training. Thus, this finding may merely reflect individual differences in learning strategies among the read subjects. However, the major finding of a generation advantage comparing read and generate subjects cannot be explained in this way because of the significant interaction between test (comparing pretest to posttest and retention test) and training condition.

Mnemonic Coding Differences Between Subjects. On the basis of the mnemonic strategy questionnaire, a mnemonic score was given to every word-nonword pair for each subject. The mnemonic score was 0 for a "no" response, 1 for a "yes" response with either an indication that the subject did not remember the mnemonic or only a description of a phonetic or graphemic mnemonic, and 2 for a "yes" response with a semantic mnemonic. The subject's total mnemonic score was simply the mean of the 30 scores of the word-nonword pairs. Two individuals separately determined the mnemonic score for every subject. In the few cases in which the individuals did not agree on the mnemonic score, discrepancies were resolved after discussion.

There was no difference between the generate ($M = 1.150$) and read ($M = 1.156$) training conditions in subjects' total mnemonic scores. However, we tested the hypothesis that this result was related to the finding that read subjects often attempted to recall the foreign word internally before seeing it. Indeed, the correlation (for the subjects in the read condition only) between internally generating and mean mnemonic score was .645 ($p = .024$).

To explore further the relation between internally generating the nonword and forming a mnemonic linking the word and nonword, we used the categorical variable based on the percentage of time subjects internally generated (high vs. low internally generate). The six read subjects who were classified as high internally generate had a mean mnemonic score of 1.500, and the six read subjects who were classified as low internally generate had a mean mnemonic score of .811. This difference was statistically reliable, $F(1, 10) = 7.4$, $MS_e = 0.1921$, $p = .021$. Thus, the subjects in the read condition who generated the word internally (and also tended to recall more nonwords) also reported more mnemonics.

To explore further the locus of the generation advantage, we used the mnemonic score from each subject as a covariate. Controlling for mnemonic scores in the analysis of covariance, the crucial interaction of training condition and test, comparing the pretest and both subsequent tests, remained significant, $F(1, 21) = 6.0$, $p = .023$. This result indicates that generating enhanced learning beyond any effect of mnemonic coding. In addition, controlling for training condition, there was an interaction of mnemonic score and test, comparing the pretest and both subsequent tests, $F(1, 21) = 6.9$, $p = .016$, reflecting the superior performance of subjects with higher mnemonic scores after training. There was in addition a marginally significant three-way interaction of condition, mnemonic score, and test, comparing the pretest and both subsequent tests, $F(1, 20) = 3.3$, $p = .082$, reflecting a greater effect of the use of mnemonics on learning for the subjects in the read, rather than the generate, condition. Alternatively, this three-way interaction reflects the fact that the generation advantage was only evident for the subjects with low mnemonic coding after the pretests.

Because accuracy was near the ceiling for the generate condition on the posttest, an additional analysis of covariance was conducted including the same covariate (mnemonic score) and the same factors (training condition and test) as in the previous analysis, but including only two levels (pretest and retention test) of the test factor. That analysis yielded, as in the previous analysis, the crucial interaction of training condition and test, $F(1, 21) = 5.2$, $p = .033$. This result implies that generating enhanced learning regardless of the degree of mnemonic coding used by the subjects, even when the immediate posttest is excluded. In addition, controlling for training condition, there remained an interaction of mnemonic score and test, $F(1, 21) = 6.7$, $p = .017$, again reflecting the superior performance of subjects with higher mnemonic scores after training. The previously marginal three-way interaction of condition, mnemonic score, and test was not significant in this analysis with the immediate posttest removed, $F(1, 21) = 2.7$, $p = .115$.

The results from the overall analysis of covariance cannot be graphically depicted. The analysis of covariance employed mnemonic score as a continuous variable, reflecting each subject's use of a mnemonic strategy for all of the 30 word-nonword pairs. However, to provide values illustrating the relationship of mnemonic score to both test and training condition, we used a mnemonic score categorical variable obtained by a median-split procedure. The median-split procedure categorized the subjects in each training condition into those with a relatively low and those with a relatively high mnemonic score. Table 5.7 presents the proportions of correct responses as a function of mnemonic score category (low, high), training condition, and test. The generation advantage, as indexed by the difference between the generate and read mean proportions correct, occurs on both the posttest ($M = .277$) and the retention test ($M = .189$), but not the pretest ($M = .011$) for subjects with low mnemonic scores. In contrast, it does not occur on any test (pretest, M = −.122; posttest, M = −.033; retention test, M = .006) for subjects with high mnemonic scores. As predicted, subjects in the read condition with high mnemonic scores (who also tended to be more likely to internally generate) have similar learning and retention to subjects trained in the generate condition, even those who also have high mnemonic scores. Thus, instructions to generate only benefited those subjects who did not already use the mnemonic strategy.

Mnemonic Coding Differences Within Subjects. The analyses reported earlier showed that subjects who used a high degree of mnemonic coding demonstrated superior performance relative to subjects who used a lower degree of mnemonic coding. A related question pertains to differences in

Table 5.7 Proportions of Correct Responses in Experiment 2 as a Function of Mnemonic Category, Training Condition, and Test

Mnemonic Category	Pretest	Test Posttest	Retention
Low			
Read	.283	.667	.517
Generate	.294	.944	.706
High			
Read	.422	1.000	.800
Generate	.300	.967	.806

mnemonic coding within subjects. Were the items for which subjects used mnemonic coding better remembered than the items for which subjects did not use mnemonic coding? To answer this question, we conducted an analysis of the proportion of correct responses dividing the items for each subject into those given a 0 (i.e., no mnemonic), a 1 (i.e., a nonsemantic mnemonic), or a 2 (i.e., a semantic mnemonic). For those cases in which a subject had no items in a particular scoring category, we replaced that missing proportion with the mean from the subjects in the same training condition (i.e., read or generate) and at the same test (i.e., pretest, posttest, or retention test). Table 5.8 presents the mean proportions of correct responses as a function of mnemonic score (0, 1, 2), training condition, and test.

A mixed factorial analysis of variance was conducted on these data including the single between-subjects factor of training condition and the two within-subjects factors of test and mnemonic score. As found in the previous analyses, there was a significant main effect of test, $F(2, 44) = 96.0$, $MS_e = 0.0661$, $p < .001$, and a significant interaction of training condition and test, $F(2, 44) = 4.0$, $MS_e = 0.0661$, $p = .025$. Of most interest, there was also a significant main effect of mnemonic score, $F(2, 44) = 7.7$, $MS_e = 0.0679$, $p = .002$. Overall, the proportion of correct responses was highest for the items given a score of 2 ($M = .714$), next highest for the items given a score of 1 ($M = .625$), and lowest for the items given a score of 0 ($M = .543$). There were no significant interactions involving mnemonic score. This finding suggests that the advantage for the high mnemonic score did not depend on either test or training condition. However, there appears to be a retention advantage (i.e., less of a difference between the posttest and the retention test) for a semantic mnemonic (i.e., a score of 2) relative to both a nonsemantic mnemonic (i.e., a score of 1) and the absence of a mnemonic (i.e., a score of 0). To establish the statistical

Table 5.8 Proportions of Correct Responses in Experiment 2 as a Function of Mnemonic Score, Training Condition, and Test

| | | Test | |
Mnemonic Score	Pretest	Posttest	Retention
No mnemonic (0)			
Read	.336	.743	.482
Generate	.197	.887	.615
Nonsemantic mnemonic (1)			
Read	.367	.916	.655
Generate	.200	1.000	.610
Semantic mnemonic (2)			
Read	.430	.908	.752
Generate	.361	.984	.846

reliability of this finding, we conducted a separate analysis of variance including only the posttest and retention test. That analysis revealed a significant main effect of test, $F(1, 22) = 38.1$, $MS_e = .0573$, $p < .001$, reflecting forgetting across the retention interval, along with a main effect of mnemonic score, $F(2, 44) = 6.5$, $MS_e = .0684$, $p = .004$, reflecting increased performance as the mnemonic score increased. Most important, there was also a significant interaction of mnemonic score and test, $F(2, 44) = 3.9$, $MS_e = .0256$, $p = .027$, in agreement with the observation that forgetting across the retention interval was least for a semantic mnemonic. However, interpretation of this effect is hindered by ceiling-level performance on the posttest, particularly for the semantic and nonsemantic mnemonics.

Summary. In Experiment 2, there was a generation advantage for learning to associate nonwords with corresponding English words, and this advantage was retained after a 1-week interval. Also, subjects in the read condition who reported trying more often to think of the foreign word before seeing it (i.e., who internally generated the word) recalled 27% more nonwords than did those subjects in the read condition who internally generated less often.

On the basis of our procedural account, we expected that subjects would be aided by the formation of a mnemonic code linking the word to its corresponding nonword. We found, as expected, advantages for mnemonic coding both between and within subjects; that is, subjects who more often reported using mnemonics showed superior learning and retention, and a given subject showed superior learning and retention for word-nonword pairs linked via a mnemonic, especially a semantic one. It was also predicted that those subjects in the read condition who used mnemonic coding would show a level of performance comparable to that shown by subjects in the generate condition. There was some support for this prediction: For subjects who were high on mnemonic coding, the level of performance on the posttest and retention test in the read condition was similar to that in the generate condition.

General Discussion

We have found a generation advantage in two experiments examining the acquisition and retention of skill and knowledge. In both experiments subjects were trained in either a read or generate condition. In Experiment 1, subjects performed simple and difficult multiplication problems, and as predicted, a generation advantage occurred only for the difficult problems. In Experiment 2, subjects learned to associate nonword vocabulary terms with common English nouns. A generation advantage occurred, and in both conditions, subjects using mnemonic strategies showed superior performance. A generation advantage was found even though training condition was varied in a between-subjects design (cf. Begg & Snider, 1987; Slamecka & Katsaiti, 1987) and even though the information to be remembered consisted of nonwords in Experiment 2 (cf. McElroy & Slamecka, 1982; Nairne et al., 1985; Payne et al., 1986). No previous investigators have found a generation advantage for nonwords in a between-subjects design.

Previous studies of the generation effect have been limited almost exclusively to examinations of episodic memory (e.g., memory for the occurrence of an item in a previously presented list). The primary goal of this study was to extend the generation paradigm to the learning or enhancement of skills and knowledge over multiple learning episodes or trials. To address this goal, we tested a generation advantage with two tasks resembling those required in real-world settings—solving multiplication problems and learning foreign vocabulary items. A generation advantage was found in both tasks. In contrast, Carroll and Nelson (1993) recently reported the findings from seven experiments that showed no evidence of a generation effect when the responses were answers to general information questions that were either read or generated from an anagram. Like us, their goal was to extend the generation paradigm to learning new information. Why did we find that the generation paradigm does indeed generalize to more naturalistic conditions whereas they did not? The two studies differ in at least two important ways. First, in contrast to the present study, Carroll and Nelson, as they admit (1993, p. 365), did not provide for test appropriateness in their experiments because solving an anagram at study was never matched by the same operations at test. Equating conditions at study and at test has been shown to be critical for the generation effect to occur, particularly for less familiar information such as nonwords (e.g., Nairne & Widner, 1987). Second, Carroll and Nelson (1993) employed single-trial learning in their experiments. In contrast, as in the majority of training studies (e.g., Atkinson & Raugh, 1975; Fendrich et al., 1993; Schneider & Shiffrin, 1977), we used multiple training trials in our study; our subjects were required to generate or read across multiple trials before being tested for the memorial benefits of the two types of study. Multiple study trials may be necessary for differences in learning between read and generate conditions to become apparent and reliable. The importance of multiple trials is evident in Nairne et al.'s (1985) first experiment, which included five study-test trials and yielded a significant interaction of trials and the read/generate variable. A generation effect for nonwords did not begin to appear until after the second trial and was not pronounced until the fifth trial.

The use of multiple study trials in our study was necessary because we were investigating learning, not just memory. Because repetitive generating may be seen as similar to repetitive testing, our paradigm may be seen as analogous to that used to explore benefits of prior tests on later tests of learning (see, e.g., Bjork, 1975; Hogan & Kintsch, 1971; Izawa, 1992; McDaniel & Masson, 1985). However, the procedures used in the earlier studies differed in many ways from the procedures used in the present paradigm; most crucially, no direct comparison of read and generate learning conditions was made in the earlier studies. The advantages of generating can also be seen as analogous to the advantages of discovery learning, as opposed to expository learning (see, e.g., Bruner, 1961; Mayer, 1975; McDaniel & Schlager, 1990), because both involve advantages of active, as opposed to passive, learning. The primary differences between these two paradigms are that this other distinction applies to more complicated problem-solving tasks than does the distinction considered in the present study and that the discovery learning paradigm does not involve repeated exposure to the same items.

Alternative Explanations of the Generation Effect

As mentioned previously, four classes of theoretical explanations of the generation effect have received the most attention: (a) those attributing the effect to the amount of effort involved, (b) those proposing the necessity of semantic activation, (c) those emphasizing the relationship between the cue and the target, and (d) those proposing that the generation effect is based on multiple factors. The strengths and weaknesses of these explanations are discussed below.

Effort. One of the most intuitively appealing explanations of the generation effect is that it is due to increased amount of effort (e.g., Griffith, 1976; McFarland et al., 1980) or arousal (Jacoby, 1978) for a generated stimulus relative to a stimulus that is only read. Indeed, many researchers have found what is called an "effort" effect, wherein the more effort that is expended during encoding, the better the subsequent recall of the encoded items (e.g., Eysenck & Eysenck, 1979; Griffith, 1976; Jacoby, Craik, & Begg, 1979; Kolers, 1973, 1975; Tyler, Hertel, McCallum, & Ellis, 1979; see also Mitchell & Hunt, 1989, for a review of the literature). In these studies, effort is generally operationalized in terms of the difficulty of the task (e.g., Jacoby, 1978) or the amount of cognitive processing resources required (e.g., Griffith, 1976). According to effort hypotheses of the generation effect, it is the increased effort associated with generating a response that results in superior performance on retention tasks. There are several problems associated with any hypothesis that the amount of effort used for a task has memorial consequences. The first problem concerns the difficulty of defining or operationalizing the construct of "effort." Once defined, a subsequent problem is the difficulty of isolating the amount of effort used for a task and keeping constant all other variables that can affect later recall. One of the most important confounding variables is the amount of time spent on a task. It is difficult, and perhaps impossible, to specify tasks that require equal amounts of time and yet varying degrees of effort. A common solution to that problem is to require subjects to spend equal amounts of time on all tasks. That solution unfortunately leaves open the question of what cognitive processing is actually occurring during the excess time for the easier tasks—although subjects may spend the same amount of time completing both a hard and an easy task, there is no guarantee that after the easy task is completed the extra time is actually allotted to processing the information in the task (e.g., they may be thinking about what to have for dinner).

Another problem with an effort hypothesis concerns the robustness of the effort effect itself. For example, Zacks, Hasher, Sanft, and Rose (1983) reported five experiments using three different means of varying effort, none of which yielded evidence of a reliable relation between encoding effort and subsequent recall. In consideration of their findings, Zacks et al.

(1983) suggested that because the generation effect is more robust than the effort effect, the two should be treated separately. Indeed, there is little evidence that effort or difficulty play a role in the generation effect. For example, Jacoby (1978) failed to find an effect of effort in a generation task wherein difficulty was varied as a function of the number of letters missing from a target word (cf. Gardiner, Smith, Richardson, Burrows, & Williams, 1985), and other researchers have found generation effects even when the process of generating required virtually no effort at all (e.g., Glisky & Rabinowitz, 1985).

Semantic Activation. The second class of explanations includes those proposing the necessity of semantic or lexical activation. There have been two major lines of research directed at determining the role of semantic processing in the generation effect. One line involved the manipulation of the meaningfulness of the generated item. Initial findings indicated that the generation effect did not occur with meaningless items, such as nonwords (e.g., McElroy & Slamecka, 1982), anomalous sentences (Graf, 1980), or meaningless bigrams (Gardiner & Hampton, 1985). However, further exploration of the issue has indicated that as long as the subject is tested on the same items as presented at test, the generation effect occurs regardless of the nature of the generated item, in accord with the principle of test appropriateness (e.g., Nairne & Widner, 1987). Another line of research was directed at the distinction between implicit and explicit memory, and the supposition that the generation effect was solely the enhancement of explicit memory and thus involved only conceptual processing. Initial findings supported this view (e.g., Jacoby, 1983). However, when Gardiner (1988, 1989) equated the conditions of study and test in an implicit memory paradigm, the generation effect reappeared.

Cue-Target Relationship Enhancement. Some researchers have hypothesized that the generation effect is due to the enhancement of the relationship between the cue and the target (e.g., Donaldson & Bass, 1980; Rabinowitz & Craik, 1986). Donaldson and Bass (1980) suggested that the act of generating resulted in a superior encoding of the cue-target relationship and that the factor underlying the generation effect is that the subject perform a check on each generated target to ensure that the response adequately meets its prescribed relation to the stimulus (i.e., the cue). They found that a read task that also required the evaluation of the goodness of the relationship resulted in a memorial advantage for the target items similar to that found for a generate task. This result is similar to our finding that the retention of the subjects in the read condition who developed mnemonics when learning word-nonword pairs resembled that of the subjects who had generated the nonword. Some researchers have argued against the importance of the relationship between the cue and the target on the basis that no memorial advantage is found for the cues in the generate task (Slamecka & Graf, 1978). Other researchers, however, have found generation effects for cues (Greenwald & Johnson, 1989). On the other hand, Glisky and Rabinowitz (1985) found a generation effect when single words were generated from word fragments; this result cannot be easily explained in terms of relational processing. These contradictory findings leave this issue unresolved, although it seems clear that relational factors are not sufficient to explain the generation effect.

Multiple Factors. It has become increasingly clear that the generation effect cannot be explained on the basis of any one of the above three factors alone (i.e., effort, semantic activation, or cue-target relationship enhancement). Because of findings inconsistent with each of these singular explanations and also because of the lack of a generation effect in between-subjects designs with free recall retention measures (Begg & Snider, 1987; Hirshman & Bjork, 1988; McDaniel et al., 1988; Nairne et al., 1991; Schmidt & Cherry, 1989; Slamecka & Katsaiti, 1987), some authors have suggested that the generation effect is due to more than a single factor (e.g., Hirshman & Bjork, 1988; McDaniel et al., 1988). Hirshman and Bjork (1988) proposed that generating is superior to reading because it both activates features of the response term in memory (i.e., lexical or semantic activation) and strengthens the stimulus-response relation in memory (i.e., enhanced cue-target relationship). They assume that free recall is facilitated by the activation of the response term but is disturbed by the strengthening of the stimulus-response relation, whereas cued recall is facilitated by the activation of both the response term and the stimulus-response relation. McDaniel et al. (1988) proposed a third factor—the use of whole list information. More specifically, free recall depends on whole list information and the task of generating enhances the stimulus-response relation at the expense of whole list information. This hypothesis was based on the finding that a generation effect did occur in a between-subjects design for free recall when the response words were structured by categories and the cue words were the category names. Thus, the three factors are three different types of information (i.e., item, relational, whole list) that are more or less useful for the generation task depending on the items and the retention measure.

Hirshman and Bjork's (1988) and McDaniel et al.'s (1988, 1990) interpretations of the generation effect are based on the lack of a generation effect in a between-subjects design with free recall used as the retention measure (in the absence of whole list structural cues). There exist, however, two studies that found generation effects under those conditions (Gollub & Healy, 1987; McFarland et al., 1980, Experiment 2). Gollub and Healy (1987) had subjects generate sentences using target words; yoked subjects evaluated target word usage in the sentences generated by the first group. Free recall performance for the target words was superior for the generate subjects than for the evaluate subjects. McFarland et al. (1980) had subjects either decide if a given word fit a specified context or generate a word to fit the context. They found a generation effect using a between-subjects design with free recall as the dependent measure, though the effect was slightly reduced from the results using a within-subjects design. It is not clear that the findings from these two studies could be accommodated by the multifactor accounts.

Procedural Account. It is evident that there have been empirical findings both supporting and contradicting the four classes of explanations reviewed above. We prefer instead a procedural account of memory (see, e.g., Crutcher & Healy, 1989; Healy et al., 1992), according to which the critical factor leading to a generation advantage for learning new facts or skills is that cognitive procedures be developed during the learning process and that these procedures be reinstated at test. We define a cognitive procedure as a mental operation linking a stimulus to a response. When the mental operation is reinstated at test, then subjects can rapidly derive the target answer given the stimulus context. In the case of multiplication, the relevant cognitive operation is the multiplication operation itself, which could be either a direct retrieval operation or an operation involving mediated retrieval. In the case of learning new word-nonword pairs, the cognitive operation is the process of associating the two items. One way to associate two items is by using a mnemonic link.

The procedural account has the advantage relative to the other accounts that it has been applied to a broad range of findings concerning learning and memory (Kolers & Roediger, 1984), long-term retention (Healy et al., 1992, 1993), and problem solving (McDaniel & Schlager, 1990), beyond just those concerning the effects of generating. As mentioned earlier, the important distinction between this account and the alternatives is that the emphasis is placed on cognitive operations rather than on specific stimuli or the target responses; that is, it focuses on the generation process rather than on the nature of the items or the relationship between the items. This account is compatible with the alternative accounts, such as McDaniel et al.'s (1988) multifactor framework, but places greater emphasis on the process side, as opposed to the structure side, of the structure-process distinction (see, e.g., Kolers & Roediger, 1984).

We extended the procedural account to accommodate learning within the generation paradigm by making the assumptions that for learning to occur mental procedures must be developed during training and that generating promotes the formation of these new procedures. With this extension, we made a set of predictions that were verified in our two experiments. In Experiment 1, we predicted and found a generation advantage for difficult, but not easy, multiplication problems. This prediction was based on the assumptions that (a) little change in cognitive procedures would be expected for easy problems, but difficult problems would be expected to require the development of new cognitive procedures; and (b) with training the generate condition would be more apt than the read condition to promote the formation of new and stable cognitive procedures (e.g., algorithms).

In Experiment 2, we predicted and found a generation advantage for the learning of nonword vocabulary terms. This finding is important because it extends the generation advantage to the learning of new material, as in foreign language acquisition. In addition, we predicted and found superior learning and retention of the word-nonword pairs by subjects who used mnemonic codes. We also predicted that the generation advantage would be eliminated for subjects who used mnemonics, and we found some support for this prediction.

To avoid circularity, our procedural account relies on our having a clear and consistent definition of what constitutes a cognitive procedure. For this account to lead to specific predictions and new insights, it is necessary that attempts be made to define and operationalize more precisely the concepts of procedures and proceduralization. In this study, we have not attempted to provide a definition of a cognitive procedure that would cover all tasks and domains. In Experiment 1, we did not provide an operational definition for a cognitive procedure relevant to mental multiplication; instead we relied on previous observations (e.g., Bourne & Rickard, 1991) that new cognitive procedures would be more likely to be developed for the difficult than for the easy multiplication problems. In contrast, in Experiment 2, we did employ a clear-cut operational criterion for what constituted one type of cognitive procedure. The criterion we used—that a mnemonic code be developed—is not meant to apply to all tasks or to be inclusive of all cognitive procedures used in our vocabulary learning task. It did, however, allow us to identify a specific type of procedure that was found to promote superior acquisition and long-term retention. Indeed, these mnemonics were found to improve the learning and retention of information in Experiment 2.

Educational Implications

As we mentioned earlier, we think that these findings have important educational implications. Previous studies of the generation effect have been limited almost exclusively to examinations of events stored in episodic memory, whereas the present study has examined the acquisition and retention of skill and knowledge. Most work in the classroom involves teaching new knowledge or skills, so our finding a generation advantage for this type of learning implies that classroom teaching would benefit by encouraging students to generate the material to be learned.

Indeed, there is a current trend in elementary schools to teach children how to use calculators for solving multiplication problems instead of requiring them to generate answers using the multiplication table. The study we have presented (which included difficult multiplication problems not already memorized by our adult subjects and new foreign vocabulary items) suggests that children, when learning new multiplication problems, should not use calculators but rather should perform the multiplication operations mentally. Generating the answers to the problems, instead of simply reading them from the calculator display, should lead to optimal acquisition and long-term retention (see McNamara, 1992). More generally, our findings point to the important implications of the generation paradigm in the applied realm outside the laboratory. Although this paradigm has been widely investigated in the laboratory, there has been little attempt to consider the possible applications of the benefits of generating to the classroom or other real-world settings. Our findings indicate that future applied research on the acquisition and retention of skill and knowledge would benefit from use of the generation paradigm. Ultimately, extending the generation advantage to instructional settings may enlighten our understanding of the factors underlying the benefits of generation, particularly the critical role of proceduralization.

Conclusions

The first goal of this study was to extend the generation paradigm to the investigation of the acquisition and retention of skill and knowledge because previous studies of the generation effect were limited almost exclusively to episodic memory tasks. The importance of this extension of the generation paradigm is highlighted by the clear deficit in the generation effect literature with respect to tasks that are relevant to educational settings and the applied realm. The second goal of this study was to investigate more thoroughly the plausibility of a procedural account and to provide concrete examples of what might constitute a cognitive procedure. Indeed, the generation advantage was found to extend to the acquisition of multiplication skill and foreign word acquisition and retention, and the results of these two studies were accommodated by a procedural account. The specific predictions of our procedural framework were tested and confirmed, thereby adding to the plausibility of this procedural account of the generation advantage. However, more empirical research is required to discover and define the specific parameters underlying the benefits of generating that we observed. Thus, the results of this study provide a promising new direction for research concerning the generation advantage for skill and knowledge acquisition.

Notes

1. Note, here and throughout this chapter, by "knowledge" we mean facts that are generalizable, context-free, and not associated with a single learning event or episode.

2. Finding the same pattern of results for both accuracy and correct response time indicates that we have no speed/accuracy trade-off problems of interpretation—that is, there was better performance in terms of *both* speed and accuracy for easy problems compared to difficult problems and for generate training compared to read training on difficult problems (but not on easy problems).

References

Ashcraft, M. H. (1992). Cognitive arithmetic: A review of data and theory. *Cognition, 44,* 75-106.

Atkinson, R. C., & Raugh, R. R. (1975). An application of the mnemonic keyword method to the acquisition of a Russian vocabulary. *Journal of Experimental Psychology: Human Learning and Memory, 104,* 126-133.

Begg, I., & Snider, A. (1987). The generation effect: Evidence for generalized inhibition. *Journal of Experimental Psychology: Learning, Memory, and Cognition, 13,* 553-563.

Begg, I., Vinski, E., Frankovich, L., & Holgate, B. (1991). Generating makes words memorable, but so does effective reading. *Memory & Cognition, 19,* 487-497.

Bjork, R. A. (1975). Retrieval as a memory modifier: An interpretation of negative recency and related phenomena. In R. L. Solso (Ed.), *Information processing and cognition* (pp. 123-144). New York: John Wiley.

Bourne, L. E., Jr., & Rickard, T. C. (1991, July). *Mental calculation: The development of a cognitive skill.* Paper presented at the Interamerican Congress of Psychology, San Jose, Costa Rica.

Bruner, J. S. (1961). The act of discovery. *Harvard Educational Review, 31,* 21-32.

Carroll, M., & Nelson, T. O. (1993). Failure to obtain a generation effect during naturalistic learning. *Memory & Cognition, 21,* 361-366.

Crutcher, R. J., & Healy, A. F. (1989). Cognitive operations and the generation effect. *Journal of Experimental Psychology: Learning, Memory, and Cognition, 15,* 669-675.

Donaldson, W., & Bass, M. (1980). Relational information and memory for problem solutions. *Journal of Verbal Learning and Verbal Behavior, 19,* 26-35.

Eysenck, M. W., & Eysenck, M. C. (1979). Processing depth, elaboration of encoding, memory store, and expended processing capacity. *Journal of Experimental Psychology: Human Learning and Memory, 5,* 472-484.

Fendrich, D. W., Healy, A. F., & Bourne, L. E., Jr. (1993). Mental arithmetic: Training and retention of multiplication skill. In C. Izawa (Ed.), *Cognitive psychology applied* (pp. 111-133). Hillsdale, NJ: Lawrence Erlbaum.

Gardiner, J. M. (1988). Generation and priming effects in word-fragment completion. *Journal of Experimental Psychology: Learning, Memory, and Cognition, 14,* 495-501.

Gardiner, J. M. (1989). A generation effect in memory without awareness. *British Journal of Psychology, 80,* 163-168.

Gardiner, J. M., Gregg, V. H., & Hampton, J. A. (1988). Word frequency and generation effects. *Journal of Experimental Psychology: Learning, Memory, and Cognition, 14,* 687-693.

Gardiner, J. M., & Hampton, J. A. (1985). Semantic memory and the generation effect: Some tests of the lexical activation hypothesis. *Journal of Experimental Psychology: Learning, Memory, and Cognition, 11,* 732-741.

Gardiner, J. M., & Rowley, J.M.C. (1984). A generation effect with numbers rather than words. *Memory & Cognition, 12,* 443-445.

Gardiner, J. M., Smith, H. E., Richardson, C. J., Burrows, M. V., & Williams, S. D. (1985). The generation effect: Continuity between generating and reading. *American Journal of Psychology, 98,* 373-378.

Glisky, E. L. (1992). Acquisition and transfer of declarative and procedural knowledge by memory-impaired patients: A computer data-entry task. *Neuropsychologia, 30,* 899-910.

Glisky, E. L., & Rabinowitz, J. C. (1985). Enhancing the generation effect through repetition of operations. *Journal of Experimental Psychology: Learning, Memory, and Cognition, 11,* 193-205.

Gollub, D., & Healy, A. F. (1987). Word recall as a function of sentence generation and sentence context. *Bulletin of the Psychonomic Society, 25,* 359-360.

Graf, P. (1980). Two consequences of generating: Increased inter- and intraword organization of sentences. *Journal of Verbal Learning and Verbal Behavior, 19,* 316-327.

Greenwald, A. G., & Johnson, M.M.S. (1989). The generation effect extended: Memory enhancement for generation cues. *Memory & Cognition, 17,* 673-681.

Griffith, D. (1976). The attentional demands of mnemonic control processes. *Memory & Cognition, 4,* 103-108.

Healy, A. F., Clawson, D. M., McNamara, D. S., Marmie, W. R., Schneider, V. I., Rickard, T. C., Crutcher, R. J., King, C., Ericsson, K. A., & Bourne, L. E., Jr. (1993). The long-term retention of knowledge and skills. In D. Medin (Ed.), *The psychology of learning and motivation* (pp. 135-164). New York: Academic Press.

Healy, A. F., Fendrich, D. W., Crutcher, R. J., Wittman, W. T., Gesi, A. T., Ericsson, K. A., & Bourne, L. E., Jr. (1992). The long-term retention of skills. In A. F. Healy, S. M. Kosslyn, & R. M. Shiffrin (Eds.), *From learning processes to cognitive processes: Essays in honor of William K. Estes* (Vol. 2, pp. 87-118). Hillsdale, NJ: Lawrence Erlbaum.

Healy, A. F., King, C. L. Clawson, D. M. Sinclair, G. P., Rickard, T. C., Crutcher, R. J., Ericsson, K. A., & Bourne, L. E., Jr. (this volume). Optimizing the long-term retention of skills. In A. F. Healy & L. E. Bourne, Jr. (Eds.), *Learning and memory of knowledge and skills: Durability and specificity.* Thousand Oaks, CA: Sage.

Hirshman, E., & Bjork, R. A. (1988). The generation effect: Support for a two-factor theory. *Journal of Experimental Psychology: Learning, Memory, and Cognition, 14,* 484-494.

Hogan, R. M., & Kintsch, W. (1971). Differential effects of study and test trials on long-term recognition and recall. *Journal of Verbal Learning and Verbal Behavior, 10,* 562-567.

Izawa, C. (1992). Test trials contributions to optimization of learning processes: Study/test trials interactions. In A. F. Healy, S. M. Kosslyn, & R. M. Shiffrin (Eds.), *From learning processes to cognitive processes: Essays in honor of William K. Estes* (Vol. 2, pp. 1-33). Hillsdale, NJ: Lawrence Erlbaum.

Jacoby, L. L. (1978). On interpreting the effects of repetition: Solving a problem versus remembering a solution. *Journal of Verbal Learning and Verbal Behavior, 17,* 649-667.

Jacoby, L. L. (1983). Remembering the data: Analyzing interactive processes in reading. *Journal of Verbal Learning and Verbal Behavior, 22,* 485-508.

Jacoby, L. L. (1991). A process dissociation framework: Separating automatic from intentional uses of memory. *Journal of Memory and Language, 30,* 513-541.

Jacoby, L. L., Craik, F.I.M., & Begg, I. (1979). Effects of decision difficulty on recognition and recall. *Journal of Verbal Learning and Verbal Behavior, 18,* 586-600.

Johns, E. E., & Swanson, L. G. (1988). The generation effect with nonwords. *Journal of Experimental Psychology: Learning, Memory, and Cognition, 14,* 180-190.

Johnson, M. K., Raye, C. L., Foley, H. J., & Foley, M. A. (1981). Cognitive operations and decision bias in reality monitoring. *American Journal of Psychology, 94,* 37-64.

Kolers, P. A. (1973). Remembering operations. *Memory & Cognition, 1,* 347-355.

Kolers, P. A. (1975). Memorial consequences of automatized encoding. *Journal of Experimental Psychology: Human Learning and Memory, 1,* 689-701.

Kolers, P. A., & Roediger, H. L. (1984). Procedures of mind. *Journal of Verbal Learning and Verbal Behavior, 23,* 425-449.

Kucera, H., & Francis, W. N. (1967). *Computational analysis of present-day American English.* Providence, RI: Brown University Press.

Logan, G. D. (1988). Toward an instance theory of automatization. *Psychological Review, 95,* 492-527.

Mayer, R. E. (1975). Information processing variables in learning to solve problems. *Review of Educational Research, 45,* 525-541.

McDaniel, M. A., & Masson, M.E.J. (1985). Altering memory representations through retrieval. *Journal of Experimental Psychology: Learning, Memory, and Cognition, 11,* 371-385.

McDaniel, M. A., Riegler, G. L., & Waddill, P. J. (1990). Generation effects in free recall: Further support for a three-factor theory. *Journal of Experimental Psychology: Learning, Memory, and Cognition, 16,* 789-798.

McDaniel, M. A., & Schlager, M. S. (1990). Discovery learning and transfer of problem-solving skills. *Cognition and Instruction, 7,* 129-159.

McDaniel, M. A., & Waddill, P. J. (1990). Generation effects for context words: Implications for item-specific and multifactor theories. *Journal of Memory and Language, 29*, 201-211.

McDaniel, M. A., Waddill, P. J., & Einstein, G. O. (1988). A contextual account of the generation effect: A three factor theory. *Journal of Memory and Language, 27*, 521-536.

McElroy, L. A., & Slamecka, N. J. (1982). Memorial consequences of generating nonwords: Implications for semantic-memory interpretations of the generation effect. *Journal of Verbal Learning and Verbal Behavior, 21*, 249-259.

McFarland, C. E., Jr., Frey, T. J., & Rhodes, D. D. (1980). Retrieval of internally versus externally generated words in episodic memory. *Journal of Verbal Learning and Verbal Behavior, 19*, 210-225.

McNamara, D. S. (1992). *The advantages of generating extended to skill acquisition and retention: Procedural implications.* Unpublished doctoral dissertation, University of Colorado, Boulder.

Melton, A. W. (1970). The situation with respect to the spacing of repetitions and memory. *Journal of Verbal Learning and Verbal Behavior, 9*, 596-606.

Mitchell, D. B., & Hunt, R. R. (1989). How much "effort" should be devoted to memory? *Memory & Cognition, 17*, 337-348.

Nairne, J. S. (1988). The mnemonic value of perceptual identification. *Journal of Experimental Psychology: Learning, Memory, and Cognition, 14*, 248-255.

Nairne, J. S., Pusen, C., & Widner, R. L., Jr. (1985). Representation in the mental lexicon: Implications for theories of the generation effect. *Memory & Cognition, 13*, 183-191.

Nairne, J. S., Riegler, G. L., & Serra, M. (1991). Dissociative effects of generation on item and order retention. *Journal of Experimental Psychology: Learning, Memory, and Cognition, 17*, 702-709.

Nairne, J. S., & Widner, R. L., Jr. (1987). Generation effects with nonwords: The role of test appropriateness. *Journal of Experimental Psychology: Learning, Memory, and Cognition, 13*, 164-171.

Payne, D. G., Neely, J. H., & Burns, D. J. (1986). The generation effect: Further tests of the lexical activation hypothesis. *Memory & Cognition, 14*, 246-252.

Peynircioglu, Z. F. (1989). The generation effect with pictures and nonsense figures. *Acta Psychologica, 70*, 153-160.

Rabinowitz, J. C., & Craik, F.I.M. (1986). Specific enhancement effects associated with word generation. *Journal of Memory and Language, 25*, 226-237.

Rickard, T. C., & Bourne, L. E., Jr. (this volume). An identical-elements model of basic arithmetic skills. In A. F. Healy & L. E. Bourne, Jr. (Eds.), *Learning and memory of knowledge and skills: Durability and specificity.* Thousand Oaks, CA: Sage.

Roediger, H. L. (1990). Implicit memory: Retention without remembering. *American Psychologist, 45*, 1043-1056.

Scapin, D. L. (1982). Generation effect, structuring and computer commands. *Behavior and Information Technology, 1*, 401-410.

Schmidt, S. R., & Cherry, K. (1989). The negative generation effect: Delineation of a phenomenon. *Memory & Cognition, 17*, 359-369.

Schneider, W., & Shiffrin, R. M. (1977). Controlled and automatic human information processing: I. Detection, search, and attention. *Psychological Review, 84*, 1-66.

Slamecka, N. J., & Fevreiski, J. (1983). The generation effect when generation fails. *Journal of Verbal Learning and Verbal Behavior, 22*, 153-163.

Slamecka, N. J., & Graf, P. (1978). The generation effect: Delineation of a phenomenon. *Journal of Experimental Psychology: Human Learning and Memory, 4,* 592-604.

Slamecka, N. J., & Katsaiti, L. T. (1987). The generation effect as an artifact of selective displaced rehearsal. *Journal of Memory and Language, 26,* 589-607.

Thompson, C. P., & Barnett, C. (1981). Memory for product names: The generation effect. *Bulletin of the Psychonomic Society, 18,* 241-243.

Tulving, E. (1984). Precis of elements of episodic memory. *Behavioral and Brain Sciences, 7,* 223-268.

Tyler, S. W., Hertel, P. T., McCallum, M. C., & Ellis, H. C. (1979). Cognitive effort and memory. *Journal of Experimental Psychology: Human Learning and Memory, 5,* 607-617.

Watkins, M. J., & Sechler, E. S. (1988). Generation effect with an incidental memorization procedure. *Journal of Memory and Language, 27,* 537-544.

Zacks, R. T., Hasher, L., Sanft, H., & Rose, K. C. (1983). Encoding effort and recall: A cautionary note. *Journal of Experimental Psychology: Learning, Memory, and Cognition, 9,* 747-756.

6 A Long-Term Retention Advantage for Spatial Information Learned Naturally and in the Laboratory

WILLIAM T. WITTMAN

ALICE F. HEALY

The long-term retention characteristics of three memory components learned both naturally and in the laboratory were investigated. Under a cued-recall procedure, 48 college students were asked to recall the spatial, temporal, and item components of their own semester class schedules (Experiment 1) or a fictitious schedule (Experiment 2). In completing class schedule questionnaires, students were both cued with and asked to recall these three components. For example, a subject might be given the name of a course (item component) and then be asked to locate on a campus map where the class was held (spatial component). In Experiment 1, a longitudinal as well as cross-sectional approach was taken wherein subjects were tested three times, each time covering three different retention intervals. In total, recall data were gathered from intervals ranging from approximately 12 to 36 months in length. In Experiment 2, subjects studied a fictitious semester schedule and were tested approximately 1 week and 6 weeks following training. Results from both experiments indicated better retention of the spatial component of class schedules over either the item or temporal components. All three components showed poorer recall over time, with the spatial component showing the greatest stability. Results are interpreted in terms of a procedural view of memory (Kolers & Roediger, 1984).

AUTHORS' NOTE: This research was supported in part by the U.S. Army Research Institute Contracts MDA903-86-K-0155 and MDA903-90-K-0066 to the Institute of Cognitive Science at the University of Colorado. It is based in part on the doctoral dissertation of William T. Wittman at the University of Colorado, Boulder, performed under the guidance of Alice F. Healy. We thank Lyle Bourne for his many hours of support and technical advice in the early stages of the project. We also thank Walter Kintsch, Dave Thomas, and Verne Keenan for their helpful comments on earlier versions.
 Correspondence concerning this chapter should be sent to William T. Wittman, AL/CFHA, Building 248, 2255 H Street, Wright-Patterson AFB, OH 45433-7200.

The aim of this research was to examine the long-term retention of spatial, temporal, and item characteristics of knowledge. These distinctions come from the work of Healy (1978, 1982; Healy, Cunningham, Gesi, Till, & Bourne, 1991), Lee and Estes (1981), and others on short-term memory, though the terms have been broadened to include a larger range of information. What we mean by the spatial characteristic of knowledge is information about locations of objects and their spatial relations and distances (Evans & Pezdek, 1980; Golledge, Smith, Pellegrino, Doherty, & Marshall, 1985), as well as knowledge of how to proceed through space (Thorndyke & Hayes-Roth, 1982). Temporal information includes knowledge of dates and times (White, 1982) and the relative order of events (Healy, 1974). Item information includes verbal information, such as facts, figures, and names (e.g., Bahrick, Bahrick, & Wittlinger, 1975).

Any distinction between these components of knowledge is useful only if it is tied to actual differences in performance. Evidence for processing differences among spatial, temporal, and item information, and more specifically a retention advantage for spatial information, is presented here. These studies have been divided into two groups—laboratory studies and those done outside the laboratory, or natural memory research.

Laboratory Studies. Some of the most direct evidence for differences in the processing and retention of spatial, temporal, and item information comes from the short-term memory research dealing with the serial position effect. Early studies suggested processing differences for item and order information in serial order recall. The basic notion is that one can remember a particular item from a list of, say, letters, yet not recall its relative position in the list. Conversely, at times one can remember something was in, for example, the third serial position of a list, yet not be able to name the item. Healy (1974) found that the serial position functions for consonants recalled in order were much more bowed than for recall of items with order constrained. This observation suggests that differences in the amount of bowing represents loss of information not needed in simple item recall and that recall of item and order (temporal) information showed some degree of independence. Similar suggestions have been provided by Murdock (1976) and Shiffrin and Cook (1978).

Healy (1978) examined memory for item, order, and spatial information. As in earlier studies, subjects were shown four consonants randomly arranged in a linear array. This time, however, order information was divided into recall of either the temporal sequence of the letters or their spatial locations in the array. Healy (1978) found that the serial position functions for spatial location were less bowed than those functions for temporal sequence information. Further, spatial information showed a flatter retention function than temporal information. Healy (1982) further tested the temporal, spatial, and item distinction, confirming their processing independence and suggesting that spatial information was retained longer and involved a different encoding strategy than temporal information.

A number of other laboratory studies of spatial memory also provide evidence for differential processing of spatial information. In a short-term memory experiment, Salthouse (1974, 1975) had subjects recall either the spatial positions or the identities of letters in a 25-letter, diamond-shaped array. Prior to recall subjects were given various intervening tasks designed to interfere selectively with remembering either letter identity or position. For example, subjects performed a same-different judgment task involving either faces or words. Memory performance was found to vary with the type of intervening task; interference was greatest if both tasks involved the same memory code. Because performance was related to the assumed memory code and the demands of the intervening tasks it was concluded that verbal and spatial information are stored and processed in separate information-processing systems. Pezdek, Roman, and Sobolik (1986) examined recall for two types of stimuli, 16 common objects and 16 one-word labels for these objects. Both objects and words were studied on a 6 × 6 matrix, arranged randomly. Subjects were tested for recall of the items (names of objects or the words) and for the location of the items (using the matrix to place correctly the actual objects or word labels) after delays up to 90 seconds. Pezdek et al. (1986) found that more objects were recalled and correctly located than words. They attributed this advantage for objects to the encoding of spatial location information in the study of the objects. In sum, there is evidence from the laboratory for processing and retention differences among the spatial, temporal, and item components of learned material.

Natural Memory Research. Natural memory research also provides evidence for differential processing of information, and in some cases, for a spatial information advantage. Several flashbulb memory studies have focused on specific classes of information evident in natural event memories (Brown & Kulik, 1977; Pillemer, 1984). These studies report that subjects followed a canonical form in describing their memories of critical events. This form included, among other categories, the "where," "what," and "who" of events, roughly equivalent to spatial and item information. These classes of information were consistently found in subjects' accounts of their memories and thus all were considered highly recalled, though no specific comparisons were reported. In another flashbulb memory study,

Yarmey and Bull (1978) more directly studied differences in the components of natural memories. They specifically questioned subjects about the *where* (spatial), *when* (temporal), and *who* and *what* (item components) of their personal circumstances at the time of the assassination of President Kennedy. Although actual differences in recall for these types of information were not reported, they did find subject ratings of the clarity of each memory component to be about equal. Wagenaar (1978) studied memory for the component parts of radio traffic reports. He found that subjects remembered where traffic jams were located better than the names of the city or roads involved (item components). Further evidence for component differences is found in Bahrick et al.'s (1975) study of long-term recognition memory for the names and faces of high school classmates. Among other memory tasks, subjects were shown either five pictures or five names of former classmates. Subjects did far better in picture recognition than in name recognition. It was concluded that visual information (faces) was retained virtually unimpaired for 35 years, whereas retention of verbal information (names) declined after 15 years. Bahrick (1979) again reported differences in the loss of spatial versus verbal information. In this case, however, spatial information (recall of the spatial sequence of streets in a familiar town) was more rapidly forgotten than verbal information (recall of street names). In a diary study of memory for daily events, Thompson (1982) found that forgetting when an event occurred (temporal component) and what occurred (item component) were related for the first few weeks following the event, but thereafter forgetting occurred at different rates. Temporal information followed a linear rate of forgetting, whereas item information loss conformed to the more familiar negatively accelerated retention function. In sum, component differences are at least suggested in the natural memory literature.

Present Research. The objective, then, of the current research was to determine whether memory performance differences could be found among the three types of information in a long-term retention paradigm. We examined whether spatial information might show a retention advantage over the other components, both in a real-world environment and in the controlled environment of the laboratory. Thus two experiments were performed, one involving natural learning, the other done in the laboratory. Details of the second experiment will be provided later in the chapter.

Experiment 1 used a cued-recall format similar to that used by Wagenaar (1986) in a natural memory study using the diary methodology. Wagenaar (1986) had his subject (himself) recall four aspects of his memories, the *who, what, where,* and *when* of daily events. He recorded these four aspects of his daily experiences for 6 years and at recall cued himself with one or more of these aspects. He found that events cued with the *what* aspect showed better recall than those cued with the *when* aspect. Unfortunately, Wagenaar (1986) did not present an analysis of recall by aspect type. Visual inspection of his reported data suggest, at the very least, that *when* information was more poorly recalled than the *who, what,* or *where.*

Like Wagenaar (1986), we addressed the *who, what, where,* and *when* of events, but we avoided the disadvantages of the diary methodology. In keeping with the temporal, spatial, and item distinction made earlier, we considered the *who* and *what* aspects as item information, with the *where* and *when* aspects considered as spatial and temporal information, respectively. Experiment 1 looked at students' memory for their course schedules learned naturally. College students were asked questions about courses they took during previous semesters. Questions explored memory using the *what, who, where,* and *when* aspects used by Wagenaar (1986), but tailored to course schedules. After pilot testing a number of specific questions, four were selected that were not on the ceiling or floor. These included memory for the name of the course (*what*), the name of the instructor (*who*), the location of the course (*where*), and the time the course took place (*when*). These four aspects are hereafter referred to as types of information. The advantage this study had over Wagenaar's (1986) approach was that answers to these questions were established prior to attempted recall, without the help or knowledge of subjects. As in Wagenaar's (1986) study, a cued-recall paradigm was used wherein subjects were both asked to recall and cued with the four types of information. By asking subjects to recall course information from three different semesters and after three retention intervals, recall was measured with delays ranging from approximately 12 to 36 months in length, in 6-month intervals. In addition to examining recall performance over time, several other factors were investigated. These included prior course experience and the effectiveness of each type of information as a recall cue.

Beyond the specific differences from Wagenaar's (1986) work, our research methodology overcame some of the typical problems of the three common approaches to the study of natural memory. With the probe word method, where specific probes or words are given to subjects to elicit recall of previous experiences, there is little control over the period of recall or the event to be recalled. In our work, each probe was specific to only one event and specific retention periods could be defined. Using the diary method, events to be remembered are identified by the subject prior to retention testing, likely contaminating recall performance. In our case, there was no prerecording of events by subjects, although specific items to be remembered were preestablished. Finally, unlike the typical questionnaire methodology where generic questions are formulated for subjects to answer about their everyday experiences, our study had some measure of what was originally learned and incorporated specific questions relevant to each individual subject. In addition to these improvements over typical methodologies, a second experiment was designed to test results from the real world in a laboratory setting.

In sum, recall performance was expected to be high, at least for the first year, because of the numerous rehearsals of the schedule information (two to three times per week for a full semester). More important, *where* information (the spatial component), was expected to produce the best performance (following Healy 1978, 1982). *When* information was predicted to be most poorly recalled and was expected to be a poor recall cue (Wagenaar, 1986). Also following Wagenaar's (1986) results, *what* information was expected to be the best recall cue, due to its uniqueness.

EXPERIMENT 1

Method

Subjects

Forty-eight University of Colorado Introductory Psychology students were used as subjects, 29 men and 19 women. All subjects had attended the University of Colorado for at least 2 years prior to initial testing. Following initial testing in fall 1987, subjects were given course credit for participation. After participating in Testing Sessions 2 and 3, subjects were paid $5 for each test day. All subjects received initial testing based on random assignment to one of three retention groups according to the semester being tested. One third (16) of the subjects were tested on courses taken during the semester approximately 12 months prior (fall 1986). The remaining two groups of 16 were tested on courses taken during the semesters 18 and 24 months prior, spring 1986 and fall 1985, respectively. In Testing Sessions 2 and 3, subjects were assigned to another of the three tested semesters so that after the last testing each subject had been tested on all three semesters. In addition, with each testing session, the retention interval increased by 6 months for each semester being tested. With the second and third test sessions, there were 39 and 28 subjects participating, respectively, out of the original 48. Two of the subjects in the third session had not participated in the second session. Most of the nonparticipants simply did not want to participate (they were no longer enrolled in an introductory psychology course). The remainder had moved or graduated. Specific subtotals of subjects participating in each condition are provided in the results section.

Materials

Subjects were asked to complete a questionnaire covering three courses randomly selected from their tested semester schedule. The questionnaire was divided into three parts, which covered information cues and questions, course experience, and semester experience, respectively.

In the first part of the questionnaire, subjects were cued with one of four types of course information, the *what, who, where,* or *when* of a course. Subjects were then asked to provide answers to questions using the remaining three types of course information. For example, subjects were cued with when a course took place (the class start time) and then asked who instructed the course, where the classroom was located (on a campus map), and what was the name of the course. On the next page of the questionnaire subjects received two cues (for the same course), the first repeating the original cue and the second adding a new cue, for example, the *when* cue again, along with the *who* cue, with subjects completing the *what* and *where* information. This same cue-then-question procedure was repeated once for each of the three courses being tested.

Cues and questions were formed in the following manner. The four types of information were combined to form 12 groups of two types, with the same type of information never grouped with itself. Thus, with each of the 12 pairs the first member served as the primary cue and the second served as the secondary cue. These cue pairs, or combinations, were assigned to subjects according to the following criteria: Three cue pairs were assigned to each subject such that the same primary cue type was never repeated and the same secondary cue was never repeated. Additionally, all four information types were used at least once for each subject (either in the first or second cuing position). Because each subject was shown 3 pairs, the full cycle of 12 cue pairs was repeated with every four subjects. Two different sets of 12 cue pairs were constructed, each meeting the above criteria. In sum, these two sets were repeated six times to account for all 48 subjects in the study. On subsequent testings, subjects received the same three cue pairs used in the first testing, albeit for different courses.

Subjects identified class locations by marking a two-dimensional, black-and-white map of the university campus. The map included trees, shadowing (giving a three-dimensional appearance), and outlines of buildings (but no building or street names). The map provided the direction of north and indicated the location of the Rocky Mountains. In addition, when given a *where* cue, the subject was shown the class location on the map by an obvious mark next to the appropriate building. See Wittman (1990) for more complete information about materials used, including a copy of the map.

In the second part of the questionnaire, subjects were given the correct answers to the questions in Part I and then were asked to make several ratings about their experience with each course. Specifically, after completing the test questions, subjects were asked to rate (on a 5-point scale from 0 to 4 or more) their experience with each of the four types of information. Subjects were asked, since the end of the test semester, how many times they took a course in the same subject area, had the same instructor, had a course in the same building, and had a course at the same time.

In the final section of the questionnaire, after answering questions for each course, subjects were asked to determine how much they had reviewed their test semester schedule since its completion and to provide other biographical information.

Procedure

Prior to testing, subjects were gathered for a presession to obtain their consent to access their university academic records. Access to records was necessary to obtain the recall cues used in the questionnaire and to evaluate responses once the questionnaires were completed. Prior to being asked for consent, subjects completed a short survey about classes taken during the immediately preceding semester (which was not one of the actual test semesters). This task was intended only as a time filler. The questions in the survey were not the same as those used in the actual test questionnaire. Subjects were told that their answers to the questions would be checked against their actual academic record for that semester. Only one subject did not grant consent. This subject was replaced with another. Before being dismissed, subjects were told only that during the return session, 1 week later, their answers to the survey questions would be evaluated. They were not told that a new questionnaire would also be administered.

In the interim, questionnaires were constructed, tailored to each subject's test semester schedule, with three courses identified for testing with the *what, who, where,* and *when* of a course not being the same for any two courses. (Note: This standard was possible for all but one subject in the initial testing, all but five subjects in Session 2, and all but three subjects in Session 3. For these exceptions, subjects had two courses in the same building.)

During the initial test session, subjects completed a questionnaire that matched their assigned semester, fall 1985, spring 1986, or fall 1986. Subjects were told they were being asked to recall information about courses taken during one of their previous semesters at the university. They were instructed to take careful note of the semester being tested before starting. They were told to answer questions as accurately as possible, proceeding one page at a time without turning back to change answers or to note previous answers. Subjects were tested in small groups, usually not more than four at a time. Sessions lasted approximately 20 minutes.

Subjects were asked to return for two subsequent testings, once in the spring 1988 semester and then again in the fall 1988 semester. Test session procedures were the same as in the initial testing. During the two return sessions, subjects were asked to recall courses for the two semesters not previously tested. Thus, using a combined cross-sectional and longitudinal approach allowed the study of five retention periods, in 6-month increments, ranging from 12 to 36 months in length.

Results

Questionnaires were scored for the percentage of correct responses. Scoring was strict, with emphasis placed on consistent scoring across information types. A *what* response (course title) received a score of 1 if it contained all the words found in the title. Responses adding or missing function words, however, like "to" or "of," were given full credit. Adding or leaving out content words resulted in only half credit (e.g., "Beginning Russian 1" changed to "Intro to Russian" or "Russian 100"), as did giving the course number instead of the title. A *who* response received full credit if it contained the correct identification and spelling of an instructor's name. Accurate identifications, but misspelled names received half credit, (e.g., "Berbernes" instead of "Bebernes"). Locations on the campus map (*where* responses) were given full credit if they precisely marked the correct building. Responses marking buildings immediately adjacent to the correct building were given half credit. A *when* response received full credit if it identified the precise time a course started. Half credit was given if the indicated start time was within 30 minutes on either side of the correct time.

The major interest in this analysis was whether information about where a course was held was retained better than information about course title, professor, or course time (the what, who, or when). Most of the analyses therefore focused on performance differences across these four informa-

Table 6.1 Mean Percentage Correct Across Information Types by Test Session for Experiment 1

Session	What	Who	Information Type Where	When	Mean
1 (n = 48)	62.50	59.19	81.27	60.77	65.93
2 (n = 39)	45.46	43.56	72.90	49.51	52.86
3 (n = 28)	42.57	36.36	69.39	46.71	48.76

tion types. Of particular interest were differences among information types over time. Several other factors were also examined to determine their relationship to information type performance. These included degree of prior experience and cue effectiveness. All statistical tests in this experiment used a .05 level of confidence.

Information Type Differences and the Retention Interval

In the following analyses, a two-way analysis of variance (ANOVA) procedure was used with information type as the single within-subjects factor and semester as the single between-subjects factor. The variable semester indicated the semester being tested, fall 1986, spring 1986, or fall 1985. At Test Session 1, these three semesters were approximately 12, 18, and 24 months, respectively, in the past, thus defining three retention intervals. At Test Sessions 2 and 3, these three intervals were increased by 6 and 12 months, respectively. In all, there were five different retention intervals, at 12, 18, 24, 30, and 36 months. The analyses below first examine differences across information types within each test session and then between sessions.

For each test session there was a significant main effect of information type; for the initial testing, $F(3, 135) = 7.62$, $MS_e = .51$; for the second testing, $F(3, 108) = 10.31$, $MS_e = .73$; and finally, for the third session, $F(3, 75) = 9.13$, $MS_e = .62$. (Note: Analyses for semester and test session were done on proportions and thus mean square error terms are appropriate for proportions. Results, however, are reported in terms of percentages.) The critical finding was that for all three test sessions, recall performance for *where* information was significantly better than for any of the other three types of information. Table 6.1 provides the mean percentages correct by information type for all three test sessions.

For the 48 subjects in the initial test session, planned analyses revealed that *where* performance was statistically superior in all cases, $F(1, 45) =$

23.93, MS_e = 1.69 for where/what; $F(1, 45)$ = 14.72, MS_e = 2.34 for where/who; and $F(1, 45)$ = 13.47, MS_e = 2.02 for where/when. There was no main effect of semester. Mean percentages correct were 57.14% for fall 1986, 66.42% for spring 1986, and 74.23% for fall 1985. Test semester did not interact significantly with information type.

For the 39 subjects in the second test session, performance for *where* was also significantly better than performance on any other information type, $F(1, 36)$ = 34.67, MS_e = 2.91 for where/what; $F(1, 36)$ = 28.99, MS_e = 3.62, for where/who; and $F(1, 36)$ = 8.47, MS_e = 1.72 for where/when. As found in Session 1, there was no main effect of semester. Mean percentages correct were 53.96%, $n = 14$, for fall 1986; 53.47%, $n = 9$, for spring 1986; and 51.55%, $n = 16$, for fall 1985. Again, test semester did not interact significantly with information type.

Finally, for the 28 subjects in the third test session, performance for *where* information was again significantly better than that for any other information type, $F(1, 25)$ = 35.61, MS_e = 2.15 for where/what; $F(1, 25)$ = 22.46, MS_e = 3.20 for where/who; and $F(1, 25)$ = 11.61, MS_e = 1.70 for where/when. As in previous sessions, there was no main effect of semester. Mean percentages were 47.94%, $n = 8$, for fall 1986; 48.14%, $n = 11$, for spring 1986; and 50.25%, $n = 9$, for fall 1985. There was a Semester × Information Type interaction, $F(6, 75)$ = 2.92, MS_e = .20. Performance for *where* appeared to improve with the shorter retention interval. Mean percentages were 89.63% for fall 1986, 64.45% for spring 1986, and 57.44% for fall 1985. Mean percentages for *when* information were 37.50%, 56.82%, and 42.56%; for *who* information percentages were 24.00%, 29.54%, and 55.67%; and for *what* information, 40.63%, 41.73%, 45.33%, for fall 1986, spring 1986, and fall 1985, respectively.

Results were also examined across the three test sessions. In this case, a two-way within-subjects ANOVA was conducted with test session and information type as factors. Twenty-six subjects were used in this analysis. (This is the number of subjects who completed all three testings.) Of interest in this analysis was whether there was a decrease in performance across testings. On average, the first test session used a retention interval of 18 months; the second session, 24 months; and the third session, 30 months. Overall percentages correct were 68.27%, 53.41%, and 48.26% for Test Sessions 1, 2, and 3, respectively. There was a main effect for test session, $F(2, 50)$ = 8.83, MS_e = 1.12. Single-degree-of-freedom tests revealed that subjects performed significantly better during Test Session 1, the shorter retention interval (18 months), than for either of the other intervals, $F(1, 25)$ = 8.50, MS_e = 9.18, for Test 1 versus Test 2 (24 months); and $F(1, 25)$ = 12.81, MS_e = 16.66, for Test 1 versus Test 3 (30 months).

Table 6.2 Mean Experience Ratings Across Information Types by Test Session for Experiment 1

| | Information Type | | | | |
Session	What	Who	Where	When	Mean
1 ($n = 47$)	3.64	0.58	4.47	4.02	3.18
2 ($n = 36$)	4.11	0.38	4.86	5.17	3.63
3 ($n = 27$)	5.37	0.85	5.75	7.01	4.75

No significant difference was found between the second and third testing sessions. In this analysis there was also a main effect for information type, $F(3, 75) = 14.76$, $MS_e = 1.35$. Mean percentages correct for *where, what, who,* and *when* were 76.32%, 51.68%, 48.68%, and 49.67%, respectively. Performance for *where* information was better than that for any of the other types of information, $F(1, 25) = 50.27$, $MS_e = 14.21$ for *where/what;* $F(1, 25) = 28.87$, $MS_e = 17.56$ for *where/who;* and $F(1, 25) = 20.84$, $MS_e = 16.62$ for *where/when*. No significant Test Session × Information Type interaction was found.

In sum, the analysis of information type differences over time revealed a consistent performance advantage for *where* information over *what, who,* and *when* information recall. This advantage was found within and across test sessions. Declines in performance as a function of increases in retention interval were evident across but not within test sessions.

Experience Ratings

In a natural learning study such as this one, it is important to determine the extent to which subsequent learning or rehearsal contributed to results. Specifically, we wanted to know if the retention advantage for *where* information was attributable to more experience with certain campus locations than with class times, professors, or courses. Subject experience ratings were used to examine this possible factor. Subjects were asked to rate their experience with the *what, who, where,* and *when* aspects of each course being tested. Ratings were summed across the three courses tested, making the range of possible scores 0 to 12. One-way within-subjects ANOVAs were performed on these rating data to examine whether the *where* advantage in recall could be attributed to greater experience with *where* information over the other types of information. Table 6.2 presents the mean experience ratings by information type for all three test sessions.

In the first test session, the main effect of information type for experience was found to be significant, $F(3, 138) = 43.06$, $MS_e = 146.35$ ($n = 47$, because one subject did not complete all ratings). Experience with *where* information was significantly greater than that for *what* information, $F(1, 46) = 5.18$, $MS_e = 32.16$, and for *who* information, $F(1, 46) = 135.09$, $MS_e = 710.66$. There was no significant difference between *where* and *when* experience ratings. Experience with *who* information was clearly the anomaly in these data. *Who* ratings were considerably below *what, when,* and *where*. This result should not be surprising, however, because having the same professor for more than one class is an unusual experience at most universities. Additional analyses were performed examining the degree of correlation between experience ratings for a particular information type and performance on that type of information. Correlation coefficients between experience and performance were .20, .01, .02, and .02 for *what, who, where,* and *when,* respectively. Only the correlation between *what* experience and *what* performance was significantly greater than zero, $F(1, 44) = 10.78$, $MS_e = .53$, though even this correlation was small.

Similar results were found in the second testing. The main effect for experience was significant, $F(3, 105) = 38.51$, $MS_e = 176.00$ ($n = 36$, because three subjects did not complete all ratings). Experience with *where* information was significantly greater than that for *who* information only, $F(1, 35) = 101.98$, $MS_e = 722.53$. Experience with *who* information again was clearly less than that for *what, when,* and *where*. Correlations between experience and performance in the second test were .10, .04, .09, and .01 for *what, who, where,* and *when,* respectively. All were nonsignificant.

Finally, results from the third testing were consistent with the first two sessions. The main effect for experience was significant, $F(3, 78) = 43.93$, $MS_e = 192.79$ ($n = 27$, because one subject did not complete all ratings). Experience with *where* information was significantly greater than that for *who* information only, $F(1, 26) = 92.11$, $MS_e = 638.31$. Experience with *who* information was again much less than that for *what, when,* and *where* information. An interesting result in this analysis was the high ratings for *when* experiences. Though subjects tended to give high ratings for *when* experiences in earlier sessions, in this session, two semesters after starting the experiment, the mean *when* experience rating was greater than those for *who,* as already noted, *what,* and *where*. This finding suggests that despite the large number of possible class times (approximately 21), some times may be more likely to be experienced. Correlations between experience ratings and performance were .11, .03, .01, and .004 for *what, who, where,* and *when,* respectively. All were nonsignificant.

Table 6.3 Mean Percentage Correct Across Cue Types by Test Session for Experiment 1

	Cue Type			
Session	What	Who	Where	When
1	72.22	71.36	61.08	60.22
2	62.28	58.58	44.19	44.36
3	60.75	63.58	29.08	35.46

In sum, the analysis of experience ratings indicates that subjects did not receive a disproportionate amount of subsequent experience with *where* information over *what* or *when* information. Thus, the *where* advantage in test performance is not likely attributable to greater experience with where courses were held. In addition, the clear lack of repeated experiences with *who* information and the tendency for slightly more experiences with the same class times should be noted, though these differences are not readily reflected in recall performance scores.

It is also important to note that for each test session subjects were asked to indicate how many times they had reviewed their schedule (of the tested semester) since the semester ended. Almost all subjects said they had not reviewed their schedule. The mean number of times reviewed were .23, .24, and .43 for Tests 1, 2, and 3, respectively.

Information Types as Cues

In addition to looking at differences in how well each type of information was remembered, ANOVAs were performed examining each type of information as a cue for recall. The primary question being addressed in these analyses was whether *where* information was distinct from the other types of information in cuing effectiveness. In these analyses, individual subjects were combined into groups of four so that in each group of subjects, all 12 cue/information combinations were found, 3 combinations per subject. For Test Session 1, 12 such grouped observations were constructed. Consistent with previous analyses, ANOVAs were conducted only for performance after one cue was given (the primary cue). Preliminary analysis of performance after two cues (the primary and secondary cues) revealed no significant effects. Table 6.3 provides mean percentages correct by cue type for all three test sessions.

Results from the first session yielded a nonsignificant main effect of cue type, $F(3, 33) = 2.10$, $MS_e = .05$, $p < .12$. Comparisons made between the *where* cue and each of the other cues were also not significant. In the second test session, 12 combined observations were constructed; however, 9 observations had data from only three, not four, subjects. Results yielded a marginally significant overall effect of cue type, $F(3, 33) = 2.80$, $MS_e = .11$, $p < .06$. Comparisons made between the *where* cue and the others showed only the *what* cue to be significantly better than *where*, $F(1, 11) = 9.30$, $MS_e = .39$.

Finally, in the third test session only eight of the combined observations could be constructed, with four of these having data from only three subjects. Results yielded a significant main effect for cue type, $F(2, 21) = 7.01$, $MS_e = .24$. Both *what* and *who* cues produced significantly better performance than did the *where* cue, $F(1, 7) = 24.90$, $MS_e = .80$, for *what*; and $F(1, 7) = 11.18$, $MS_e = .95$, for *who*. The *where* and *when* cues did not differ significantly.

In sum, the analysis of retrieval cues suggests that differences do exist among information types in their usefulness as cues during recall. The *where* cue along with the *when* cue appear to be less effective than the *what* and *who* cues.

Discussion

The results from all three test sessions in this experiment demonstrated a clear advantage in recall of *where* information over *what, who,* or *when* information. Analysis of recall performance over time suggests that *where* information retains its advantage for several years, even as the other types of information show substantial loss. This advantage cannot be attributed simply to subjects having more experience with where a course was held than with courses in the same subject area, with the same professor, or at the same time. In addition, the analysis of cue effectiveness revealed that *where* information was a relatively poor cue, but so was *when* information.

It can be argued that the advantage found for the retention of *where* information is due to some unique characteristic of the *where* recall task. Possibly it was having the campus map that helped *where* information recall. Subjects could have used the features depicted on the map (e.g., buildings, roads, trees) as additional cues for recall. The problem with this multiple-cues hypothesis is that subjects are likely to find many familiar features on the map. Unless these features were somehow associated with the particular course in question, they would be of little help. Further, the map was available to subjects for all tasks and thus could have served as a cue for all four types of information.

A second possible advantage of the campus map was that it might have converted the *where* task into a recognition task rather than a recall task (the recognition hypothesis). With the map, subjects were provided with all the possible responses to a *where* question. The map presented subjects with a visual display of all the buildings on campus. Of the over 100 locations, one of them was the correct one for a given course. In actuality, there were fewer alternatives. Given some familiarity with the campus, a number of buildings were not likely locations (e.g., dormitories, administration buildings). In contrast, for the *what, who,* and *when* tasks subjects had to recall the information explicitly. Consequently, the *where* task, given that it involved recognition memory, yielded better performance. As a counterargument, the *when* task was similar to the *where* task in this respect. For the *when* task, the possible class times (approximately 21 of them) were available to subjects much as the buildings on the map were. However in this case, the alternatives were not presented visually, but were part of a subject's general knowledge about class schedules. It is common student knowledge, especially for the juniors and seniors employed in this experiment, that classes start on the hour or half hour, depending on the day of the week. Consequently, as with a *where* response, subjects could select *when* responses from among a finite set of alternatives. Despite this similarity in tasks, *where* information was still better retained than *when* information.

A third hypothesis addresses the characteristics of the *where* task. It is plausible that the *where* task involved the use of some form of spatial information (the spatial procedures hypothesis). The unique processing characteristics of spatial information have been suggested in the literature, as previously discussed. In getting from class to class during a semester, subjects are likely to learn specific routes through the campus and come to associate these routes with specific buildings and other campus features. Assuming that knowledge can be both declarative and procedural (Anderson, 1982; Cohen, 1984), it could be said that over the course of a semester, subjects lose declarative knowledge of their course schedule—the *what, who, where* (building name), and *when*—but develop and maintain their procedural knowledge of their schedule (getting to and from their classes). There is evidence that spatial knowledge acquired by way of actual navigation does have a routing or procedural component (see Golledge et al., 1985; Thorndyke & Hayes-Roth, 1982). The *where* task might tap into this proceduralized knowledge and thus show an advantage at recall.

In summary, three possible explanations have been proposed for the consistent advantage for *where* information found in this experiment: the multiple-cues, recognition, and spatial procedures hypotheses.

To explore further the *where* task advantage, a second experiment was conducted. This experiment asked subjects to learn a semester schedule in a controlled, laboratory setting. Moving into the laboratory provided a test of the spatial procedures hypothesis. Performance could be examined when learning did not involve proceeding to classes. Second, the possible contributions of the campus map were examined more closely by constructing two recall tasks for *where* information. One task used the campus map as in Experiment 1. The other task was a verbal task that required subjects to name the buildings where classes were held. If the *where* advantage was found for both the spatial location and location naming tasks, the multiple-cues and recognition hypotheses would not be supported.

The second experiment was also designed to determine if the *where* advantage was due to some natural learning factor beyond the explanations already considered. One possible factor was the effect of spacing learning across a full semester. Repeated practice over many weeks could have a differential effect on the four types of information. Subjects in Experiment 2, therefore, either received massed training all in one day or had training spaced across 3 weeks. A second training factor examined was the amount of practice each type of information received. In studying long-term retention of Spanish learned in school, Bahrick (1984) found that degree of original learning was a major predictor of memory performance. In the real world, learning where and when a class is held may receive greater emphasis or practice over a semester than would learning what a course is called and who is teaching the course. It is possible in the case of *where* information that knowledge necessary for getting to classes received greater practice than knowledge of building names. Similarly, subjects may have practiced simply the sequential order of their classes during the school week more than the actual start times. Thus, an additional manipulation in this experiment was to give one group of subjects extra practice in recall of building names and class start times, and another group, extra practice recalling building locations and class order. If spatial knowledge is implicated in the *where* advantage, subjects practicing building locations more than names would likely show a stronger *where* advantage at recall.

EXPERIMENT 2

Method

Subjects

As in Experiment 1, 48 University of Colorado undergraduates enrolled in Introductory Psychology participated in this study for course credit. Also as before, subjects were restricted to only those students who had attended the university for at least two years, essentially only juniors and seniors.

Materials

Subjects were asked to learn a fictitious class schedule. These schedules were constructed from the actual schedules of subjects used in Experiment 1. Twenty-four of the fictitious schedules contained four courses and 24 had five courses. The three courses used in the questionnaire in Experiment 1 were always used in the fictitious schedules. The remaining one or two courses were constructed using previously unused courses from Experiment 1. Thus, each fictitious schedule was made up of courses, buildings, times, and so forth found in real schedules.

Class schedules were in two parts. The class listing looked much like a standard university class schedule. Classes were described, one per line, using eight column headings: department, course number, course title, instructor, class time (start to finish), days of the week, building name, and room number. The department, days, and building names were always abbreviated, and at times, so was the course title, just as in actual schedules. The second part of the schedule was the campus map. The map was a two-dimensional, black-and-white drawing of the university campus. It included trees, shadowing (for a three-dimensional appearance), street names, and an index to the building names (each building was marked with a number that matched a directory of names and location coordinates). The buildings where classes were held were marked with blank yellow circles (numbers were removed). The map also showed the relative location of the Rocky Mountains to the campus and the direction of north.

During the training phase of the experiment, subjects were asked to recall their schedule information based on their task assignment, either to the class listing or map task. The class listing task involved completing the missing information on a form much like the class schedule used during study. The form, however, differed in that it had only six rather than eight headings: department, course number, course title, instructor, class time (but no days of the week), and building name (but no room number). In addition, the class listing forms had four columns left blank: course title, instructor, class time, and building (what, who, when, and where information). The department and course number were provided and served as recall cues. Those subjects assigned to the map task used a slightly modified form. On this form subjects marked the buildings on a map indicating where their classes were held. The maps in this task were the same as the maps used during study except the numbers on all buildings were omitted and no building name directory or street names were included. In addition to completing the map (where information), a modified class listing was included on the map form. The five column headings on the map task form included department and course number (which were filled in), and course title, instructor, and class order (what, who, and when information), which required completion. The class order heading required listing of the order of classes during the school week: first, second, third, and so on.

In addition to the new materials used in this experiment, the class schedule questionnaire from Experiment 1 was also used for testing recall. The same cue-then-question format was used wherein subjects were given one and then two cues for recalling the what, who, where, and when information for each of three courses. The questionnaire used in this experiment differed only in the questions asked following recall. Instead of questions about course and semester experience, this version of the questionnaire focused on the differences and similarities subjects found between studying their fictitious schedule and studying their own schedule in real life.

Design and Procedure

A $2 \times 2 \times 2 \times 4$ mixed factorial design was used combining the following between-subjects variables: (a) training type (spaced or massed), (b) orienting task (class listing or map), and (c) number of courses (4 or 5). Information type (what, who, where, or when) was the single within-subjects factor. All subjects received nine study-then-recall training trials spread equally across three sessions (spaced training) or grouped in one session (massed training). During Week 4 of the experiment all subjects were administered the class schedule questionnaire followed by both the map and class listing recall tasks. Approximately 5 weeks following this first test session, the questionnaire and both the map and class listing tasks were again administered.

Subjects in all conditions were told that the experiment was designed to examine how well students remember their university class schedules. They were informed that during the course of the experiment they would repeatedly study and then recall a fictitious schedule. They were instructed to study their schedule as if they were learning their own schedule at the start of the semester.

In the training phase of the experiment, subjects were given nine study trials where they were asked to study both their class listing and their class map. Each trial lasted 5 minutes. Subjects were told that each trial would be followed by a recall test. Precisely how recall would be tested was not specified. Subjects were simply instructed to study their schedule as if it was their own. The type of recall test was determined by which orienting task the subject was assigned to, either the class listing or map task. Those assigned to the class listing task were asked to fill in a blank class listing following eight of the nine study trials. Following one study trial, the fifth, these subjects were asked to complete the map task. Including one trial with the alternate task was done to discourage subjects from completely ignoring, during study, the information not being tested during training. In the class listing task, for example, the subjects could neglect studying the map and class order information. For the subjects assigned to the map condition, the reverse was true. Subjects could neglect study of building names and class start times. Therefore, in the map task, a map form was used for recall on eight trials, with a class listing form used after the fifth study trial. Subjects were instructed to recall all required information as accurately as possible and were given a maximum of 5 minutes to complete their recall, though few took this long after the first two study trials.

As for the type of training, subjects were randomly assigned to either the massed- or spaced-training condition. The 24 subjects receiving massed training were given all nine study/recall trials in a 1½-hour period. Brief breaks (approximately 5 minutes each) occurred after the third and sixth trials. Subjects were allowed to stand up, go to the rest room, and so forth during breaks, but were not permitted to discuss the experiment. These subjects were divided into three groups, with each group of eight subjects receiving training either 1, 2, or 3 weeks prior to the test trial during Week 4. This division was made to equate the average retention interval for massed training with that received by subjects in the spaced-training condition. The 24 subjects in the spaced condition received their nine study/recall trials, three per week, in 30-minute sessions spaced over 3 weeks. Testing occurred on the fourth week. Both the massed and spaced groups had training trials separated by 1-week intervals (precisely 7 days). However, six subjects missed a scheduled training session and came 1 day late (five in the spaced condition, one in the massed) and two subjects had to reschedule 1 day earlier than their scheduled session (both in the spaced group).

In the testing phase of the experiment, both training groups followed identical sequences. All subjects were first asked to complete the class schedule questionnaire. The questionnaires followed the cued-recall format described above. Three courses were randomly selected from the four or five courses in each class schedule for testing. Following completion of the questionnaire, subjects were asked to complete both the blank class listing and map tasks, with the order of these two tasks counterbalanced across subjects in the training groups. Test trials lasted approximately 30 minutes. All subjects were scheduled for testing precisely 1, 2, or 3 weeks after completing the last training trial, depending on their assigned training condition. However, five subjects missed their scheduled test time and were tested 1 day late (four in spaced training, one in massed). Approximately 5 weeks after testing, subjects were asked to participate in an unexpected retest session following the same procedures used in the first testing. Subjects were not informed of the precise nature of this last session, but were simply told that it would be similar to earlier sessions. Subjects had already met course requirements at time of retest and were thus paid $5 each for participating. In spite of upcoming final exams, 36 of the 48 original subjects volunteered to take part in retesting.

Results

The questionnaire, map test, class listing test, each retest, and the training type data were scored for percentage of correct responses using the same criteria as in Experiment 1. Unique to this experiment was the requirement to provide building names (in the class listing test) and class order (in the map test). Full credit for building names was given only when the precise name provided in the schedule was used. Shortened names or misspellings received half credit. When subjects were required to provide the temporal order of classes during the school week, full credit was given only for the precise order. Half credit was given when the order was off by one, for example, the 4th and 5th classes were exchanged.

Unless otherwise stated, a $2 \times 2 \times 2 \times 4$ analysis of variance (ANOVA) was performed for each test and retest and for the training data, with training type, orienting task, and number of courses as between-subjects factors and the four types of information as the single within-subjects factor.

Analysis of Questionnaire Test Data

Mean percentages correct as a function of information type, training type, and orienting task for test data can be found in Table 6.4. The main effect of training type (massed or spaced) proved to be significant, $F(1, 40)$ = 21.83, MS_e = 3.78, with spaced training yielding better recall performance than massed training. (Note: Though tables and figures report percentages, all analyses in this experiment were done on proportions; thus, all mean square errors are appropriate for proportions.) Training type

Table 6.4 Mean Percentage Correct for Questionnaire Test and Retest Data Across Information Types as a Function of Training and Task Type for Experiment 2

			Information Type		
	What	*Who*	*Where*	*When*	*Mean*
Questionnaire Test					
Training					
Massed	55.21	53.79	77.46	44.08	57.64
Spaced	85.75	89.25	82.67	85.08	85.69
Task					
Map	64.58	62.50	77.46	58.67	65.80
Class Listing	76.38	80.54	82.67	70.50	77.52
Mean	70.48	71.52	80.06	64.58	71.66
Questionnaire Retest					
Training					
Massed ($n = 19$)	56.58	51.79	55.74	33.79	49.47
Spaced ($n = 17$)	64.24	74.00	74.00	64.24	69.12
Task					
Map ($n = 15$)	70.60	59.47	77.27	42.80	62.53
Class Listing ($n = 21$)	52.76	64.29	55.14	52.00	56.05
Mean	60.19	62.28	64.36	48.17	58.75

NOTE: Number of subjects per cell was 24 unless otherwise stated.

did not interact significantly with orienting task or number of courses, but did with information type, $F(3, 120) = 5.83$, $MS_e = .30$. Separate $2 \times 2 \times 2$ ANOVAs for each information type revealed significant training type differences for all but *where* information, with spaced training yielding the best performance for *what*, $F(1, 40) = 15.72$, $MS_e = 1.12$; for *who*, $F(1, 40) = 22.08$, $MS_e = 1.51$; and for *when*, $F(1, 40) = 19.75$, $MS_e = 2.20$. For *where* information spaced and massed subjects showed no significant difference in performance, $F(1, 40) < 1$.

Orienting task also had a significant effect on performance, $F(1, 40) = 3.81$, $MS_e = .66$, with subjects training under the class listing task performing better than those using the map completion task. This task type difference did not interact significantly with training or information type, but it did vary with the number of courses in a student's schedule, $F(1, 40) = 5.28$, $MS_e = .91$. Differences in orienting task were evident only for subjects with five courses in their schedule and not for those with four courses. With five courses, performance was at 83.69% for the class listing task and only 58.17% in the map task.

The main effect of number of courses in the schedule was not significant. The mean percentage correct for four courses was 72.40%, and 70.93% for five courses. Number of courses did interact with task type as described above. No other interactions with number of courses were significant.

Of primary interest in this study were performance differences among information types. The main effect of information type proved to be significant, $F(3, 120) = 3.80$, $MS_e = .20$. Of more interest were the comparisons of *where* information with performance on the other three types of information. Consistent with Experiment 1, *where* information was found to have the best recall performance. Performance for *where* information was significantly higher than performance on any of the other information types; for *what*, $F(1, 40) = 6.22$, $MS_e = .44$; for *who*, $F(1, 40) = 5.38$, $MS_e = .35$; and for *when*, $F(1, 40) = 6.90$, $MS_e = 1.15$. As described earlier, there was an Information × Training Type interaction. No other interactions with information type were significant.

Analysis of Questionnaire Retest Data

In the questionnaire retest, 36 subjects were tested again using the same three courses as in the initial testing. The same cue-question combinations were used, but in a different order. Despite retesting with the same courses, the mean overall performance on the questionnaire retest was only 58.75%. This performance was significantly below that on the initial test, 72.10%, for the same 36 subjects, $F(1, 28) = 15.33$, $MS_e = .60$.

Mean percentages correct as a function of information type, training type, and orienting task for retest data can also be found in Table 6.4. As in the test data, training type proved to be a significant factor, $F(1, 28) = 7.94$, $MS_e = 1.35$. Subjects undergoing spaced training performed better than those given massed training. Training type did not interact significantly with task or number of courses. More important, there was no interaction of training with information type, as was found in the test data. This finding suggests that the test data Training × Information Type interaction was likely due to a ceiling effect for *where* information.

For orienting task, no main effect was found. Orienting task did interact significantly with information type, $F(3, 84) = 2.96$, $MS_e = .20$. Separate ANOVAs for each information type revealed that subjects assigned to the map task did significantly better at recalling *what* information than those assigned to the class listing task, $F(1, 28) = 5.11$, $MS_e = .33$. The same appeared true for *where* information, though the difference between tasks was only marginally significant, $F(1, 28) = 3.93$, $MS_e = .44$, $p < .06$.

Table 6.5 Mean Percentage Correct by Information Type for Questionnaire, Map, and Class Listing Test and Retest for Experiment 2

| | Information Type | | | | |
	What	*Who*	*Where*	*When*	*Mean*
Questionnaire					
Test	71.28	71.06	82.89	63.19	72.10
Retest	60.19	62.28	64.36	48.17	58.75
Map					
Test	92.17	79.32	95.18	87.88	88.63
Retest	84.85	70.71	92.44	76.62	81.15
Class Listing					
Test	90.34	80.91	81.14	77.80	82.55
Retest	83.51	70.49	66.51	61.94	70.61

Differences for *who* and *when* were not significant, though the class listing task tended to show better performance.

As in the test data, number of courses was not a significant factor in retest data. Mean percentages correct for 4 and 5 courses were 58.00% (n = 18) and 59.50% (n = 18), respectively. No interactions with this factor were significant as well.

As for information type, there was a significant main effect, $F(3, 84)$ = 3.26, MS_e = .22. Recall performance from highest to lowest started with *where,* followed by *who, what,* and *when.* This was the same ordering found in the test data. However in this case, statistically *where* was significantly better than *when* information only, $F(1, 28)$ = 6.79, MS_e = 1.14. No interactions with information type were significant (excluding the orienting task interaction cited above).

Additional ANOVAs were performed specifically comparing test to retest performance for each type of information. All four types of information showed worse performance at retest than at test, suggesting forgetting had occurred between tests. Mean percentages correct by information type for both the test and retest are provided in Table 6.5. Means for the test reflect only scores from the 36 subjects participating in the retest. Differences among information types from test to retest were significant for *what,* $F(1, 28)$ = 5.18, MS_e = .33; for *where,* $F(1, 28)$ = 8.41, MS_e = 1.03; and for *when,* $F(1, 28)$ = 4.18, MS_e = .86; and marginally significant for *who,* $F(1, 28)$ = 3.86, MS_e = .32, $p < .06$.

Results of the questionnaire test analysis lend clear support for the superior memory of spatial location information *where* over temporal *when* or item information *what* and *who* in retention of class schedules. In the retest, the advantage of spatial information was not as evident, possibly due to the fact that retesting involved the same class information used during initial testing.

Analysis of Questionnaire Cue Data

As in Experiment 1, the four types of information were also examined for their effectiveness as retrieval cues. As before, subjects were grouped in fours such that each set of four subjects (one supersubject) included data from all 12 cue combinations. In total there were 12 supersubjects. The analysis performed here was simply a one-way ANOVA with cue type as the single, within-subjects variable. As in previous analyses, results are reported only for performance after one cue was given (the primary cue). Performance after two cues did not yield significant differences.

The overall effect of cue type following the primary cue was significant, $F(3, 33) = 4.11$, $MS_e = .10$. *Who* information was the best cue with a mean of 81.97% correct, followed closely by *what* information at 75.89%. *When* and *where* information showed the poorest performance, at 65.89% and 62.50%, respectively. Statistically, the *who* cue was not better than the *what* cue, but was significantly better than the *when* and *where* cues, $F(1, 11) = 8.40$, $MS_e = .31$, $p < .01$; and $F(1, 11) = 7.93$, $MS_e = .46$, respectively. The *what* cue was not significantly better than the *when* cue, but was marginally better than the *where* cue, $F(1, 11) = 4.26$, $MS_e = .22$, $p < .06$.

In the analysis of cue type on the questionnaire retest, data were also grouped into 12 observations as described previously. However, because there were only 36 subjects in the retest, not all observations contained data from 4 subjects. In contrast to the test results, no significant effect of cue type was found. Despite this fact, the same pattern across cues appeared. As in the test data, *what* and *who* cues appeared to produce the best recall at 64.58% and 61.14%, respectively. Conversely, the *where* and *when* cues appeared less efficient at 54.47% and 52.14%, respectively.

Analysis of the Map and Class Listing Test Data

During testing, each subject completed the questionnaire discussed above and then completed the same map and class listing recall tasks used in the training procedure. The map and class listing tests were administered in a counterbalanced manner across subjects in each condition. Scoring of the two tests was identical to that used in the questionnaire data. Subjects were assigned a percentage correct for each of the four types of

Table 6.6 Mean Percentage Correct for Map Test and Retest Data Across Information Types as a Function of Training and Task Type for Experiment 2

| | Information Type | | | | |
	What	*Who*	*Where*	*When*	*Mean*
Map Test					
Training					
Massed (*n* = 22)	85.00	68.59	89.91	83.32	81.70
Spaced (*n* = 24)	97.92	94.75	99.50	97.29	97.36
Task					
Map (*n* = 24)	90.58	76.33	95.00	93.33	88.81
Class Listing (*n* = 22)	93.00	88.68	94.82	87.64	91.03
Mean	91.74	82.24	94.91	90.61	89.87
Map Retest					
Training					
Massed (*n* = 17)	81.24	60.12	88.06	66.76	74.04
Spaced (*n* = 17)	88.47	81.29	96.82	86.47	88.26
Task					
Map (*n* = 15)	88.27	65.13	94.53	81.33	82.32
Class Listing (*n* = 19)	82.16	75.11	90.79	72.89	80.24
Mean	84.85	70.71	92.44	76.62	81.15

information in their schedule, the *what, who, where,* and *when* of each course. Of primary interest in these data were differences across information types and their interactions with the three between-subjects factors, training type, orienting task, and the number of courses. First, it is important to note several significant main effects for these other variables.

Table 6.6 provides the mean percentages correct across information types by training and task type for the map test data. Two subjects neglected to fill in the campus map and were not used in the analysis. Of the three between-subjects factors, only training type had a significant main effect, $F(1, 38) = 25.36$, $MS_e = 1.12$, with spaced training again yielding better performance than massed training. Surprisingly, there was no main effect of task, $F(1, 38) < 1$. Subjects who trained with the map task did not do better on the map test than those who trained using the schedule task. Number of courses was also not a significant factor in the map test data.

There was a main effect for information type on the map test, $F(3, 114) = 7.35$, $MS_e = .13$. Single-degree-of-freedom tests revealed that performance for the *where* information was significantly better than that for

Table 6.7 Mean Percentage Correct for Class Listing Test and Retest Data
Across Information Types as a Function of Training and Task Type
for Experiment 2

| | Information Type | | | | |
	What	Who	Where	When	Mean
Class Listing Test					
Training					
Massed	83.13	73.08	71.21	65.13	73.14
Spaced	97.42	94.75	89.21	95.42	94.20
Task					
Map	87.04	77.17	73.08	77.50	78.70
Class Listing	93.50	90.67	87.33	83.04	88.64
Mean	90.27	83.92	80.21	80.27	83.67
Class Listing Retest					
Training					
Massed ($n = 19$)	80.47	63.95	52.89	44.21	60.38
Spaced ($n = 16$)	87.13	78.25	82.69	83.00	82.77
Task					
Map ($n = 14$)	86.71	59.79	66.50	60.57	68.39
Class Listing ($n = 21$)	81.38	77.62	66.52	62.86	72.10
Mean	83.51	70.49	66.51	61.94	70.61

NOTE: Number of subjects per cell was 24 unless otherwise stated.

when, $F(1, 38) = 4.71$, $MS_e = .10$, and *who,* $F(1, 38) = 24.49$, $MS_e = .73$.
Though performance for *where* was numerically higher than that for *what,*
this difference was not statistically significant, possibly because performance was so close to the ceiling. The map test data also revealed an
Information × Training Type interaction, $F(3, 114) = 2.99$, $MS_e = .05$. Here
again, it is likely that differences among information types were not so
apparent for spaced trained subjects because performance was at the
ceiling.

Table 6.7 provides the mean percentages correct across information
types by training and task type for the class listing test data. In terms of
main effects, both training and task type effects were significant, $F(1, 40)$
$= 23.08$, $MS_e = 2.13$, for training type; and $F(1, 40) = 5.14$, $MS_e = .47$, for
task type. As in the map test data, spaced-training subjects showed better
performance than those receiving massed training. Unlike the map test
data, however, subjects who trained using the class listing task did better
on the class listing test than those who trained using the map task. Number
of courses was not a significant factor in the class listing test data.

A significant main effect of information type was also found in the class listing test, $F(1, 40) = 4.43$, $MS_e = .11$. However, the pattern of differences was not the same as found in the map test data. Performance for *where* information was not different from that for *who* and *when* information. For the class listing test data, *what* information showed the best recall. Performance for *what* information was marginally better than that for *who* information, $F(1, 40) = 3.75$, $MS_e = .19$, $p < .06$, and significantly better than that for *where*, $F(1, 40) = 18.55$, $MS_e = .49$, and *when* information, $F(1, 40) = 9.62$, $MS_e = .48$. In addition, information type was not found to interact with training type as found in the map test data.

Analysis of Map and Class Listing Retest Data

Table 6.6 also provides mean percentages correct across information types by training and task types for map retest data. Two subjects neglected to fill in the campus maps. The mean overall performance on the map retest was significantly below the overall performance on the initial map test for the same 34 subjects, $F(1, 26) = 15.19$, $MS_e = .15$.

As with the map test data, performance on the map retest revealed a main effect of training type, $F(1, 26) = 7.14$, $MS_e = .38$. Spaced training was shown to yield better performance than massed training. Unlike in the map test, however, training type did not interact significantly with information type. Similar to test results, task type and number of courses did not show significant main effects. Further, there were no significant interactions with these factors.

The most important results of the map retest data come from the analysis of information type. There was a main effect of information type, $F(3, 78) = 7.33$, $MS_e = .28$, but more critically, *where* information was better recalled than any of the other three types of information. All three other means were significantly below the mean for *where*, $F(1, 26) = 9.20$, $MS_e = .19$, for *where* versus *what*; $F(1, 26) = 9.87$, $MS_e = .70$, for *where* versus *when*; and $F(1, 26) = 18.89$, $MS_e = 1.49$, for *where* versus *who*. Further, comparisons made by information type from test to retest showed significant forgetting between tests for *what* information, $F(1, 26) = 11.44$, $MS_e = .14$; for *when*, $F(1, 26) = 5.13$, $MS_e = .33$; and for *who* information, $F(1, 26) = 8.22$, $MS_e = .22$. In contrast, *where* information showed no significant loss between test and retest, despite the 5-week delay. Mean percentages correct for the test-retest comparisons can be found in Table 6.5 for the 34 subjects participating in the retest. These results suggest a certain durability in memory for the spatial location of courses. The same cannot be said for memory for the names of the buildings where courses were held, as is shown next in the class listing retest data.

Table 6.7 also provides mean percentages correct across information types by training and task type for class listing retest data. One subject neglected to fill in the *when* information on the test and was excluded from the analysis. The mean overall performance on the class listing retest was significantly below the overall performance on the class listing test for the same 35 subjects, $F(1, 27) = 20.31$, $MS_e = .42$.

Consistent with the test data, the class listing retest results revealed a significant main effect of training type, $F(1, 27) = 16.26$, $MS_e = 1.52$. As in all the previous analyses, spaced training produced significantly better performance than massed training. There was also a significant Information × Training Type interaction, $F(3, 81) = 2.90$, $MS_e = .16$. As can be seen in Table 6.7, the advantage of spaced over massed training was less pronounced for *what* and *who* information than for *where* and *when*.

Unlike in the test results, there was no significant main effect found for task type, nor was there a significant effect for number of courses. Neither of these two factors yielded any significant interactions.

For information type, class listing test and retest results were very consistent. As for the test results, the main effect of information type was significant, $F(3, 81) = 4.41$, $MS_e = .24$. Also consistent was the superior performance for *what* information, followed by *who, where,* and *when*. Performance for *where* information was not significantly different from *who* or *when* and was significantly below performance for *what* information, $F(1, 27) = 12.34$, $MS_e = .81$. This finding suggests that recalling a building's name is not the same as recalling its spatial location on a map. Further, in the class listing data there was a significant decrease in performance from test to retest for *where* information, $F(1, 27) = 7.74$, $MS_e = .64$, in contrast to the lack of forgetting of *where* information in the map test-retest data. In addition to the decline in performance for *where* information, *what, who,* and *when* information also showed significant decreases, for *what, F(1, 27) = 7.15, MS_e = .15$; for *who, F(1, 27) = 10.74, MS_e = .36$; and for *when, F(1, 27) = 6.60, MS_e = .66$. Mean percentages correct for the test-retest comparisons can be found in Table 6.5 for the 35 subjects completing the retest.

Results of the map and class listing tests provide further support and clarification of the role of spatial information in class schedule recall. Two observations are particularly important. First, in the map test and retest, not only did *where* information (in this case, the spatial location of classes on a map) show superior performance over the other types of information, but there was also no loss of this information over the 5-week retention interval. *What, who,* and *when* information all showed significant losses. Second, in the class listing test, *where* information (in this case, the name of the building where classes were held) showed no superior performance over the others and showed significant loss at retest, 5 weeks later.

Analysis of Training Data

The main concern in this analysis was that at the conclusion of training subjects had learned the four types of information in their schedules equally well. This result was found to be the case. Analysis of performance during the last training trial revealed no significant main effect of information type. Mean percentages correct following Trial 9 for *what, who, where,* and *when* information were 99.58%, 97.96%, 98.43%, and 100.00%, respectively.

Discussion

Results of this experiment lend further support for the superior long-term retention of *where* information, relative to *what, who,* and *when* information. More specifically, results suggest the *where* advantage holds only for identification of map locations and not for recall of names of locations. A number of factors may contribute to this spatial location advantage. In discussing Experiment 1, three specific accounts of the *where* recall advantage were considered. Each of these hypotheses will be considered in light of new evidence from this experiment. The first two hypotheses considered were the multiple-cues and recognition hypotheses. Both suggest that the *where* advantage was due to a direct contribution of the map's presence during testing. The multiple-cues hypothesis simply holds that, unlike in the *what, who,* and *when* tasks, the *where* task boosted recall because the map provided additional retrieval cues. This hypothesis could explain the *where* advantage in the questionnaire test, but is weakened by the *where* advantage found in the map test. In the map test, the *what, who,* and *when* tasks also received multiple cuing, albeit in a different form. Subjects were asked to recall information using the same forms used in training. These recall forms presented the department of the course, the course number, and the column labels, all information studied during training. In spite of this additional cuing, *where* information continued to be recalled better.

The recognition hypothesis holds that because the map provided the subjects with all the possible alternative locations, the *where* task was really a recognition test, not a recall test. This hypothesis is thus consistent with the significant advantage for *where* information found in the questionnaire test and in the map test and retest. The lack of a *where* information advantage in the class listing test and retest also provides support for this hypothesis. The *where* task in this case was clearly a cued-recall test because only building names were required and no map was used.

The spatial procedures hypothesis assumes that knowledge can take both a declarative and a procedural form (Anderson, 1982). Through extended practice, a behavior such as going to and from classes can become proceduralized. In the process, the declarative components of the behavior, the names of buildings, courses, and so on, are forgotten. This account had a certain intuitive appeal in Experiment 1 where schedules were learned naturally over the course of a semester. In Experiment 2 subjects did not actually proceed to and from classes, yet *where* information was found to have an advantage on the questionnaire and map test. This finding would suggest that the *where* advantage is attributable to something other than, or at least more than, the procedural knowledge gained by walking to one's classes.

Before drawing any conclusions about the value of these explanations in accounting for the *where* advantage, it is necessary to review findings for the between-subjects variables in this experiment, specifically, training and task effects.

Spaced training yielded better performance than did massed training in almost all cases. The one exception was in the questionnaire test. In this case, spaced training led to superior performance for *what, who,* and *when* information, but not for *where*; massed- and spaced-trained subjects performed equally well on *where* information recall. As suggested earlier, this interaction is likely due to performance for *where* information being at the ceiling. Thus, differences in training type provide little further help in identifying the locus of the *where* advantage. Some other factor, such as encoding variability (Glenberg, 1979), may be responsible for the spacing effect.

Results of the training task analysis, however, suggest yet another view of the *where* information advantage. Task assignment directly determined how much practice subjects received in recalling course information. Though all subjects had the same amount of study time and practiced recall using both the map and class listing recall forms, there were differences in the amount of practice on each form. Reviewing briefly, subjects participated in nine study-then-recall trials during the training phase of the experiment. Subjects assigned to the map task during training performed recall using the map test format on eight trials and on one trial used the class listing test format. The reverse was true for those subjects assigned to the class listing task. It would seem reasonable to expect that the task most practiced would yield the best performance at test. To some extent, this expectation was supported in the data. Those assigned to the class listing task did better overall on the class listing test, but there was no overall task effect for the map test. What is critical here is the suggestion that the degree of match between training and testing might be a factor in the *where* information advantage. Results of both experiments are worth considering from this perspective.

General Discussion

In Experiment 1, *where* information showed a strong advantage across even the longest retention intervals. Experiment 2 also demonstrated superior retention for *where* information. In this case the *where* advantage varied with the experimental manipulations. The results of both experiments might best be explained using the procedural reinstatement perspective.

Following Kolers and Roediger (1984), memory performance is believed to reflect the degree to which subjects reinstate learned operations or procedures (see, e.g., Fendrich, Healy, & Bourne, 1991; Healy et al., 1992; Healy, Fendrich, & Proctor, 1990: Healy et al., this volume, for further support of this point of view). This definition is of little use unless one gets more specific about just what is proceduralization. Proceduralization as used here is defined as the process of encoding, rehearsing, and retrieving temporally sequenced information. Proceduralization simply involves learning information in a specific temporal sequence, with each sequence having a starting and ending point. Proceduralization or temporal sequencing need not involve explicit motor behavior such as walking through a campus. Some temporal sequences might be learned and practiced simply through active observation, for example, when studying a map.

Within this framework it is important to make one further specification. It is suggested that spatial memories should not be thought of as simply information about the spatial relationships of objects, that is, their relative distances and directions, but must also be viewed in terms of the temporal order relationships of objects. A similar proposal was made by Healy (1978, 1982) in suggesting that spatial information was retained by means of temporal-spatial patterns. Objects in the natural environment as well as those studied in two dimensions are easily temporally related. The same point was made by Sholl (1987), who suggested that spatial experiences are often sequential, that is, extended over time. What is being proposed here is different from the distinction between routing versus survey knowledge suggested by Thorndyke and Hayes-Roth (1982), or the types of spatial knowledge identified by Golledge et al. (1985). Here it is suggested that all knowledge, including words and numbers, can be temporally sequenced or proceduralized. Examining memory performance in this light may provide a better accounting of experimental results.

Evidence for procedural reinstatement can be found in both experiments of this research. The questionnaire results of Experiment 1 provide a good example of temporal sequencing involving overt motor procedures during acquisition. *Where* information, in all three testings in this experiment, was better recalled than any of the other kinds of information. This supports short-term memory studies in the laboratory showing a similar advantage across time (e.g., Healy, 1982; Pezdek et al., 1986). The long-term advantage found here might be attributable to the encoding and reinstatement of temporally sequenced spatial information, that is, learned procedures. Subjects in this case acquired procedures both in direct study of their schedules and by going to class.

Results of Experiment 2 suggest that map study can also yield procedural learning, even when procedures involve little overt motor behavior. The *where* recall task in the map test and retest provides evidence for this view. In this task, subjects had to identify all building locations on a single map. Subjects did exceptionally well at this task, showing a strong *where* advantage on both test and retest performance. It is conceivable that during training subjects learned a specific temporal-spatial sequence suggested by the pattern of marks denoting building locations on the study map. Depending on the pattern, a starting and end point were selected and the locations were learned in this order. At recall, this learned temporal-spatial sequence was reinstated, prompted by the map. Further, half the subjects practiced reinstatement of this pattern on eight of the nine training trials. The other half practiced reinstatement on only one trial. Despite differences in practice, both training task groups performed equally well. These results suggest that overt motor behavior, more specifically, direct navigation, is not necessary in the learning of procedures.

The *where* advantage in the questionnaire test results of Experiment 2 provides further evidence for proceduralization in map study. Here again, subjects performed equally well on the *where* task in spite of differences in training. This evidence for temporal sequencing is particularly important because in the questionnaire test subjects were not asked to reinstate explicitly the temporal-spatial pattern of class locations on the map, unlike in the map test. Subjects instead located classes one at a time, on separate maps. Further, in contrast to the natural learning of class locations, subjects never had the benefit of actually proceeding to and from classes.

These differences might explain why the *where* advantage did not reach statistical significance in all of the comparisons of the questionnaire retest. It is important to note that the proposed procedural account of the *where* advantage is incomplete and tentative at best. For example, it does not easily account for the better recall of building locations over building names in the map versus the class listing tasks. It could be argued that people simply are more efficient at sequencing spatial information than verbal information. Retrieval of temporally sequenced spatial information is a daily event for most people, a well-practiced, "effortless" skill. As previously discussed, several other explanations for the *where* advantage are possible. Some have suggested (McNamara, 1986) that spatial knowledge is stored in both imagelike networks and propositionally, the redundancy in representation thus enhancing recall. It cannot be completely ruled out that the map did not provide additional retrieval cues or make the spatial task a recognition versus a recall test. Further, it has been assumed that the *where* advantage in Experiments 1 and 2 can be accounted for using the same explanation, the temporal sequencing of spatial information. Training in each experiment was different, even though the laboratory training in Experiment 2 was designed to be as similar as possible to the natural training of Experiment 1. It is certainly possible that some other learning factor not yet considered was operative in either or both experiments.

References

Anderson, J. R. (1982). Acquisition of cognitive skill. *Psychological Review, 89,* 369-406.

Bahrick, H. P. (1979). Maintenance of knowledge: Questions about memory we forgot to ask. *Journal of Experimental Psychology: General, 108,* 296-308.

Bahrick, H. P. (1984). Semantic memory content in permastore: Fifty years of memory for Spanish learned in school. *Journal of Experimental Psychology: General, 113,* 1-29.

Bahrick, H. P., Bahrick, P. O., & Wittlinger, R. P. (1975). Fifty years of memory for names and faces: A cross-sectional approach. *Journal of Experimental Psychology: General, 104,* 54-75.

Brown, R., & Kulik, J. (1977). Flashbulb memories. *Cognition, 5,* 73-99.

Cohen, N. J. (1984). Preserved learning capacity in amnesia: Evidence for multiple memory systems. In L. R. Squire & N. Butters (Eds.), *Neuropsychology of memory* (pp. 83-103). New York: Guilford.

Evans, G. W., & Pezdek, K. (1980). Cognitive mapping: Knowledge of real-world distance and location information. *Journal of Experimental Psychology: Human Learning and Performance, 6,* 13-24.

Fendrich, D. W., Healy, A. F., & Bourne, L. E., Jr. (1991). Long-term repetition effects for motoric and perceptual procedures. *Journal of Experimental Psychology: Learning, Memory and Cognition, 17,* 137-151.

Glenberg, A. M. (1979). Component-levels theory of the effects of spacing repetitions on recall and recognition. *Memory & Cognition, 7,* 95-112.

Golledge, R. G., Smith, T. R., Pellegrino, J. W., Doherty, S., & Marshall, S. P. (1985). A conceptual model and empirical analysis of children's acquisition of spatial knowledge. *Journal of Environmental Psychology, 5,* 125-152.

Healy, A. F. (1974). Separating item from order information in short-term memory. *Journal of Verbal Learning and Verbal Behavior, 13,* 644-655.

Healy, A. F. (1978). A Markov model for the short-term retention of spatial location information. *Journal of Verbal Learning and Verbal Behavior, 17,* 295-308.

Healy, A. F. (1982). Short-term memory for order information. In G. H. Bower (Ed.), *The psychology of learning and motivation* (Vol. 16, pp. 191-238). New York: Academic Press.

Healy, A. F., Cunningham, T. F., Gesi, A. T., Till, R. E., & Bourne, L. E., Jr. (1991). Comparing short-term recall of item, temporal, and spatial information in children and adults. In W. E. Hockley & S. Lewandowsky (Eds.), *Relating theory and data: Essays on human memory in honor of Bennet B. Murdock* (pp. 127-154). Hillsdale, NJ: Lawrence Erlbaum.

Healy, A. F., Fendrich, D. W., Crutcher, R. J., Wittman, W. T., Gesi, A. T., Ericsson, K. A., & Bourne, L. E., Jr. (1992). The long-term retention of skills. In A. F. Healy, S. M. Kosslyn, & R. M. Shiffrin (Eds.), *From learning processes to cognitive processes: Essays in honor of William K. Estes* (Vol. 2, pp. 87-118). Hillsdale, NJ: Lawrence Erlbaum.

Healy, A. F., Fendrich, D. W., & Proctor, J. D. (1990). Acquisition and retention of a letter-detection skill. *Journal of Experimental Psychology: Learning, Memory, and Cognition, 16,* 270-281.

Healy, A. F., King, C. L., Clawson D. M., Sinclair, G. P., Rickard, T. C., Crutcher, R. J., Ericsson, K. A., & Bourne, L. E., Jr. (this volume). Optimizing the long-term retention of skills. In A. F. Healy & L. E. Bourne, Jr. (Eds.), *Learning and memory of knowledge and skills: Durability and specificity.* Thousand Oaks, CA: Sage.

Kolers, P. A., & Roediger, H. L., III. (1984). Procedures of mind. *Journal of Verbal Learning and Verbal Behavior, 23,* 425-449.

Lee, C. L., & Estes, W. K. (1981). Item and order information in short-term memory: Evidence for multilevel perturbation processes. *Journal of Experimental Psychology: Human Learning and Memory, 7,* 149-169.

McNamara, T. P. (1986). Mental representations of spatial relations. *Cognitive Psychology, 18,* 87-121.

Murdock, B. B., Jr. (1976). Item and order information in short-term serial memory. *Journal of Experimental Psychology: General, 105,* 191-216.

Pezdek, K., Roman Z., & Sobolik, K. G. (1986). Spatial memory for objects and words. *Journal of Experimental Psychology: Learning, Memory, and Cognition, 12,* 530-537.

Pillemer, D. B. (1984). Flashbulb memories of the assassination attempt on President Reagan. *Cognition, 16,* 63-80.

Salthouse, T. A. (1974). Using selective interference to investigate spatial memory representations. *Memory & Cognition, 2,* 749-757.

Salthouse, T. A. (1975). Simultaneous processing of verbal and spatial information. *Memory & Cognition, 3,* 221-225.

Shiffrin, R. M., & Cook, J. R. (1978). Short-term forgetting of item and order information. *Journal of Verbal Learning and Verbal Behavior, 17,* 189-218.

Sholl, M. J. (1987). Cognitive maps as orienting schemata. *Journal of Experimental Psychology: Learning, Memory, and Cognition, 13,* 615-628.

Thompson, C. P. (1982). Memory for unique personal events: The roommate study. *Memory & Cognition, 10,* 324-332.

Thorndyke, P. W., & Hayes-Roth, B. (1982). Differences in spatial knowledge acquired from maps and navigation. *Cognitive Psychology, 14,* 560-589.

Wagenaar, W. A. (1978). Recalling message broadcast to the general public. In M. M. Gruneberg, P. E. Morris, & R. N. Sykes (Eds.), *Practical aspects of memory* (pp. 128-136). New York: Academic Press.

Wagenaar, W. A. (1986). My memory: A study of autobiographical memory over six years. *Cognitive Psychology, 18,* 225-252.

White, R. T. (1982). Memory for personal events. *Human Learning, 1,* 171-183.

Wittman, W. T. (1990). A long-term retention advantage for spatial information learned naturally and in the laboratory. *University Microfilms International,* 4405.

Yarmey, A. D., & Bull, M. P., III. (1978). Where were you when President Kennedy was assassinated? *Bulletin of the Psychonomic Society, 11,* 133-135.

7 Long-Term Performance in Autobiographical Event Dating

Patterns of Accuracy and Error Across a Two-and-a-Half-Year Time Span

JOHN J. SKOWRONSKI

ANDREW L. BETZ

CHARLES P. THOMPSON

STEEN F. LARSEN

For up to 2½ years, the six subjects in this study listed events in a diary. The subjects later provided dates for these events. Analyses of these dates examined (a) exact dating frequencies and error magnitudes across the 2-year retention interval; (b) possible alterations in the relation between several predictors and measures of dating accuracy with increases in the retention interval; (c) subjects' perceptions of the memory sources used in event dating, and how these sources changed with increases in the retention interval; (d) the impact of the temporal landmarks provided by the start date and the end date of the study on time expansion and telescoping effects in event dating; (e) how the day of the week on which an event occurs is related to the day of the week on which an event is dated; and (f) the stability of these day-of-week relations with increases in the retention interval.

AUTHORS' NOTE: We wish to extend our thanks to Dan Aeschliman, Minida Dowdy, Will Eckels, Cosima Hadidi, Tricia Hoard, and Grant Nurnberg, who served as our stalwart subjects. The research reported here was supported by National Institute of Mental Health Grant MH44090 with the third author as principal investigator.

The year 1993 was momentous for many people living in the central United States. Heavy rains forced the Mississippi River and many of its tributaries over their banks, flooding those who lived nearby. Residents in West Quincy, Missouri, waged a tireless battle against the floodwaters, yet were inundated when a river levee suddenly and catastrophically failed. Residents of Des Moines, Iowa, were without potable water after the city's water treatment plant was flooded.

Those who experienced such dramatic, emotional, and life-altering events will likely not forget them. However, people's ability to place these events correctly in time may not be so robust. If West Quincy residents were asked the *exact date* the levee broke, or if Des Moines residents were asked the *exact date* the treatment plant was flooded, how accurate would those dating attempts be? If attempts at dating these events were inaccurate, would there be any patterns that might characterize the errors made?

For over a decade, we have conducted research looking at precisely these types of questions (Betz & Skowronski, 1993a, 1993b; Larsen, 1988, 1992; Larsen & Thompson, 1993; Skowronski, Betz, Thompson, & Shannon, 1991; Skowronski, Betz, Thompson, Walker, & Shannon, 1994; Skowronski & Thompson, 1990; Thompson, 1982, 1985a, 1985b; Thompson, Skowronski, & Lee, 1988a, 1988b; Thompson, Skowronski, & Betz, 1993). Through these studies we have discovered several factors related to dating accuracy and dating error. However, excepting several studies by Larsen (e.g., Larsen, 1992, Larsen & Thompson, 1993), our research has employed a 10- to 15-week interval between event occurrence and dating attempt. Logically, the concern arises whether the factors related to event dating performance in this relatively short retention interval also relate to dating performance in the long term. The study discussed in the present chapter addresses this concern.

In this study, six undergraduate students at Kansas State University kept personal diaries for relatively long periods of time, ranging from $1\frac{1}{2}$ to $2\frac{1}{2}$ years. They entered one event a day, with the events collected each week. The students were requested to include a wide range of events (e.g., memorable and nonmemorable; pleasant and unpleasant) each week. At the time an event was recorded in the diary, the subjects rated the pleasantness of the event (-3 = *very unpleasant* to $+3$ = *very pleasant*), rated the degree of emotion engendered by each event (1 = *none* to 5 = *extreme*), and provided a base rate estimate of each event's frequency (1 = *once a day* to 7 = *once in a lifetime*). Finally, they estimated the memorability of the event on a 3-point scale (1 = *will forget the event in a couple of weeks* and 3 = *will remember the event a year from now*).

During interview sessions conducted after event recording ended, the events in each person's diary were read back to that person, one event at a time, with the events randomly ordered. During this diary interview session, subjects provided a rating of how well they remembered each event (1 = *no memory*, 7 = *perfect memory*) and were asked to recall two attributes of the events (the location of the event and who was with them); if they could not recall these attributes, the information was provided. Next they were asked how often they rehearsed each event (continuous scale from 0 to infinity). Finally, they were asked for information on the date of the event. Using a blank calendar providing only the usual year, month, and day-of-the-week information, subjects were asked to provide an exact date for each diary event. They then reported on the memory information that they used to come up with the date estimate (1 = *knew the exact date; 2 = related the event to another event that served as a dating reference point; 3 = knew the general period in which the event occurred; 4 = estimated the number of events that have happened in the intervening retention interval; 5 = used the clarity of memory to estimate the event's date* [e.g., clear = recent, poor = old]; 6 = *used a prototypic date* [e.g., if this was a class it had to be on a Monday]; 7 = *guessed;* and 8 = *used another source not listed*).

The diaries provide an objective record of each event's actual date, so that measures of accuracy and error can be derived by comparing each estimated date to the exact date obtained from the diaries. We shall focus on four measures of accuracy and error. The first of these is exact accuracy: whether or not an event was exactly dated. The second of these measures is the absolute value of the dating error (error magnitude): regardless of direction, the discrepancy between the date estimate and the provided date. The third of these measures is signed dating error, which incorporates both the magnitude and the direction of the discrepancy between the estimated date and the exact date. The fourth of these measures is modulo 7 error, which is the remainder when the dating error is divided by 7. This measure allows us to evaluate whether the student picked the correct day of week in estimating the date of the event (i.e., a correct-day judgment will produce a remainder of zero).

This multiple-measures approach is justified in light of the many different factors involved in event dating. For example, event dates are occasionally recallable from a time tag attached to a specific event (e.g., I wrecked my car on January 10), or from time tags that are part of real-world knowledge (e.g., Christmas is on December 25). A more frequent possibility is that event dates are reconstructed from partial temporal information stored with the event (e.g., it happened in June), or from real-world knowledge that provides such information (e.g., it happened at church, so it must have been on a Sunday). Further, event dates can be affected by one's knowledge of general time periods and landmarks (e.g., I know that school started on January 10, so the event couldn't have happened before that).

The alternative measures of dating accuracy and error are differentially sensitive to these processes. For example, signed error is sensitive to distortions due to temporal boundaries, which sometimes serve as dating landmarks (e.g., Rubin & Baddeley, 1989; Thompson et al., 1988b; Thompson et al., 1993). The modulo 7 measure is sensitive to dating attempts that use the day of the week on which an event occurred, as well as other within-week information (Larsen & Thompson, 1993; Skowronski et al., 1991; Thompson et al., 1993).

Exact Dating Accuracy and Error Magnitude

The Impact of Retention Interval

Because the time frame for this study was much longer than we typically used in our previous research, one of our primary concerns was to evaluate the impact of lengthening the retention interval on our dependent measures. Consequently, we first looked at the impact of retention interval on exact dating accuracy. For the exact accuracy measure, each event dated by our subjects was scored as correct or incorrect. Figure 7.1 plots the proportion of events dated correctly as a function of the interval (or event age) between the occurrence of the event and the time of the diary interview session. As illustrated by the data in Figure 7.1, subjects' exact dating performance decreased (lower accuracy proportion) with increasing retention interval. This conclusion is verified by the results of a pooled within-subjects regression analysis in which retention interval (in days) is regressed against whether an event was correctly or incorrectly dated, $b = -.00037$, $F(1, 3501) = 171.77$, $p < .0001$.[1]

The data in Figure 7.1 also suggest that the impact of retention interval on correct dating varies across retention interval. Specifically, dating accuracy decreases rapidly at short retention intervals (less than 5 months) but decreases more gradually at longer intervals. This interpretation is confirmed by the results of an analysis in which both linear and quadratic retention interval are entered into the regression model: The quadratic

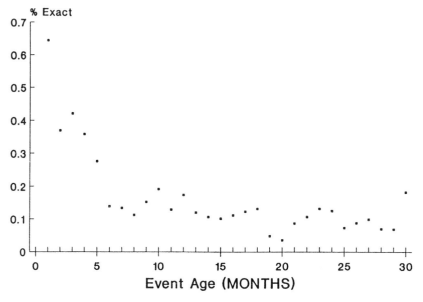

Figure 7.1. The Relation Between Retention Interval and Exact Dating Accuracy

component of the retention interval effect was statistically reliable, $b =$ .000001, $F(1, 3500) = 77.51$, $p < .0001$.

A somewhat different picture emerges from the second measure of dating performance, the magnitude of the errors made by the subjects (see Figure 7.2). This measure is derived by calculating the days of difference between the exact date and the estimated date, ignoring the direction of the difference.

Figure 7.2 reveals a linear increase in error magnitude with increases in retention interval. The rate of increase in error magnitude, roughly .83 days of error per week, is similar to that obtained in our earlier short-term dating studies (e.g., Thompson, 1982; Skowronski et al., 1991). In contrast to the exact dating data depicted in Figure 7.1, there does not appear to be substantial curvilinearity. Regression analyses confirm these perceptions. Subjects' dating performance worsened linearly (larger error magnitude) with increasing retention interval, $b = .1175$, $F(1, 3501) = 229.12$, $p <$ .0001. By comparison, the quadratic effect of retention interval on error magnitude was not statistically reliable.

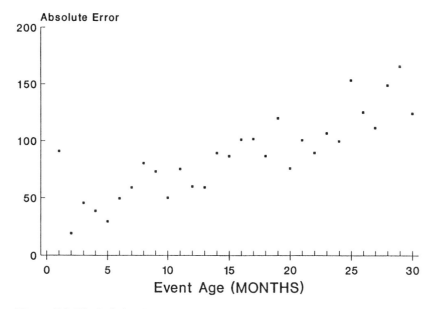

Figure 7.2. The Relation Between Retention Interval and Dating Error Magnitude

The Impact of Event Characteristics and
Their Action Across Lengthening Retention Intervals

Our previous research looked at how various event characteristics are related to event dating accuracy and error. One of our typical stratagems asks subjects to rate the events along several dimensions as the events are entered into the diaries. These ratings are later examined in relation to dating accuracy and error. As we indicated earlier in this chapter, in this study we asked our diary keepers to rate the pleasantness of each event, to rate the degree of emotion engendered by each event, and to provide a base rate estimate of each event's frequency.

Pleasantness. Several theoretical reasons suggest that pleasant events should be dated more accurately than unpleasant events. First, certain events probably capitalize on the cyclical nature of the calendar year. Examples of these include birthdays, anniversaries, and repetitive holidays such as Christmas. Because events that occur on these days are usually positive, the presence of pleasantness effects in event dating could partially reflect this real-world cyclicity.

Second, pleasant events might induce spontaneous associations with event dates. For example, dating couples often celebrate such personal landmarks as their 1-month and 2-month "anniversaries." Special pleasant landmark events such as weddings and graduations may also tend to be associated with specific event dates.

A third possible reason for a relation between event pleasantness and event dating accuracy lies in event memory. When people are unable to recall an event's exact date, they may often use their recall of the event content to concoct an estimate, and this event content may provide information as to the likely date of an event. Because pleasant events are recalled better than other types of events (Skowronski et al., 1991), such events might contain more date-relevant cues, which in turn could be used to produce more accurate date estimates.

We also had practical reasons to expect pleasantness effects to emerge: They have done so in past research (e.g, Skowronski et al., 1991; Thompson, 1985b). Based on this past research, two specific effects were expected. First, pleasant events should be dated more accurately than unpleasant events. Second, more extreme events should be more accurately dated than less extreme events.

The mean dating error and mean percentage of exact dates associated with each level of rated event pleasantness in the present study (−3 = *very unpleasant* to +3 = *very pleasant*) are presented in Table 7.1. Regression analyses indicated that controlling for subjects, linear age, and quadratic age, the linear effect of pleasantness on dating was significant, but only for the exact dating accuracy measure. Pleasant events were more frequently dated correctly than unpleasant events, $b = .0264$, $F(1, 3496) = 26.18$, $p < .0001$,[2] but pleasant events were not significantly associated with smaller error magnitudes than unpleasant events. Similarly, the quadratic effects of pleasantness on dating were statistically reliable for the exact correctness measure, $b = .0156$, $F(1, 3495) = 26.08$, $p < .0001$, but not for the error magnitude measure.

Although the quadratic pleasantness effect in dating accuracy was reliable, close scrutiny of Table 7.1 suggests that this quadratic effect is not indicative of a pure extremity effect. If this were the case, then extreme events, both positive and negative, would be more accurately dated than neutral events. Instead, increases in event extremity were related to exact dating accuracy only when the events were rated positively. Increases in extremity were unrelated to exact accuracy when the events were rated negatively. Similar trends, although not statistically reliable, held for the error magnitude measure.

Table 7.1 Raw Means Describing the Relation Between Levels of Perceived
Event Pleasantness, Perceived Event Frequency, and Perceived
Emotional Involvement and Exact Dating Accuracy and Magnitude of
Dating Error

| | Pleasantness Rating | | | | | | |
	−3	−2	−1	0	1	2	3
Exact Dating % Correct	.114	.094	.124	.121	.167	.270	.345
Error Magnitude in Days	70.17	82.34	63.66	60.85	55.76	39.82	33.18

| | Frequency Rating | | | | | | |
| | High | | | | | | Low |
	1	2	3	4	5	6	7
Exact Dating % Correct	.125	.116	.099	.197	.226	.188	.381
Error Magnitude in Days	26.59	48.09	57.19	58.71	56.93	60.02	28.63

| | Perceived Emotion | | | | |
	1	2	3	4	5
Exact Dating % Correct	.089	.120	.224	.283	.436
Error Magnitude in Days	76.47	58.67	46.72	44.69	48.17

Although these data resemble those from earlier short-term studies,
they are not exact replications. Earlier studies (Skowronski et al., 1991;
Thompson, 1985b) found that pleasantness was related to error magnitude,
whereas this study did not. Further, the extremity effect observed in earlier
studies was symmetric, with extreme ratings related to dating accuracy for
both positive and negative events. In the present study, extremity was
related to accuracy only when the events were positive.

One possible explanation for these differing outcomes is that the interview procedure used in the present study differed slightly from that used
previously. In prior studies, subjects were first asked to provide a memory
rating, then asked to provide an event date. In the present study, subjects
were asked to recall two attributes of the events (the location of the event
and who was with the subject) prior to dating the event; if they could not
recall these attributes, the information was provided. Because event memory is related to dating accuracy (e.g., Skowronski et al., 1991), it could
be the case that providing memory cues to subjects helped to neutralize

the memory-based advantage of pleasant and extreme events for event dating. However, for this explanation to be valid, exact date accuracy must be, to some extent, independent of event recall. After all, although error magnitude was not related to event pleasantness, exact accuracy certainly was. This finding suggests that pleasant and extreme events can have a higher probability of being dated exactly independently of one's ability to recall the event. We will present evidence for such independence later in this chapter.

The long-term nature of this study additionally provides the opportunity to test whether the relation between event pleasantness and dating accuracy holds over increasing retention intervals. This relation can be assessed by looking at the interaction between pleasantness and retention interval. Controlling for subjects, the linear and quadratic effects of retention interval, and the linear effects of event pleasantness, the Pleasantness × Age interaction was not statistically reliable for the error magnitude measure. However, this interaction was statistically reliable for the exact dating measure, $b = -.00006$, $F(1, 3495) = 6.82$, $p < .01$.

To examine this interaction further, the retention interval was parsed into three categories—short (100 days or less), intermediate (101 days to 1 year), and long (greater than 1 year)—and the relation between event pleasantness and exact dating accuracy was examined within each time category. Increases in event pleasantness were related to smaller increases in exact dating accuracy when the events were old ($b = .0194$) than when they were of intermediate age ($b = .0362$) or were of relatively recent origin ($b = .0302$). However, even when the events were in the old category, event pleasantness was still predictive of exact accuracy, $F(1, 1888) = 10.38$, $p < .01$. Thus, despite some alteration in the pleasantness/accuracy relation across retention intervals, pleasant events are associated with greater exact dating accuracy than unpleasant events across the entire retention interval used in the study.

Perceived Event Frequency. Subjects recorded their perception of event frequency as each event was entered into the diary. This frequency estimate ($1 = once a day$ to $7 = once in a lifetime$) is tantamount to a perception of the event's population base rate. For very different reasons, both very frequently occurring and very infrequently occurring events might show evidence of enhanced dating accuracy relative to events of middling frequency. Frequently occurring events may often tie into some temporal cycle that can enhance dating accuracy, for example, "I listened to a sermon about the evils of money in church today—the event probably happened on a Sunday." Infrequently occurring events, such as one's graduation day, may tend both to be both well remembered and to have an enhanced likelihood of being tagged with a specific date. Thus, there is reason to suspect enhanced dating accuracy for both very frequent and very infrequent events. However, given the mechanisms that may underlie these accuracy enhancements, it is difficult to predict whether an accuracy difference between frequently occurring or infrequently occurring events will exist.

One might suspect that the results of our previous research would provide some clues about whether such differences exist. This research shows that dating is more accurate for events that are atypical than typical for a person, and that both highly atypical and typical events are dated better than events of middling typicality (Skowronski et al., 1991). However, there may be a difference between person typicality and base rate frequency in the population. In theory, an event might be typical for a person but unusual for the population. For example, if a straight-A student received an A on a test, it would be very typical for the student but atypical for the student population. Hence, our previously obtained person-typicality results are not necessarily indicative of results that one might obtain with a perceived frequency measure.

The data from the present study indicate that there are, indeed, differences between the base rate frequency/dating accuracy relation examined in the present study and the person-typicality/dating accuracy relation examined in our prior research. The raw dating magnitude and exact dating accuracy means for the perceived frequency variable are presented in Table 7.1. Regression analyses indicate that controlling for subjects and both the linear and quadratic effects of event age, events perceived to occur infrequently were more likely to be exactly dated, $b = .0554$, $F(1, 3499) = 116.91$, $p < .0001$, but were less accurately dated, $b = -4.05$, $F(1, 3499) = 6.76$, $p < .01$, than events perceived to be frequent. We also examined the quadratic frequency effect to determine whether frequently and infrequently occurring events were dated more accurately than events of middling frequency. Controlling for subjects, the linear effects of age, the quadratic effects of age, and the linear effects of frequency, the quadratic effect was significant for the error magnitude measure, $b = -2.02$, $F(1, 3498) = 4.55$, $p < .05$, but not for the exact dating measure.

The results of these analyses suggest that the exact dating measure and the error magnitude measure are affected by perceived event frequency in different ways. The nature of this divergence is illustrated by the means in Table 7.1. For very frequent events, the exact dating likelihood is low and error magnitude is low, but for very infrequent events, the exact dating likelihood is high and error magnitude is low. One possible explanation for this divergence is that different memory cues may be associated with the high-frequency and low-frequency events. High-frequency events allow the use of one's store of life and world knowledge to date events and allow relatively precise estimation of the dates of events that occur cyclically. By comparison, the better dating for infrequent events might be due to a couple of factors. First, the exact dates for these infrequent events may be more often remembered than the exact dates of frequently occurring events. Second, these infrequent events may be better recalled than frequently occurring events, and this enhanced memory may yield more precise date estimates.

As with the pleasantness measure, the long-term nature of this study also allowed us to examine whether the relation between rated frequency and dating accuracy changed across retention interval. It did not. The Retention Interval × Frequency Rating interaction was not statistically reliable for either the exact correctness measure or the error magnitude measure. In sum, as with the pleasantness measure, the rated frequency and dating accuracy relation was consistent over the retention interval.

Perceived Emotion Resulting From the Event. Subjects provided a rating of the emotionality (emotional intensity) of the event (1 = *none* to 5 = *extreme*). We suspected that this variable would be related to dating accuracy in much the same way as event extremity, a variable that can be derived from the pleasantness ratings. Our previous research (Skowronski et al., 1991) suggests that extremely positive and extremely negative events are more accurately dated than events of middling pleasantness, and given this outcome, we had originally suspected that high emotionality would lead to greater accuracy than low emotionality. However, recall that our earlier analyses of the pleasantness variable in this study indicated that the extremity effect (tested by the quadratic pleasantness factor in the analysis) was statistically reliable only for the exact accuracy measure, not for the error magnitude measure. To the extent that emotionality is related to the pleasantness of events (extremely pleasant and unpleasant events causing the most emotion), one would expect to obtain a similar outcome for the perceived emotion variable.

The raw means for the perceived emotion variable are presented in Table 7.1. Regression analyses using this variable as a predictor indicate that controlling for individual differences as well as the linear and quadratic effects of age, events perceived to produce high levels of emotion were more often exactly dated than events low in emotional content, $b = .0640$, $F(1, 3499) = 78.63$, $p < .0001$. The trend toward greater accuracy for emotion-producing events also characterizes the error magnitude measure

(b = -2.37), but the effect is not statistically reliable. These data thus converge nicely with the indirect extremity ratings, derived from the pleasantness ratings, which also found that extremity predicted exact accuracy but not error magnitude.

As with the pleasantness and perceived frequency measures, the long-term nature of this study allowed us to examine whether the relation between emotionality and dating accuracy changed across retention interval. There was not a significant Retention Interval × Emotionality Rating interaction for either the exact correctness measure or for the error magnitude measure. The results therefore show that the relation between the rated emotion produced by the event and dating accuracy was consistent across the retention interval.

The Independent Contributions of Perceived Frequency, Perceived Emotionality, and Event Pleasantness in Dating Accuracy. One area of interest with respect to the descriptive variables that we have so far used as predictors of dating accuracy concerns their independent contributions to dating accuracy; that is, one might imagine that these predictor variables are correlated, so that infrequent events are also emotion-producing events, which also tend to be pleasant events. Thus, it could be the case that all of these effects are really being driven by one of the variables. For example, it could be the case that emotionality is really the key variable, and that the effects of pleasantness and frequency on event dating are a result of the correlation of these variables with emotionality.

Given this possibility, we conducted a regression analysis that simultaneously evaluated the independent relation between each of the three predictors and event dating. The results of the analysis of the exact dating measure suggests that each of the three variables has an effect on dating accuracy that is independent of the other two variables: rated event frequency b = .050, $F(1, 3494)$ = 74.54, p < .0001; event pleasantness b = .026, $F(1, 3494)$ = 26.17, p < .0001; and emotionality b = .043, $F(1, 3494)$ = 32.77, p < .0001. The results of the analysis of error magnitude suggest that only rated frequency has an effect on dating that is independent of the other two variables, b = -3.95, $F(1, 3494)$ = 5.76, p < .02.

Does Event Memory Mediate the Impact of Event Characteristics on Dating Accuracy? Our discussion of relations between pleasantness, frequency/infrequency, and emotionality and dating accuracy implied that memory may be a crucial mediating process, that is, these variables affect event dating because of the impact that they have on memory. However, implicit in this discussion is the possibility that at least three different types of memory cues are used to construct event dates. The first of these is direct recall of a date, which assumes that the event date is a part of the memory trace (e.g., I wrecked my car on January 15). A second memory cue is "real-world knowledge." This is temporal information that comes from what we generally know about our lives and the world around us (e.g., That happened on Christmas, and Christmas is on December 25). The third type of cue comes from details of the event itself and from temporal information implied by those details (e.g., I remember that it was hot, so it must have happened in the summer).

Two ratings provided by our subjects allowed us to assess whether memory for event details, as opposed to the other two types of cues, was crucial to exact dating accuracy and error magnitude. As we indicated earlier in this chapter, these ratings were collected during the diary interview session. The first was a memory rating: Subjects reported how well they remembered the event described by each diary entry ($1 = no\ memory$, $7 = perfect\ memory$). The second was a rehearsal rating: Subjects reported how often they thought that they had recalled or rehearsed each event since it happened (continuous scale from 0 to infinity).

Prior research indicates that memory and rehearsal are related to dating accuracy (Betz & Skowronski, 1993a; Skowronski et al., 1991). Unknown, however, is whether these variables mediate the effect of the descriptive variables on dating accuracy. Specifically, if the inclusion of these two ratings in our regression equation eliminates the predictive effects of the three descriptive variables, then event memory could have been mediating those effects. On the other hand, if the effects of the descriptive variables persist even after the memory and rehearsal are entered into the model, then we can conclude that event recall did not mediate the effects of these descriptive variables on dating accuracy.

The results of the analyses diverge with respect to the question of mediation. In the analysis of error magnitude, only the memory rating, $b = -11.17$, $F(1, 3492) = 35.67$, $p < .0001$, and the rehearsal rating, $b = -1.12$, $F(1, 3492) = 10.87$, $p < .001$, were reliable predictors; the pleasantness rating, the frequency rating, and the emotionality rating were not. By comparison, even after entry of the memory and rehearsal variables into the model (memory rating $b = .0512$, $F[1, 3492] = 60.96$, $p < .0001$; rehearsal rating $b = .0040$, $F[1, 3492] = 11.54$, $p < .001$), the three descriptive variables continued to predict exact accuracy: pleasantness $b = .0227$, $F(1, 3492) = 20.45$, $p < .0001$; rated frequency $b = .0351$, $F(1, 3492) = 34.99$, $p < .0001$; and rated emotionality $b = .0257$, $F(1, 3492) = 11.11$, $p < .001$.

Given these data, it follows that pleasantness, emotionality, and perceived frequency contribute to dating accuracy in at least two ways. The first of these works through event memory. Pleasant, infrequent, and emotional events are better recalled, and the corresponding event cues aid date estimation (e.g., Skowronski et al., 1991). The second contribution works independently of event recall. Perhaps temporal information is more often stored or is more reconstructible for pleasant, frequent, and emotional events.

Regardless of the exact memory mechanisms involved, these data emphasize the fact that event dating performance is partially related to event characteristics. Pleasant, frequent, and emotional events are dated exactly with higher frequency (in this study) and with less error (in our earlier studies) than unpleasant, infrequent, and unemotional events. Further, pleasantness, frequency, and emotionality were consistently related to event dating for the entire 2½-year time span encompassed by this study.

Subjects' Perceptions of Information Use
Across Retention Interval

As we indicated earlier in this chapter, subjects were asked to provide us with self-report information about *how* they arrived at their event date estimates. Thus, after providing a date, subjects were asked to report whether that date was generated as a result of (a) knowing the exact date, (b) relating the event to another event that served as a dating reference point, (c) knowing the general period in which the event occurred, (d) estimating the number of events that happened in the intervening retention interval, (e) using the clarity of memory to estimate the event's date (e.g., clear = recent, poor = old), (f) using a prototypic date (e.g., if this was a class it had to be on a Monday), (g) a guess, or (h) another source not listed (data using these information types are also reported in Thompson et al., 1988b, 1993; also see Linton, 1975). Regression analyses indicate that these sources are significantly related to both exact dating accuracy, $F(7, 3493) = 144.15$, $p < .0001$, and error magnitude, $F(7, 3493) = 34.44$, $p < .0001$.

To examine the relation between these strategies and retention interval, we tabulated the data separately within the old, intermediate, and recent retention intervals. The relative proportions of events dated using each information type were calculated within each time segment, along with their associated means for error magnitude and exact dating accuracy. These are presented in Table 7.2.

Table 7.2 Subjects' Reports of Information Use in Event Dating by Retention Interval: Percentage Used, Error Magnitude, and Exact Dating Accuracy

| | | Retention Interval | | |
		Recent	Intermediate	Old
Exact Date Known	% Used	20.58	6.65	3.16
	Error Magnitude	6.82	8.91	61.38
	% Exactly Correct	87.32	88.09	71.67
Used Reference Event	% Used	18.55	15.91	8.95
	Error Magnitude	4.26	20.88	50.63
	% Exactly Correct	40.62	28.36	25.29
Knew General Reference Period	% Used	37.10	57.80	55.89
	Error Magnitude	15.78	28.24	56.99
	% Exactly Correct	26.56	11.37	8.38
Estimated # Intervening Events	% Used	.29	0	.53
	Error Magnitude	63.00	—	46.60
	% Exactly Correct	0	—	10.00
Used Memory Clarity to Estimate	% Used	7.54	2.45	6.16
	Error Magnitude	18.15	53.62	130.38
	% Exactly Correct	38.46	16.13	2.56
Used Prototypic Information	% Used	8.99	3.80	2.79
	Error Magnitude	28.32	11.17	75.81
	% Exactly Correct	35.48	31.25	32.07
Guess	% Used	4.64	11.96	20.68
	Error Magnitude	81.63	85.13	135.74
	% Exactly Correct	6.25	1.99	1.53
Other	% Used	2.32	1.43	1.84
	Error Magnitude	1.88	108.00	83.31
	% Exactly Correct	62.50	5.56	5.71

Several effects in this table are worth noting. From a metamemory perspective, these data should be fairly comforting. When subjects report that they know the exact date, they are correct 87% of the time if the event is less than 100 days old and 71% of the time if the event is greater than 1 year old. However, as one might expect, subjects report recalling the exact date of an event far less frequently as retention interval increases. In short, subjects seem to have a good (albeit not perfect) sense of when they know the exact date of an event.

Use of reference information and prototypic information both produced high levels of exact dating accuracy, and the use of these strategies also declined with longer retention times. However, note that if this time-specific information is available, it leads to relatively high rates of exact dating, even for events that are over 1 year old. For those old items, exact dating percentages were 25% when subjects used some reference event and 32% when subjects used a prototypic strategy. These percentages do not decline much as retention interval increases. In conjunction with subjects' self-reports of knowing exact dates, these data suggest that exact dating accuracy is heavily dependent on recall of relatively specific time-based information (e.g., dates of events, event orders).

As these types of temporally specific information are forgotten, subjects must resort to other, less precise information to generate event dates. Evidence for this strategic change is reflected in the usage rates for other information types as retention interval increases. For example, use of the general reference period jumped from 37% of the time for events under 100 days old to 55% of the time when events were over 100 days old. Further, subjects reported that they resorted to a self-described "guess" strategy only 5% of the time for events in the most recent interval, but for older events (over 1 year old) guessing was used over 20% of the time. As one might suspect, these alternative information sources provide relatively imprecise temporal information, and they lead to poor dating. For example, for older events the exact correctness rates are about 1.5% for guess and about 8% for general reference period.

To the extent that subjects can accurately access their own cognitive processes, then, these self-report data link differing types of dating cues and dating accuracy across an expansive retention interval. In brief, these self-reports suggest that event dating involves different types of recalled information. The types of information recalled are related to dating accuracy, and over time people switch to less precise types of information to date events.

Signed Dating Error

Another dependent measure that can be assessed is signed dating error. In contrast to the error magnitude measure, which is calculated without regard to the direction of the discrepancy between the actual and estimated dates, the signed dating error retains this directional information. Hence, from this measure, we can assess whether a date estimate is one that places an event at a date that is more recent than its actual date of occurrence (a *telescoping* error), or whether it places an event at a date that is later than its actual date of occurrence (a *time expansion* error).

The systematic biases of telescoping and time expansion have surfaced at least twice in the event-dating literature. In the first of these episodes, the specific issue was the impact of temporal boundaries on event dating. In the second of these episodes, the issue was the possibility that people use the clarity of memory as a cue for constructing date estimates.

Temporal Boundaries and Distortion in Date Estimates

By necessity, many dating studies have definite temporal boundaries. Participants can often recall the approximate start date of a study and can almost certainly recall when the study ended. As noted by Thompson et al. (1988b; also see Huttenlocher, Hedges, & Bradburn, 1990; Huttenlocher, Hedges, & Prohaska, 1988; Rubin & Baddeley, 1989), event-date estimates are systematically distorted near these boundaries. Events near the older boundary, around the time a study begins, are subject to telescoping, whereas events near the recent boundary, around the time the diary interview is conducted, are subject to time expansion.

The data in the present study show these boundary effects. The mean signed dating errors are plotted as a function of retention interval in Figure 7.3. Our algorithm for calculating signed dating error subtracts the actual date from the estimated date, so that positive error values reflect time expansion and negative error values reflect telescoping. As illustrated by the data in Figure 7.3, dating errors for recent events tend to be time expansion errors, whereas dating errors for older events tend to be telescoping errors. Regression analyses indicate that this effect is statistically reliable. Controlling for subjects, signed dating error became increasingly negative with event age, $b = -.151$, $F(1, 3501) = 301.98$, $p < .0001$. An additional analysis revealed that there was a significant quadratic component to the interval-signed error relation, $b = -.00016$, $F(1, 3500) = 21.37$, $p < .0001$.

These data support the explanations for boundary effects offered by Huttenlocher et al. (1990) and Rubin and Baddeley (1989). These explanations center on the notion that boundaries restrict the direction of possible errors. Near the oldest date boundary, if the boundary is known, dating errors can only be telescoping errors; otherwise an event would be outside the retention interval investigated by the study. Similarly, near the most recent date boundary, if the boundary is known, dating errors can only be time expansion errors; otherwise, an event would be outside the retention interval.

Thus, because our methodology imposes boundaries on event dates, the event dates that we collected were partly affected by the study itself. Although the telescoping and time expansion effects we obtained are

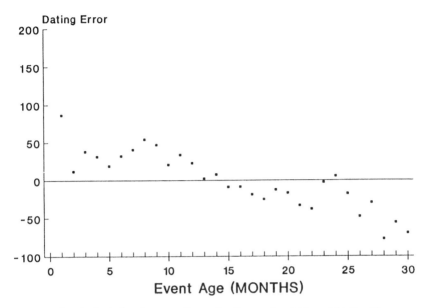

Figure 7.3. The Relation Between Retention Interval and Signed Dating Error

likely a consequence of methodology, real-world dating attempts may be subject to similar effects; people sometimes have some knowledge of the general time period in which an event occurred. Indeed, that is what our subjects told us in their self-reports of information use. Further, these general time periods may have fairly definite boundaries. Accordingly, imprecise temporal knowledge such as "the event occurred sometime in winter" should induce boundary effects similar to those observed in the present study. Specifically, events that occurred in early winter will show telescoping, whereas events that occurred in late winter will show time expansion.

In principle, the explanation by Huttenlocher et al. (1990) and Rubin and Baddeley (1989) should apply to any period with date boundaries, regardless of event age or the period in which the event occurred. The present study was not designed to evaluate this idea. However, this idea could be systematically tested in future studies. For example, one simple way would be to ask subjects (a) if they estimated an event's date (as opposed to recalling it) and (b) if they used boundaries to estimate the date of an event. If the answer to both of these queries is yes, then systematic distortion in date estimation relative to those boundaries should be evident.

Memory Clarity and Date Estimation

Signed dating error is also useful for evaluating the hypothesis that people use memory clarity to estimate event dates. This suggestion was offered by Bradburn, Rips, and Shevell (1987), who proposed that well-remembered events will tend to be dated more recently than poorly remembered events. The reason for this tendency lies in metamemory. People know that they have a more detailed recall of recent events than of older events. A clearly recalled memory, in the absence of other temporal cues, should be judged to have occurred relatively recently. Thus, in our study, if the clarity hypothesis were correct higher memory clarity should be associated with increasingly negative error magnitudes.

Based on the three studies reported by Thompson et al. (1988b), we concluded that memory clarity was not strongly related to telescoping. However, the limited retention interval used in those studies may have been insufficient for memory clarity to affect directional dating error. The current study suggests that the limited retention interval was not the problem. Regression analyses indicate that, controlling for subjects and the linear and quadratic effects of age, subjects' self-rated memory was not reliably related to signed dating error. In fact, the slope of this effect is positive ($b = .0773$), opposite of that predicted by the clarity hypothesis. Thus, the data indicate that higher memory ratings are associated (albeit nonsignificantly) with less negative error values (e.g., the raw error magnitude mean when self-rated memory is poor $= -40.73$, and when self-rated memory is excellent $= -4.42$).

Another way to test the memory clarity hypothesis is to analyze only those events for which subjects reported using memory clarity information in date estimation. We conducted this analysis. Controlling for subjects and the linear and quadratic effects of age, the relation between reported event memory and age was consistent with the memory clarity hypothesis, evidencing some telescoping, $b = -4.94$, but this date underestimation effect was not statistically reliable. As with our earlier studies, these data suggest that telescoping due to memory clarity occurs infrequently, at best, and its impact on overall dating accuracy is minimal.

Modulo 7 Error

As we have argued so far, event dating often involves cues that yield partial temporal information. The color of the leaves on the trees, the sport one is watching on television, or the fact that an event happened in a psychology classroom may all to a greater or lesser extent help narrow the range of possible event dates. Perhaps one of the more typical types of temporal information available is within-week time. For example, sometimes people may remember or reconstruct the exact day of the week on which an event occurred. At other times, they may be only able to recollect or reconstruct that an event occurred sometime during the workweek.

Evidence for such processes was first provided by Skowronski et al. (1991), who observed that error frequency tended to peak at every seven days of error magnitude, that is, error frequencies were highest at error magnitudes of 0, 7, 14, 21, 28, and so on days of error. Skowronski et al. (1991) speculated that this pattern was produced by subjects' ability to remember or reconstruct the day of the week on which an event occurred. Thus, dating errors tended to be off by multiples of seven days (right day, wrong week).

Thompson et al. (1993) extended this logic further, attempting to account for the systematic error pattern that occurred *between* the 7-day peaks. To account for this systematicity, Thompson et al. (1993) suggested that subjects use other types of within-week information to aid in date estimation. Instead of knowing only the exact day of the week on which an event occurred, subjects might instead remember that an event occurred sometime in midweek (Tuesday through Thursday), during the workweek (Monday through Friday), or on the weekend (Saturday or Sunday).

Investigation of these within-week error patterns is facilitated using base 7 arithmetic. Unlike base 10 arithmetic, in which the numeral cycle repeats after every 10 increments, in base 7 arithmetic the cycle repeats after only 7 increments. Therefore, in base 7, counting would proceed as follows: 0, 1, 2, 3, 4, 5, 6, 10, 11, 12, 13, 14, 15, 16, 20, 21, and so forth. For reasons that shall become apparent shortly, we are only interested in the *remainder* values that occur when a dating error is divided by 7. For example, error magnitudes of 1 day, 8 days, 15 days, and so on are assigned the modulo 7 error value of 1; dating errors of 2 days, 9 days, 16 days, and so on are assigned the modulo 7 error value of 2.

Each type of within-week information implicates a different pattern of modulo 7 values. For example, assume that a person knows that an event occurred on a weekend but is unsure if it happened Saturday or Sunday. By guessing randomly, the person will be correct (mod 7 error value of 0) 50% of the time. The remaining estimates will be split evenly between a day long (mod 7 error value of 1) and a day short (mod 7 error value of 6). Similar arguments can be developed for workweek and midweek estimates. A first approximation of the overall modulo 7 error pattern is obtained by assuming that the four types of within-week information are

Table 7.3 Mod 7 Error Percentages for Estimated Dates by Partial Information Type and Overall

| | Error (Mod 7) | | | | | | |
	0	1	2	3	4	5	6
Exact Day of Week	100	0	0	0	0	0	0
Weekend	50	25	0	0	0	0	0
Midweek	33	22	11	0	0	11	22
Weekday	20	16	12	12	12	12	16
Overall	50.8	15.8	5.8	3	3	5.8	15.8

used equally often (but see Larsen & Thompson, 1993). The error probabilities at each remainder value are then averaged across the four information types, yielding an overall error pattern for estimated dates. As indicated by Table 7.3, this overall pattern is asymmetric and curvilinear: The highest proportion of errors are calculated to occur at 0 mod 7, the second highest proportion at 1 mod 7 and 6 mod 7, the third highest proportion at 2 mod 7 and 5 mod 7, and the lowest proportion at 3 mod 7 and 4 mod 7.

As illustrated in Figure 7.4, the predicted pattern closely resembles the actual pattern observed in this study. This result replicates earlier research (Larsen & Thompson, 1993; Skowronski et al., 1991; Thompson et al., 1993); however, the long time frame used in this study affords the opportunity to investigate whether this pattern was maintained across time. We calculated the modulo 7 error for each subject's most recent 100 events, for their middling 100 events, and for their oldest 100 events. The frequencies for each mod 7 error value within each event block are plotted in Figure 7.5. Note that as events become older, there is a relatively large reduction in the proportion of 0 mod 7 errors and an increase in the proportion of other error values. However, the overall curvilinear, asymmetric pattern of mod 7 dating errors is clearly maintained across all retention intervals.

Larsen and Thompson (1993) argue that the relative stability of this pattern over time derives from people bringing their real-world knowledge into play when dating events. For example, many people work on a regular schedule. If an event took place at work, a reasonable guess can be made about the days of the week on which the event occurred. If we assume that this real-world knowledge is relatively impervious to time, then the pattern of mod 7 dating errors observed should remain, even with increasing retention intervals.

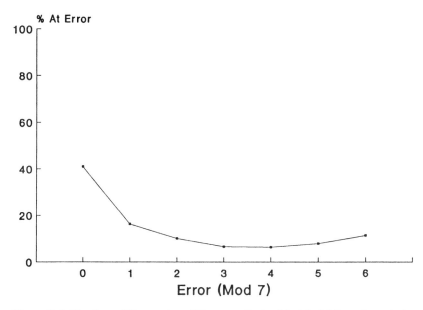

Figure 7.4. The Overall Proportion of Events at Each of the Mod 7 Error Remainder Values

By comparison, people are likely to rapidly lose the specific memory cues that allow reasonably precise dating to occur. Certainly, looking at the exact date known data in Table 7.2 suggests that subjects seem to perceive this relationship themselves. The substantial decrease in the proportion of 0 mod 7 events that occurs as one moves from recent events to events of middling age likely reflects the loss of temporally specific memory cues. Note that this decrease is not repeated, however, in the transition from middle-aged to older events, suggesting that a substantial portion of the errors at 0 mod 7 result from the world and life knowledge that persists across time.

Similar conclusions come from inspection of the mod 7 data for each individual subject. Each subject's data resembled the aggregated pattern, especially in the longer retention intervals. For example, Figure 7.6 presents the data for the two subjects with the largest difference in their dating patterns. The difference between these two subjects emerges primarily in the recent retention interval—Subject A's curve is much steeper than Subject B's, and in fact, Subject A has no errors at some of the mod 7 values. However, in the intermediate and older retention intervals, although

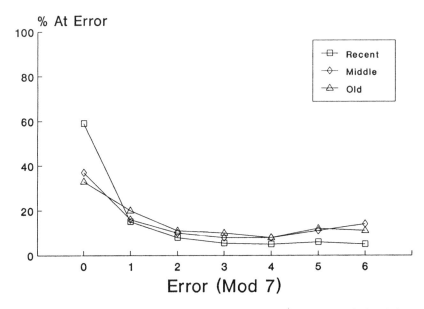

Figure 7.5. The Proportion of Events at Each of the Mod 7 Error Remainder Values for Each Subject's Most Recent 100 Events, for Middling 100 Events, and Oldest 100 Events

Subject A's error curve still is a bit steeper than Subject B's, the curves were quite similar. This suggests that Subject A was able to rely more strongly on temporally specific dating cues than Subject B, particularly in the most recent retention interval. However, at longer intervals, Subject A's recall of temporally specific information likely dissipated, forcing her to rely on more general types of available temporal information, thus producing an error curve resembling Subject B's. Both the individual and aggregate data therefore implicate the use of within-week information to date events. Further, these data suggest that within-week information sometimes comes from event-specific memories, but at other times from general world and personal knowledge.

It is possible that our subjects' use of this type of information was an artifact of our procedure. Subjects were shown a calendar on which the days of the week were listed. However, there is reason to believe that this within-week information would be used regardless of the test format. Huttenlocher, Hedges, and Prohaska (1992) proposed that subjects' temporal estimates follow a "5 + 2" cycle—essentially corresponding to a

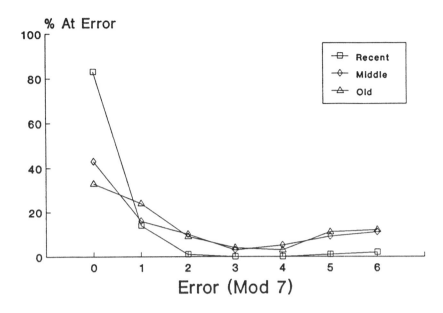

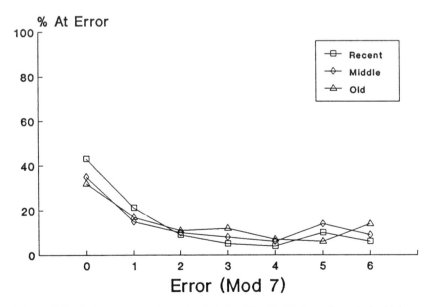

Figure 7.6. The Proportion of Events at Each of the Mod 7 Error Remainder Values for Subject A's (Top) and Subject B's (Bottom) Most Recent 100 Events, Middling 100 Events, and Oldest 100 Events

discrimination between a weekday and a weekend event. A test of this idea provided some support. This outcome is noteworthy, for the temporal estimation task used by Huttenlocher et al. (1992) was different from ours. In contrast to our "Here is a calendar, what is the exact date?" task, Huttenlocher et al. (1992) did not provide subjects with a calendar, and instead asked subjects "How old is the event?" That evidence for within-week dating emerges even in the absence of an overt calendar strongly suggests that our dating task does not introduce this bias into the dates provided by subjects.

Even if it did, our data would remain valid for those real-world cases in which a calendar accompanied a date estimation. Such circumstances perhaps occur with some regularity in legal proceedings. For example, the oft-discussed testimony of John Dean in the Watergate hearings hinged on the question "What did Nixon know, and when did he know it?" To come up with the exact dates that he used in his testimony, along with other aids (e.g., newspaper accounts), Dean probably used a calendar (and a diary) to assist his date reconstruction efforts. Hence, one would suspect that Dean's reconstructions for the dates of some events would be subject to the same sort of within-week biases observed in this chapter.

Summary and Implications

It is now clear that exact event dates are recalled with relative rarity. More frequently, people use information stored in memory to concoct an estimate of an event's date. The data in this chapter document patterns of accuracy and error in dating performance over the long term and suggest various memory mechanisms that might be responsible for these patterns.

Often, the patterns of accuracy and error that are observed emerge from the temporal cyclicity in the world. Holidays and anniversaries tend to occur on or near specific dates, so that if an event is linked to a holiday, a reasonably accurate estimate can be made. Similarly, our lives have within-week regularities that allow us to guess the day of the week on which an event may have occurred. Event recall is also related to dating accuracy. For example, particular details (leaf color, weather, activities) imply different times of the year, helping to narrow the range of possible event dates. Sometimes, however, event date estimates can be influenced by factors transcending schematic cyclicity. Dating performance generally declines as retention intervals increase. Memory for temporal boundaries produces telescoping and time expansion.

One of the implications of the fact that people use differing sources of information to construct event dates is that the event dates that people provide should show elements of both temporal instability and temporal durability. Both of these characteristics were observed in the present research. Memory for event-specific details (including both episodic details and specific temporal details) certainly declines over time, and the decrease in exact dating frequency and the increase in dating error magnitude that we observed in our research likely reflects this decline.

However, it should also be emphasized that some of the error patterns that emerged in the data showed considerable evidence of stability across retention interval. For example, the pattern of 0 mod 7 errors seemed to stabilize at longer retention intervals. Such stability suggests that a relatively enduring memory source is involved in the construction of at least some event dates. In the case of 0 mod 7 errors, we have suggested that the source of this consistency is an individual's real-world knowledge about the kinds of events that tend to occur on specific days. Individuals, after all, are repeatedly exposed to recurring patterns in their lives and overlearn these so that they are readily available for long periods of time. In a real sense, people become experts on the patterns of their lives. Thus, such real-world knowledge is relatively durable and could easily account for the stabilization of the 0 mod 7 error pattern across time. The durability of day-of-week information is completely consistent with the durability found in expert performance that is reported throughout this book.

In considering the evidence for these various types of memory and their impact on event dating, one should remember that the data reported in the present chapter are still only observational in nature. The observations are certainly valid, but the inferences allowed by those observations are not as strong as one would like. This is especially true with regard to the memory systems involved in event dating and the independent impact of those memory systems on event dating. Nonetheless, we believe that our data have begun to lay a solid foundation for understanding event-dating performance and for suggesting some of the memory-based mechanisms underlying that performance. This foundation gives future researchers an idea of the kinds of effects that characterize event-dating performance and of the kinds of memory cues that may be related to those effects.

Notes

1. Unless noted otherwise, all regression analyses reported in this chapter are pooled within-subject regressions, a technique that bears some similarity to a repeated-measures

ANOVA. As in a repeated-measures ANOVA, this analysis allows the use of repeated measures from the same subject. In a pooled within-subjects regression, the effects reported for the predictors of interest are controlled for subjects. In addition, all bs that we report are raw score slopes (e.g., not standardized). These bs reflect the impact of an independent variable on the dependent variable controlling for all other variables entered into the model. For further information, see Cohen and Cohen (1983).

2. All valid event date estimates are used in the regression analyses. However, occasionally subjects neglected a rating or listed an invalid rating. Consequently, the error degrees of freedom vary slightly across analyses.

References

Betz, A. L., & Skowronski, J. J. (1993a). *Social memory in everyday life: II. Event rehearsal and event involvement in the recall of self-events and other-events.* Unpublished manuscript.

Betz, A. L., & Skowronski, J. J. (1993b). *Temporal order judgments of personal life experiences in naturalistic settings.* Paper presented at the fifth annual meeting of the American Psychological Society, Chicago.

Bradburn, N. M., Rips, L. J., & Shevell, S. K. (1987). Answering autobiographical questions: The impact of memory and inference on surveys. *Science, 236,* 151-167.

Cohen, J., & Cohen, P. (1983). *Applied multiple regression/correlation analysis for the behavioral sciences* (2nd ed.). Hillsdale, NJ: Lawrence Erlbaum.

Huttenlocher, J., Hedges, L., & Bradburn, N. (1990). Reports of elapsed time: Bounding and rounding processes in estimation. *Journal of Experimental Psychology: Learning, Memory, and Cognition, 16,* 196-213.

Huttenlocher, J., Hedges, L., & Prohaska, V. (1988). Hierarchical organization in ordered domains: Estimating the dates of events. *Psychological Review, 95,* 471-484.

Huttenlocher, J., Hedges, L., & Prohaska, V. (1992). Memory for day of the week: A 5 + 2 day cycle. *Journal of Experimental Psychology: General, 121,* 313-325.

Larsen, S. F. (1988). Remembering reported events: Memory for news in ecological perspective. In M. M. Gruneberg, P. E. Morris, & R. N. Sykes (Eds.), *Practical aspects of memory: Current research and issues* (Vol. 1, pp. 440-445). New York: John Wiley.

Larsen, S. F. (1992). Personal context in autobiographical and narrative memories. In M. A. Conway, D. C. Rubin, W. Wagenaar, & H. Spinnler (Eds.), *Theoretical perspectives on autobiographical memory* (pp. 53-71). Amsterdam: Kluwer.

Larsen, S. F., & Thompson, C. P. (1993). *Modeling day-of-week memory.* Unpublished manuscript.

Linton, M. (1975). Memory for real-world events. In D. A. Norman & D. E. Rumelhart (Eds.), *Explorations in cognition* (pp. 376-404). San Francisco: Freeman.

Rubin, D. C., & Baddeley, A. D. (1989). Telescoping is not time compression: A model of the dating of autobiographical events. *Memory & Cognition, 17,* 653-661.

Skowronski, J. J., Betz, A. L., Thompson, C. P., & Shannon, L. (1991). Social memory in everyday life: Recall of self-events and other events. *Journal of Personality and Social Psychology, 60,* 831-843.

Skowronski, J. J., Betz, A. L., Thompson, C. P., Walker, W. R., & Shannon, L. (1994). The impact of differing memory domains on event dating processes in self and proxy reports. In S. Sudman & N. Schwarz (Eds.), *Autobiographical memory and the validity of retrospective reports* (pp. 217-234). New York: Springer-Verlag.

Skowronski, J. J., & Thompson, C. P. (1990). Reconstructing the dates of personal events: Gender differences in accuracy. *Applied Cognitive Psychology, 4,* 371-381.

Thompson, C. P. (1982). Memory for unique personal events: The roommate study. *Memory & Cognition, 10,* 324-332.

Thompson, C. P. (1985a). Memory for unique personal events: Some effects of the self-schema. *Human Learning, 4,* 267-280.

Thompson, C. P. (1985b). Memory for unique personal events: The effects of pleasantness. *Motivation and Emotion, 9,* 277-289.

Thompson, C. P., Skowronski, J. J., & Lee, D. J. (1988a). Reconstructing the date of a personal event. In M. M. Gruneberg, P. E. Morris, & R. N. Sykes (Eds.), *Practical aspects of memory: Current research and issues* (Vol. 1, pp. 241-246). New York: John Wiley.

Thompson, C. P., Skowronski, J. J., & Lee, D. J. (1988b). Telescoping in dating naturally occurring events. *Memory & Cognition, 16,* 461-468.

Thompson, C. P., Skowronski, J. J., & Betz, A. L. (1993). The use of partial temporal information in dating personal events. *Memory & Cognition, 21,* 352-360.

8 Training and Retention of the Classic Stroop Task

Specificity of Practice Effects

DEBORAH M. CLAWSON

CHERI L. KING

ALICE F. HEALY

K. ANDERS ERICSSON

Effects of practice on the classic Stroop color-word task were explored using two different practice tasks, the Stroop task itself and simple color naming. Stroop practice, but not color-naming practice, led to a pattern of improvement from pretest to posttest pointing to an advantage for practiced stimuli over unpracticed stimuli on both Stroop and color-naming tests but a disadvantage for practiced stimuli on word reading and "reverse Stroop" tests. The advantage for practiced stimuli was maintained on versions of the Stroop test that used orthographic manipulations of the stimuli, and it persisted across a 1-month delay. Thus, practice effects may be specific to colors, to semantic or phonetic aspects of the words, or to a combination of these two, but probably not to word form.

O ne of the most studied phenomena of the last two decades is the Stroop effect (MacLeod, 1992), the finding that subjects show interference

AUTHORS' NOTE: This research was supported in part by Army Research Institute Contract MDA903-90-K-0066. We are grateful to Nancy Befort for transcribing the protocol data, to Brooke E. Schefrin for conducting the color vision tests, to William R. Marmie for help designing the experiment, to Robert J. Crutcher for assistance designing the verbal protocol instructions, and to Gary H. McClelland and Charles M. Judd for statistical advice. An earlier report of this experiment was given by Clawson, King, Healy, and Ericsson (1993) at the 15th Annual Conference of the Cognitive Science Society.

when naming the ink color of an incongruous color word. Its popularity as a research task is due both to its implications for automatic processing (e.g., Anderson, 1992) and its use in neuropsychological testing (e.g., Connor, Franzen, & Sharp, 1988). Despite the large and increasing body of research on the Stroop effect (see Dyer, 1973; Jensen & Rohwer, 1966; MacLeod, 1991), the present study is the first to examine the extent to which practice, either on the color-word interference task or on a simple color-naming task, is specific to the particular colors used during training.

In his recent comprehensive review of the literature on the Stroop effect, MacLeod (1991) remarked, "Practice may turn out to be one of the most effective manipulations for disentangling theories of the Stroop effect" (p. 182). Stroop (1935) himself trained subjects for 8 days on the color-word interference task and found considerable improvement across days, with the most striking improvement from the first to the second day of training. Even before Stroop, a study by Brown (1915) examined the effects of practice on color naming, although that study did not include incongruous color words and hence did not examine color-word interference.

The two most prominent sets of theories explaining the Stroop effect are relative speed of processing theories and automaticity theories (see MacLeod, 1991, for a thorough discussion of theoretical accounts of the Stroop effect). The relative speed of processing explanation envisions Stroop processing as similar to a horse race: Word reading and color naming compete, with word reading as the faster process. The resulting response competition causes interference. According to automaticity theories, the interference is caused not by a difference in processing speed but rather by a difference in automaticity between word reading and color naming. Word reading, being more automatic, requires less attention and may be irresistible. According to these theories, the more automatic process, word reading, interferes with the less automatic color naming. Both the automaticity theory of the Stroop effect and the horse race theory predict that training on simple color naming, by increasing either the speed of color naming or its degree of automaticity, should improve Stroop performance.

The present study is the first to examine the effects of simple color-naming practice alone on color-word interference (other investigators, e.g., Connor et al., 1988, examined the effects of combined practice on all three Stroop-related tasks: color naming, word reading, and Stroop). Further, as mentioned earlier, the present study is the first to examine the extent to which practice either on the color-word interference task or on the simple color-naming task is specific to the particular colors used during training.

A recent study by Musen and Squire (1993) investigated specificity of training in the classic Stroop task. Subjects (who included amnesic patients as well as normal controls) practiced the Stroop task on a set of seven stimuli. Each of seven different color words was shown six times in one of seven different incongruent colors. After this practice, subjects were tested on a transfer set of stimuli that included the same colors and words in different incongruous combinations. Response latencies increased for the transfer set relative to the original set. These results suggested that subjects implicitly learned the color-word combinations that were used during practice.

Specificity of training has also been explored in nonstandard versions of the Stroop task. For example, in a digit-counting task, Reisberg, Baron, and Kemler (1980) trained subjects to ignore a pair of digits (e.g., 2 and 4) and found that this training did not transfer perfectly to ignoring other digits (e.g., the digits 1 and 3), nor did it transfer to ignoring homophonic words (e.g., *to* and *for*). Some transfer was obtained, however, to the task of ignoring the digits printed as words (e.g., *two* and *four*).

Ménard-Buteau and Cavanagh (1984) used a Stroop task with incongruously colored objects. Subjects practiced naming the ink color of a word representing an incongruously colored object (e.g., the word *carrot* printed in green ink). They found that this training did not transfer to a version of their task with drawings of the objects rather than words.

To explore the effects of practice on the Stroop phenomenon, the present study provided subjects with 12 sessions of practice either on the Stroop task itself or on simple color naming; subjects in a control condition received no training. The subjects were tested in a pretest previous to training as well as in a posttest after training and in a retention test after a month-long delay. Each test session included a set of tests related to Stroop interference: one test each on word reading and on simple color naming plus a Stroop test and a test with Stroop stimuli but requiring word-reading responses (reverse Stroop). Additional orthographic manipulation tests consisted of a Stroop test in which the letters of the color words were bracketed by asterisks and one in which the letters were all uppercase (in contrast to the lowercase letters used in the other tests). These orthographic manipulations provided an indication of specificity to the word form. Another measure of specificity was provided by the use of two different color sets. Although the trained subjects were presented with only one color set during their practice, with the set counterbalanced across subjects, all subjects were tested on both color sets.

It was predicted that specificity of training effects would lead to less improvement from pretest to posttest on the orthographic manipulations than on the normal Stroop test and to less improvement on the untrained color set than on the trained set. It was further predicted that practice on simple color naming would improve Stroop performance. On the basis of our previous studies showing extremely good retention of procedural skills (Healy et al., 1992), we also predicted relatively little forgetting across the 1-month delay interval. Of greatest interest is whether any specificity effects persist across this long retention interval.

Method

Subjects

Six female students from the University of Colorado participated as subjects for payment at the rate of $5 per hour. Subjects were assigned to training condition and training color set on the basis of their time of arrival for testing according to a fixed rotation. All subjects demonstrated normal color vision.

Design

The experiment included a standardized paper test (Golden, 1978) followed by 15 successive computer tests. The 15 computer tests included 12 that were the focus of this investigation. The remaining 3 tests were baseline word-reading measures for words and nonwords printed in white on black. The 12 focal tests were divided into two categories, which partly overlapped: (a) 8 color interference assessment measures and (b) 6 orthographic color interference measures.

A mixed factorial design was employed for the 8 color interference assessment measures, with one between-subjects factor, training condition (control, patches training, Stroop training), and three within-subjects factors, test time (pretest, posttest, retention test), color set (trained, untrained), and test type. The four test types were (a) reading color words in white on black, (b) color-patch naming, (c) naming colors of incongruous words (Stroop), and (d) reading incongruous color words (reverse Stroop).

A second mixed factorial design was employed for the six orthographic color interference measures, with one between-subjects factor, training condition, and three within-subjects factors, test time, color set, and orthographic test type (standard, asterisks, uppercase).

Apparatus

A DTK Data-1000 personal computer with a Zenith Data Systems color monitor was employed for training and for the computer tests. A MEL (Schneider, 1988) Version 5.0 voice key-button box and an Electret microphone were used for measuring the subjects' verbal response latencies and for recording the experimenter's indications of response accuracy.

Materials

The test materials were identical for the pretest, posttest, and retention test. They consisted of the standardized paper test and 15 computer tests.

Standardized Paper Test

The standardized paper test consisted of three pages that were shown in a fixed sequence: black-and-white color-word reading, colored-XXXX naming, and naming colors of incongruous color words (i.e., Stroop). Each page included 100 items arranged in five columns of 20 items each. The colors used were red, green, and blue.

Computer Tests

Each computer test consisted of 24 trials, which occurred in a pseudorandom order with the constraint that the stimuli possible for a given test were used equally often in each block of 6 trials.

The color stimuli from Set 1 consisted of pink, blue, and orange. The colors from Set 2 consisted of purple, green, and red. One of the two subjects in each condition was trained on Set 1, and the other was trained on Set 2. For all subjects tests on the trained set always preceded the corresponding tests on the untrained set.

The 12 color interference and orthographic color interference assessment tests occurred in a fixed sequence, with each test type presented first with the words and colors from the subjects' trained set, then with the words and colors from the untrained set:

Tests 1 and 2 (*color patches*): naming colors (i.e., subjects named the colors of patches).

Tests 3 and 4 (*Stroop*): naming colors of incongruous color words (i.e., subjects named the colors of words denoting incongruent colors; the color of a given word was different from the one denoted by the word itself).

Tests 5 and 6 (*Stroop asterisks*): naming colors of incongruous color words with asterisks surrounding each letter (e.g., the word *blue,* displayed as *b*l*u*e* in pink letters).

Tests 7 and 8 (*Stroop uppercase*): naming colors of incongruous color words printed in all capital letters (e.g., the word *blue,* displayed as BLUE in pink letters).

Tests 9 and 10 (*black-and-white word-reading colors*): reading color words (i.e., subjects read color words that were displayed on the screen in white letters on a black background).

Tests 11 and 12 (*reverse Stroop*): reading incongruous color words (i.e., subjects read color words that were displayed in an incongruent color).

Three baseline word-reading measures occurred between Tests 10 and 11. There was a no-training control and two training conditions, patches and Stroop, corresponding to Tests 1 and 3, respectively. There were 240 trials in each training session, divided into 10 blocks of 24 trials. As in the test, the stimuli occurred in a pseudorandom order with the constraint that the possible stimuli were used equally often in each subblock of six trials. Four versions of the training stimulus sequence were constructed, which differed only in the order of the stimuli within a given subblock of six trials. The four versions were shown to all subjects in a fixed rotation, with every version shown once in each successive set of four sessions.

Procedure

Before any testing, subjects were assigned to training condition and training color set, with one subject in each combination of condition and set. Before the first experimental session of testing, subjects were given a standardized color vision test (Farnsworth Panel D-15 test, and F-2 plate; National Research Council, 1981) in a room with controlled lighting. This testing took approximately 5 minutes. In the first experimental session, a pretest was administered consisting of the standardized paper test (which took 10 minutes) and the 15 computer tests (which took approximately 30 minutes). On each of the following 12 experimental sessions (i.e., Sessions 2-13), subjects were given training that lasted approximately 30 minutes. At the next session (i.e., Session 14), subjects were given the posttest, which was identical to the pretest except that the standardized paper test was administered after (instead of before) the 15 computer tests. The retention session (i.e., Session 15), which occurred 28 days later, was identical to Session 14. The acquisition sessions (the first 14 sessions) occurred on successive weekdays (i.e., Monday-Friday, with no testing on the weekend and one day off due to snow closure).

Standardized Paper Test

We used the standard instructions for individualized administration included with the test. Subjects were told to read down each column progressing through the columns from left to right, beginning again at the top of the first column if they finished all the columns. Subjects were told that if they made any incorrect response, they were to correct the error and continue without stopping. Each subject was timed for 45 seconds for each of the three test pages. They were told when to begin each page by the experimenter's saying, "Then begin." At the end of 45 seconds, the experimenter said "Stop, circle the item you are on. If you finished the entire page and began again, put a one by your circle." For the first task, subjects were told to read the color words red, green, and blue, which were printed in black ink. For the second task, they were told to name the color of colored XXXXs, which were printed in red, green, or blue ink. For the third task, they were told to name the ink color of the words. These words were incongruent color words also from the set red, green, and blue. For each of the three tasks, subjects were told to proceed as quickly as they could.

Computer Tests

All instructions and trials were self-paced. To progress from a given screen of instructions to the first trial, subjects had to press the "c" (i.e., "continue") key. Subjects then progressed from one trial to the next by pressing the space bar.

Immediately preceding the set of computer tests, subjects were asked to read aloud 20 numbers shown one at a time on the screen, and they were given feedback informing them whether their verbal response was loud enough for the voice key to register. If the response was not sufficiently loud, the following warning message was displayed: "Sorry, I could not hear you. Please answer more loudly next time."

Throughout all test trials, subjects were given the warning message whenever their vocal response was not registered by the voice key (but the experimenter's response was registered by the button box). Any response not registered by the voice key was discarded from the data analyses.

The instructions for each computer test were shown on the computer screen. For each test the instructions described the stimuli to be presented and the expected response. All instructions directed subjects to respond as accurately and as quickly as possible. For the tests involving incongruous color words, the instructions included a single example from the appropriate set. For instance, for the Stroop trained test with Set 1 stimuli, subjects were given the following instructions: "In the next task I'll show you a color word printed in pink, orange, or blue. For example, I might show you the word 'blue' but written in orange letters. Your job is to say the color of the letters. Don't read the word out loud; just say the color of the letters." Below these instructions, subjects saw the word *blue* printed in orange letters. Below that example, the instructions continued as follows: "Here you would say 'orange.' If you have any questions, please ask the experimenter now. As always, please be as correct and as fast as you can. PRESS THE c TO CONTINUE."

The procedure on a given test trial was as follows: First, subjects viewed a screen with the instructions: "PRESS THE SPACE BAR TO CONTINUE." When the subject pressed the space bar, the screen became blank for 300 ms. Next the stimulus appeared on the screen, and the subject responded. The experimenter, who sat behind the subject, compared the subject's responses to a list of the correct answers and entered a response on the button box, indicating the accuracy (correct or incorrect) of the subject's vocal response. The experimenter's response prompted the computer to replace the stimulus with the instruction: "PRESS THE SPACE BAR TO CONTINUE."

Training

Each training session started with the number-reading warm-up task used for the purpose of voice volume feedback, as described above. The training procedure was the same as the procedure used for the computer tests except that feedback was provided. Immediately after each trial, accuracy and reaction time feedback were displayed on the screen for correct responses, as in the following example: "CORRECT; reaction time = .76 seconds." For incorrect responses, only the word "INCORRECT" was displayed. Both displays lasted for 1,600 ms. In addition, a summary feedback of the number of correct responses and the average correct reaction time was shown for 2,000 ms at the end of every block of 24 trials, as in the following example: "You got 23 of the last 24 correct. Your average correct reaction time was .73 seconds."

Retrospective verbal protocols were collected during each of the first 12 and last 12 trials of each training session; protocols were not collected, however, on any of those responses that did not trigger the voice key. At the beginning of the first training session, subjects were given instructions and training in how to give verbal reports, following the procedures recommended by Ericsson and Simon (1984). Arithmetic problems were used as examples and for practice in giving both think-aloud and retrospective reports. To confirm that subjects could generalize the reporting procedures from the arithmetic domain to a new domain, a final practice question was asked that concerned the number of windows found in a house the subject had lived in. At the beginning of each following training session, the experimenter reviewed the instructions on verbal protocols before the commencement of training. During the protocol trials, after the subject responded but before the subject received feedback, the prompt "Retrospective report" was displayed on the screen.

Results

Standardized Paper Test

Table 8.1 presents the results of the standardized paper test in terms of number of items completed (from the page of 100 items) within 45 s as a function of test time (pretest, posttest, retention test) and test page (black-and-white color-word reading, colored-XXXX naming, and Stroop). It should be noted that the scores on the Stroop page at posttest and at retention test were above the "normal limits" of performance (2.0 and 1.6 standard deviations above the mean, respectively) according to the test manual's normative scale. All of the other scores were within normal limits. Table 8.1 does not include a breakdown by training condition, because we found no significant main effect or interactions involving that factor in a mixed analysis of variance that also included the within-subjects factors of test time and test page.

There was overall improvement from the pretest ($M = 80.4$ items completed) to the posttest ($M = 85.2$) with no loss from the posttest to the retention test one month later ($M = 86.1$), $F(2, 6) = 6.17$, $MS_e = 27.11$, $p < .05$. As expected from previous research, performance was best on the black-and-white color-word reading test ($M = 108.3$) and was better on the colored-XXXX naming test ($M = 83.8$) than on the Stroop test ($M = 59.7$), $F(2, 6) = 98.54$, $MS_e = 107.67$, $p < .001$. The change across test times was biggest for the Stroop test and absent for the word-reading test; this interaction of test time and test page was significant, $F(4, 12) = 3.35$, $MS_e = 22.78$, $p < .05$. Thus, the degree of improvement seems to be related to the degree of subjects' prior familiarity with the test: Word reading is a

Table 8.1 Number of Items Completed on the Standardized Paper Test as a Function of Test Time and Test Page

Test page	Pretest	Posttest	Retention
Word reading	108.5	106.5	109.8
Colored XXXX	79.7	84.3	87.3
Stroop	53.2	64.8	61.2

common activity, color naming is less common, and the Stroop task is rarely encountered outside the laboratory. The improvement must be due to the experience with the tests themselves rather than to training, because no differences were found for subjects in the three training conditions. The absence of a training effect could be due either to the use of different colors in the paper test than in training or to the use of different procedures in the two cases or to both. Note that by far the largest improvement in training found by Stroop (1935) was between the first and the second sessions of Stroop practice. Because performing a session of practice in Stroop's experiment was comparable to completing our standardized paper test, it is not surprising that we found considerable improvement from the pretest to the posttest even for the control group of subjects.

Computer Tests

Error rates were very low throughout testing. The combined proportion of trials on which either the voice key did not register a response or the response was an error was lower than .02 overall for both the color interference assessment measures and the orthographic color interference measures. Therefore, in the following discussion, performance is reported only in terms of reaction time for correct responses.

Comparing Pretests and Posttests

Color Interference Assessment Measures. Table 8.2 presents log (to the base 10) correct reaction times as a function of training condition (patches training, Stroop training, control), test type (color patches, Stroop, word reading, reverse Stroop), test time, and color set (trained, untrained). The effects of training are evident by comparing the results for the pretest and posttest. A mixed analysis of variance was conducted on these acquisition results with the between-subjects factor of condition and the within-subjects factors of test time (pretest and posttest only), test type, and color set.

Table 8.2 Reaction Time (log ms) as a Function of Training Condition, Test Type, and Test Time for the Trained (Tr) and Untrained (Untr) Color Sets

	Pretest		Posttest		Retention	
Condition and Test	Tr	Untr	Tr	Untr	Tr	Untr
Patches training						
Color patches	2.768	2.743	2.667	2.673	2.674	2.666
Stroop	2.825	2.831	2.764	2.779	2.745	2.749
Word reading	2.666	2.633	2.604	2.596	2.619	2.596
Reverse Stroop	2.721	2.701	2.656	2.643	2.636	2.652
Stroop training						
Color patches	2.804	2.811	2.701	2.732	2.688	2.740
Stroop	2.863	2.880	2.738	2.797	2.777	2.829
Word reading	2.704	2.674	2.685	2.649	2.697	2.667
Reverse Stroop	2.794	2.763	2.734	2.694	2.742	2.720
Control (no training)						
Color patches	2.768	2.731	2.677	2.678	2.693	2.688
Stroop	2.901	2.833	2.815	2.794	2.821	2.783
Word reading	2.673	2.652	2.670	2.666	2.677	2.669
Reverse Stroop	2.695	2.681	2.666	2.680	2.700	2.662

The effectiveness of training was evinced by faster overall reaction times on the posttest ($M = 2.698$ log ms, antilog $M = 499$ ms) than on the pretest ($M = 2.755$ log ms, antilog $M = 569$ ms), $F(1, 3) = 16.37$, $MS_e = .0047$, $p < .05$. As in previous research (see MacLeod, 1991), reaction times were faster for the test types involving word reading than those involving color naming and were slower for the test types involving incongruous stimuli than for those that did not; the main effect of test type was significant, $F(3, 9) = 27.56$, $MS_e = .0041$, $p < .001$. Specifically, the test types in order of fastest to slowest were word reading ($M = 2.656$ log ms, antilog $M = 453$ ms), reverse Stroop ($M = 2.702$ log ms, antilog $M = 504$ ms), color patches ($M = 2.729$ log ms, antilog $M = 536$ ms), and Stroop ($M = 2.818$ log ms, antilog $M = 658$ ms). Importantly, training differentially affected the four test types; there was a significant interaction of test time and test type, $F(3, 9) = 6.44$, $MS_e = .0007$, $p < .05$. Training led to decreased reaction times from the pretest to the posttest more for color patches (pretest $M = 2.771$ log ms, antilog $M = 590$ ms; posttest $M = 2.688$ log ms, antilog $M = 488$ ms) and for Stroop (pretest $M = 2.856$ log ms, antilog $M = 718$ ms; posttest $M = 2.781$ log ms, antilog $M = 604$ ms) than for reverse Stroop (pretest $M = 2.726$ log ms, antilog $M = 532$ ms; posttest $M = 2.679$ log ms, antilog $M = 478$ ms) and word reading (pretest $M =$

Table 8.3 Reaction Time (log ms) as a Function of Training Condition, Orthographic Test Type, and Test Time for the Trained (Tr) and Untrained (Untr) Color Sets

Condition and Test	Pretest		Posttest		Retention	
	Tr	*Untr*	*Tr*	*Untr*	*Tr*	*Untr*
Patches training						
Standard	2.825	2.831	2.764	2.779	2.745	2.749
Asterisks	2.807	2.829	2.762	2.752	2.742	2.770
Uppercase	2.809	2.815	2.774	2.749	2.788	2.791
Stroop training						
Standard	2.863	2.880	2.738	2.797	2.777	2.829
Asterisks	2.885	2.904	2.787	2.820	2.807	2.837
Uppercase	2.881	2.872	2.762	2.806	2.803	2.848
Control (no training)						
Standard	2.901	2.833	2.815	2.794	2.821	2.783
Asterisks	2.817	2.840	2.803	2.781	2.808	2.823
Uppercase	2.852	2.818	2.795	2.792	2.810	2.783

2.667 log ms, antilog $M = 465$ ms; posttest $M = 2.645$ log ms, antilog $M = 442$ ms). This finding of a larger effect of training on test types involving color naming than on those involving word reading can be explained either by the fact that training involved color naming rather than word reading or by the fact that reaction times on the word-reading test (and to a lesser extent on the reverse Stroop test) were closer to the floor initially. Note that in his classic study, Stroop (1935) found that training in the Stroop task actually led to slower reaction times in a posttest than in a pretest (i.e., interference) on the reverse Stroop task. Also note that reaction times for the color patches posttest approached those for the word-reading pretest for all three training groups. Thus, the training given to subjects was sufficient for them to make color-naming responses that were almost as rapid as were their word-reading responses before training.

The specificity of training is reflected by a significant interaction of test time and color set, $F(1, 3) = 38.51$, $MS_e = .0001$, $p < .05$. Reaction times decreased from the pretest to the posttest more for the trained set (pretest $M = 2.765$ log ms, antilog $M = 582$ ms; posttest $M = 2.698$ log ms, antilog $M = 499$ ms) than for the untrained set (pretest $M = 2.744$ log ms, antilog $M = 555$ ms; posttest $M = 2.698$ log ms, antilog $M = 499$ ms).

Orthographic Color Interference Measures. Table 8.3 presents log correct reaction times as a function of training condition (patches training, Stroop training, control), test time, orthographic test type (standard, asterisks, uppercase), and color set (trained, untrained). Again, the effects of training are evident by comparing the results for the pretest and posttest. A mixed analysis of variance was conducted on these acquisition results with the between-subjects factor of condition and the within-subjects factors of test time (pretest and posttest only), orthographic test type, and color set.

There was no effect of orthographic test type, and that factor did not enter into any significant interactions. However, as in the analysis of the color interference assessment measures, there was a significant speedup from the pretest (M = 2.848 log ms, antilog M = 705 ms) to the posttest (M = 2.782 log ms, antilog M = 605 ms), $F(1, 3)$ = 81.75, MS_e = .0010, $p <$ .01. Further, importantly, there was a significant three-way interaction of training condition, test time, and color set, $F(2, 3)$ = 11.50, MS_e = .0001, $p < .05$. This interaction reflects the observation that the greatest decrease in reaction time from the pretest to the posttest occurred for the Stroop training condition with the trained color set. The stimuli used during training and the stimuli used during all three of the trained orthographic tests (standard, asterisks, and uppercase) shared the same colors and color words but differed in their orthographic forms. Hence, these results are consistent with the hypothesis that training is specific to the colors employed or to the meaning of the color words, but probably not to the orthographic form of the color words.

Comparing Posttests and Retention Tests

Color Interference Assessment Measures. The effects of retention can be examined in Table 8.2 by comparing the results of the posttest and the retention test. A mixed analysis of variance was conducted on the retention results including the between-subjects factor of training condition and the within-subjects factors of test time (posttest and retention test only), test type, and color set.

There was no reliable forgetting from the posttest to the retention test; the main effect of test time was not significant and that factor was not involved in any significant interactions. The other results of the retention analysis are consistent with those from the training analysis and provide even stronger evidence for the specificity of training effects on reaction time performance.

As in the training analysis, the test types in order of fastest to slowest were word reading (M = 2.650 log ms, antilog M = 447 ms), reverse Stroop (M = 2.682 log ms, antilog M = 481 ms), color patches (M = 2.690 log ms, antilog M = 490 ms), and Stroop (M = 2.783 log ms, antilog M = 607 ms), $F(3, 9)$ = 21.84, MS_e = .0036, $p < .001$.

The specificity of training is reflected by a significant two-way interaction of test type and color set, $F(3, 9) = 6.91$, $MS_e = .0002$, $p < .05$, as well as a significant three-way interaction of test type, color set, and training condition, $F(6, 9) = 6.95$, $MS_e = .0002$, $p < .01$. The two-way interaction may be due to the observation that subjects were faster on the trained set than on the untrained set only when naming colors, that is, in the Stroop test (trained $M = 2.777$ log ms, antilog $M = 598$ ms; untrained $M = 2.788$ log ms, antilog $M = 614$ ms) and in the color-patches test (trained $M = 2.683$ log ms, antilog $M = 482$ ms; untrained $M = 2.696$ log ms, antilog $M = 497$ ms), but not in either the word-reading test (trained $M = 2.659$ log ms, antilog $M = 456$ ms; untrained $M = 2.640$ log ms, antilog $M = 437$ ms) or the reverse Stroop test (trained $M = 2.689$ log ms, antilog $M = 489$ ms; untrained $M = 2.675$ log ms, antilog $M = 473$ ms). For these last two tests, reaction times were faster for the untrained set than for the trained set, presumably because the test on the untrained set always followed that on the trained set. The three-way interaction corresponded to an advantage for the trained set on color-naming responses and an advantage for the untrained set on word-reading responses that was only found for subjects in the Stroop training condition, not for subjects in either the color-patch training or control conditions. Because in the Stroop task subjects name colors and ignore words, Stroop training may be likely to facilitate color-naming responses but suppress word-reading responses.

Orthographic Color Interference Measures. The effects of retention on the orthographic color interference measures can be examined in Table 8.3 by comparing the results of the posttest and the retention test. Another mixed analysis of variance was conducted on the retention results including the between-subjects factor of training condition and the within-subjects factors of test time (posttest and retention test only), orthographic test type, and color set.

As in the analysis of the pretest and posttest, there was no effect of orthographic test type, and that factor was not involved in any significant interactions. Further, as in the analysis of the color interference assessment measures, there was no reliable forgetting; that is, there were no significant main effect or interactions involving the factor of test time.

In accord with the previous observations concerning specificity of training, there was a significant interaction of training condition and color set, $F(2, 3) = 12.56$, $MS_e = .0005$, $p < .05$. This interaction reflected the observation that on these three orthographic versions of Stroop stimuli only Stroop training yielded faster reaction times for the trained set than for the untrained set (trained $M = 2.779$ log ms, antilog $M = 601$ ms; untrained $M = 2.823$ log ms, antilog $M = 665$ ms); for color-patch training there was no difference between the two color sets (trained M = 2.762 log ms, antilog M = 578 ms; untrained M = 2.765 log ms, antilog M = 582 ms); and for the control condition there was a difference in the opposite direction (trained M = 2.809 log ms, antilog M = 644 ms; untrained M = 2.793 log ms, antilog M = 621 ms). Because the same pattern was found for all three orthographic test types, the results again are consistent with the hypothesis that training is specific to the colors or to the word meanings, but not to the orthographic form of the color words.

Item Analyses for Stroop Training

To gain insight into the specificity effects found for subjects given training in the Stroop condition, we conducted two analyses of variance on log correct reaction times on the first session of training and another two on the last (i.e., 12th) session of training, one analysis on each session for each of the two subjects. In those sessions each subject had been presented with 240 stimuli (i.e., each allowable combination of word and color was shown 40 times). Each analysis examined three nonorthogonal effects—word, color, and the interaction of the two. Because of the nonorthogonal nature of this design, due to the fact that no congruous stimuli were presented to the subjects, the degrees of freedom for the interaction were reduced to one.

The specificity of training effects could be illuminated by any item advantages found during training. In particular, specificity of training effects could be due to specific improvement on particular words, colors, or word-color combinations. Specificity to words, to colors, or to particular combinations of words and colors could be suggested in the item analyses by a main effect of word, a main effect of color, or an interaction, respectively. The relevant means for both subjects are shown in Table 8.4. For the first of the two subjects, the analysis on Session 1 reaction times yielded a significant main effect of color, $F(2, 231)$ = 27.78, MS_e = .0075, $p < .001$; a significant main effect of word, $F(2, 231)$ = 19.93, MS_e = .0075, $p < .001$; and a significant interaction of color and word, $F(1, 231)$ = 16.50, MS_e = .0075, $p < .001$. The analysis on Session 12 yielded only a significant interaction of color and word, $F(1, 232)$ = 3.91, MS_e = .0073, $p < .05$. The main effects of color and word in Session 1 reflect the fact that this subject was fastest for the color pink and slowest for the word *pink*.

For the second subject, the analysis on Session 1 yielded a significant main effect of color, $F(2, 232)$ = 24.87, MS_e = .0052, $p < .001$, and a significant interaction of color and word, $F(1, 232)$ = 15.37, MS_e = .0052, $p < .001$. The analysis on Session 12 yielded a significant main effect of

Table 8.4 Reaction Time (log ms) for Subjects 1 and 2 During Training
Sessions 1 and 12 as a Function of Color and Word

	Color					
Word		*Session 1*			*Session 12*	
Subject 1	Blue	Pink	Orange	Blue	Pink	Orange
Blue	—	2.775	2.859	—	2.848	2.865
Pink	2.874	—	2.887	2.877	—	2.828
Orange	2.820	2.771	—	2.860	2.849	—
Subject 2	Green	Red	Purple	Green	Red	Purple
Green	—	2.747	2.844	—	2.603	2.739
Red	2.783	—	2.807	2.714	—	2.706
Purple	2.822	2.745	—	2.724	2.617	—

color, $F(2, 228) = 106.27$, $MS_e = .0029$, $p < .001$; a significant main effect of word, $F(2, 228) = 13.33$, $MS_e = .0029$, $p < .001$; and a significant interaction of color and word, $F(1, 228) = 57.87$, $MS_e = .0029$, $p < .001$. The main effects of color in Sessions 1 and 12 and word in Session 12 reflect the complementary observations that this subject was fastest for the color red and after training gave the slowest responses for the word *red*.

The fact that the pattern of reaction times changed, at least for Subject 1, from the first to the last session suggests that the item advantages are modified as a function of practice and hence may contribute to the practice specificity effects. The significant interactions for both subjects in both sessions suggest that the practice specificity effects may be due in part to an advantage for selected color-word combinations.

Protocol Analyses for Stroop Training

All subjects gave verbal retrospective reports immediately after each of the first 12 and last 12 trials of every training session. The protocols for the two subjects given Stroop training were analyzed to assess the cognitive processes that mediate performance on the Stroop task. Each of the subjects' responses was categorized into one of three classes: (a) color, in which the subject reported noticing only the color of the stimulus; (b) word then color, in which the subject reported first noticing the word and only thereafter the color; and (c) other (i.e., a class of miscellaneous responses). For Subject 1, 15% of all protocols were categorized as color, 81% as word then color, and 4% as other. For Subject 2, 71% of all protocols were categorized as color, 14% as word then color, and 15% as other. An analysis of covariance was conducted for each subject to compare reaction times for responses that were categorized in the first two protocol classes, controlling for training session. Both subjects showed a significant effect of protocol response category on reaction times: for Subject 1, $F(1, 270)$ = 4.17, MS_e = .0086, $p < .05$; for Subject 2, $F(1, 240)$ = 63.19, MS_e = .0049, $p < .001$. Color trials yielded faster reaction times (Subject 1 M = 2.816 log ms, antilog M = 655 ms; Subject 2 M = 2.767 log ms, antilog M = 585 ms) than did word-then-color trials (Subject 1 M = 2.857 log ms, antilog M = 719 ms; Subject 2 M = 2.859 log ms, antilog M = 723 ms). It is interesting to compare the mean reaction time for the color protocol trials during Stroop training (M = 2.792 log ms, antilog M = 619 ms) with the mean reaction times for the same subjects on the patches test involving the trained colors both before (M = 2.804 log ms, antilog M = 637 ms) and after (M = 2.701 log ms, antilog M = 502 ms) training. This comparison leads to the intriguing suggestion that some subjects can produce responses to the Stroop task as fast as they can name color patches, thus possibly overcoming completely the interference created by the words in the Stroop stimuli.

Discussion

The question of practice specificity in the Stroop task has been addressed. We found clear evidence for specificity of practice effects, which persisted across a 1-month delay interval. Subjects showed differential effects of color set, with better performance on the trained set than on the untrained set. Further, in the analyses of color interference at the posttests and retention tests, the effects differed according to test and training condition, with the Stroop-trained subjects showing an advantage for the trained set on the tests that required color naming and a disadvantage for the trained set on the tests that required word reading. Performance on the orthographic tests provides insight into whether the observed specificity was due to the colors or due to the words.

In the orthographic tests the colors were identical to the colors used during training, but the word forms were different. Because for the Stroop-trained subjects the orthographic Stroop measures yielded the same trained color set advantage as did the standard Stroop test, it can be concluded that the specificity was not due solely to word form. The finding for the asterisks test is particularly interesting in light of results from letter detection studies (Healy, Conboy, & Drewnowski, 1987; Schneider, Healy, & Gesi, 1991) that suggest that asterisks disrupt unitization of words, which would be expected to disrupt the word-reading process (but perhaps not when the words are limited to a small set). The finding for the uppercase test is similar to one reported recently by Musen and Squire (1993), who noted that implicit learning on a Stroop task was not disrupted by a change in type case. The lack of effect of the orthographic manipulations suggests that the observed specificity is probably mediated by the colors. Indeed, the item analyses revealed advantages for the colors red and pink. The alternative possibility that there are specific practice effects for the semantic or phonetic aspects of the item to be ignored (in this case, the word) is one put forward by Reisberg et al. (1980). There was some evidence for this possibility from the item analyses, which yielded disadvantages for the words *red* and *pink* (i.e., disadvantages related to the aspect of the stimuli to be ignored).

One additional possibility is that practice is actually specific to the individual color-word combinations; that is, practice may improve performance at the level of individual combinations rather than at the level of words or colors. This possibility gained support from the item analyses at the end of training for both subjects, who showed significant interactions of color and word. This possibility was also supported by Musen and Squire's (1993) recent study of implicit learning in the Stroop task.

Further experiments using testing materials with colors and color words that are not completely corresponding (e.g., with the words *red, green,* and *purple* in the colors pink, blue, and orange) could further differentiate between specificity to trained words and specificity to trained colors, as could experiments using different shades of the same colors. Future experiments using training materials that do not include the full complement of possible color-word combinations could further explore the possibility that training effects are specific to the trained color-word combinations.

In contrast to the clear evidence on the specificity of training, the effects of simple color-naming practice on overall Stroop performance were much less clear-cut. We found that all subjects' performance—even that of the control subjects—improved from pretest to posttest. This finding suggests that the lion's share of the improvement was due to learning on the pretest. If our pretest is equivalent to one session of practice, our finding agrees with Stroop's (1935) data showing the greatest improvement after the first session of practice. Sacks, Clark, Pols, and Geffen (1991) also reported improvement only between their first two blocks of training, after which performance was asymptotic. The improvement we observed from pretest to posttest was different, however, for different tests. On the standardized paper test, it was only the Stroop page that showed improvement to a level beyond normal performance, as defined by the normative scale included in the test manual. Among the computer tests, the tests requiring naming colors showed more improvement than did the tests requiring reading words.

Because there were no significant differences among the different training groups on either the standardized paper test or the computer tests except those involving color set (i.e., those relating to the specificity of training), it is unclear what our current findings imply about the underlying cause of Stroop interference. On one hand, both the relative speed of processing and the automaticity theories suggest that if simple color-naming practice results in improved color naming, then it should improve Stroop performance as well, and the differential improvement on the different tests implies that there was improvement in color naming. However, because this differential improvement was not reliably influenced by training condition, it may be that practice did not lead to noticeable improvement beyond learning on the pretest. Alternatively, the effects of training condition may not have been reliable simply because of the small number of subjects in our study. (Note that training condition is a between-subjects factor, whereas our reliable specificity effects reflected more sensitive within-subjects comparisons.) Thus, the question of whether color-naming practice alone—without the large amount of Stroop experience on the pretest—would improve Stroop performance cannot be given a definite answer in this study. However, there is a suggestion from the protocol analyses for Stroop training that practice in the Stroop task may help the subject learn to overcome the interference created by the words in the Stroop stimuli, and color-naming practice could not help in this way.

It should be noted that our main finding, the specificity effects we found for training on the Stroop task, has implications beyond those for performance on tasks involving color naming. These effects suggest that other types of training may also yield advantages that are specific to the materials or stimuli used during training. Converging evidence for this hypothesis can be found in recent work showing training specificity in mental arithmetic tasks (see Fendrich, Healy, & Bourne, 1993; Rickard, Healy, & Bourne, in press; Rickard & Bourne, 1992). These studies of mental arithmetic, like the present one of the Stroop task, showed durable retention of the acquired skill across long delay intervals. Perhaps both the durability and specificity of these skills can be understood in terms of the importance of procedural reinstatement in skill acquisition, retention, and transfer.

References

Anderson, J. R. (1992). Automaticity and the ACT* theory. *American Journal of Psychology, 105,* 165-180.

Brown, W. (1915). Practice in associating color names with colors. *Psychological Review, 22,* 45-55.

Clawson, D. M., King, C. L., Healy, A. F., & Ericsson, K. A. (1993). Specificity of practice effects in the classic Stroop color-word task. *Proceedings of the Fifteenth Annual Conference of the Cognitive Science Society* (pp. 324-329). Hillsdale, NJ: Lawrence Erlbaum.

Connor, A., Franzen, M., & Sharp, B. (1988). Effects of practice and differential instructions on Stroop performance. *The International Journal of Clinical Neuropsychology, 10,* 1-4.

Dyer, F. N. (1973). The Stroop phenomenon and its use in the study of perceptual, cognitive, and response processes. *Memory & Cognition, 1,* 106-120.

Ericsson, K. A., & Simon, H. A. (1984). *Protocol analysis: Verbal reports as data.* Cambridge, MA: Bradford Books/MIT Press.

Fendrich, D. W., Healy, A. F., & Bourne, L. E., Jr. (1993). Mental arithmetic: Training and retention of multiplication skill. In C. Izawa (Ed.), *Cognitive psychology applied* (pp. 111-133). Hillsdale, NJ: Lawrence Erlbaum.

Golden, C. J. (1978). *Stroop color and word test (Cat. No. 30150M): A manual for clinical and experimental uses.* Wood Dale, IL: Stoelting Company.

Healy, A. F., Conboy, G. L., & Drewnowski, A. (1987). Characterizing the processing units of reading. In B. K. Britton & S. M. Glynn (Eds.), *Executive control processes in reading* (pp. 279-296). Hillsdale, NJ: Lawrence Erlbaum.

Healy, A. F., Fendrich, D. W., Crutcher, R. J., Wittman, W. T., Gesi, A. T., Ericsson, K. A., & Bourne, L. E., Jr. (1992). The long-term retention of skills. In A. F. Healy, S. M. Kosslyn, & R. M. Shiffrin (Eds.), *From learning processes to cognitive processes: Essays in honor of William K. Estes* (Vol. 2, pp. 87-118). Hillsdale, NJ: Lawrence Erlbaum.

Jensen, A. R., & Rohwer, W. D., Jr. (1966). The Stroop color-word test: A review. *Acta Psychologica, 25,* 36-93.

MacLeod, C. M. (1991). Half a century of research on the Stroop effect: An integrative review. *Psychological Bulletin, 109,* 163-203.

MacLeod, C. M. (1992). The Stroop task: The "gold standard" of attentional measures. *Journal of Experimental Psychology: General, 121,* 12-14.

Ménard-Buteau, C., & Cavanagh, P. (1984). Localization of the form/colour interference at the perceptual level in a Stroop task with stimuli drawings. *Canadian Journal of Psychology, 38,* 421-439.

Musen, G., & Squire, L. R. (1993). Implicit learning of color-word associations using a Stroop paradigm. *Journal of Experimental Psychology: Learning, Memory, and Cognition, 19,* 789-798.

National Research Council. (1981). *Procedures for testing color vision: Report of working group 41.* Washington, DC: National Academy Press.

Reisberg, D., Baron, J., & Kemler, D. G. (1980). Overcoming Stroop interference: The effects of practice on distractor potency. *Journal of Experimental Psychology: Human Perception and Performance, 6,* 140-150.

Rickard, T. C., & Bourne, L. E., Jr. (1992, November). *Cross-operation transfer of mental arithmetic skill.* Paper presented at the 33rd Annual Meeting of the Psychonomic Society, St. Louis, MO.

Rickard, T. C., Healy, A. F., & Bourne, L. E., Jr. (in press). On the cognitive structure of basic arithmetic skills: Operation, order, and symbol transfer effects. *Journal of Experimental Psychology: Learning, Memory, and Cognition.*

Sacks, T. L., Clark, C. L., Pols, R. G., & Geffen, L. B. (1991). Comparability and stability of performance of six alternate forms of the Dodrill-Stroop colour-word test. *The Clinical Neuropsychologist, 5,* 220-225.

Schneider, V. I., Healy, A. F., & Gesi, A. T. (1991). The role of phonetic processes in letter detection: A reevaluation. *Journal of Memory and Language, 30,* 294-318.

Schneider, W. (1988). Micro Experimental Laboratory: An integrated system for IBM PC compatibles. *Behavior Research Methods, Instruments, & Computers, 20,* 206-217.

Stroop, J. R. (1935). Studies of interference in serial verbal reactions. *Journal of Experimental Psychology, 18,* 643-662.

9 An Identical-Elements Model of Basic Arithmetic Skills

TIMOTHY C. RICKARD

LYLE E. BOURNE, JR.

In this chapter, we review evidence from five experiments supporting an *identical-elements* model of the structure and specificity of adult mental arithmetic skill. The model specifies a single and distinct "chunk" of arithmetic knowledge corresponding to each unique combination of the elements that make up an arithmetic fact (i.e., the arithmetic operation, the operands, and the answer). Experimental results support the model by showing that the effects of practice on a selected subset of multiplication and division problems transfer to altered problems on a subsequent test if and only if the elements of the test problem are identical to those of a practice problem. Implications for general issues relating to the structure of factual knowledge are discussed. Factors mediating the retention of arithmetic skill are also discussed.

In this chapter, we review several experiments in which basic mental arithmetic problems (e.g., $4 \times 7 = ?$) were used to explore the structure and specificity of highly practiced factual knowledge. Mental arithmetic is well suited for investigating these issues because it is (a) generally believed to reflect fact retrieval for skilled subjects, (b) a highly practiced and well-established skill for virtually any college student, (c) a well-defined task based on knowledge that is relatively distinct, and (d) easy to investigate in the laboratory.

The organization of knowledge in highly practiced, conceptually based domains like arithmetic is likely to differ markedly from that of less practiced and more arbitrary domains. For example, if a child were taught

AUTHORS' NOTE: This research was supported in part by Army Research Institute Contract MDA903-90-K-0066 to the University of Colorado. We wish to thank Alice Healy for her valuable comments concerning this chapter.

to respond with "28" to the stimulus, "$4 \times 7 = ?$" with no reference to the concept of multiplication, and with no exposure to any other multiplication problem, then there is little doubt that what would be learned would be very specific and might not transfer even to a very similar problem such as "$7 \times 4 = ?$" Arithmetic facts, however, are not learned in conceptual vacuums, and they are practiced in many different contexts and formats. Under these learning conditions, questions about the structure and specificity of the skill become interesting theoretically and are not easy to answer on a priori grounds. For example, do complementary operand orders within a commutative operation (e.g., $7 \times 4 = ?$ and $4 \times 7 = ?$) access the same or different underlying memory structures? Do complementary problems from two operations (e.g., $6 \times 7 = ?$ and $6 \times \_\_ = 42$) or related problems within a noncommutative operation (e.g., $6 \times ? = 42$ and $7 \times ? = 42$) access the same or different memory structures?

There are several results in the literature that speak to the first question. First, Siegler (1986) showed that during initial learning children often use algorithms that are "order specific" in that a different sequence of adding steps is required for each operand order (e.g., 4×7 is solved by adding four 7s). This conceptual distinction may carry over and influence the kind of structure that characterizes adult factual knowledge. Consistent with this possibility, Siegler (1986) demonstrated that children often acquire order-specific memory structures for arithmetic problems, and Reder and Ritter (1992) showed a similar effect for adults learning novel pseudoarithmetic problems. On the other hand, there is also evidence from Fendrich, Healy, and Bourne (1993) suggesting that for college students, knowledge structures for complementary operand orders are closely related. These researchers gave subjects extensive practice on a set of simple, single-digit multiplication problems, and then tested them on problems seen during practice; on practice problems for which the operand order was reversed; and on new, unpracticed problems. Performance at test was fastest on practiced problems, intermediate for reversed order problems, and slowest for new problems. The faster performance on reversed order problems relative to new problems indicates that knowledge structures for both operand orders are accessed when either order is encountered, and this result also hints at the possibility that memory representations for complementary orders overlap in some fundamental way.

The second basic question stated above addresses the representational relations, if any, among problems that are derived from different combinations of a single number relation (e.g., 4, 7, 28). Clearly there are mathematical similarities among different problems derived from a single number relation (e.g., $4 \times 7 = \_\_$, $4 \times \_\_ = 28$, and $7 \times \_\_ = 28$). It follows that there are likely to be cognitive similarities as well. How these relations are built into the memory structure that develops with experience is, however, an open question. Perhaps a single representation exists for all problems corresponding to a number relation, such that practice on any of the problems in the preceding example would transfer to any of the other problems. Alternatively, there may be separate representations for multiplication ($4 \times 7 = ?$ and $7 \times 4 = ?$) and division ($28 \div 4 = ?$ and $28 \div 7 = ?$) problems within a number relation. There are other possibilities, and we know of no existing theory (other than the identical-elements model that we propose below) that makes strong predictions that discriminate among them.

Although for the time being we focus on arithmetic, the basic questions about the structure of factual knowledge discussed above are not limited to this domain. Virtually any cognitive skill requires fact retrieval, and the basic questions relating to the order, the combination, and the modality of retrieval cues that we address in the experiments discussed below are quite general. It is our hope that a sound model of the organization of arithmetic facts will provide a useful starting point for future investigations into the organization of factual knowledge in other highly practiced domains.

We begin by reviewing our initial experiment exploring these issues. Next, we will describe an identical-elements model of the structure of adult arithmetic skill that we developed based on the results of the first experiment. We then discuss several follow-up experiments that provide surprisingly strong support for this relatively simple model. We conclude with a discussion of some implications of our results for general models of fact retrieval, concept formation, and skill retention.

Effects of Operand Order, Operation, and Symbol on the Transfer of Mental Arithmetic Skill

The purpose of the first two experiments (see Rickard, Healy, & Bourne, in press) was to provide preliminary data addressing the structure and specificity of basic arithmetic skills, using a practice-transfer approach. Subjects received practice on a set of basic multiplication and division problems and were then tested on the practice problems as well as on various altered problems as discussed below. A basic assumption of this approach is that good transfer of learning from practice to test provides evidence of access to a common knowledge unit, and that poor transfer provides evidence of access to different knowledge units.

In the first experiment, 12 college students were given three sessions of repeated practice on 36 simple multiplication and division problems pre-

Table 9.1 Test Conditions for an Example Problem at Test in Experiment 1 of Rickard, Healy, and Bourne (in press)

Test Condition	Practice	Test
Multiplication		
No change	__ = 4 × 7	__ = 4 × 7
Order change	__ = 7 × 4	__ = 4 × 7
Operation change	28 = __ × 7	__ = 4 × 7
Order & operation change	28 = __ × 4	__ = 4 × 7
Division		
No change	28 = __ × 7	28 = __ × 7
Order change	28 = __ × 4	28 = __ × 7
Operation change	__ = 4 × 7	28 = __ × 7
Order & operation change	__ = 7 × 4	28 = __ × 7

sented on a CRT one at a time. There was a total of 40 exposures to each problem (i.e., 40 *blocks* of practice) across all three sessions. On subsequent immediate and delayed (after a 1-month retention interval) tests, subjects solved three blocks of 144 problems. Each block consisted of one presentation of each practice problem and one presentation of each of three altered versions of each practice problem, yielding four test conditions: no change, operand order change, operation change, and operation and operand order change (see Table 9.1). Multiplication and division problems are presented separately in Table 9.1 because the results depended critically on this distinction. Note that here and throughout the chapter, we a priori define a problem as involving either multiplication (e.g., __ = 4 × 7) or division (e.g., 35 = __ × 5) according to the arithmetic operation that is formally required to produce the answer. Counterbalancing and random presentation of items within each block ensured that during both practice and test any differences obtained did not reflect spurious effects such as that of problem difficulty. See Rickard et al. (in press) for the details of the methodology.

Response times (RTs) on the first block of practice were approximately 1,000 ms and 1,300 ms for multiplication and division, respectively. There was substantial and reliable speedup (following a power function) with practice for both multiplication (about 450 ms) and division (about 650 ms). The RT advantage for multiplication was reliable both at the beginning and at the end of practice.

Collapsing across the three blocks of the immediate test, error proportions for multiplication problems in the no change, operand order change, operation change, and operation and operand order change conditions were .013, .032, .112, and .115, respectively. On the delayed test, these values were .043, .035, .088, and .080. On both tests, there was a reliable effect of operation, reflecting fewer errors in the no change and operand order change conditions (the same operation conditions) than in the operation change and operation plus operand order change conditions (the different operation conditions), but there were no reliable effects of operand order, and there was no reliable interaction between these variables. RT results for multiplication are shown in the top panel in Figure 9.1, again collapsed across the three blocks of each test. As with the error patterns, there was a strong performance advantage for same-operation problems on both the immediate and delayed tests. There was also a weaker effect of operand order, reflecting faster performance overall in the no change and operation change conditions than in the operand order change and operation plus operand order change conditions. More focused post hoc analyses showed that on both the immediate and the delayed tests the effect of operand order was reliable for same-operation problems but was not reliable for different-operation problems.

Error proportions for division on the immediate test, collapsed across block, were .022, .105, .108, and .092 for the no change, operand order change, operation change, and operation plus order change conditions, respectively. On the delayed test, these values were .034, .076, .093, and .080. On both tests, there were reliable effects of operation, operand order, and the interaction of these variables. Post hoc comparisons showed no reliable differences among the operand order, operation, and operation plus operand order conditions on either test. RT results for division are shown in the lower panel in Figure 9.1, collapsed across block within each test. As with the error patterns, there were strong effects on both tests of operation change, operand order change, and their interaction. Post hoc analyses again revealed no differences among the operand order, operation, and operand order plus operation conditions. In sum, both the error and the RT results for division on both tests reflected an advantage for the no change condition over all other conditions but revealed no differences among the other conditions.

The performance at test for both multiplication and division is easily summarized. When the presented numbers (disregarding operand order) and the formally required arithmetic operation of a test problem were exactly the same as those of a problem solved during practice (as in the no change conditions for both operations, and the operand order change condition for multiplication), test performance was relatively good, although there was some increase in RTs for the operand order change condition for multiplication. When the presented numbers and the required

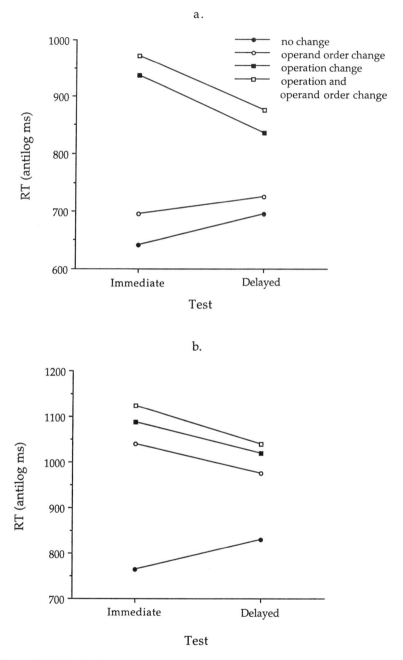

Figure 9.1. RTs for Correctly Solved Problems in Experiment 1 of Rickard, Healy, and Bourne (in press) as a Function of Test (immediate or delayed) and Test Condition. (Panel a shows the results for multiplication problems, and Panel b shows the results for division problems.)

operation of a test problem did not completely match those of a practice problem (as in the operation and operation plus operand order change conditions for both operations and the operand order change condition for division), test performance suffered substantially; error rates were three to five times higher on the immediate test, and RTs were over 300 ms slower.

These results suggested to us a relatively simple working model of the structure of skilled arithmetic knowledge that we term an *identical-elements* model, according to which there is a single and functionally distinct "unit" of arithmetic knowledge corresponding to each unique combination of the two numbers (ignoring order) that constitute a problem (e.g., 4 and 7), the number that is the answer (e.g., 28), and the arithmetic operation formally required to produce the answer (e.g., multiply).[1] Note that "the operation formally required" refers to the operation required in the mathematical sense rather than to the arithmetic symbol present in the problem. For example, the answer to $28 = \_\_ \times 4$ requires division. The model assumes distinct perceptual, cognitive, and motor stages of arithmetic fact retrieval (see also McCloskey, Caramazza, & Basili, 1985) and it applies only to the structure of knowledge as represented within the cognitive stage. Numbers are treated as abstract elements superordinate to the perceptual characteristics of the modality or physical format in which problems are presented.[2] Problems that have exactly the same elements access the same knowledge unit within the cognitive stage, despite any perceptual differences, such as format or modality of presentation. For example, multiplication problems that differ only in operand order, such as 3×8 and 8×3, access the same knowledge unit. Similarly, a problem presented in Arabic format, such as "4×7," and the same problem presented in a written verbal format, such as "four times seven," access the same knowledge unit. Indeed, any problems that differ only with respect to detailed characteristics of the format (e.g., horizontal versus vertical presentation, variations in the symbol used to denote an operation) access the same knowledge unit. In contrast, problems that differ with respect to even one element access completely different knowledge units. So, for example, complementary problems from two operations (e.g., $4 \times 7 = \_\_$ and $4 \times \_\_ = 28$) and related problems within a noncommutative operation (e.g., $28 = \_\_ \times 4$ and $28 = \_\_ \times 7$) access completely different knowledge units. Although somewhat counterintuitive, this model is consistent with the pattern of results observed in this experiment and makes some interesting predictions that we tested in the follow-up experiments.

Assuming that practice strengthens only the knowledge units corresponding to the practiced problem, the identical-elements model makes straightforward predictions about positive transfer of learning to the various test conditions. If the elements of the test problem match exactly with the elements of a problem seen during practice, there will be substantial positive transfer of learning to the test problem, despite any other problem differences. Note, though, that the model does not necessarily predict complete transfer in this case, because some perceptual processing advantage (in the model's presumed perceptual stage) could accrue for the practiced problem. Thus, for example, the model is not necessarily inconsistent with the small but reliable increase in RT that was observed in the operand order change condition relative to the no change condition for multiplication, here and in the previous study by Fendrich et al. (1993). It could be the case that a perceptual advantage accrued for the practiced operand order, but that the same knowledge units were accessed for corresponding problems in the two conditions. In contrast, if the elements of the test problem do not exactly match the elements of at least one practice problem, and if there are no general transfer effects from practice to test (e.g., no improvements with practice in general perceptual or motor processes), then the identical-elements model makes a prediction of absolutely no positive transfer. Consistent with the prediction, performance in the operation change and operation plus operand order change conditions for both operations, and in the operand order change condition for division, was much poorer than performance in the other conditions.

A comparison of performance on the immediate and delayed tests reveals surprisingly good retention in terms of both error proportions and RTs (see also Fendrich et al., 1993, for similar findings). The procedural reinstatement framework (Healy et al., this volume) states that retention will be relatively good when performance is largely skill based and when the retention test reinstates the procedures acquired or strengthened during practice. Assuming that basic mental arithmetic is largely a procedural skill, then procedural reinstatement provides an appropriate framework within which to account for these findings.

The second experiment of Rickard et al. (in press) explored transfer of arithmetic skill manipulating operation, as in the first experiment, and a new variable, symbol, as shown in Table 9.2. The symbol variable replaces the operand order variable at both practice and test. In all other respects, the design was identical to that of the first experiment. Based on the identical-elements model, we expected a substantial overall performance advantage for all problems in the same operation conditions (the no change and symbol change conditions) for which the elements match exactly with those of a problem seen during practice, relative to problems in the different operation conditions (the operation and operation plus symbol

Table 9.2 Examples of Each of the Four Problem Types Seen at Practice and the Corresponding Test Conditions in Experiment 2 of Rickard, Healy, and Bourne (in press)

| | | Test Condition | | |
| | | Symbol | Operation | Operation & |
Practice	No Change	Change	Change	Symbol Change
__ = 4 × 7	__ = 4 × 7	__ ÷ 4 = 7	28 = __ × 7	28 ÷ __ = 7
__ ÷ 9 = 5	__ ÷ 9 = 5	__ = 9 × 5	45 ÷ __ = 5	45 = __ × 6
48 = __ × 6	48 = __ × 6	48 ÷ __ = 6	__ = 8 × 6	__ ÷ 8 = 6
18 ÷ __ = 3	18 ÷ __ = 3	18 = __ × 3	__ ÷ 6 = 3	__ × 6 = 3

NOTE: From top to bottom, the four types of problems at practice represented above are multiplication with symbol "×," multiplication with symbol "+," division with symbol "×," and division with symbol "+."

change conditions), for which the elements do not match exactly with those of a problem seen at practice.

Note that it is not clear a priori whether subjects will treat problems that differ only in the arithmetic symbol as the same problem, as predicted by the identical-elements model. For example, subjects may interpret "__ = 4 × 7" as "what is four times seven?" whereas they may interpret "__ ÷ 4 = 7" as "what divided by four is seven?" Similarly, subjects may interpret "28 = __ × 7" as "twenty-eight equals what times seven?" whereas they may interpret "28 ÷ __ = 7" as "twenty-eight divided by what equals seven?" It is quite possible that the knowledge structures that are accessed and presumably strengthened with practice are strongly dependent on these potential differences in how the problems are interpreted. The identical-elements model, however, makes the strong prediction that the same knowledge structure is accessed regardless of symbol, and thus we expect substantial transfer of learning to symbol change problems at test.

The results for all four problem types at test in this experiment were essentially the same as those for multiplication in the first experiment, if symbol is substituted for operand order as a transfer variable. Collapsing across format, the overall error proportions on the immediate test were .042, .042, .100, and .090 in the no change, symbol change, operation change, and operation plus symbol change conditions, respectively. These values on the delayed test were .053, .066, .091, and .093. The RTs for both the immediate and the delayed tests are shown in Figure 9.2. Consistent with the predictions of the identical-elements model, there were strong effects of a change in operation on both the immediate and delayed tests as measured by both error proportions and RTs. There were no effects of symbol in the error analyses, although there were reliable symbol

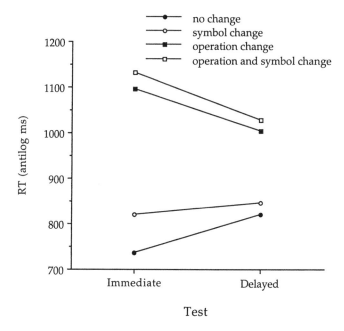

Figure 9.2. RTs for Correctly Solved Problems in Experiment 2 of Rickard, Healy, and Bourne (in press) as a Function of Test (immediate or delayed) and Test Condition

effects in the RT analyses. Post hoc tests showed the symbol effects on the RTs to be reliable for same operation problems, but not for different operation problems, on both the immediate and delayed tests.

The results of this experiment were generally consistent with the identical-elements model. The major new result was that syntactic changes in the ways in which problems are presented (i.e., the symbol manipulations) had only relatively minor effects on performance at test. The slight RT advantage of no change problems over symbol change problems is at least potentially consistent with the model assuming that it reflects only a perceptual level processing advantage for no change problems over symbol change problems, analogous to the advantage observed for no change problems over operand order change problems in the first experiment.

Additional Tests of the Identical-Elements Model

Although there were large performance decrements with a change in operation at test in both of the Rickard et al. (in press) experiments, a more direct test of the identical-elements prediction of no positive transfer to operation change problems would require a comparison of performance on these problems at test with performance on the same problems on a pretest. If this comparison yielded no differences, then the prediction of no positive transfer to operation change problems at test would be verified. A valid test using this pretest-posttest design, however, is complicated by a variety of potential general transfer effects that would yield better performance on the posttest than on the pretest and yet would not be inconsistent with the identical-elements model. As examples, practice might result in a general speedup in perceptual and/or motor processes that would facilitate performance on all problems at test (see Rickard et al., in press, for more discussion of this point). Campbell (1987), however, successfully conducted just such a transfer experiment in which he pretested subjects on two sets of simple multiplication problems, trained them on one of these sets, and then tested them again on both sets. Because Campbell (1987) used a voice key response mode and presented problems in a familiar digit format, general perceptual and motor transfer effects were probably minimized. Pre-post comparisons for the unpracticed problem set showed a slight *negative* transfer effect in both the error proportions and the RTs.

The Campbell (1987) results are relevant to the work discussed in this chapter in two respects. First, the finding of no positive transfer to the unpracticed problem set is consistent with the identical-elements model because none of the problems in the practiced and unpracticed sets shared the same elements. Second, it opens the door to a strong test of the identical-elements prediction of no transfer to operation change problems at test that is not plagued by general transfer factors. Consider an extension of Experiment 1 of Rickard et al. (in press) in which, in addition to the test conditions of that experiment, a new problems condition is included that contains problems not seen during practice in either operation, as shown in Table 9.3 (see Rickard & Bourne, 1993, for a detailed discussion of this experiment). The Campbell (1987) results demonstrate that practice does not transfer to new problems. Given this fact, a finding of no performance differences among operation change problems, operation plus order change problems, and new problems would allow for the inference that there was no transfer of learning to either the operation change or the operation plus operand order change conditions.

Note that the test conditions in this experiment (and in all of the other experiments we discuss in this chapter) can be divided into *noncritical* change conditions, within which problems have elements exactly the same as a problem seen during practice (as defined by the identical-elements model), and *critical* change conditions, within which problems do not have

Table 9.3 Test Conditions for an Example Problem at Test in Experiment 1 of Rickard and Bourne (1993)

Test Condition	Practice	Test
Multiplication		
No change	__ = 4 × 7	__ = 4 × 7
Order change	__ = 7 × 4	__ = 4 × 7
Operation change	28 = __ × 7	__ = 4 × 7
Order & operation change	28 = __ × 4	__ = 4 × 7
New problems	—	__ = 4 × 7
Division		
No change	28 = __ × 7	28 = __ × 7
Order change	28 = __ × 4	28 = __ × 7
Operation change	__ = 4 × 7	28 = __ × 7
Order & operation change	__ = 7 × 4	28 = __ × 7
New problems	—	28 = __ × 7

exactly the same elements as a problem seen during practice. To facilitate and simplify discussion, we use this distinction throughout the remainder of the chapter when discussing the various test conditions.

The method was similar to that of Rickard et al. (in press, Experiment 1), with the following primary changes: (a) 90 blocks of practice were given over three sessions; (b) the test was given 2 days after the third practice session; (c) there was no retention test; (d) 24 problems were used in each problem set, all of which had double-digit answers; and (e) 16 problems were seen during practice by each subject, with the remaining 8 problems constituting the new problems at test (see Rickard & Bourne, 1993, for details).

Error proportions for multiplication problems in the no change, operand order change, operation change, operation plus operand order change, and new problems conditions were .027, .027, .073, .072, and .077, respectively. The RT results for multiplication, collapsed across the first two blocks of the test, are shown in the top panel of Figure 9.3. As predicted by the identical-elements model, there was a large and reliable difference between the no change and operand order change conditions, and all other conditions, for both the error and RT data. There were no reliable differences between the no change and operand order change conditions in the error analysis, but these differences were reliable in the RT analysis. In both the error and RT analyses, there were no reliable differences among the operation, operation plus operand order, and new problems conditions.

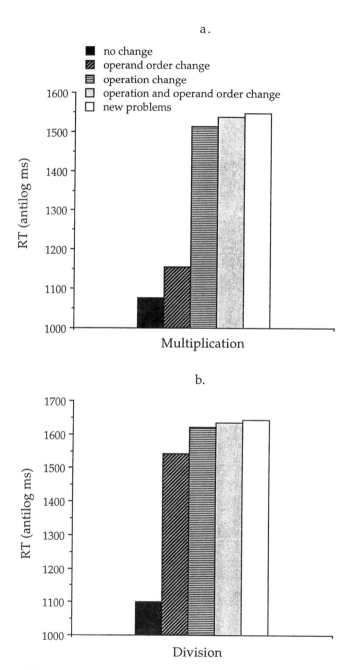

Figure 9.3. RTs for Correctly Solved Problems in Experiment 1 of Rickard and Bourne (1993) as a Function of Test Condition. (Panel a shows results for multiplication problems, and Panel b shows results for division problems.)

Error proportions for division problems in the no change, operand order change, operation change, operation plus operand order change, and new problems conditions were .033, .094, .087, .083, and .075, respectively. The RT results for division, collapsed across the first two blocks of the test, are shown in the lower panel in Figure 9.3. There was a large and reliable difference between the no change condition and all other conditions, for both the error and RT data. There were no reliable differences among the operand order, operation, operation plus operand order, and new problems conditions.

To summarize, as predicted by the identical-elements model, there were substantial performance differences between problems with noncritical and critical changes, but there were no reliable differences among problems with critical changes (in either RTs or error rates) for either multiplication of division. The lack of any performance differences between the new problems condition and the other critical change conditions for both multiplication and division, in conjunction with the Campbell (1987) finding of no positive transfer to his equivalent of our new problems condition, is consistent with the identical-elements assumption that independent knowledge units support performance on complementary multiplication and division problems and also on related problems within division (e.g., 4 × __ = 28 and 7 × __ = 28).

Rickard and Bourne (1993) conducted a second experiment to test the assumption that any advantage for no change problems over operand order change problems at test reflects purely a perceptual processing advantage for the no change problems. Subjects received practice on a set of 16 multiplication problems, half of which were presented in an Arabic format (e.g., "4 × 7"), and half of which were presented in a written verbal format (e.g., "six × nine"). They were then tested on both operand orders of each practiced problem in the practiced format (e.g., "six × nine" and "nine × six"), on both operand orders of each practiced problem in a different format (e.g., "6 × 9" and "9 × 6"), and on new problems in both formats and in both operand orders (see Table 9.4). Based on earlier results, we expected an advantage for the practiced operand order over the unpracticed operand order in the practiced format. The identical-elements model made two additional predictions. First, there should be a substantial performance advantage for all noncritical change problems (no change, operand order change, format change, and operand order plus format change) over critical changes problems (new problems), even when the format and/or order is changed from practice to test. Second, any performance advantage for no change over operand order change problems should disappear when these problems are presented in an unpracticed

Table 9.4 Test Conditions for an Example Problem at Test in Experiment 2 of Rickard and Bourne (1993)

Test Condition	Practice	Test
Arabic format		
No change	4×7	4×7
Order change	7×4	4×7
Format change	four times seven	4×7
Order & format change	seven times four	4×7
New problems	—	4×7
Written verbal format		
No change	four times seven	four times seven
Order change	seven times four	four times seven
Format change	4×7	four times seven
Order & format change	7×4	four times seven
New problems	—	four times seven

format. This second prediction follows from the model under the assumption that perceptual processing of complementary operand orders presented in an unpracticed format will be equivalent.

The error proportions for Arabic problems in the no change, operand order change, format change, operand order plus format change, and new problems conditions were .037, .038, .054, .047, and .055, respectively. The RT results for the first two blocks of the test are summarized in the top panel in Figure 9.4. Contrasts comparing the noncritical change conditions (no change, operand order change, format change, and operand order plus format change) with the critical change condition (new problems), and comparing the same format and different format conditions, were strongly reliable for both errors and RTs. In both the error and RT analyses, there were no reliable differences between the same and different operand order conditions, and there was no reliable interaction between format and operand order. More focused post hoc RT analyses, however, comparing the no change and operand order change conditions separately for each block of test, showed reliable order effects for Blocks 1 and 2, but not for the remaining blocks. Thus, there does appear to have been an RT advantage for no change over order change problems initially, although, for reasons unknown, the effect was less persistent than in previous experiments.

The error proportions for written verbal problems in the no change, operand order change, format change, operand order plus format change, and new problems conditions were .047, .072, .071, .057, and .092,

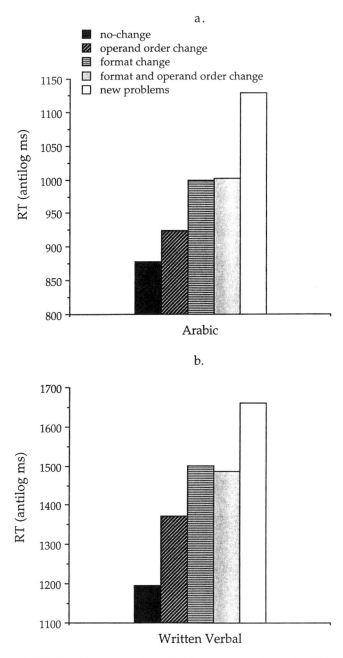

Figure 9.4. RTs for Correctly Solved Problems in Experiment 2 of Rickard and Bourne (1993) as a Function of Test Condition. (Panel a shows results for Arabic problems, and Panel b shows results for written verbal problems.)

respectively. The RT results are shown in the lower panel in Figure 9.4. A contrast comparing the noncritical change conditions (no change, operand order change, format change, and operand order plus format change) with the critical change condition (new problems) was reliable for both error and RTs. The only other reliable contrast for errors was the interaction of operand order and format. This effect reflects primarily lower error rates in the no change condition relative to the other conditions. Contrasts testing for the effects of operand order, format, and the interaction of operand order and format were all reliable for RTs.

Two basic predictions of the identical-elements model were confirmed in the test data. First, for both formats, performance in the new problems condition (the only critical change condition) was worse than performance in the other conditions. Additional post hoc comparisons confirmed this conclusion by showing faster performance in the operand order and format plus operand order change conditions than in the new problems conditions for both the Arabic and the written verbal format. Second, although there were clear differences between the no change and operand order change conditions in terms of RTs (especially for the written verbal format), when perceptually specific practice effects were factored out, there were no performance differences between these problems (i.e., between problems in the format change and format plus operand order change conditions). Most impressively, the RT difference between no change and operand order change problems in the written verbal format was a substantial 180 ms on the first two blocks of the test, but when these problems were presented in the Arabic format, this difference essentially disappeared. These findings are remarkably consistent with the identical-elements assumption that a single knowledge unit, operative in the cognitive stage of processing, supports performance on complementary operand orders.

Tests of the Model Using a Pseudoarithmetic Task

Rickard (1993) tested the generalizability of the identical-elements model to a novel pseudoarithmetic task that we termed *pound arithmetic.* Two types of math problems were derived using a simple arithmetic series in which the third element of the series is the difference between the first two elements, plus 1, added to the second element. Thus, the third element of the number sequence 4, 15, ?, is $[(15 - 4) + 1] + 15 = 27$. In Type 1 problems, the third element was unknown (e.g., 4 # 15 = __). In Type 2 problems, the second element of the series was unknown (e.g., 4 # __ = 27). Problems were presented in a traditional arithmetic format (as in the examples above) with a blank holding the place of the missing element and with the # symbol used as the arithmetic symbol. Subjects were taught a three-step algorithm, as shown above, for solving Type I problems, and a similar four-step algorithm for solving Type II problems. They then practiced for four sessions on a set of six Type I and six Type II problems. On one third of the practice problems (chosen randomly) subjects were probed to determine whether they (a) used the algorithm, (b) retrieved the answer directly from memory, or (c) used some other approach. During a fifth session (immediate test) and a sixth session (delayed test), they were tested three times on each of the problems seen during test (no change problems), on type changes of each of the problems seen during practice (i.e., a Type I problem seen during practice was presented as a Type II problem), and on new problems not seen during practice. Strategy probes (as described above) were collected on every trial during the tests.

The identical-elements model predicted that practice will result in a transition to retrieval only for no change problems despite the strong similarity of each type change problem to its corresponding no change problem (e.g, $4 \# 15 = \_\_$ and $4 \# \_\_ = 27$). Thus, performance on no change problems at test should be significantly faster than performance on either type change or new problems. Also, because type change problems and new problems are both solved using the algorithm, performance in these test conditions should not differ.

The acquisition results are discussed in detail in Rickard (1993). For our current purposes, it is sufficient to summarize two basic findings. First, the strategy-probing data revealed a complete transition to retrieval for all problems and all subjects by about the 60th block of practice. Second, there was substantial RT speedup with practice, from around 12 s on the first block in Session 1 to about 1,200 ms on the last block of Session 5. RTs of around 1,200 ms are very close to fact retrieval RTs established in other domains (Olson & Olson, 1990), and thus provide converging evidence for the claim based on the strategy-probing data that a complete transition to retrieval took place during practice.

The probability of using the algorithm as indicated by the strategy probes for the three conditions on the immediate test is shown in Figure 9.5, collapsed across block. No change problems show nearly total retrieval, not surprising given the complete transition to retrieval indicated for these problems during practice. In contrast, the algorithm was reported nearly always for new and type change problems. A contrast performed on the proportion retrieved, comparing the no change condition with the other conditions, was reliable, but a second contrast comparing the type

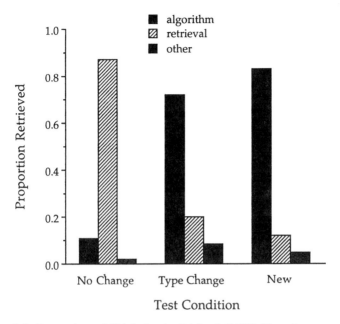

Figure 9.5. Proportion of Trials in the Rickard (1993) Experiment on Which Subjects Reported Algorithm, Retrieval, or Other as a Function of Test Condition

change and new problems conditions was not reliable. Thus, the transition to retrieval was quite specific to the problems on which subjects practiced.

Errors proportions and RTs at test show similar results. The overall error proportions on the immediate test for the no change, type change, and new problems conditions were .024, .250, and .283, respectively. The difference between no change problems on one hand, and type change and new problems on the other hand, was reliable, but the difference between type change and new problems was not reliable. The average RTs on the immediate test were about 2,000, 6,200, and 6,700 ms in the no change, type change, and new problems conditions, respectively. RTs in the no change condition were reliably faster than in the other conditions, but there was no difference between the other two conditions.

The trends toward slightly fewer errors and slightly faster performance in the type change condition than in the new problems condition might reflect a generate-and-test strategy that subjects adopt for unfamiliar problems at test: Subjects could first generate a candidate answer based on the answers encountered during practice (e.g., 15 for 4 # __ = 27), and

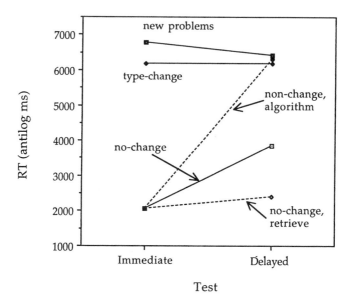

Figure 9.6. RTs for Correctly Solved Problems in the Rickard (1993) Experiment as a Function of Test and Test Condition

then retrieve the answer for the reverse problem type and test to see if it matches the given value (e.g., 4 # 15 = __). This strategy would work for type change problems but not for new problems and could potentially be executed faster than the algorithm. The most important point of the test results, however, is unaffected by the possibility that a generate-and-test strategy was used: Performance on both type change and new problems was far too slow to reflect direct retrieval from memory. Thus, the results are in basic agreement with the identical-elements model.

A comparison of RTs on the immediate and delayed tests is shown in Figure 9.6 (solid lines represent overall results within each test condition). RTs for no change problems on the delayed test were about halfway between RTs for no change and new problems on the immediate test, indicating some skill retention. Nevertheless, the substantial increase in RT for no change problems on the delayed test indicated a much greater loss in skill across the retention interval than we had observed in our previous work on arithmetic (see Rickard et al., in press, Experiment 1; Fendrich et al., 1993). To investigate this finding further, we plotted the

RTs for no change problems on the delayed test separately by strategy, as shown by the dotted lines in Figure 9.6. When retrieval was the reported strategy for no change problems on the delayed test, RTs were only slightly slower than those for no change problems on the immediate test. When the algorithm was the reported strategy, the RTs were nearly exactly the same as those for new and type change problems. This result suggests that the effects of the retention interval were primarily to decrease the probability with which the retrieval strategy was used, without changing substantially the time required to execute that strategy when it was used. Thus, a training procedure that promotes the use of an optimal strategy for a given task appears to contribute to the maintenance of training levels of performance on later tests of retention. See also Healy et al. (this volume) for a discussion of this point.

General Discussion and Conclusions

In this chapter, we summarized results from a series of experiments exploring the structure and specificity of basic arithmetic skills. The major findings are that (a) speedup with practice on one subset of multiplication and division problems does not transfer to another subset of problems with different operand combinations (see also Campbell, 1987), (b) speedup with practice on either multiplication or division problems does not transfer to complementary problems in the other operation, (c) speedup with practice transfers substantially when only syntactic changes (such as a change in symbol) are introduced, and (d) speedup with practice transfers completely to reversed operand order problems in a commutable operation (multiplication) if speedup in perceptual processing of the practiced operand order is factored out.

These results indicate that adult arithmetic skill can be characterized in part as a large set of essentially independent facts, each of which is constructed from a unique combination of existing elements, or chunks of knowledge, about numbers and arithmetic operations. The identical-elements model provides a detailed account of how these facts are organized in memory. To summarize, the model specifies a single and distinct chunk of arithmetic knowledge corresponding to each unique combination of the elements that make up an arithmetic fact (i.e., the arithmetic operation, the operands, and the answer). Three central predictions of the model were supported empirically: (1) the two operand orders of a multiplication problems (e.g., 4×7 and 7×4) are represented as a single fact within the cognitive stage of processing, (2) related problems from complementary operations (e.g., $3 \times 8 = \_\_$ and $3 \times \_\_ = 24$) are represented as completely separate facts, and (3) related problems within division (e.g., $6 \times \_\_ = 42$ and $7 \times \_\_ = 42$) are represented as completely separate facts. The identical-elements model and the data supporting it have notable implications for several computational models of arithmetic fact retrieval currently under development (e.g., Campbell & Oliphant, 1992; McCloskey & Lindemann, 1992; Rickard, Mozer, & Bourne, 1992), and these implications are discussed in detail in Rickard et al. (in press) and Rickard and Bourne (1993). In the current discussion, however, we focus on the potential implications of our results for three different although related issues: the structure of factual knowledge in nonnumerical domains, the nature of conceptual generalization processes, and factors mediating the retention of cognitive skills.

The Structure of Factual Knowledge
in Nonnumerical Domains

A natural next step is to ask whether this model might generalize to skills other than arithmetic. Certainly, there are other types of factual knowledge that can be characterized naturally in terms of a discrete set of constituent elements. For example, Morse code translation is easily characterized in terms of the dots, dashes, and letters. Question-answering processes can also be viewed as a set of critical elements (i.e., words) corresponding to critical concepts. Thus, the question "Who is the current president of the United States?" can be characterized as a set of elements (i.e., president, United States, Bill Clinton) that constitute a unique chunk of knowledge.

Broadly speaking, the identical-elements model makes two basic predictions about the organization and specificity of knowledge and skill in such domains. First, there is a maximal level of generality of facts in memory, at the level of each unique chunk as defined by the model, which cannot be exceeded. In the case of Morse code translation, this level corresponds simply to each code-letter combination. Given that general transfer factors are controlled, the model predicts that practice on one set of letters will not transfer to another set. In the case of question answering, the model makes a similar but perhaps less intuitive prediction: If the difficult job of controlling for general transfer factors is attended to, the model predicts not only that speedup with practice retrieving the answer to one set of facts will not transfer to another set involving different elements, but it also predicts that speedup with practice on one fact, such as "Who is the current president of the United States?," will not transfer even to another fact that has the same elements, such as "Bill Clinton is the president of what country?" Verification of this prediction would suggest that the identical-elements model provides a quite general account of the organization of facts in memory. Failure to verify this prediction would raise some interesting questions about differences in the representation of quantitative and qualitative knowledge.

A second and related prediction of the identical-elements model is that after sufficient experience in a domain, the level of generality, or abstraction, of facts in memory will converge on the maximum level allowed by the model. In mental arithmetic, for example, a single knowledge unit supports adult performance on problems that vary with respect to noncritical factors such as modality, format, operand order, and arithmetic symbol. Whether this prediction will hold in general depends largely on whether generalization occurs as an automatic (i.e., nonstrategic) consequence of experience or whether conscious recognition of the "superficial" nature of certain differences between items is needed for generalization to take place. Consider the representation of operand order in mental multiplication. One possibility is that order is abstracted out of the representations in the cognitive stage as an automatic consequence of experience and without conscious awareness. If this type of automatic generalization is ubiquitous across tasks, then the organization of factual knowledge may always take the form predicted by the model, given sufficient experience. Alternatively, conscious recognition of the conceptual equivalence of two items may be necessary for generalization to take place. This recognition could occur by way of (a) explicit instruction (e.g., instruction on the commutativity principle in multiplication), or (b) independent discovery by way of an unspecified process. If conscious recognition is necessary, then the extent to which the generality of the knowledge approaches the predictions of the model would vary from task to task and depend on both availability of instruction about a task and the ease with which underlying conceptual equivalences can be induced.

Operand Order Transfer Effects and
Conceptual Generalization Processes

Our explorations of operand order transfer in multiplication (see also Fendrich et al., 1993; Reder & Ritter, 1992; Siegler, 1986) represent an interesting case study of the development and stability of conceptual generalizations in human memory. As discussed earlier, representations of arithmetic facts appear to develop initially in an order-specific way. Our transfer results show clearly, however, that with sufficient experience they can take on a more generic form that does not include representation of order information. An additional and particularly interesting implication of our results is that even under conditions of extensive practice on one operand order, the nature of these generalized representations is left unchanged. This result suggests a principle of generalization such that once a generalization has taken place, the representations mediating performance will never revert to an earlier, more specific form, even under extreme conditions of extensive practice on items corresponding to that earlier form.

The prospect of such a simple and potentially far-reaching principle warrants additional research, especially in light of the current interest in distributed, connectionist models of memory and generalization. These models exhibit varying degrees of *catastrophic forgetting* (McCloskey & Cohen, 1989), such that exposure to new items tends to overwrite representations of old items. Even models that can largely overcome this extreme interference problem (see Kruschke, 1992, for a discussion) would probably have difficulty accounting for the combined findings of (a) order specificity on initial learning, (b) generalization across operand order with experience, and (c) remarkable stability of these generalized representations even under conditions of extensive practice on a more specific, earlier instance of the representation. Additional empirical investigations into the nature and stability of generalization effects thus have potential implications not only for the understanding of basic abstraction phenomena in human memory but also for evaluating the plausibility of various types of connectionist accounts of these processes.

Implications for Skill Retention

Both experiments of Rickard et al. (in press) showed that improvements in performance with practice on already existing skills (simple multiplication and division) were retained substantially across a 1-month interval. In contrast, the pound arithmetic experiment, which explored the effect of practice on a novel task, showed more significant decrements in performance on the delayed test. As we discussed earlier, the critical difference between these experiments is probably the fact that in the Rickard et al. (in press) experiments, the effect of practice was limited largely to improving the speed and accuracy with which existing factual information could be retrieved, whereas in the pound arithmetic experiment, improvements with practice reflected a strategy shift from the use of a slow algorithm to direct and relatively fast retrieval of answers from memory. One can invoke a simple strength-threshold model of memory to understand why skill retention was so different in these two cases. This model assumes that practice continually strengthens a memory trace for each problem. Before the strength reaches some criterion threshold, the answer to the problem cannot be retrieved, and performance will reflect alternative strategies, such as execution of a general algorithm (as in the pound arithmetic experiment). After the threshold is reached, the more efficient retrieval strategy will be used. The model assumes further that the memory trace will decay to some extent as a direct function of the time since the last retrieval. This decay process, however, is assumed to take place very slowly, perhaps over a period of months or years.

This model can account for the retention differences between the Rickard et al. (in press) experiments and the pound arithmetic experiment, in the following way. In the Rickard et al. (in press) experiments, subjects practiced on existing arithmetic facts that had above-threshold strengths at the onset of practice. Practice strengthened the traces substantially (as reflected in the speedup), and the decay of strength across the retention interval resulted in a slight reduction in strength, as reflected in somewhat slower RT in the noncritical change conditions on the delayed test in comparison to the immediate test. (Note that the speedup in the critical change conditions across the retention interval reflects practice effects on the immediate and the delayed tests.) On both tests, however, strengths presumably remained above threshold at all times. In the pound arithmetic experiment, however, memory traces were well below threshold at the beginning of practice (indeed, they were nonexistent), but they were above threshold by the end of practice (as evidenced by the data indicating a complete transition to retrieval by the end of the last practice session). Nevertheless, the memory traces would likely be much closer to threshold at the end of practice on this novel task than they were at the end of practice on the very familiar multiplication and division tasks of Rickard et al. (in press). Thus, decay across the delay interval in the pound arithmetic experiment was sufficient to push the strength of some of the memory traces below threshold, causing the observed reversion to use of the much slower algorithm strategy for many problems on the delayed test.

A strength-threshold approach to understanding these effects underscores two basic but important points concerning factors that are relevant to skill retention on tasks that can be performed using either a slow algorithm or fast memory retrieval. First, overlearning during initial acquisition is important for maximizing the probability that the memory trace will still be above threshold after a delay. Second, periodic retraining is necessary to keep the strength of memory traces above threshold and thus ensure continued availability of the memory retrieval strategy.

Notes

1. The reader may question whether one or more of these elements is redundant. The model, however, would make substantially different and often untenable predictions if any one of the elements that we have defined were excluded. For example, if the answer were excluded as an element, the model would predict that the same knowledge unit would be accessed by $28 \div 4 =$ __ and $4 \div 28 =$ __. Note also that the model can be restated equivalently in terms of the two numbers presented in the problem, the formal operation to be performed, and if and only if the operation is noncommutative, the order of the presented numbers.

2. Although our use of the term identical-elements is similar to and strongly motivated by its previous uses by Thorndike (1906) and Singley and Anderson (1989), there are also some differences. Thorndike's (1906) elements were the stimulus items themselves. Taken literally, this position predicts no transfer any time there is any change whatsoever in the makeup of the stimulus items (such as a change in operand order). Our elements are abstract representations of numbers and arithmetic operations. Singley and Anderson (1989) also proposed a general abstract identical-elements model of skill acquisition and transfer, framed within the ACT* architecture (Anderson, 1983). However, arithmetic facts could potentially be modeled using the ACT* architecture in many different ways that would yield many different predictions about transfer. In contrast, our identical-elements model, although much narrower in scope, makes very specific predictions regarding mental arithmetic.

References

Anderson, J. R. (1983). *The architecture of cognition.* Cambridge, MA: Harvard University Press.

Campbell, J.I.D. (1987). Network-interference and mental multiplication. *Journal of Experimental Psychology: Learning, Memory, and Cognition, 13,* 109-123.

Campbell, J.I.D., & Oliphant, M. (1992). Representation and retrieval of arithmetic facts: A network-interference model and simulation. In J.I.D. Campbell (Ed.), *The nature and origins of mathematical skills* (pp. 331-364). Amsterdam: Elsevier.

Fendrich, D. W., Healy, A. F., & Bourne, L. E., Jr. (1993). Mental arithmetic: Training and retention of multiplication skill. In C. Izawa (Ed.), *Cognitive psychology applied* (pp. 111-133). Hillsdale, NJ: Lawrence Erlbaum.

Healy, A. F., King, C. L., Clawson, D. M., Sinclair, G. P., Rickard, T. C., Crutcher, R. J., Ericsson, K. A., & Bourne, L. E., Jr. (this volume). Optimizing the long-term retention of skills. In A. F. Healy & L. E. Bourne, Jr. (Eds.), *Learning and memory of knowledge and skills: Durability and specificity.* Thousand Oaks, CA: Sage.

Kruschke, J. K. (1992). ALCOVE: An exemplar-based connectionist model of category learning. *Psychological Review, 99,* 22-44.

McCloskey, M., Caramazza, A., & Basili, A. (1985). Cognitive mechanisms in number processing and calculation: Evidence from dyscalculia. *Brain and Cognition, 4,* 171-196.

McCloskey, M., & Cohen, N. J. (1989). Catastrophic interference in connectionist networks: The sequential learning problem. In G. Bower (Ed.), *The psychology of learning and motivation* (Vol. 24, pp. 109-165). San Diego, CA: Academic Press.

McCloskey, M., & Lindemann, A. M. (1992). MATHnet: Preliminary results from a distributed model of arithmetic fact retrieval. In J.I.D. Campbell (Ed.), *The nature and origins of mathematical skills* (pp. 365-409). Amsterdam: Elsevier.

Olson, J. R., & Olson, G. M. (1990). The growth of cognitive modeling in human-computer interaction since GOMS. *Human-Computer Interaction, 5,* 221-265.

Reder, L. M., & Ritter, F. E. (1992). What determines initial feeling of knowing? Familiarity with question terms, not with the answer. *Journal of Experimental Psychology: Learning, Memory, and Cognition, 18,* 435-451.

Rickard, T. C. (1993). *Bending the power law: A quantitative model of the transition from algorithm to association.* Unpublished manuscript.

Rickard, T. C., & Bourne, L. E., Jr. (1993). *On the cognitive structure of basic arithmetic skills: Some tests of an identical elements model.* Unpublished manuscript.

Rickard, T. C., Healy, A. F., & Bourne, L. E., Jr. (in press). On the cognitive structure of basic arithmetic skills: Operation, order, and symbol transfer effects. *Journal of Experimental Psychology: Learning, Memory, and Cognition.*

Rickard, T. C., Mozer, M. C., & Bourne, L. E., Jr. (1992). *An interactive activation model of arithmetic fact retrieval* (Institute of Cognitive Science Technical Report number 92-15). University of Colorado, Boulder.

Siegler, R. S. (1986). *Children's thinking.* Englewood Cliffs, NJ: Prentice-Hall.

Singley, K., & Anderson, J. R. (1989). *The transfer of cognitive skill.* Cambridge, MA: Harvard University Press.

Thorndike, E. L. (1906). *Principles of teaching.* New York: A. G. Seiler.

10 Acquisition and Retention of Skilled Letter Detection

JANET D. PROCTOR

ALICE F. HEALY

Literature on the acquisition and retention of skilled letter detection is reviewed in two sections. The first section concerns the observation that extensive training in letter detection leads to automaticity. The conditions necessary for automaticity are summarized, and two different conceptions of the nature of automaticity are compared: process-based, or strength-based, theories and item-based, or instance-based, theories. Studies exploring the extent of transfer and retention of automaticity are shown to provide mixed support for the two types of theories. The second section of the review concerns the word frequency disadvantage that occurs with letter detection in prose. Work in our laboratories is summarized that shows a reduction of the word frequency disadvantage with practice and a persistence of this change across lengthy retention intervals. A strategy shift explanation for this change is ruled out, and it is shown that the practice necessary to elicit this change depends on a prose context and is highly specific to the particular target letters and test words used during training. These findings are compatible with item-based, or instance-based, theories.

In 1901, Thorndike and Woodworth reported one of the earliest studies of the effects of practice on letter detection performance. They compared the speed and accuracy of letter detection before and after practice involving different or similar target letter sets. As expected, letter detection performance improved in accuracy or speed with practice. Also, the greatest improvement was found when target letter sets overlapped in the test and practice phases.

AUTHORS' NOTE: Preparation of this chapter was supported in part by Army Research Institute Contract MDA903-93-K-0010 to the University of Colorado. We are grateful to Robert Proctor and Lyle Bourne for helpful comments on an earlier version of this chapter.

Thorndike and Woodworth (1901) were interested in the interdependence of mental functions. Having established that one mental function could affect another by demonstrating that the type of practice influenced the magnitude of a practice effect, they called for further research to determine the nature of this influence and to specify the particular aspects of skill that are affected by training. Cognitive psychology has since directed great attention to the nature of cognitive processes and skill acquisition. In this chapter, we examine the subset of this research concerning the acquisition of letter detection skill and the factors that influence letter detection performance.

The letter detection task typically involves the search for one or more target letters appearing in an array of unrelated letters (e.g., Neisser, 1963), a multiframe presentation of letters (e.g., Schneider & Shiffrin, 1977), or a display of one or more words (e.g., Healy & Drewnowski, 1983). When the target set consists of a single item and the display contains more than one item (e.g., Neisser, 1963), the task is sometimes referred to as "pure" visual search. When the target set contains more than one item but the display contains only one item or a constant number of items (e.g., Sternberg, 1963), the task is referred to as memory search. Tasks in which both the target set and the display contain more than one item are referred to as hybrid memory search tasks (e.g., Fisk & Hodge, 1992).

The acquisition of increased skill in letter detection has been the focus of an extensive body of research. The majority of this research has focused on the finding that after extensive practice, increases in target set size (e.g., Neisser, Novick, & Lazar, 1963; Schneider & Shiffrin, 1977) and display size (e.g., Schneider & Shiffrin, 1977) have little or no effect on search accuracy or search speed. For example, Neisser et al. (1963) found that subjects could search simultaneously for 10 items as well as they could search for one item. Likewise, Schneider and Shiffrin (1977) found equal performance across processing loads (target set size × display size) of up to 16 items after significant practice. They argued that the absence of an effect of processing load reflected a shift from an effortful and serial-like, or "controlled," process to one with few attentional demands and parallel in nature, termed "automatic." This type of improvement in performance occurs not only for letter detection but also for a wide variety of other target and task variations (see, e.g., Fisk & Hodge, 1992; Fisk, Lee, & Rogers, 1991; Logan, 1992; Treisman, Vieira, & Hayes, 1992).

Issues in Automaticity of Letter Detection

Much of the body of research on automaticity in detection has addressed three issues. First, substantial research has delineated conditions necessary for the development of automaticity. Second, a great deal of attention has been devoted to developing models to explain the nature of the changes in processing that produce automaticity. Third, research has examined the transfer and retention of automaticity.

Necessary Conditions for Automaticity

There is no great consistency in the data concerning the amount of practice necessary for the development of automaticity. Schneider and Fisk (1983) report that automaticity can develop in as few as 200 trials if appropriate training procedures are employed. However, many studies show much more substantial practice to be required. Schneider and Fisk (1982), for example, reported asymptotic letter search performance after approximately 1,000 trials, but when the task involved a very high workload from a concurrent task, automaticity development continued through 2,600 trials. Dumais (1979, cited in Shiffrin & Dumais, 1981) gave 4,000 trials of practice and found only incomplete automaticity. In her study, response latencies for 4-item displays were approximately 50 ms faster than were latencies for 16-item displays, and thus, display size slope was greater than zero. Czerwinski, Lightfoot, and Shiffrin (1992) also obtained only partial automaticity after over 4,000 trials, as did Healy, Fendrich, and Proctor (1987, 1990). Perhaps the most surprising failure to obtain full automaticity occurred in a study by Rabbitt, Cumming, and Vyas (1979). In this study, subjects practiced for 60,000 trials over 25 sessions of a hybrid memory search task. Memory set size and display size each included up to nine letters. Full automaticity was present only based on memory set size, not when defined by the display size effect.

Stimulus characteristics are a likely explanation for some of these very different results. Schneider and Fisk (1982), for example, purposefully selected stimuli from different categories (letters vs. digits) for their target and distractor sets so as to facilitate the acquisition of automaticity. Czerwinski et al. (1992) and Healy, Fendrich, et al. (1987, 1990) employed letters for both distractor sets and target sets, and Dumais (1979) employed sets of letters mixed with foreign alphabetic characters. In these cases the target-distractor discriminability was reduced, increasing the difficulty of automaticity development.

A second important variable is the nature of practice. Schneider and Shiffrin (1977; Shiffrin & Schneider, 1977) propose that for automatic processing to develop, mapping of target stimuli to responses must be consistent; stimuli that appear as members of the target set on some trials cannot appear as distractors on other trials. When target mapping is variable and stimuli appear as both targets and distractors across trials, no automaticity occurs. According to their theory of automaticity (e.g., Schneider, 1985; Schneider & Detwiler, 1987; Schneider & Fisk, 1983; Shiffrin & Czerwinski, 1988; Shiffrin & Schneider, 1977), variability in stimulus to response mapping prevents the development of automatic productions in which the appearance of the stimulus directly attracts attention and activates the appropriate response.

Certainly the necessity of consistent mapping has been the most common finding. However, recent research (Czerwinski et al., 1992) suggests that automaticity can also develop with a varied mapping procedure. Czerwinski et al. (1992) note that in previous consistent versus variable mapping studies the amount of practice given a particular stimulus item is greater in the consistent mapping condition than in the varied mapping condition. The consistent mapping superiority, then, could be due to an inequality of production strength caused by unequal practice. When Czerwinski et al. (1992) equated practice for each stimulus in the two mapping conditions, consistent mapping and variable mapping both produced the same increase in automaticity. Thus, varied mapping-consistent mapping differences in automaticity development might well result from a procedural artifact common to most procedures and not from changes in the nature of processing unique to practice with consistently mapped stimuli.

The Nature of Automaticity

The conceptualizations of the nature of automaticity are too numerous to discuss in detail here. However, two contrasting views receiving current attention should be noted. Logan (1988) has described theories of automaticity as two types. First, and most common, are theories that propose that automaticity reflects a greater efficiency in processing and reduced demands on attention (e.g., LaBerge & Samuels, 1974; Schneider, 1985; Shiffrin & Schneider, 1977). In this approach, performance improves because practice strengthens representations or productions of the task, eliminates or reduces attentional requirements, increases the discriminability of target items through the development of automatic detection, and allows bypassing of early stages of processing. Logan (1988) classifies this type of theory as process based, because it proposes that processes involved in task performance become more efficient, rather than different, and as strength based, because practice strengthens a production or stimulus-response link.

The alternative approach is Logan's (1988) instance theory of automaticity. This theory is a memory theory, rather than a theory emphasizing attention. It is item based in that it proposes that practice allows the subject to learn specific stimulus-response relationships rather than improving process efficiency. It is instance based in that practice increases the number of memory traces concerning the stimulus and response rather than increasing the strength of a task production or representation. In sum, Logan's (1988) theory proposes that each stimulus presentation produces an individual memory trace for the stimulus-response relationship. Practice increases the number of memory traces for each stimulus, increasing the probability that the stimulus-response relationship can be directly retrieved from memory.

Transfer of Automaticity

In comparison to the research examining other aspects of automaticity, transfer and retention of performance have been relatively neglected. However, the limited range of research contains some studies that are particularly interesting. Once again, though, the results sometimes conflict.

In the standard automaticity experiments, transfer manipulations have typically been limited to reversals of target and distractor sets. Shiffrin and Schneider (1977, Experiments 1 and 2) initially had subjects practice with one set or category of targets and distractors in a hybrid memory search task (letters and letters or letters and digits) and then reversed the target and distractor stimuli. The result was a serious decline in performance. Shiffrin and Schneider (1977) concluded that subjects were not simply learning some categorical discrimination, but instead were learning a stimulus to response relationship that depends on consistent mapping.

Dumais (1979) moved beyond the simple reversal conditions. She trained subjects in a pure visual search task with one target set and one distractor set and then introduced either a new target set while maintaining the original distractors or a new distractor set while maintaining the original targets. Here, performance was not affected; transfer performance showed no decrement at all when either the targets or the distractors maintained their assignment. Again, the data were interpreted in terms of the development of stimulus to response relationships in which, for this experiment, targets may be thought of as associated with a response or attention mode, whereas distractors become associated with a no response or "ignore" mode.

Similar effects have been obtained with semantic category visual search. Fisk, Lee, and Rogers (1991) gave subjects substantial consistent mapping practice searching for words belonging to a target semantic category and then examined several transfer conditions. Unique to this experiment is the simultaneous training of four different consistently mapped relationships. Four different target sets were separately paired with four different distractor sets. These pairings allowed seven different transfer manipulations: a trained target with an untrained distractor (target transfer); an untrained target with a trained distractor (distractor transfer); a previous distractor as target with an untrained distractor (distractor reversal); a previous target as distractor with an untrained target (target reversal); two previous targets, one now the distractor (target conflict); two previous distractors, one now a target (distractor conflict); and two previous variable mapping sets now used in a consistent mapping condition (new consistent mapping).

All conditions showed some decrement in performance relative to the end of the original training sessions. However, the decrement was smallest for the target transfer and distractor transfer conditions, and performance in those conditions was superior to performance in the new consistent mapping condition (however, see Kristofferson, 1977, for a case in which memory search practice fully transferred to entirely new items). All reversal and conflict conditions showed serious declines in performance such that they did not differ from the new consistent mapping condition.

Although both target and distractor conflict conditions were characterized by poor performance, the disruption was greatest in target conflict conditions. Apparently, learning to suppress stimuli formerly attended to is more difficult than learning to respond to formerly ignored stimuli. Fisk et al. (1991) interpreted these findings as supporting strength models of automaticity (e.g., Schneider, 1985) and these models' proposal that both target and distractor stimulus to "response" relationship strengths are increased by automaticity training.

In another semantic category search experiment, Fisk and Hodge (1992) again looked at transfer effects. In this experiment the transfer manipulations included previously untrained target categories or previously untrained target exemplars paired with trained target categories and exemplars. Performance was best maintained when both category and exemplars had been trained, but new exemplars from previously trained categories produced reasonable performance; detection of untrained exemplars was significantly faster than detection of varied mapping stimuli in all cases.

Based on these findings (see Pashler & Baylis, 1991, for additional evidence), it can be concluded that automaticity that develops from training with exemplars of a semantic category at least partially transfers to other exemplars; the training not only strengthens the individual exemplars but also strengthens the category.

Transfer of the influence of automaticity training also can extend to significantly different tasks. When consistent mapping training in a letter search task preceded a task in which subjects were asked to count the number of letters in a display, counting performance was improved (Dumais, unpublished research, cited in Shiffrin & Dumais, 1981). Shiffrin and Dumais (1981) suggest that the improvement in counting accuracy was the result of increased saliency of the letter (category) stimuli.

Up to this point the research provides a fairly orderly picture of transfer effects and similar insights as to underlying aspects of automaticity. Specifically, the findings tend to support the strength or process models (e.g., Schneider, 1985) and to indicate that training effects can extend beyond the individual stimuli given practice. As noted previously, however, research findings are not entirely consistent. Other research tends to support a more highly specialized automaticity effect compatible with Logan's (1988) instance-based theory. These studies do not show general transfer across conditions.

Treisman and her colleagues (Treisman et al., 1992; Vieira & Treisman, 1988) investigated whether automatic processing was preattentive processing and included manipulations to examine transfer of automaticity across stimuli and tasks. Subjects practiced a hybrid memory search task with random-line figure and letter stimuli. These stimuli and unpracticed stimuli were then used in a variety of transfer tasks (e.g., texture segregation, probe recognition, mental integration, part-whole perception, etc.) and transfer across tasks and stimuli were examined. Little evidence of transfer was obtained. In fact, seemingly irrelevant changes in stimulus presentation sometimes prevented transfer of training (e.g., Treisman et al., 1992). Switching from presenting the stimuli in a diamond-shaped array to a linear array or reversing the display and background colors slowed visual search performance. Based on these results, Treisman and her colleagues concluded that the mechanisms of automaticity best corresponded with the specific instance, memory model of Logan (1988).

Other evidence that practice effects are highly specific is available from studies of a variety of other tasks. Some of the best-known data supporting specificity comes from Kolers's inverted text research (e.g., Kolers, 1979). Kolers (1979) found that reading performance was best when the same typography was used for each passage. Likewise, in a more recent study,

Masson (1986) found that identification of typographically transformed words was aided by training only when training and testing instances shared common letters printed in the same case. Similarly, proofreading was improved by passage familiarity, but only if all aspects (type, modality, and wording) of the passage were exactly the same (Levy, 1983; but see Levy, Newell, Snyder, & Timmins, 1986, for a case of transfer across typescript). Clearly, there is a need for additional research to clarify the origin of the inconsistencies between those studies showing transfer across stimuli or tasks and those studies showing only highly specific effects of experience.

Retention of Automaticity

Like transfer, retention has not been a primary focus for work on automaticity. However, some of the transfer research also examined retention. The Rabbitt et al. (1979) study retested subjects in their hybrid memory search task 2, 4, or 6 weeks after they completed 3,000 trials of practice. Although the advantage of automaticity gained through practice showed no reduction at tests up to 4 weeks, Rabbitt et al. (1979) report significant decay at 6 weeks. Subjects retested on the same targets and distractors had mean reaction times approximately 34 ms slower than on the last day of practice, or a loss of approximately 20% of the improvement in reaction time shown from the first session to the last session of practice. In contrast, Healy et al. (1990) found full retention of performance after at least 1 month following automaticity training in a visual search task. In fact, two of their subjects who were tested at 6 months and over 1 year following training still showed full retention.

Retention of training effects was also found by Fisk and Hodge (1992). They retested subjects 30 days after completing a substantial amount of practice with a memory scanning task (almost 8,000 trials), a visual search task (almost 6,000 trials), or a hybrid memory search task (700-4,300 trials, depending on group). For the memory search task, little decay occurred. For pure visual search, only the subjects practiced and tested for transfer with the same items showed small (7%), but significant, decay. Decay in the hybrid memory search task occurred only for the multiple target set-multiple distractor set conditions (13%-18%), not for the visual search component (target set = 1, multiple distractors; nonsignificant 8%). Additional tests after a 1-year delay found no further deterioration of performance.

The Fisk and Hodge (1992) study provides important information. First, it indicates that the pattern of retention of practice effects is specific to

particular tasks. The more complex hybrid memory search is more susceptible to decay than is the visual search task. Also, this research seems to
explain the different retention patterns reported by Rabbitt et al. (1979)
and by Healy et al. (1990). Recall that Rabbitt et al. (1979) found significant decay at 1 month with memory search, whereas Healy et al. (1990)
found no decay after longer intervals with visual search. Fisk and Hodge
(1992) suggest that this discrepancy is attributable to task differences.
They propose that the more complex hybrid memory search, particularly
conditions with multiple targets and distractors, requires more integrative
functions, which are susceptible to decay.

At this point, we will shift away from research primarily devoted to
aspects of automaticity and examine instead letter detection practice in a
different environment. Recent work in our laboratories has investigated
the effects of practice on a particular letter detection familiarity effect
obtained in a reading environment.

Practice and the Word Frequency Disadvantage

Our interest in the underlying causes of improvements in letter detection
developed as we investigated possible loci for the word frequency disadvantage. When subjects perform a letter detection task while simultaneously reading a prose passage, they miss the target letter more frequently
when it appears in a very high frequency word (such as *the* or *and*) than
when it appears in other, lower frequency words (e.g., Healy, 1976; Healy
& Drewnowski, 1983; Healy, Oliver, & McNamara, 1987; Proctor &
Healy, 1985; see Healy, in press, for a review). Drewnowski and Healy
(1977; see also Hadley & Healy, 1991) proposed the unitization model to
account for this effect. This model suggests that very high frequency
words often can be identified before letters are fully processed and that,
after word identification, letter processing is terminated. Thus, letter-level
information in these very high frequency words is not available, and the
probability of letter detection is reduced.

An alternative to the assertion of the unitization hypothesis that letter
information is not available is the possibility that letter information is available but not easily accessible (see, e.g., Healy, Conboy, & Drewnowski,
1987). For example, Johnson, Turner-Lyga, and Pettigrew (1986) proposed that responses to targets were dependent on the cognitive codes
assigned to target detectors. The assignment of these cognitive codes may
be influenced by task demands. If the task is simply letter detection or
letter identification in single words (e.g., Reicher, 1969), the letter-level

detectors would be activated by the letters in words. However, if the task emphasizes semantic, word-level information (e.g., Healy, 1976), the cognitive code that determines the response would be assigned to the semantic, word level, rather than to the letter level. Therefore, even if letter-level information accumulates fully, it might not be accessible for response. Some subsequent research is consistent with this proposal (e.g., Greenberg, 1988; Greenberg & Vellutino, 1988).

We investigated the accessibility alternative by giving subjects substantial letter detection training in order to automatize detection of the target letter (Healy, Fendrich, et al., 1987; Healy et al., 1990). If letters are fully processed but not easily accessed for a detection response, automaticity training should allow subjects better access to the letter-level information, and thus greatly reduce or eliminate the word frequency disadvantage for letter detection in prose.

The automaticity training employed a pure visual search task with displays of up to 16 items. We varied across two experiments the type of training (letter detection in random letter strings vs. digit detection in random digit strings) and the amount of letter detection training (none, in the digit detection control task, to over 3,700 trials). As cited earlier, letter detection performance did improve substantially in the automaticity training task (although complete automaticity, as defined by zero-slope frame-size functions, was not obtained). However, letter detection in prose was not affected; the beneficial effect of practice in detecting letters in random letter strings did not transfer to detecting letters in prose. The magnitude of the word frequency effect was the same for all practice groups following automaticity training.

These data suggest that either the processes required for detecting letters in prose and for detecting letters in random letter strings are not the same, as might follow from process models of automaticity (e.g., Schneider, 1985), or that the stimuli, and therefore the memory traces, in the two contexts are too different for effective transfer of skills (e.g., Logan, 1988), or perhaps, that some combination of these factors operates.

Although the automaticity training did not influence subsequent letter detection in prose, we found a very large reduction in the magnitude of the word frequency disadvantage or a reversal to a word frequency advantage on the posttest prose letter detection task as compared to a pretest prose letter detection task. As confirmed by subsequent unpublished experiments by Fendrich, Healy, and Proctor, the cause of the reduction of the word frequency disadvantage was the practice obtained when performing letter detection in prose in the pretest, not the letter detection practice given in the automaticity training tasks. Experience with the letter detection in prose task in a single, moderate length passage is sufficient to reduce significantly or even eliminate or reverse the word frequency disadvantage in subsequent tests.

The rapid disappearance of an effect that is so reliably obtained and supposedly based on extensive experience with particular words raises many of the same questions addressed in the main body of research on standard automaticity situations. First, of course, is the question of what processes are changing. Is there a true shift in the way in which letters are handled, or are letter detection processes relatively unchanged but subject strategies are being altered? What type of practice is necessary to reduce the word frequency disadvantage? Is practice detecting letters in a prose context necessary? Does letter detection practice with one target letter or one familiar test word transfer to other letters and words, or is the practice effect highly specific? Also, how durable is the practice effect? We have begun to answer some of these questions.

Process or Strategy?

We have concluded that the practice effect for letter detection in prose is not the result of a simple shift in subject strategy in which subjects realize that certain words (e.g., *the*) always contain the target and begin to look specifically for those words. Experiments have repeatedly shown little influence of either reported or induced subject strategies (Proctor & Healy, 1993; Proctor, Healy, & Fendrich, 1988).

Two experiments (Proctor et al., 1988) manipulated information given to subjects that might influence their chosen strategies. In the first (explicit hint) experiment, we included the word *the* in the example given in the instructions to one group of subjects (e.g., "Jack saw the dogs"). Also, this group was explicitly told that the word *the* contains the target letter and to be careful not to forget to mark the target letter in the word *the*. The other group's instructions did not contain the word *the* or any special instructions about the task. The explicit hint did increase the number of targets detected in the word *the,* thus reducing the magnitude of the word frequency disadvantage, but a substantial effect remained.

In the second (subtle hint) experiment, either the example used in the instructions included the word *the* (but without any explicit statement about its particular importance) or the example did not include the word *the*. Although some subjects (approximately 20%) reported on a follow-up questionnaire that they had used a "look for *the*" strategy, no differences in the word frequency disadvantage were found for either the subtle hint versus no hint conditions, or between subjects who reported using the strategy and those who did not.

A third experiment (Proctor & Healy, 1993) examined the influence of strategy on the word frequency disadvantage practice effect. Here, subjects performed the letter detection task in two passages and then responded to a strategy questionnaire. When the data from subjects reporting a "look for *the*" strategy were compared to the data from subjects who did not report this strategy, no differences in the word frequency disadvantage practice effect were found. Strategy did increase the number of targets detected in the word *the,* but the practice effect matched that of subjects using other strategies. Therefore, the practice effect does not appear to involve a realization that a particular word always contains a target letter and a strategy to search explicitly for that word.

Clearly, although a "look for *the*" strategy can reduce the magnitude of the basic word frequency disadvantage, most subjects do not spontaneously adopt that strategy, and when they do, the practice effect is not different from that obtained with other strategies. These findings suggest that changes in the magnitude of the word frequency disadvantage are probably not due to conscious shifts in strategy.

Practice Characteristics

Although strategy is not particularly important in the word frequency disadvantage and is even less important in its practice effect, the nature of the practice is quite critical. Our most recent research (Proctor & Healy, 1993) has examined the essential characteristics of practice necessary to reduce or eliminate the word frequency disadvantage. We have found that the practice effect is highly specific and does not reflect a general improvement in letter detection skill.

First, the word frequency disadvantage is reduced most when letter detection practice is given in a normal prose context. Remember that automaticity training for target letter detection improved letter detection, but only for the automaticity task itself; it did not transfer to a subsequent letter detection task in prose. Proctor and Healy (1993) manipulated the contexts in which the detection practice was given. Specifically, subjects first were given letter detection practice in a prose passage, a scrambled words passage, or a scrambled letters passage. All subjects then performed the letter detection task in a normal prose context. The magnitude of the word frequency disadvantage for this second passage was examined as a function of the type of practice given. The word frequency disadvantage was smallest after practice with a normal prose passage, of intermediate magnitude when practice involved words in scrambled order, and largest after practice with a scrambled letter passage.

Practice also must be consistent in terms of target letter. When different target letters are used in the two passages, a practice effect is generally not found (Proctor & Healy, 1993) and the word frequency disadvantage maintains its original magnitude. This maintenance occurs even when the critical high-frequency word that contains the target letter is consistent across passages and only the target letter changes.

We (Proctor & Healy, 1993) varied the target letter and high-frequency test word across two prose passage letter detection tasks. Subjects circled the letter *h, t,* or *n* (one target only) in the first passage and *h, t,* or, *n* in the second passage. Those switched between *t* and *h* maintained the same high-frequency word (*the*) for both passages, whereas those switched to or from *n* had different high-frequency words (*the* and *and*) for the two passages. In general, the word frequency disadvantage was as large after practice with a different letter as it was before practice. In fact, there was generally no advantage of maintaining a constant high-frequency test word compared to switching both high-frequency test word and target letter (e.g., *t/the,* switched to *n/and*). However, in another set of experiments, we held target letter constant (*h* or *t*) and varied instead only the high-frequency test word (*the, this,* or *their*). The word frequency disadvantage for the word *the* was reduced by practice with a prose passage including that word but not by practice with the same prose passage with the word *the* replaced either by the word *this* or by the word *their* (Proctor & Healy, 1993). Thus, the practice effect is word specific as well as letter specific.

The highly specific nature of practice found in our research with letter detection in prose contrasts with the transferability of practice found for semantic category search (e.g., Fisk et al., 1991) and letter detection in typical automaticity research paradigms (e.g., Shiffrin & Dumais, 1981). Instead, our results are more compatible with the transfer data of Treisman et al. (1992), Kolers (1979), and Masson (1986). These latter studies found little transfer of skill to new stimuli or tasks, and as noted previously, modification of even nominally irrelevant details of the task was found to disrupt transfer.

Retention of Practice Effects

The studies reviewed previously indicate that the effects of automaticity training practice can be retained often with little or no loss of efficiency for periods of up to 1 year (e.g., Fisk & Hodge, 1992; Healy et al., 1990;

Kolers, 1976, 1979; Rabbitt et al., 1979). Durability also appears to be the case for the letter detection task in prose. Healy et al. (1990) found that the effects of practice in letter detection in prose are retained for at least 30 days, and perhaps to 15 months. Their subjects read three passages and searched for a target letter. The tests included a retention test after a delay of either approximately 1 month (Experiment 1) or up to 15 months (Experiment 2). Subjects in Experiment 1 displayed essentially perfect retention for 30 days. One subject in Experiment 2 performed the task with perfect accuracy 15 months after automaticity training, but the other subject showed a word frequency disadvantage after 6 months that was very similar to that found in the first passage. Although the magnitude of the word frequency disadvantage after 6 months matched the magnitude of the initial word frequency disadvantage for this subject, the accuracy overall of detecting the target letter remained substantially higher than in earlier tests.

Summary and Conclusions

In the first part of this chapter, we reviewed work concerning the development of automaticity in letter detection. Extensive training was generally found to be necessary for the development of automaticity, but automaticity development was shown to depend on both the stimulus characteristics (e.g., targets and distractors from same or different categories), and perhaps the nature of the practice that is given (consistent mapping or varied mapping). Following Logan (1988), we compared two different conceptions of the nature of automaticity: process-based, or strength-based, theories, such as that of Schneider (1985), and item-based, or instance-based, theories, such as that of Logan (1988). Because of mixed results from studies exploring the extent of transfer and retention of automaticity, we did not find clear support for one of these types of theories over the other. In the second part of the chapter, we reviewed our work concerning a word frequency disadvantage found with letter detection in prose and its reduction as a function of practice. In contrast to the mixed results of the automaticity research, our studies exploring the extent of transfer and retention of the word frequency disadvantage practice effect provide consistent evidence supporting highly specific processes compatible with the item-based or instance-based theories. We showed that the change in the word frequency disadvantage persists across long retention intervals, cannot be explained as a shift in the subjects' strategies, depends on practice in a prose context, and is highly specific to the particular target letters and test words used during training.

The highly specific nature of the practice effects reviewed here for letter detection in prose closely resembles the specificity of transfer in other visual pattern recognition tasks. For example, Kolers (1975, 1976) reported that transfer of practice effects for reading inverted text was greatest when the same text was read again, rather than a new text. Also, Kolers, Palef, and Stelmach (1980) found that variations in the case in which words were presented influenced subjects' ability to recognize them at a later test. Whittlesea and Brooks (1988) have shown that the particular types of experiences and contexts are highly influential in determining the perceptibility and recognizability of letters and words. Likewise, as reviewed elsewhere in this volume (Healy et al., this volume), the highly specific practice effects found for visual pattern recognition tasks are consistent with similar effects found for tasks in other domains, including Stroop color-word interference (Clawson, King, Healy, & Ericsson, this volume) and mental arithmetic (Rickard & Bourne, this volume). This highly specific nature of practice effects is compatible with models (e.g., Logan, 1988) based on specific memory representations. If physical appearance and context differences occur, new representations will not match earlier ones stored in memory.

References

Clawson, D. M., King, C. L., Healy, A. F., & Ericsson, K. A. (this volume). Training and retention of the classic Stroop task: Specificity of practice effects. In A. F. Healy & L. E. Bourne, Jr. (Eds.), *Learning and memory of knowledge and skills: Durability and specificity*. Thousand Oaks, CA: Sage.

Czerwinski, M., Lightfoot, N., & Shiffrin, R. M. (1992). Automatization and training in visual search. *American Journal of Psychology, 105*, 271-315.

Drewnowski, A., & Healy, A. F. (1977). Detection errors on *the* and *and*: Evidence for reading units larger than the word. *Memory & Cognition, 5*, 636-647.

Dumais, S. T. (1979). *Perceptual learning in automatic detection: Processes and mechanisms*. Unpublished doctoral dissertation, Indiana University.

Fisk A. D., & Hodge, K. A. (1992). Retention of trained performance in consistent mapping search after extended delay. *Human Factors, 34*, 147-164.

Fisk, A. D., Lee, M. D., & Rogers, W. A. (1991). Recombination of automatic processing components: The effects of transfer, reversal, and conflict situations. *Human Factors, 33*, 267-280.

Greenberg, S. N. (1988). Are letter codes always activated? *Perception and Psychophysics, 44*, 331-338.

Greenberg, S. N., & Vellutino, F. R. (1988). Evidence for processing of constituent single- and multiletter codes: Support for multilevel coding in word perception. *Memory & Cognition, 16*, 54-63.

Hadley, J. A., & Healy, A. F. (1991). When are reading units larger than the letter? A refinement of the unitization reading model. *Journal of Experimental Psychology: Learning, Memory, and Cognition, 17,* 1062-1073.

Healy, A. F. (1976). Detection errors on the word *the*: Evidence for reading units larger than letters. *Journal of Experimental Psychology: Human Perception and Performance, 2,* 235-242.

Healy, A. F. (in press). Letter detection: A window to unitization and other cognitive processes in reading text. *Psychonomic Bulletin and Review.*

Healy, A. F., Conboy, G. L., & Drewnowski, A. (1987). Characterizing the processing units of reading: Effects of intra-and interword spaces in a letter detection task. In B. K. Britton & S. M. Glynn (Eds.), *Executive control processes in reading* (pp. 279-296). Hillsdale, NJ: Lawrence Erlbaum.

Healy, A. F., & Drewnowski, A. (1983). Investigating the boundaries of reading units: Letter detection in misspelled words. *Journal of Experimental Psychology: Human Perception and Performance, 9,* 413-426.

Healy, A. F., Fendrich, D. W., & Proctor, J. D. (1987, November). *The effects of training on letter detection.* Paper presented at the 28th Annual Meeting of the Psychonomic Society, Seattle, Washington.

Healy, A. F., Fendrich, D. W., & Proctor, J. D. (1990). Acquisition and retention of a letter-detection skill. *Journal of Experimental Psychology: Learning, Memory, and Cognition, 16,* 270-281.

Healy, A. F., King, C. L., Clawson, D. M., Sinclair, G. P., Rickard, T. C., Crutcher, R. J., Ericsson, K. A., & Bourne, L. E., Jr. (this volume). Optimizing the long-term retention of skills. In A. F. Healy & L. E. Bourne, Jr. (Eds.), *Learning and memory of knowledge and skills: Durability and specificity.* Thousand Oaks, CA: Sage.

Healy, A. F., Oliver, W. L., & McNamara, T. P. (1987). Detecting letters in continuous text: Effects of display size. *Journal of Experimental Psychology: Human Perception and Performance, 13,* 279-290.

Johnson, N. F., Turner-Lyga, M., & Pettigrew, B. S. (1986). Part-whole relationships in the processing of small visual patterns. *Memory & Cognition, 14,* 5-16.

Kolers, P. A. (1975). Memorial consequences of automatized encoding. *Journal of Experimental Psychology: Human Learning and Memory, 1,* 689-701.

Kolers, P. A. (1976). Reading a year later. *Journal of Experimental Psychology: Human Learning and Memory, 2,* 554-565.

Kolers, P. A. (1979). A pattern analysing basis of recognition. In L. S. Cermak & F.I.M. Craik (Eds.), *Levels of processing in human memory* (pp. 363-384). Hillsdale, NJ: Lawrence Erlbaum.

Kolers, P. A., Palef, S. R., & Stelmach, L. B. (1980). Graphemic analysis underlying literacy. *Memory & Cognition, 8,* 322-328.

Kristofferson, M. (1977). The effects of practice with one positive set in a memory scanning task can be completely transferred to a new set. *Memory & Cognition, 5,* 177-186.

LaBerge, D., & Samuels, S. J. (1974). Toward a theory of automatic information processing in reading. *Cognitive Psychology, 6,* 293-323.

Levy, B. A. (1983). Proofreading familiar text: Constraints on visual processing. *Memory & Cognition, 11,* 1-12.

Levy, B. A., Newell, S., Snyder, J., & Timmins, K. (1986). Processing changes across reading encounters. *Journal of Experimental Psychology: Learning, Memory and Cognition, 12,* 467-478.

Logan, G. D. (1988). Toward an instance theory of automatization. *Psychological Review,* *95,* 492-527.

Logan, G. D. (1992). Attention and preattention in theories of automaticity. *American Journal of Psychology, 105,* 317-339.

Masson, M.E.J. (1986). Identification of typographically transformed words: Instance-based skill acquisition. *Journal of Experimental Psychology: Learning, Memory, and Cognition, 12,* 479-488.

Neisser, U. (1963). Decision time without reaction time: Experiments in visual scanning. *American Journal of Psychology, 76,* 376-385.

Neisser, U., Novick, R., & Lazar, R. (1963). Searching for ten targets simultaneously. *Perceptual and Motor Skills, 18,* 785-793.

Pashler, H., & Baylis, G. C. (1991). Procedural learning: 1. Locus of practice effects in speeded choice tasks. *Journal of Experimental Psychology: Learning, Memory, and Cognition, 17,* 20-32.

Proctor, J. D., & Healy, A. F. (1985). A secondary-task analysis of a word familiarity effect. *Journal of Experimental Psychology: Human Perception and Performance, 3,* 286-303.

Proctor, J. D., & Healy, A. F. (1993, May). *The effects of practice on the word frequency disadvantage in letter detection.* Paper presented at the Annual Meeting of the Midwestern Psychological Association, Chicago.

Proctor J. D., & Healy, A. F., & Fendrich, D. W. (1988, March). *The disappearance of the word inferiority effect: Strategy shift or perceptual effect?* Paper presented at the Annual Meeting of the Southeastern Psychological Association, New Orleans, Louisiana.

Rabbitt, P., Cumming, G., & Vyas, S. (1979). Improvement, learning, and retention of skill at visual search. *Quarterly Journal of Experimental Psychology, 31,* 441-459.

Reicher, D. (1969). Perceptual recognition as a function of meaningfulness of stimulus material. *Journal of Experimental Psychology, 81,* 274-280.

Rickard, T. C., & Bourne, L. E., Jr. (this volume). An identical-elements model of basic arithmetic skills. In A. F. Healy & L. E. Bourne, Jr. (Eds.), *Learning and memory of knowledge and skills: Durability and specificity.* Thousand Oaks, CA: Sage.

Schneider, W. (1985). Toward a model of attention and the development of automaticity. In M. I. Posner & O. S. Martin (Eds.), *Attention and performance* (Vol. 11, pp. 475-492). Hillsdale, NJ: Lawrence Erlbaum.

Schneider, W., & Detwiler, M. (1987). A connectionist/control architecture for working memory. In G. H. Bower (Ed.), *The psychology of learning and motivation* (Vol. 21, pp. 53-119). New York: Academic Press.

Schneider, W., & Fisk. A. D. (1982). Concurrent automatic and controlled visual search: Can processing occur without resource cost? *Journal of Experimental Psychology: Learning, Memory and Cognition, 8,* 261-278.

Schneider, W., & Fisk. A. D. (1983). Attention theory and mechanisms for skilled performance. In R. A. Magill (Ed.), *Memory and control of action* (pp. 119-143). Amsterdam: North-Holland.

Schneider, W., & Shiffrin, R. M. (1977). Controlled and automatic human information processing: I. Detection, search, and attention. *Psychological Review, 84,* 1-66.

Shiffrin, R. M., & Czerwinski, M. P. (1988). A model of automatic attention attraction when mapping is partially consistent. *Journal of Experimental Psychology: Learning, Memory, and Cognition, 14,* 562-569.

Shiffrin, R. M., & Dumais, S. T. (1981). The development of automatism. In J. R. Anderson (Ed.), *Cognitive skills and their acquisition* (pp. 111-140). Hillsdale, NJ: Lawrence Erlbaum.

Shiffrin, R. M., & Schneider, W. (1977). Controlled and automatic human information processing: II. Perceptual learning, automatic attending, and a general theory. *Psychological Review, 84,* 127-190.

Sternberg, S. (1963). High speed scanning in human memory. *Science, 153,* 652-654.

Thorndike, E. L., & Woodworth, R. S. (1901). The influence of improvement in one mental function upon the efficiency of other functions. *Psychological Review, 8,* 553-564.

Treisman, A., Vieira, A., & Hayes, A. (1992). Automaticity and preattentive processing. *American Journal of Psychology, 105,* 341-362.

Vieira, A., & Treisman, A. (1988, November). *Automatic search: Changing perceptions or procedures.* Paper presented at the 29th Annual Meeting of the Psychonomic Society, Chicago.

Whittlesea, B.W.A., & Brooks, L. R. (1988). Critical influence of particular experiences in the perception of letters, words, and phrases. *Memory & Cognition, 16,* 387-399.

11 Acquisition and Transfer of Response Selection Skill

ROBERT W. PROCTOR

ADDIE DUTTA

We review the primary findings of our research on the acquisition and transfer of response selection skill in choice-reaction tasks and discuss studies that examine the influence of practice on responding to spatial location and symbolic stimuli in stimulus-response compatibility, precuing, and categorical learning tasks. The influence of practice in these tasks is such that performance improvements occur rapidly and are retained well for at least 1 week. Stimulus-response compatibility effects endure throughout practice, but a pattern of differential precuing benefits tends to disappear. Transfer findings show that the performance improvements that occur with practice involve primarily the speed with which response locations assigned to stimuli can be selected, although direct associations between stimuli and effectors seem to play a role in the spatial precuing task.

When someone first performs a perceptual-motor task, considerable mental effort is required and responses tend to be relatively slow and inaccurate. As skill at the task is acquired, performance becomes more efficient and fluid, and less effort needs to be devoted to the determination and execution of responses. On the basis of changes such as these, some authors, most notably Welford (1968, 1976), have proposed that the primary influence of practice is on the processes that translate stimuli into responses, or on what we will call the response selection stage of human information processing. If this proposal is correct, one potentially fruitful strategy for studying skill acquisition is to examine changes in performance with practice for tasks that are presumed to provide relatively pure measures of response selection processes. This is the strategy that we and our colleagues have taken in much of our research.

Perhaps the most direct measures of response selection processes can be obtained in choice-reaction tasks. Such tasks use two or more stimuli assigned to two or more responses. On any trial, only a single stimulus is presented, and the response assigned to it is to be made as quickly as possible. The contribution of stimulus identification processes is minimized by using the same, easily discriminable stimuli in different conditions and by not including extraneous noise stimuli from which the target must be distinguished. The contribution of motoric processes is minimized by using simple responses, usually key presses, which are the same across the conditions of interest. Consequently, several phenomena that occur in choice-reaction tasks can be attributed relatively unambiguously to response selection processes.

As with virtually any task, when subjects practice choice-reaction tasks their performance typically improves. In many cases, the speedup in reaction times (RTs) follows a power function (Newell & Rosenbloom, 1981). Moreover, in agreement with the general point that performance in choice-reaction tasks is primarily determined by response selection requirements, the consensus is that the observed practice effects are attributable to changes in response selection efficiency (Pashler & Baylis, 1991; Teichner & Krebs, 1974).

During the past several years, we have been engaged in a research program to examine systematically the nature of the changes in response selection that occur as skill is acquired in choice-reaction tasks. In the present chapter, we review our primary findings, along with related work of other authors, to illustrate properties of the acquisition, transfer, and retention of response selection skill. Two categories of studies, those in which spatial location stimuli are assigned to key press responses and those in which symbolic stimuli are assigned to the key presses, are discussed.

Skill at Responding to Spatial Location Stimuli

In many choice-reaction tasks, the stimuli are spatial locations and the responses are key presses made at assigned locations. Considerable evidence indicates that response selection in such tasks is mediated initially by spatial codes for the stimulus and response sets (see, e.g., Umiltà & Nicoletti, 1990). Specifically, for two-choice reaction tasks in which left and right stimulus locations are assigned to left and right response locations, a stimulus-response (S-R) compatibility effect is obtained based on the mapping of stimulus locations to response locations. Responses are faster when the mapping of stimuli to response locations is direct (i.e., left stimulus mapped to left response and right stimulus to right response) than when it is not (i.e., left stimulus to right response and right stimulus to left response), regardless of whether the left response key is operated by the left index finger and the right key by the right index finger or vice versa (Brebner, Shephard, & Cairney, 1972). Similarly, for four-choice reaction tasks in which pairs of locations are precued, differences in the relative precuing benefits for different pairs of locations are a function of the spatial locations of the response keys and not the fingers assigned to the locations (Reeve & Proctor, 1984). We have examined effects of practice and transfer in both the spatial S-R compatibility and spatial precuing tasks. The primary questions of interest are whether spatial coding ceases to be a factor as subjects become practiced at the task, perhaps because a direct association between the stimulus and the response effector is formed, and the extent to which the benefits of practice transfer to altered task conditions.

Spatial Compatibility Effects

The basic spatial S-R compatibility effect is the one described above in which a direct mapping of left and right stimulus locations leads to faster RTs and fewer errors than does an indirect mapping. As with most other S-R compatibility effects, this effect is thought to reflect the additional processing required to determine the correct response under the indirect mapping as opposed to the direct mapping (Proctor & Reeve, 1990). It is often presumed that the necessity for mediation by such translation processes diminishes as subjects become practiced at a task. This presumption is apparent in models of attention for which it is proposed that automaticity develops (e.g., Schneider & Shiffrin, 1977) and in models of skill that propose that task-specific procedures are acquired (e.g., Anderson, 1982) when the S-R mapping is kept constant across the period of practice. The implication of this view seems to be that S-R compatibility effects should be eliminated with practice. Yet, such is not the case for the spatial two-choice task or for the other spatial compatibility tasks that we have examined.

The initial examination of practice in the two-choice task was conducted by Brebner (1973). Subjects in his experiment performed 120 trials on each of 10 days with each of four conditions comprising direct and indirect spatial S-R mappings and uncrossed (left index finger on left key; right index finger on right key) versus crossed (left index finger on right key; right index finger on left key) placement of the hands on the response keys.

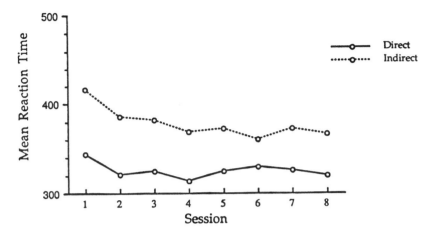

Figure 11.1. Mean Reaction Times (ms) as a Function of Session and Mapping in Dutta and Proctor's (1992) Experiment 1

Of concern here, the benefit for the spatially direct mapping did not disappear over practice. With the normal, uncrossed hand placement, the compatibility effect averaged over the first two sessions was approximately 70 ms and averaged over the last two sessions was approximately 50 ms. However, because subjects in Brebner's experiment switched between the four conditions each day of the experiment, the mapping of stimuli to responses varied within each session. It has been shown in many situations that consistent mappings are necessary for practice to be most beneficial (e.g., Schneider & Shiffrin, 1977), so the persistence of the compatibility effect could have been due to the varied mapping procedure that was employed.

To optimize any benefits of practice, we conducted an experiment in which each subject performed with only either the indirect or direct spatial mapping for eight sessions of 300 trials each (Dutta & Proctor, 1992, Experiment 1), using the uncrossed hand placement exclusively. Thus, a given subject performed in just one condition throughout the experiment. As shown in Figure 11.1, the initial compatibility effect was 72 ms. The magnitude of the effect decreased reliably across the first few sessions but little thereafter. In the eighth session, the RTs were still 46 ms faster for the direct mapping than for the indirect mapping. Thus, our results are very similar to those of Brebner (1973) and indicate that even when conditions of practice are consistent, performance with the indirect spatial mapping

Table 11.1 Mean Reaction Times (MRTs) in ms, Percent Error (PE), and Percent of Trials With Missed Deadline (MD) as a Function of Deadline and Assignment

Measure	Deadline									
	500	485	470	455	440	425	410	395	380	365
Direct Mapping										
MRT	298	288	277	275	267	268	265	264	260	256
PE	0.9%	1.5%	1.9%	2.6%	2.2%	2.5%	4.0%	4.4%	2.5%	4.4%
MD	1.2%	1.7%	1.3%	1.5%	1.1%	1.5%	2.2%	2.6%	1.3%	2.5%
Indirect Mapping										
MRT	328	315	306	296	293	288	280	279	276	267
PE	4.8%	3.8%	4.2%	5.3%	4.8%	6.9%	7.9%	7.8%	6.7%	8.1%
MD	4.0%	1.8%	1.2%	1.9%	1.9%	2.9%	2.6%	2.9%	3.1%	4.3%

remains at a disadvantage relative to that with the direct spatial mapping after considerable practice.

Although there was no sign of the compatibility effect disappearing with extended practice, it could be argued that with additional incentives to improve performance, the effect would disappear. Provision of feedback that supports setting or attainment of more stringent performance goals is one factor that has been shown to facilitate performance (e.g., Tubbs, 1986). Thus, we conducted two experiments in which subjects practiced for five sessions of 480 trials each, in blocks of 40 trials (Dutta & Proctor, 1993). In the first experiment, summary feedback in the form of mean RT and percentage correct was provided at the completion of each 40-trial block. The results were similar to those of our previous experiment. An initial compatibility effect of 91 ms was obtained that decreased in magnitude across the first three sessions. There was little subsequent change, and the effect was still 52 ms in the last session.

Because summary feedback alone was not sufficient to eliminate the spatial compatibility effect, a deadline procedure was introduced in the second experiment. Across 10 sessions of 240 trials each, the deadline was decreased in successive steps of 15 ms from 500 ms to 365 ms. As shown in Table 11.1, the deadline procedure was effective at decreasing the mean RTs. Even in the initial session, responses were fast, and the compatibility effect (30 ms) was smaller than in the previous experiments. Despite the reduced magnitude of the initial effect, it decreased reliably with practice to a value of 11 ms in the last session, which was still significant. Moreover, considerably more incorrect responses and missed deadlines occurred for the indirect condition than for the direct condition over all sessions, with the disparity in missed deadlines increasing significantly and the disparity in incorrect responses increasing by a nonsignificant amount as the deadline decreased. In short, the basic two-choice spatial compatibility effect is a phenomenon that persists throughout extended practice, even when summary feedback and deadlines encourage the setting of strict performance goals.

The persistence of the spatial compatibility effect found in the two-choice task is not unique. Fitts and Seeger (1953) showed such persistence across 25 sessions for compatibility effects obtained with an eight-choice task in which different stimulus displays were paired with different response arrangements and responses were executed by moving one or two styluses to assigned locations. Additionally, Dutta and Proctor (1992, Experiment 2) found that a compatibility effect obtained when stimuli above and below a fixation point are mapped to left and right key press responses (the mapping above-right/below-left leads, in most cases, to faster and more accurate responding than does the reverse mapping) was slightly larger in the last of eight sessions of 300 trials each than in the first session. Finally, Simon, Craft, and Webster (1973) examined responses to high- and low-pitched tones, with the ear in which the tone was heard varying randomly from trial to trial. Even though stimulus location was irrelevant to the task, RTs were slowed in the first of five sessions of 218 trials by approximately 60 ms when the stimulus location did not correspond to that of the assigned response (this phenomenon has subsequently come to be called the Simon effect). This effect of irrelevant location on RTs decreased across sessions but still was approximately 30 ms in the fifth session.

The persistence of spatial compatibility effects across practice suggests, contrary to the view that stimuli come to activate automatically their assigned responses, that translation processes continue to mediate response selection. A question that can be asked is whether any qualitative changes in these processes occur as subjects become practiced or whether the changes are strictly quantitative. By orthogonally varying hand placement with spatial mapping, as in Brebner's (1973) experiment, three different relations for which compatibility may be crucial can be isolated (see Figure 11.2): (a) stimulus locations to response locations, (b) response locations to the effectors (e.g., fingers) assigned to them, and (c) stimulus locations to effectors. Predictions for the ordering of the RTs can be made based on these relationships between stimulus locations, response locations, and effectors, which are illustrated in Figure 11.2. The general logic is that if a particular relation is important, RTs should depend on whether that relation is compatible or incompatible. Thus, faster RTs for

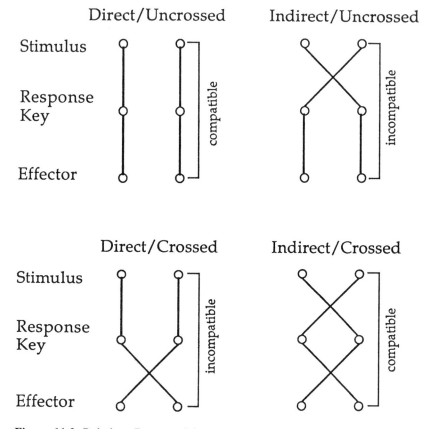

Figure 11.2. Relations Between Stimulus Locations, Response Key Locations, and Effectors for the Direct-Uncrossed, Direct-Crossed, Indirect-Uncrossed, and Indirect-Crossed Conditions. (For the relations between stimuli and response keys and between response keys and effectors, crossed lines indicate incompatibility and parallel lines indicate compatibility.)

SOURCE: From Proctor and Dutta (1993). Copyright 1993 by the American Psychological Association. Reprinted by permission.

the direct mapping than for the indirect mapping would indicate an effect of the relation between stimulus and response locations, and faster RTs for the uncrossed placement than for the crossed placement would indicate an effect of the relation between response locations and effectors. If the effects of spatial mapping and hand placement are underadditive, we can conclude that the relation between stimulus locations and effectors is of consequence, because this relation is compatible for the indirect-crossed condition.

The typical finding is that RTs are slower with the indirect spatial mapping than with the direct mapping and when the hands are crossed than when they are uncrossed, with these effects of spatial mapping and hand placement being additive (e.g., Brebner, 1973; Brebner et al., 1972). This pattern of results implicates spatial coding as the basis for the difference in compatibility between the direct and indirect mappings, with an additional contribution of the compatibility between the response location and the effector used to respond. It suggests no role of the stimulus location to effector relation.

To determine whether subjects continue to rely on spatial coding as they become practiced, we had subjects practice for three sessions of 300 trials each with one of the four conditions created by a factorial manipulation of direct versus indirect spatial mapping and crossed versus uncrossed hand placement (Proctor & Dutta, 1993, Experiment 1). As in previous studies, these two variables exerted independent effects in the initial session. More important, the functions remained parallel across the three sessions of practice. In other words, there was no evidence of a shift from spatial coding to direct specification by a stimulus of the responding finger.

After the three sessions of practice, one fourth of the subjects from each practice condition were tested in a transfer session with one of the four Mapping × Placement conditions. Positive transfer was evident for those conditions in which the spatial mapping was the same in the transfer session as in practice, with no evidence for transfer based on either of the other two possible compatibility relations. This finding indicates that the benefit of practice involved primarily the relation between stimulus and response locations. In subsequent experiments, subjects alternated between two of the four conditions every 42 trials. When alternation was between the indirect-uncrossed and indirect-crossed conditions, for which the spatial mapping is consistent, performance was similar to that of control subjects who did not alternate between conditions. However, when alternation was between the direct-uncrossed and indirect-crossed conditions, for which the stimulus location to effector relation is consistent but the spatial mapping is not, the alternation had strong interfering effects. Thus, the alternation data are consistent with the practice and transfer data in suggesting that the changes that occur with practice reflect quantitative changes in processing efficiency and not qualitatively different modes of processing.

Spatial Precuing Effects

Another line of research has examined practice and transfer effects in a four-choice spatial precuing task. For this task, a row of four stimulus locations is mapped compatibly to a row of four response locations, and subjects respond, usually with the index or middle finger of the left or right hand, to a target stimulus in one of the four locations. A precue row precedes the target at an onset interval that varies from 0 s (simultaneous presentation) to 3 s. When the precue is informative, it validly indicates two of the four locations as possible target locations; otherwise, the precue indicates all four locations. The primary outcome of interest is a pattern of differential precuing benefits that is most evident at precuing intervals of 1 s or less: RTs are fastest when the cues indicate either the two leftmost or two rightmost locations and slowest when the cues indicate either pair of alternate locations (e.g., Miller, 1982; Reeve & Proctor, 1984). As with the two-choice compatibility task, this pattern of precuing benefits is primarily a function of the spatial relations between the stimuli and responses. When the hands are overlapped so that the fingers from each hand are placed on alternate response locations, the benefit remains with the precues associated with the two leftmost or rightmost locations (Reeve & Proctor, 1984).

Proctor and Reeve (1988, Experiment 1) examined performance of this task across three sessions of 310 trials each. As with other spatial choice-reaction tasks, three sessions seem to be sufficient for most of the benefit of practice to occur. However, contrary to what is found for spatial compatibility effects, the pattern of differential precuing benefits virtually disappeared by the third session. In that session, all precue conditions produced precuing effects of approximately equal magnitudes. A subsequent experiment established that this change in performance is relatively durable. When performance of subjects tested in a fourth session the next day was compared to that of subjects tested a week later, no reliable differences between the two retention conditions were found (Proctor, Reeve, Weeks, Dornier, & Van Zandt, 1991, Experiment 1A).

Proctor and Reeve (1988, Experiment 2) evaluated whether transfer occurred when the hand placement was changed from overlapped to adjacent, or vice versa, in a fourth session. In contrast to the Proctor and Dutta (1993) study reported above, little evidence for transfer was apparent. The performance of subjects who switched from the overlapped to the adjacent hand placement not only showed a pattern of differential precuing benefits similar to that shown by subjects in their initial session of performance with the adjacent placement, but the overall level of the RTs was also equivalent. Subjects who switched from the adjacent placement to the overlapped placement also showed a reinstated pattern of differential benefits, but the magnitude was reduced somewhat from that typically evident in the initial session.

The relative lack of transfer between the adjacent and overlapped hand placements could be due at least in part to the relative difficulty associated with executing the appropriate finger response when using the overlapped placement. Proctor and Reeve (1988, Experiment 3) evaluated this possibility by requiring subjects to switch from the adjacent hand placement to a crossed-hand placement for which the fingers were not alternated. For this placement, the hands were crossed completely, as in the two-choice compatibility tasks, with the two leftmost responses made by the right index and middle fingers and the two rightmost responses by the left index and middle fingers. Again, the pattern of differential precuing benefits in the transfer session was comparable to that shown by subjects who had not first performed with the adjacent hand placement. The lack of transfer in the spatial precuing task suggests that subjects may have acquired direct associations between stimulus locations and their assigned fingers, contrary to the implication of the results obtained for the two-choice compatibility task.

Although little or no transfer occurs in the spatial precuing task when the mapping of fingers to locations is altered by changing hand placement, positive transfer is evident when the orientation of the stimulus or response set is changed. A pattern of differential precuing benefits similar to that obtained with horizontal stimulus and response sets is obtained when the stimulus set is oriented vertically on the display screen and the response set is oriented vertically along the transverse plane at the body midline (Proctor & Reeve, 1986), as well as when one set is oriented vertically and the other horizontally (Proctor, Campbell, Reeve, Weeks, & Dornier, 1994). Proctor et al. (1994) assigned one group of subjects to practice the spatial precuing task for three sessions with a vertically oriented stimulus display and a horizontally oriented response array, with the bottom-to-top order of stimulus locations mapped to the responses in a left-to-right order. The typical practice effect, in which the pattern of differential precuing benefits diminishes, was observed when the stimulus and response sets were oriented orthogonally in this manner. In a fourth session, the orientation of the stimulus display was changed to horizontal, making it parallel to the orientation of the response arrangement. The performance of subjects in this transfer session did not differ from that of a group of subjects who had practiced with the horizontal arrangements for all four sessions. This transfer when stimulus orientation was changed from vertical to horizontal suggests that with the exception of an additional transformation process, the processes used to perform the task with orthogonal orientations are the same as those used with parallel orientations.

Changing the orientation of the response arrangement from vertical to horizontal (or vice versa) introduces a methodological complication that is not a factor when display orientation is changed. This complication arises from the fact that for the vertical response arrangement, each hand must be turned inward for placement of the fingers on the keys. Consequently, when the response orientation is changed from vertical to horizontal, a minimum of two fingers will change their relative locations (e.g., if the bottom-to-top ordering of fingers with the vertical arrangement is left middle, left index, right index, and right middle, the relative locations of the left index and middle fingers will be switched with the horizontal arrangement, for which the left-to-right ordering is left middle, left index, right index, and right middle). Because little transfer occurs when the orientation of the response set is not changed but the mapping of fingers to locations is (Proctor & Reeve, 1988), any change in mapping of fingers to relative locations accompanying a change in response-set orientation could preclude transfer that might otherwise occur.

To address this issue, Proctor et al. (1994) conducted two experiments in which groups of subjects practiced with a horizontal stimulus display and a vertical response arrangement (with the stimuli from left to right mapped to the keys from bottom to top) for three sessions. This was followed by a transfer session in which both the stimulus and response sets were arrayed horizontally. In one experiment, a two-hand placement was used for the vertical response arrangement (bottom-to-top ordering of right index, right middle, left index, and left middle fingers) that allowed all four fingers to change relative locations when changed to a normal, adjacent placement with the horizontal arrangement. In the other experiment, all four responses were made with the fingers from the right hand (excluding the thumb), thus allowing the relative locations to be the same for the vertical and horizontal arrangements (bottom-to-top and left-to-right orderings of index, middle, ring, and little fingers). With the two-hand placement, for which the relative locations of the fingers changed from the practice sessions to the transfer session, performance with the horizontal arrangement in the transfer session was like that of subjects performing in an initial session with that arrangement, that is, there was no transfer. However, with the single-hand placement, for which the relative locations of the fingers were maintained in the transfer session, the results were similar to those of the experiment in which display orientation was changed: Performance with the horizontal arrangement in the transfer session was comparable to that of subjects who had performed with the horizontal arrangement all along. That transfer was apparent only when the relation between fingers and stimulus locations remained unaltered supports the findings of Proctor and Reeve (1988) in suggesting that this relation is part of what is learned in spatial precuing tasks.

At present, we can only speculate about why spatial precuing tasks suggest learning of direct stimulus-finger associations but two-choice compatibility tasks do not. There are numerous differences between the tasks that may be important. Most obvious, the phenomenon of concern in two-choice compatibility tasks is a comparison between spatially compatible and incompatible mappings, whereas the phenomenon of interest in the spatial precuing tasks is the relative efficiency of precuing within a single, usually spatially compatible, mapping. Another difference is that whereas the compatibility effects reflect the ease with which a single response to a target stimulus can be selected and executed, the differential precuing benefits reflect the ease with which two of the four responses can be selected as possible alternatives. Associated with this distinction is the fact that the event of interest in the compatibility task is a single stimulus location, whereas in the precuing task it is a pattern of locations. It is possible that the intent to prepare specific subsets of responses may lead to the acquisition of direct associations between specific precue stimulus patterns and their assigned fingers.

Skill at Responding to Symbolic Stimuli

For many skills, performance involves responding to symbolic stimuli and not to spatial locations. In choice-reaction tasks, stimuli such as letters and digits are often used. Such stimuli have been the focus of studies investigating symbolic compatibility effects and categorization phenomena.

Symbolic Compatibility Effects

Several studies have shown that when four two-dimensional, symbolic stimuli (e.g., the letters *O, o, Z, z*) are assigned to four key press responses, RTs are faster if the more salient letter identity feature of the stimulus set corresponds to the salient left-right feature of the horizontal response set (e.g., a left-to-right mapping of *O, o, z, Z*—the *OozZ* mapping) than if there is no systematic relation between stimulus features and the left-right feature of the response set (e.g., a left-to-right mapping of *O, z, o, Z*—the *OzoZ* mapping; e.g., Miller, 1982, Proctor & Reeve, 1985). The *OozZ* mapping also yields faster RTs than a mapping for which the less salient size feature of the stimulus set corresponds with the left-right feature of the response set (e.g., a left-to-right mapping of *o, z, O, Z;* De Jong, Wierda, Mulder, & Mulder, 1988). This symbolic compatibility effect seems to reflect differences in the amount of required S-R translation, in much the same way that the spatial compatibility effects do (De Jong et al., 1988; Proctor & Reeve, 1985).

The magnitude of the symbolic compatibility effect also decreases across three sessions of practice. In an initial experiment reported by Proctor et al. (1991, Experiment 1B), the difference in RTs between the *OozZ* and *OzoZ* mappings decreased from 88 ms in the first session to 2 ms in the third session. In a retention session conducted one week later, the difference between the mappings was 25 ms. This value was considerably smaller than that of the first session and did not differ reliably from that of the third session (although tending to be larger), indicating that the benefit of practice is retained relatively well. Although that experiment suggested that the symbolic compatibility effect disappeared with suffi-cient practice, subsequent experiments have not borne this out. For exam-ple, Dutta and Proctor (1992, Experiment 3) tested subjects for eight sessions of 310 trials and found compatibility effects of 88 ms in the first session, 42 ms in the third session, and 47 ms in the eighth session. Thus, as with the spatial compatibility effects discussed earlier, practice reduces but does not seem to eliminate the symbolic compatibility effect.

One of the most interesting cases of positive transfer that we have observed involves performance of the symbolic compatibility task follow-ing practice with the spatial precuing task (Proctor et al., 1991, Experiment 3). When subjects practiced with all of the spatial precue conditions for one session and then were transferred to the symbolic compatibility task, the typical large advantage (in this case, 111 ms) for the *OozZ* mapping over the *OzoZ* mapping was obtained. However, subjects who practiced exclusively with the subset of precues for the alternate locations showed only a nonsignificant advantage of 21 ms for the *OozZ* mapping, with the error rate being higher for this mapping (8%) than for the *OzoZ* mapping (5%). Similarly, in another experiment, subjects who had practiced solely with the precues that indicated either pair of extreme positions showed a symbolic compatibility effect of 89 ms, whereas subjects who had prac-ticed solely with the alternate location cues showed a difference between the *OozZ* and *OzoZ* mappings of just 8 ms. In short, practice with just the alternate locations seems to have increased the salience of those pairs of locations. For the *OzoZ* mapping, which is normally at a disadvantage relative to the *OozZ* mapping, the salient letter identity feature now corresponds with a salient feature of the response set, leading to decreased RTs for that condition relative to those customarily obtained.

Categorical Learning Effects

Pashler and Baylis (1991) conducted experiments in which the stimuli were selected from categories (letters, digits, and nonalphanumeric symbols), and the responses were key presses made with the index, middle, and ring fingers of the right hand. Following practice for 15 blocks of 50 trials each with a subset of category members, both old and new category members were tested for five additional transfer blocks. In experiments for which the mapping of stimuli to responses was categorizable (i.e., digits were assigned to one response, letters to a second, and symbols to a third), a high degree of transfer to new items in the category and little disruption of responding to the old items were observed in the transfer session. In contrast, when the mapping was uncategorizable (i.e., all stimuli were letters or both letters and digits were assigned to each of the three fingers), little transfer was evident. These data led Pashler and Baylis (1991) to conclude that the learning that occurs when symbolic stimuli are assigned to key press responses is primarily of the relation between the category representations and the responses.

This learning could involve the relations between categories and fingers or between categories and response locations. To evaluate these possibilities, Pashler and Baylis (1991) conducted an experiment with a categorizable mapping in which the hand used for responding (right or left) was changed for the transfer blocks. As with spatial S-R compatibility tasks, considerable transfer to the new hand was evident. This suggests that the relation learned is between the categories and response locations, rather than between categories and specific effectors.

Another outcome of interest in Pashler and Baylis's (1991) study is that with noncategorizable mappings, adding new stimuli to responses disrupted responding to the stimuli with which subjects had practiced. In fact, little transfer was evident and responses to old items were almost as slow as those to new items. Most accounts of practice effects, such as those in which the development of automaticity is postulated, would seem to predict little effect of new stimuli on responses to old stimuli. Because only a relatively small amount of practice, 750 trials, was given in these experiments, it is possible that the disruptive influence of new items would decrease if more extended practice were given. Dutta (1993, Experiment 2) gave subjects 1,200 trials of practice (25 blocks of 48 trials each) and found, to the contrary, that RTs for the old items were virtually identical to those for the new items in the first transfer block, as well as in the other transfer blocks. Moreover, when she varied amount of practice within a single experiment (Experiment 2A), the magnitude of interference for old items in the first transfer block, relative to the last practice block, increased monotonically (increases in RT of 37, 57, 98, 100, and 121 ms for groups receiving 5, 10, 15, 20, and 25 blocks of practice, respectively). Thus, the disruptive influence of new stimuli on responses to old stimuli clearly is not due to insufficient practice with the old stimuli.

Pashler and Baylis (1991) proposed an *ad hoc category node* hypothesis to account for the disruption in responding to old stimuli. According to this hypothesis, ad hoc category nodes are created to encompass groups of stimuli that were unrelated prior to the experiment but that are related within the experiment through being assigned to the same responses. The addition of new stimuli in the transfer blocks renders the original ad hoc categories inapplicable and requires that new category nodes be created. Hence, responding to the old stimuli is disrupted.

One implication of the ad hoc category node hypothesis is that if new members are introduced for only some of the three S-R sets in the transfer blocks, no new ad hoc category node would have to be created for the unchanged sets. Consequently, there should be no disruption of responding to old stimuli for unchanged sets. Dutta (1993, Experiment 4) tested this implication by introducing a new stimulus item for either one or two of the three stimulus sets during the transfer blocks. In contrast to the prediction of the ad hoc category node hypothesis, performance was disrupted for both changed and unchanged sets when either one or two of the sets were changed.

The fact that introduction of new stimuli produces disruption in responding even for stimuli in sets that remain unchanged suggests that some learning of the entire stimulus set in relation to the response set occurs. This finding poses problems not only for the ad hoc category node hypothesis but also for associationistic accounts in which an S-R bond is strengthened by the coactivation of a stimulus and response. It seems that the efficiency of response selection depends also on the similarity between a specific stimulus and the alternative members of the stimulus set. Just as S-R compatibility effects depend on the ensemble of stimuli assigned to a response set, so does the entire set of stimuli influence choice reactions when multiple stimuli are assigned to each response. Only if the stimulus set has some structure to it (e.g., letters, numbers, and nonalphanumeric stimuli, examined in Pashler & Baylis, 1991, or groups of visually similar stimuli assigned categorically, examined in Dutta, 1993, Experiment 5) does category-based translation seem to occur.

Conclusions

Several empirical generalizations emerge from the research that we have reviewed in this chapter. First, practice effects in a range of choice-reaction tasks develop during the first 500-1,000 trials and remain relatively stable thereafter. Both spatial and symbolic S-R compatibility effects show a reduction in magnitude during this period, but little further change with more extended practice (Dutta & Proctor, 1992). Also, the pattern of differential precuing benefits in spatial precuing tasks is virtually eliminated within this period (Proctor & Reeve, 1988), and relations between symbolic stimuli and their assigned responses for both categorizable and uncategorizable mappings show evidence of having been learned (Pashler & Baylis, 1991).

A second empirical generalization is that the benefits of practice seem to be retained well. After practicing the spatial precuing task for three sessions, the performance for subjects tested 1 week later is comparable to that of subjects who are tested on the next day (Proctor et al., 1991). Also, subjects who practice the symbolic compatibility task for three sessions continue to show the reduced effect typical of practiced subjects 1 week later (Proctor et al.,1991).

A third generalization is that positive transfer to altered task conditions occurs in several situations. These situations include modifications in the assignments of fingers to response keys (Pashler & Baylis, 1991; Proctor & Dutta, 1993), changes in orientations of the stimulus arrays and response arrays (Proctor et al., 1994), and switches from spatial to symbolic stimulus sets (Proctor et al., 1991).

There is widespread agreement that performance of choice-reaction tasks at early stages of practice relies on the efficiency of response selection (e.g., Umiltà & Nicoletti, 1990). The codes for key press responses are presumed to be spatial, with the stimulus codes also being spatial if location is the defining stimulus property and symbolic if the stimuli are alphanumeric. A significant question is whether the codes that mediate response selection initially continue to play a mediating role as subjects become practiced, or whether direct associations between stimuli and effectors are acquired. The results from all of the tasks, except perhaps spatial precuing, converge on the answer that there is no qualitative change in the nature of response selection.

In the two-choice compatibility task, the role of spatial coding does not seem to diminish and direct associations between stimuli and fingers apparently are not learned. This is evidenced by the findings of Proctor and Dutta (1993) that (a) RTs for the four conditions created by the combinations of direct/indirect spatial mappings and crossed/uncrossed hands maintain the same ordering across three sessions of practice, (b) transfer occurs only for conditions in which the spatial mapping used in practice is maintained, and (c) subjects can switch between hand placements without apparent cost if the spatial mapping is constant but not if the spatial mapping is changed. The studies with symbolic stimuli paint a similar picture. The symbolic compatibility effect obtained with two-dimensional stimuli assigned to four key press responses apparently does not disappear with extended practice (Dutta & Proctor, 1992). Also, after practicing with a categorizable mapping of stimuli to responses, the hand with which the responses are executed can be changed with little consequence (Pashler & Baylis, 1991), suggesting that the relation between categories and response locations is crucial. With a noncategorizable mapping, adding a new stimulus member to the set of stimuli assigned to one or two of three responses increases the RTs of the responses for which the stimulus sets have not been changed (Dutta, 1993), implying that direct associations between the stimuli and the response are not the basis of response selection skill.

In contrast to the findings from the spatial compatibility task and the symbolic stimulus tasks, the results from the spatial precuing task suggest that direct associations between stimuli and specific fingers are acquired with practice. Unlike the S-R compatibility effects, which persist throughout extensive practice, the pattern of differential precuing benefits is virtually eliminated (Proctor & Reeve, 1988; Proctor et al., 1991). More important, although transfer can occur when spatial properties, such as orientation, are changed (Proctor et al., 1994), there is scant indication of transfer when the assignment of fingers to locations is altered. Proctor and Reeve (1988) found that the precuing pattern was reinstated when subjects switched hand placements from adjacent to crossed, from overlapped to adjacent, and to a lesser extent, from adjacent to overlapped. The importance of maintaining the relation between locations and fingers was confirmed by Proctor et al. (1994), who showed that transfer from a vertical orientation of the response set to a horizontal orientation occurred when the assignment of fingers to stimulus locations (and relative response locations) remained constant but not when the assignment of fingers to response locations also changed.

In an earlier review of the research on response selection skill, Proctor, Reeve, and Weeks (1990) concluded, primarily on the basis of the results from the spatial precuing task, that precues come to activate directly the fingers used to execute the assigned responses. Although the data from the precuing task continue to be consistent with such an interpretation, the data from the other tasks that we have discussed in this chapter clearly are not. At present, it is unclear why the relation of stimuli to the responding fingers seems to be important for skilled performance of the precuing task but not of the other tasks. The use of more than two response alternatives does not seem to be the crucial factor, because the experiments with symbolic stimuli used three or four responses. Rather, the distinction likely lies in the fact that the pattern of differential precuing benefits reflects the ease with which a subset of the possible responses can be selected and subsequently prepared, whereas the other phenomena all reflect the ease with which a single response to a target can be selected and executed. The act of preparing a subset of responses from the initial set may cause an association to be acquired between the specific precue stimulus patterns and the effectors that they specify.

To summarize, the changes in processing that lead to more efficient performance of choice-reaction tasks occur with relatively little practice and are retained with little decrease in efficiency for a period of at least 1 week. These changes predominantly concern the response location assigned to stimuli. When the stimulus set is categorizable, or structured in some other manner, the response selection processes utilize this structure. Positive transfer is often obtained when the assignment of effectors to response locations is changed and the mapping of stimuli to response locations held constant, although such does not occur in the spatial precuing task. Transfer also occurs when relative location is maintained, but orientation is altered, and when response locations that correspond with a salient feature of a stimulus set are made more salient. Most of the findings suggest that a qualitative shift with practice to direct specification of responses by stimuli does not occur.

References

Anderson, J. R (1982). Acquisition of cognitive skill. *Psychological Review, 89*, 369-406.

Brebner, J. (1973). S-R compatibility and changes with practice. *Acta Psychologica, 37*, 93-106.

Brebner, J., Shephard, M., & Cairney, P. (1972). Spatial relationships and S-R compatibility. *Acta Psychologica, 36*, 1-15.

De Jong, R., Wierda, M., Mulder, G., & Mulder, L.J.M. (1988). Use of partial information in response processing. *Journal of Experimental Psychology: Human Perception and Performance, 14*, 682-692.

Dutta, A. (1993). *Categorical learning in choice-reaction tasks.* Unpublished doctoral dissertation, Purdue University, West Lafayette, IN.

Dutta, A., & Proctor, R. W. (1992). Persistence of stimulus-response compatibility effects with extended practice. *Journal of Experimental Psychology: Learning, Memory, and Cognition, 18,* 801-809.

Dutta, A., & Proctor, R. W. (1993). The role of feedback in learning spatially indirect choice reaction tasks: Does it have one? In *Proceedings of the Human Factors and Ergonomics Society 37th Annual Meeting* (pp. 1320-1324). Santa Monica, CA.

Fitts, P. M., & Seeger, C. M. (1953). S-R compatibility: Spatial characteristics of stimulus and response codes. *Journal of Experimental Psychology, 46,* 199-210.

Miller, J. (1982). Discrete versus continuous stage models of human information processing. *Journal of Experimental Psychology: Human Perception and Performance, 8,* 273-296.

Newell, A., & Rosenbloom, P. (1981). Mechanisms of skill acquisition and the law of practice. In J. R. Anderson (Ed.), *Cognitive skills and their acquisition* (pp. 1-56). Hillsdale, NJ: Lawrence Erlbaum.

Pashler, H., & Baylis, G. (1991). Procedural learning: 1. Locus of practice effects in speeded choice tasks. *Journal of Experimental Psychology: Learning, Memory, and Cognition, 17,* 20-32.

Proctor, R. W., Campbell, K. C., Reeve, T. G., Weeks, D. J., & Dornier, L. (1994). *Translating between orthogonally oriented stimulus and response arrays in four-choice reaction tasks.* Manuscript submitted for publication.

Proctor, R. W., & Dutta, A. (1993). Do the same stimulus-response relations influence choice reactions initially and after practice? *Journal of Experimental Psychology: Learning, Memory, and Cognition, 19,* 922-930.

Proctor, R. W., & Reeve, T. G. (1985). Compatibility effects in the assignment of symbolic stimuli to discrete finger responses. *Journal of Experimental Psychology: Human Perception and Performance, 11,* 623-639.

Proctor, R. W., & Reeve, T. G. (1986). Salient-feature coding operations in spatial precuing tasks. *Journal of Experimental Psychology: Human Perception and Performance, 12,* 277-285.

Proctor, R. W., & Reeve, T. G. (1988). The acquisition of task-specific productions and modification of declarative representations in spatial-precuing tasks. *Journal of Experimental Psychology: General, 117,* 182-196.

Proctor, R. W., & Reeve, T. G. (Eds.). (1990). *Stimulus-response compatibility: An integrated perspective.* Amsterdam: North-Holland.

Proctor, R. W., Reeve, T. G., & Weeks, D. J. (1990). A triphasic approach to the acquisition of response-selection skill. In G. H. Bower (Ed.), *The psychology of learning and motivation* (Vol. 26, pp. 207-240). San Diego, CA: Academic Press.

Proctor, R. W., Reeve, T. G., Weeks, D. J., Dornier, L., & Van Zandt, T. (1991). Acquisition, retention, and transfer of response selection skill in choice reaction tasks. *Journal of Experimental Psychology: Learning, Memory, and Cognition, 17,* 497-506.

Reeve, T. G., & Proctor, R. W. (1984). On the advance preparation of discrete finger responses. *Journal of Experimental Psychology: Human Perception and Performance, 10,* 541-553.

Schneider, W., & Shiffrin, R. M. (1977). Controlled and automatic human information processing: I. Detection, search, and attention. *Psychological Review, 84,* 1-66.

Simon, J. R., Craft, J. L., & Webster, J. B. (1973). Auditory S-R compatibility: Analysis of correct responses and errors over a five-day period. *Journal of Experimental Psychology, 101,* 175-178.

Teichner, W. H., & Krebs, M. J. (1974). Laws of visual choice reaction time. *Psychological Review, 81,* 75-98.

Tubbs, M. E. (1986). Goal setting: A meta-analytic examination of the empirical evidence. *Journal of Applied Psychology, 71,* 474-483.

Umiltà, C., & Nicoletti, R. (1990). Spatial stimulus-response compatibility. In R. W. Proctor & T. G. Reeve (Eds.), *Stimulus-response compatibility: An integrated perspective* (pp. 89-116). Amsterdam: North-Holland.

Welford, A. T. (1968). *Fundamentals of skill.* London: Methuen.

Welford, A. T. (1976). *Skilled performance: Perceptual and motor skills.* Glenview, IL: Scott, Foresman.

12 The Specificity and Durability of Rajan's Memory

RODNEY J. VOGL

CHARLES P. THOMPSON

A series of studies on the skilled memorist, Rajan Mahadevan, showed that his performance is both very specific and very durable. Rajan demonstrated exceptional memory performance on numerical tasks such as the recitation of the digits of Pi, memory span for digits, and learning number matrices. However, the skill Rajan has developed working with digits has not transferred to letter memory span or other nonnumerical tasks. Generally, his performance on nonnumerical tasks fell within the range of normal memory performance.

As Rajan was given each new task in this series of studies, he became faster (and/or more accurate) with practice. The durability of Rajan's skill was reflected in the maintenance over time (without practice) of his speed and accuracy, and especially his performance on the learning of number matrices. Once Rajan increased his speed of learning, he needed less time to learn later matrices. He did not need to relearn that skill.

We also looked at the specificity of the skill of other memorists. Research on some of the memorists (Inaudi, Diamandi, Finkelstein, SF and DD, JC, and Bubbles P.) suggests that their memory skills were quite specific. In contrast, research on the memorists Rückle, Shereshevskii, VP, TE, and Aitken suggests that their skills were quite generalizable. One is tempted to speculate that the latter set of memorists such as Rückle, Shereshevskii, and Aitken have naturally powerful memories whereas those showing specific skills (including Rajan) do not.

Mnemonists have routinely astounded audiences with their extraordinary feats of memory. Their performance is so facile and unusual that one tends to assume that they have exceptional, almost superhuman,

AUTHORS' NOTE: We wish to extend our thanks to Dan Aeschliman, Minida Dowdy, Will Eckels, Cosima Hadidi, Tricia Hoard, Grant Numberg, and David Welch, who served as our stalwart control subjects and testers. The research reported here was supported by National Institute of Mental Health Grant MH44090 with the second author as principal investigator.

ability. There is another possibility, however. The mnemonists may have taken good or very good memory abilities and developed them with practice to the point where their performance is extraordinary. Chase and Ericsson (1981, 1982) demonstrated that ordinary subjects can develop memory skills sufficient to show exceptional memory performance. That demonstration leads to two important questions: First, is the memory skill specific to a certain type of material or task—or does the memory skill generalize to increased performance on all kinds of memory tasks? Many of the chapters in this book present evidence, as have Ericsson and his colleagues (Chase & Ericsson, 1981, 1982; Ericsson, 1985, 1988; Ericsson & Faivre, 1988) to suggest that skilled performance is very specific. We will show that the observations we made of a skilled memorist, Rajan Mahadevan, are consistent with that view. We will also discuss the specificity of skilled memory in several other memorists.

Second, how durable is the memory skill (i.e., how long does it last)? That question is more difficult to answer because it is impossible to control for potential practice outside the laboratory. However, we collected data from Rajan on matrix learning that we believe relevant to that question.

We begin by presenting evidence of Rajan Mahadevan's skilled memory. One can see evidence of Rajan's exceptional memory performance on numerical tasks such as his recitation of the digits of pi, memory span for digits, learning number matrices, and ability to conduct a memory search of a very large set of digits (the first 10,000 digits of pi). Following that evidence, we show that his exceptional memory performance is specific to digits. Next, we present evidence regarding the durability of Rajan's skill. Last, we discuss the performance of other skilled memorists, focusing on the specificity of their skill.

The data we use to demonstrate the specificity and durability of Rajan's skill are drawn from a series of experiments reported in two sources (Thompson, Cowan, Frieman, Mahadevan, Vogl, & Frieman, 1991; Thompson, Cowan, & Frieman, 1993). The data presented here are derived both from those reports and from the experiments reported there. The two sources also provide more detailed descriptions of the experimental procedures and results that we have summarized here.

Evidence for Rajan's Memory Skill

Recitation of Pi

Rajan Mahadevan earned a place in the *Guinness Book of World Records* on July 5, 1981, by reciting the first 31,811 digits of pi from memory in 3 hours 49 minutes (including 65 minutes of rest breaks). His record stood until March 9, 1987, when Hideaki Tomoyori recited 40,000 digits of pi in 17 hours 21 minutes (including 255 minutes of rest breaks). Rajan's recitation of pi is impressive for the speed at which he recited the digits as well as the number of digits he recited. Rajan's rate of recitation for the first 10,000 digits of pi was 4.9 digits per second. He gradually slowed down as he progressed through the digit string, but his average rate of recitation for the entire list of 31,811 digits of pi was 3.5 digits per second.

Rajan's rapid rate of presentation is impressive and suggests that he was not using a mnemonic device to retrieve the digits from memory. In contrast, Tomoyori recited the 40,000 digits of pi at an average rate of .85 digits per second. Tomoyori used a mnemonic to retrieve the digits, thus slowing his rate of recitation in comparison to Rajan.

Memory Span for Digits

Several years after Rajan's recitation of pi for the *Guinness Book of World Records,* he enrolled at Kansas State University as a graduate student in psychology. When Rajan agreed to have his memory investigated, we began with one of the most stable measures of memory ability: memory span.

In the memory span task, subjects attempt to recall a sequence of digits in the order in which the digits were presented. The digits are presented either visually or auditorially at a rate of one digit per second. A person's memory span is the number of digits that can be consistently recalled in the correct order. Most unpracticed individuals can recall between five and nine items on such a task. It is rare to find someone that has a memory span less than four digits or greater than eleven digits.

Rajan was first tested on the memory span task when he was visiting friends at the University of Minnesota in 1980 (Hanson, 1980; Horn, 1981). At that time, Rajan had a digit span of 15 digits when the digits were presented auditorially. We assumed that Rajan had not practiced this task previously so we took 15 digits as a first approximation of his baseline (i.e., unpracticed) memory span.

That estimate was supported by the results of an experiment in which we measured Rajan's responses when learning digit sequences of various lengths. We hypothesized that Rajan mastered long strings of digits in the memory span task by systematically encoding short sequences equal to or less than his baseline span. We speculated further that he rehearsed those short strings together with the order of their occurrence so that he could recite the entire string in the correct order. This process of decoding a series of short strings into the proper order should take some time. It follows from our speculations that recital of subspan strings should be essentially immediate whereas recital of supraspan sequences should be delayed because of the decoding entailed.

To test our speculations, we gave Rajan both ascending and descending series in the memory span task. In an ascending series, Rajan started at a span of 7 digits with the span increased by one following each errorless recall until he successfully completed the final span of 30 digits. In a descending series, Rajan started with 30 digits, and the span was decreased by one following each errorless recall until the lower bound of 7 digits was reached.

We designated the time between the end of the presentation of a sequence and the beginning of the recitation of that sequence as *rehearsal time*. We measured the rehearsal time for each span in 20 ascending and 20 descending sequences. We calculated the median rehearsal time for correctly recited spans of each length. These data are shown in Figure 12.1. As can be seen, Rajan's rehearsal time remained quite low and constant for spans ranging between 7 and 14 digits for both ascending and descending sequences. From that point on, his rehearsal time increased systematically as span length increased. The break point between constant and increasing rehearsal time supported our hypothesis that Rajan's baseline span was about 15 digits.

When we began testing Rajan's memory in 1988 we measured his digit memory span to be 43 digits when presentation was auditory and 28 digits with visual presentation. This level of performance was well above his baseline of about 15 digits. We suspected that Rajan became intrigued with the task after being tested at the University of Minnesota and thus practiced this task in the 8 years preceding our tests. In fact, Rajan's digit span continued to improve with practice. We tested Rajan's memory span approximately 2 years after we had conducted our initial tests. Rajan's digit span had increased to 59 digits when the digits were presented visually on a computer screen. His span for strings presented auditorially by the experimenter was 63 digits.

Rajan's digit memory span of about 60 digits (59 for visual presentation and 63 for auditory presentation) is clearly exceptional memory performance. However, others have been able to achieve even greater digit spans by using strategies to develop skilled memories. Ericsson and Chase (Chase & Ericsson, 1981, 1982; Ericsson & Chase, 1982; Ericsson, Chase, & Faloon, 1980) studied two individuals who learned to increase their memory span from around 7 digits to over 80 digits. The two memorists learned to encode the digits in the memory span task as running times

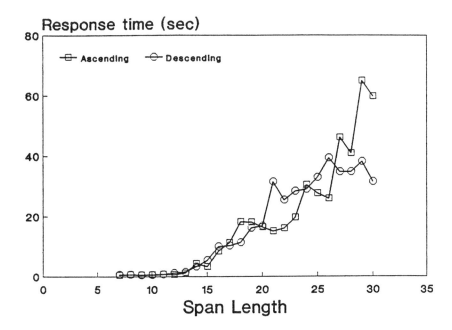

Figure 12.1. Rajan's Median Rehearsal Times for Each Memory Span Length for Ascending and Descending Series

because both of them were long-distance runners. For example, the digits 2, 1, and 8 would be remembered as 2 minutes and 18 seconds (which is close to the world record for running 1,000 meters).

Compared to other memorists, Rajan uses a conceptually barren strategy to remember digits. Other memorists, like the two studied by Chase and Ericsson (1981, 1982), attempt to relate "chunks" of digits to previous knowledge (e.g., 357 is a type of gun). By contrast, Rajan states that he uses a modified paired-associate strategy. In paired-associate (or cue-target) learning, a subject learns a list of word pairs. One word in the pair acts as a cue for recall for the target word. In Rajan's version, the cues are the location within the digit sequence and the correct digits are the targets (e.g., the 15th digit is a 4).

Memory for Number Matrices

We also tested Rajan on his ability to learn number matrices and recall them at a later time. Using a random number generator, we constructed

Table 12.1 Mean Time (s) per Digit to Learn Matrices

Matrix Size	Rajan	Control Subjects
5 × 5	2.1	6.6
6 × 6	1.5	8.3
7 × 7	1.7	8.2
9 × 9	2.7	12.1
10 × 10	3.1	13.5
12 × 12	3.5	
14 × 14	4.3	
20 × 20	5.8	

five different matrices for each of six different sizes (5 × 5, 7 × 7, 9 × 9, 10 × 10, 14 × 14, and 20 × 20). We also constructed eight 6 × 6 and eight 12 × 12 matrices for a total of 46 matrices. Thus, the matrices ranged in size from 25 to 400 digits.

Beginning with Ebbinghaus (Ebbinghaus, 1885/1964; Strong, 1912; Gillund & Shiffrin, 1984), many investigators have shown that the study time per item increases as the list gets longer. This well-established phenomenon is referred to as the *list length effect*. We used a large range of matrix sizes because we wanted to determine whether Rajan's study time per digit would increase as the matrix sizes increased. In short, we were interested in whether Rajan would demonstrate a standard list length effect.

Rajan's rate of learning was well beyond normal performance. Rajan was able to learn a 10 × 10 matrix in 5 minutes and a 20 × 20 matrix in about 30 minutes. By comparison, the mean study time for a group of control subjects to learn the same 10 × 10 matrix was approximately 22 minutes. For humanitarian reasons, the control subjects were asked to learn only those matrices that were equal to or less than 100 digits (the 10 × 10 matrices). Those data are shown in Table 12.1.

Rajan did show a list length effect. His study time per digit increased at a rate of .7 s per digit for every additional 25 digits. By contrast, the control subjects' mean study time per digit increased at a rate of 2.3 s per digit with each additional 25 digits. Thus, not only did Rajan learn the matrices at a much faster rate than the control subjects, but he was less susceptible to the list length effect.

Rajan not only showed great speed in learning the matrices; he also recalled them with considerable accuracy. Rajan made only four errors in recalling 46 matrices. He gave an incorrect digit on two matrices, omitted a digit on a third matrix, and inverted three digits on a fourth matrix. All of Rajan's errors occurred on either 12×12 or 20×20 matrices. This error rate is very low considering the number and size of the matrices he was asked to recall.

By contrast, the control subjects exhibited a wide range of error performance. The best control subject made a single error on one of the 5×5 matrices. The worst control subject found the task very aversive and made extensive errors on all of the larger (9×9 and 10×10) matrices. That subject also made one or more errors on 6 of the 18 remaining matrices. The other two control subjects made errors on five and seven matrices, respectively.

Rajan's strategy for learning number matrices was a minor modification of the procedure he used in learning long strings in the memory span task. Investigation of his pauses while reciting showed that Rajan used each row of the matrix (no matter what length) as a chunk. He then identified each digit in the row by its location (e.g., the fourth digit in Row 3 is a 2). In addition, further investigation showed that he could recall any row and the first column with great speed, but took much longer to recall columns. Rajan stated that he memorized the first column of the matrix so that he would recite the rows in the correct order.

It should be pointed out that Rajan's chunks almost always appeared to be devoid of meaning. By contrast, other people typically break up strings of digits or letters into units that can be encoded as meaningful chunks. This was not the case with Rajan. He relied on encoding the location of the digits into memory rather than producing some meaningful association for the sequence of digits.

After determining that Rajan used a modified paired-associate strategy to learn the matrices, we tested whether he relied entirely on that strategy. If Rajan only used the location of the digits within the rows to learn the matrix, it should not matter whether the individual digits in the matrix were presented in a systematic or in a random order (providing the location for each digit was specified). Therefore, as a strong test of the hypothesis that he relied on a paired-associate strategy, we predicted that Rajan's study time for matrices should be the same for both presentation of the digits in normal reading order (designated serial presentation) and random presentation of the digits.

In this experiment, Rajan was given 60 matrices with half presented randomly and half presented serially. Six matrix sizes were used (3×3, 4×4, 5×5, 7×7, 9×9, and 10×10) with five matrices for each size. Serial presentation of the matrix began with displaying the digit in the upper left-hand corner of the matrix and displaying the other digits successively in normal reading order. Random presentation of matrices was computer determined by randomly sampling the digit locations without replacement. During presentation, the matrix was outlined on the computer screen as a square array of boxes. For example, a 5 × 5 matrix was displayed as 25 boxes in a 5 × 5 array. A digit appeared in one of the boxes. Rajan pressed the space bar when he was ready to advance to the next digit. The computer recorded the study time for each digit.

Analysis of Rajan's study times demonstrated that he benefited from information other than the location within the matrix. The mean time per digit to study matrices presented serially (2.4 s) was much shorter than the mean time to study matrices presented randomly (14.7 s). Thus, Rajan used more information than digit location. We speculate that he used serial information (e.g., 2 follows 7) as well as location information in constructing his mental representation of a matrix.

Memory Search of Pi

Rajan demonstrated his memory skill in a very impressive way when he conducted a memory search of the first 10,000 digits of pi. For example, Rajan was able to report correctly that the 4,063rd decimal digit of pi is a 6. In the experiment on memory search of pi, we randomly sampled 2,000 digit locations from the first 10,000 digits of pi. The digit locations were randomly presented on a computer monitor. We measured Rajan's response time to produce the target digit.

Three important aspects of Rajan's performance were considered. These were the speed with which he correctly recalled the digits, his accuracy, and the nature of his errors.

Rajan's median response time to find the correct digit was 13.0 s. For the last 1,000 trials, his median search time was 11.6 s. It is evident that he was fast and his performance on this task improved with practice.

Rajan's overall error rate was 4.2% for 2,000 trials. However, his error rate on the last 1,000 digits was 1.0%. Thus, he was both fast and accurate.

Rajan's errors reflected the organization of the source from which he learned the digits of pi, a reproduction of a paper by Shanks and Wrench (1962). The digits are grouped in 10-digit strings with 10 strings in a row, hence 100 digits. The rows are grouped into 10-row blocks, thus, 1,000 digits in a block. There are five 1,000-digit blocks (or 5,000 digits) on each page.

Upon examining Rajan's errors closely, we determined that 63% (52 out of 83) of his errors were counting errors, that is, he was in error either by 1 digit (in the correct 10-digit block—14 such errors), 10 digits (right row and right location within the block, wrong 10-digit block—18 such errors), or 100 digits (right location in the row, wrong row—20 such errors).

According to Rajan's self-report and analysis of his response times, it appeared that he was able to locate the correct row of 100 digits of pi quickly. Once Rajan found the correct row, he simply counted across the row until he arrived at the correct location in the row (e.g., the 63rd digit is 6). To test Rajan's claim that he was able to arrive at the correct row quickly, we gave Rajan the starting location of a row in the first 10,000 digits of pi and asked him to recite the first five digits from that row. Rajan was able to find the correct row in about 1.5 s (the median search time for incorrect responses was 2.1 s). His error rate for finding the correct row was 3.1%. Thus, Rajan was able to respond very quickly as well as accurately.

Rajan reported that he had the digits of pi in chunks of 10 digits as printed in his source. That self-report was supported by the prevalence of counting errors in the error data. Given such chunks, we hypothesized that Rajan would be able to locate a string of 10 digits in pi quickly if the string of 10 digits corresponded to a printed string (a complete block of digits). Further, the critical comparison was that it should take Rajan longer to find a group of 10 digits that spanned two successive strings in pi. To test our speculation, Rajan was presented 80 cards that contained 10 successive digits in pi and was required to give us the following 5 digits. Forty-one of the digit sequences were complete strings and 39 of the sequences were spanning strings. The two types of strings were randomly presented. Rajan's response time to call out the five digits that followed the target string was recorded.

Rajan was able to locate the complete strings in about 8 s whereas location of the spanning blocks of digits took about 81 s. These results strongly suggest that Rajan has the digits in groups of 10. This task was very difficult for Rajan, and he was not able to locate 22.5% of the strings presented to him. Nevertheless, his performance was still impressive. He was, after all, locating the correct sequence of 10 digits in the first 10,000 digits of pi using a memory search. This feat strikes us as much like searching for the proverbial needle in the haystack.

It is clear that Rajan demonstrated exceptional memory performance on several memory tasks. His digit memory span was well beyond the normal range. He was able to learn number matrices much more rapidly than the control subjects. His ability to search for digit sequences in pi has, to our knowledge, never been duplicated.

Rajan's exceptional memory performance could be described according to the theory of skilled memory developed by Chase and Ericsson (Chase & Ericsson, 1981, 1982). These theorists proposed three characteristics of skilled memory. First, people use preexisting knowledge to encode presented information (i.e., meaningful encoding). Second, people explicitly attach retrieval cues to the encoded material to facilitate retrieval. Third, there is a reduction in study time to learn new material with further practice. Rajan demonstrated some of the characteristics of skilled memory. He has a retrieval structure for recalling the digits of pi, for memory span, and for number matrices. He also demonstrated speedup and improved his performance with practice. He has developed a strategy for encoding digit sequences (note, however, that his paired-associate strategy does not add meaning to the sequence). In short, Rajan demonstrated skilled memory based on highly efficient procedures or operations that do not embellish representations with new facts or associations. We now turn to the issues of the specificity and duration of his memory skill.

The Specificity of Rajan's Skill

In this section, we show that the skill Rajan has developed working with digits has not transferred to letter memory span or other nonnumerical tasks. Generally, his performance on nonnumerical tasks falls within the range of normal memory performance.

Letter Memory Span

We presented letters to Rajan in the same manner in which we presented the digit memory span task. Letters were either presented visually on a computer screen or auditorially by the experimenter. When we initially tested Rajan's memory, his letter memory span was the same for both auditory and visual presentation (13 letters). Note that we estimated Rajan's baseline (i.e., unpracticed) digit span to be approximately the same length (15 digits).

Over 2 years after the project had begun and many hours of practice on the digit span task, Rajan's digit span had increased to around 60. We thought it likely that Rajan's improvement with practice on digit memory span would transfer to the very similar letter span task. However, when we tested his letter span, it was 12 digits—essentially the same as when originally tested (13 digits). Somewhat to our surprise, Rajan's skill at the memory span task was specific to digits and did not transfer to letters.

Word Lists

As we have noted, Rajan's strategy for memorizing strings of digits (digit span, number matrices, or digit sequences in pi) focused on memorizing the location of the digit within the digit string (e.g., the 14th digit is 3). This strategy may work for strings of digits that are not meaningful, but it should not work as well for lists that can be organized into a meaningful structure (i.e., categorized word lists). When people are given a list of categorized words to remember, they usually organize the words by category in recall. Indeed, if the words cannot be organized into distinct categories, people tend to impose their own subjective organization on the list of words. Rajan, on the other hand, had used location as a tool to memorize digits in a number of tasks. Therefore, we thought Rajan would ignore any categorical organization in word lists and rely on some version of his standard strategy.

We presented Rajan and the control subjects with three of each of the following types of word lists: low-frequency uncategorized words, high-frequency uncategorized words, and categorized words. The uncategorized word lists contained 50 eight-letter, two-syllable nouns. The classification by frequency of occurrence used the Kucera and Francis (1967) norms. Low-frequency words had a frequency count of 1 and the high-frequency words ranged from 50 to 847. The categorized word lists were composed of words from seven categories with seven words from each category for a total of 49 words. The words in the categorized lists were taken from Battig and Montague's (1969) category norms and ranged in frequency from 1 to 200. Each word list was presented for three trials. The words were presented in a random order, one every 2 seconds.

Rajan's recall performance strongly suggested that he continued to use a version of his location strategy. On each trial for each list, Rajan attended to the first 12 to 15 words presented that had not yet been learned. He spent the remainder of the recall period rehearsing those items. He used that strategy on all lists and ignored the categorical structure in the categorized lists.

The data from two measures of organization in recall support our view that Rajan's strategy ignored categorical structure. We used a measure of subjective organization (ARC'; Pelligrino, 1971) for the low-frequency and high-frequency word lists. Subjective organization (Tulving, 1962) refers to the subject's tendency to recall a list of unrelated words in the same order even though the list is presented in a different random order on each trial. Rajan consistently scored higher on the subjective organization measure than the control subjects. For example, on the third trial with high-frequency unrelated words, his mean ARC' score was .69, whereas the mean ARC' score for the control subjects was .21. His strategy of recalling successive subsets of 12 to 15 words should (and did) lead to a high subjective organization score.

Our second measure of organization was a measure of the clustering in recall of categorized words (ARC; Roenker, Thompson, & Brown, 1971). Clustering (Bousfield, 1953; Thompson & Roenker, 1971) refers to the subject's tendency to recall a list of categorized words by category even though the words are presented in a random order. In the ARC measure, a score of one (1) indicates perfect organization and a score of zero (0) indicates that organization is occurring at a chance level. For the categorized lists, the control subjects' ARC scores ranged from .70 to .77, whereas Rajan's scores ranged from .04 to .13. Clearly, Rajan ignored the structure of the categorized material, whereas the control subjects did not.

Rajan's recall performance was superior to the controls for the low-frequency and high-frequency lists, but the control subjects recalled the categorized words better than Rajan did. After three recall trials, the control subjects remembered 26 low-frequency words and 32 high-frequency words. Rajan remembered 10 more words than the control subjects (36 low-frequency words and 42 high-frequency words). However, the control subjects remembered more of the categorized words (41 words) compared to Rajan (35 words).

Rajan's performance on word lists suggested that his memory skill could be modified to aid his performance under certain circumstances. Rajan's strategy, in a modified form, worked for unrelated words, that is, his performance was substantially better than that of the control subjects. Note, however, that his performance was about 25% better, rather than as in the case of digit performance, several hundred percent better. Most important, his strategy resulted in inferior performance when the word lists could be organized.

Story Memory

Given Rajan's rather poor performance on categorized word lists, we were interested in examining his ability to recall other organized textual material, such as stories. A common test is Bartlett's (1932) "War of the Ghosts" story, but Rajan had been exposed to the story earlier and had been tested on it. Thus, we used three Eskimo stories with characteristics similar to "The War of the Ghosts." The three Eskimo stories were taken from Rice (1980) and were titled "The Dog Wife," "Nakkayaq and His Sister," and "Kayatuq the Red Fox."

Rajan and the control subjects followed the same procedure. Only one story was given per session. The subjects were allowed to read each story twice at their own rate. The subjects were asked to produce a written

Table 12.2 Mean Study Time and Recall of Idea Units for Control Subjects and Rajan for Eskimo Stories

	"Dog Wife"	"Sister"	"Red Fox"
Idea Units Recalled			
(Total Possible)	(60)	(77)	(71)
Rajan	42	30	52
GN	31	41	34
TH	32	45	35
MD	48	65	59
DA	49	68	63
Study Time (s)			
Rajan	277	249	593
GN	175	202	248
TH	132	145	107
MD	258	227	241
DA	279	325	239

version of the story after performing other tasks for about 45 minutes. The subjects were instructed to be as accurate as possible in their reconstruction.

The mean study time and recall data for both Rajan and the control subjects are shown in Table 12.2. These data show that Rajan's recall of the story was low or intermediate compared to the performance of the control subjects. Rajan's study times were similar to the control subjects' times, with the exception of one story on which he spent much more time than did the control subjects. Again, these data suggest Rajan's exceptional memory performance is specific to digits. He is quite ordinary at remembering textual material.

Complex Figure Test

We asked Rajan to recall figures that were too complex to be encoded verbally. We used the Rey-Osterrieth Complex Figure Test (Rey, 1942; Osterrieth, 1944), which was developed to measure visual-spatial memory. Good imagery should aid performance on these tasks. Rajan claimed that he did not use imagery when memorizing any material (digits or text). If his claim were true, Rajan's memory skill should have no effect on his ability to recall a complex figure.

Rajan and the control subjects were asked to recall two complex figures both 30 minutes and 48 hours after they had originally copied the figures. Time to study and to reproduce the figures was recorded, and the reproduced figures were scored for accuracy. In brief, the results showed that Rajan's accuracy and production time for the first figure was close to the mean for the control subjects. On the second figure, his performance was nearly identical to the performance of the two best control subjects, but he took an unusually long time to study the figure.

Rajan's description of his strategy for recalling the figures lacked imagery. Rajan described the figures in terms of the number of lines in a quadrant and symmetrical properties such as five parallel lines. The control subjects, on the other hand, relied heavily on visual imagery. One subject described a figure as a house with a person inside and a TV antennae and kite flying on top of the house. The contrast suggests that Rajan was correct in claiming that he does not use imagery when memorizing material.

All of the evidence from Rajan's performance on nonnumerical tasks leads to one general finding. The skill that Rajan has developed to demonstrate exceptional memory for digits produces exceptional performance only with digits. Rajan's strategy is a conceptually barren strategy that generally cannot be applied to nonnumerical material. We found a version of his strategy to produce better performance than that produced by control subjects only in the case of unrelated word lists. However, the same strategy produced poorer performance than controls for categorized word lists. Most surprising, given the nature of his strategy (i.e., pairing locations with target digits), his skill at digit memory span did not transfer to the very similar task of letter span.

The Durability of Rajan's Memory Skill

We have provided strong evidence that Rajan's memory skill is specific to digits. It is much more difficult to provide evidence of the durability of Rajan's skill. The problem is that Rajan was continually practicing his skills. He sought out opportunities to demonstrate his skill in public, and of course, he was continually being tested in our laboratory. Thus, his skills were being maintained.

Nevertheless, we observed a phenomenon in all the tasks we gave him (with the exception of memory span) that convinced us of the durability of his skill. Specifically, Ericsson and Chase (Chase & Ericsson, 1981, 1982; Ericsson, 1985, 1988; Ericsson & Faivre, 1988) suggest that skilled memory is quite task specific and a memorist should speed up when learning a new task. Indeed, as Rajan was given each new task, he became faster (and/or more accurate) with practice. The important point is that the speed and accuracy were maintained when we encountered breaks of days or weeks in testing. Thus, the durability of Rajan's skill is reflected in the maintenance over time (without practice) of his speed and accuracy.

The best data we have to demonstrate the durability of Rajan's skill comes from the experiments we conducted on Rajan's ability to remember number matrices. Although Rajan had some practice in learning number matrices, he had never been systematically exposed to a set of matrices as large as the set we required him to learn. Further, although we presented the matrices randomly, we did so with the restriction that Rajan was exposed to each matrix size in each group of seven matrices. Thus, we expected that we should be able to observe the predicted speedup by examining the time to learn each group of seven matrices. Providing we observed the initial speedup, the durability of Rajan's expertise would be evidenced by the degree to which he maintained the final speed of performance.

In our experiment, we used a random number generator to construct five different matrices for each of six different sizes (5 × 5, 7 × 7, 9 × 9, 10 × 10, 14 × 14, and 20 × 20). Thus, the matrices ranged in size from 25 to 400 digits. We tested Rajan's memory for a subset of this original set of matrices 6 months after he had learned the matrices. In this test, Rajan attempted to recognize and recall the old matrices. He had to relearn any matrix he could not recall. Also, we added two new matrices of each size (as recognition foils), which he had to learn.

We look first for evidence of speedup while learning the initial matrices. The mean time per digit to learn each group of seven matrices is shown in Figure 12.2. As can be seen, the time to learn each matrix group decreases systematically over groups. Thus, there was a clear speedup effect for Rajan while learning the initial matrix set.

The question is whether Rajan would maintain his speed when learning new matrices some months later. In short, evidence for the durability of Rajan's skill would be seen in his time to learn new groups of number matrices 6 months later. Thus, we measured the mean time per digit to learn each of the two groups of six new matrices. Those data also are shown in Figure 12.2.

Rajan's performance demonstrates that he retained the skill obtained while learning the initial matrices. Rajan's study time to learn the first group of new matrices after a 6-month interval was slightly shorter than his time to learn the last group (i.e., Group 5) of the initial matrix set. It is important to point out that the skill demonstrated in this task was specific to the task we set in the laboratory. Although Rajan was performing and practicing his number-learning skills outside the laboratory, the

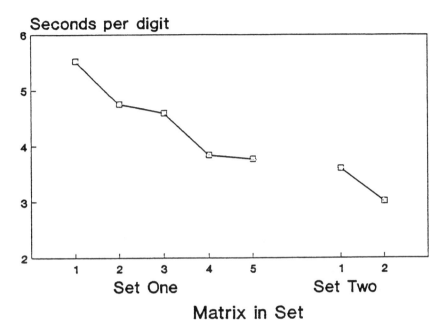

Figure 12.2. Rajan's Mean Time per Digit to Learn Each Group of Seven Matrices in the Original Matrix Set (Set One) and the New Matrix Set (Set Two) Presented 6 Months Later

speedup he demonstrated made it obvious that Rajan learned and maintained the specific skill needed in our matrix task.

In summary, Rajan's performance on the learning of number matrices provides evidence of the durability of his memory skill. Once Rajan increased his speed to learn the original matrices, he needed less time to learn later matrices. He did not need to relearn that particular skill.

The Specificity of Other Memorists' Skills

In addition to Rajan, there have been investigations of 15 other memorists. These investigations vary in sophistication, but most of them provide enough data to allow informed speculation about the specificity of the skill of these memorists. Seven of those memorists, like Rajan, show striking specificity in their skill. Five of them do not. The remaining three are difficult to characterize. One of them, Arnould, was used as a comparison subject (to Inaudi and Diamandi; Binet, 1894; see Brown and Deffenbacher, 1975, 1988) and was tested only on digits. Two others, Bergh (Hegge, 1918-1919) and Isihara (Susukita, 1933, 1934), performed on a variety of materials but worked with a single mnemonic system (the method of loci). We will begin our discussion with the seven memorists who demonstrated specific memory skills.

Memorists With Specific Memory Skills

Inaudi. Inaudi was a mental calculator who was studied by Binet (1894; see Brown & Deffenbacher, 1975, 1988). This memorist relied on auditory imagery to remember digits. Inaudi's level of performance was well above the normal digit span. His memory span was 25 digits when the digits were presented at a rate of one digit per second. Binet reported that Inaudi's skilled memory was limited to digits.

Diamandi. Diamandi was a mental calculator who used visual imagery to remember digits (Binet, 1894; see Brown & Deffenbacher, 1975, 1988). Although his ability to learn digits was above average, other memorists (e.g., Rajan and Inaudi) were at least three times faster at learning digit sequences. His performance on materials other than digits was average.

Finkelstein. Like Diamandi, the memorist Finkelstein (Sandor, 1932; Weinland, 1948) visualized digits written in his own handwriting on a mental chalkboard. He also claimed to use his knowledge of the properties of numbers to remember digit strings. His digit span was well above average. His visual digit span was 39 digits and his auditory digit span was 20 digits (Weinland, 1948). Finkelstein's skill was limited to digits. According to Sandor (1932), his letter span was average and his memory for visual forms was below average.

SF and DD. SF and DD were studied by Ericsson and Chase (Chase & Ericsson, 1981, 1982; Ericsson & Chase, 1982; Ericsson et al., 1980). Both of these individuals learned to increase their memory span from around 7 digits to over 80 digits with about 200-300 hours of practice. They learned to encode the digits as running times because both of them were long-distance runners. For example, the digits 4, 1, and 6 would be remembered as 4 minutes and 16 seconds (a very respectable time in which to run 1 mile). Their skill was specific to digits because their strategy was dependent on the relationship between running times and digits. Their skill did not cross over to other tasks such as learning word lists or even the apparently comparable task of letter memory span.

JC. Ericsson and Polson (1988) studied a waiter who could take up to 20 dinner orders without writing anything down. He would remember the orders by breaking them down into their various components. He would begin by grouping together all of the salad dressings by their first letter (e.g. t = Thousand Island, h = house). Next, he would list the starches (e.g. baked potato or fries). Lastly, he would group together the meat items by temperature (e.g., rare, well done).

Ericsson and Polson (1988) conducted an experiment to determine if JC's skill was specific to restaurant orders. The experimenters substituted categorized words from Battig and Montague's (1969) category norms for the food items. They chose each category based on its structural similarity to the food category with which it was paired. The results indicated that there was some transfer of the skill from food orders to the list of categorized words. The patterns of data for both groups looked similar. However, JC was able to learn the food orders more quickly than the categorized words. Therefore, there was some transfer of skill but not complete transfer. We would like to point out that because the categories were chosen for their similarity to the food items, JC could use his encoding strategy to remember the words.

In a second experiment on transfer of skill, the experimenters presented JC with words from categories that were not compatible with his mnemonic encoding process. According to Ericsson and Polson (1988), JC's performance was dramatically impaired but still superior to that of naïve college students. The experimenters argued that JC's "superior" performance provides evidence for the generalizability of his skill.

Ericsson and Polson (1988) conclude from their experiments that JC was able to generalize his skill to other tasks. This seems true, but the results also suggest that the transfer is quite limited. Because transfer to a task that was not designed to be extremely similar to the food-ordering task greatly impaired his performance, we conclude that his skill was fairly specific.

Bubbles P. Bubbles P. was a 33-year-old professional gambler at the time his memory was tested (Ceci, DiSimone, & Johnson, 1993). His digit span was 15-20 digits, which is outside the range of average performance. Bubbles was able to repeat the digits both forward and backward without any decrement in his performance. This level of performance is unusual in that most people's performance is halved when they are asked to repeat the digits backward. For example, the average college student's digit span is 8 digits for forward recall but only 4 digits for backward recall. Although we made no formal tests of Rajan's performance on recalling spans backward, we did observe that he could recall rows of matrices either forward or backward. However, unlike Bubbles, his performance on backward recall was slower than on forward recall. Bubbles's performance and strategies are very similar to those of Rajan. Rajan was also able to repeat digit strings both forward and backward. Both memorists encoded digits in a string or matrix according to the location of the digits within the string.

Bubbles's exceptional performance was limited to tasks involving digits or activities related to gambling. Bubbles performed well on the digit span task and learned number matrices quickly. He could also memorize matrices of playing cards. Bubbles was good at recognizing faces. He claimed he needed to be good at reading people's faces to do well in poker. On tasks involving memorizing words or other materials, his performance was unexceptional.

Memorists With General Memory Skills

Rückle. Müller (1911; see Brown & Deffenbacher, 1975, 1988) studied Rückle, a German memorist who used both visual imagery and meaningful associations when learning different types of material. Rückle studied the meaningful relationships between digits when performing the memory span task. His memory span was about 60 digits, which was similar to Rajan's level of performance.

Rückle's extraordinary memory extended beyond digits. He also had an excellent memory for nonsense syllables, colors, and nonsense figures. He reportedly used visual imagery on these nonnumerical tasks. Therefore, Rückle's extraordinary memory performance did not appear to be task specific.

Shereshevskii. Shereshevskii (S), perhaps the world's most famous memorist, was unaware of his unusual memory until he was referred to the Russian psychologist Luria by his employer. S used three processes to encode information into memory: mental imagery, creating stories with visual images, and the method of loci.

Luria (1968) claimed that Shereshevskii used visual imagery to remember matrices of numbers. Shereshevskii reported that he could "see" the matrix written on a chalkboard in his mind. If he could "read" the matrix off of his mental chalkboard then he should have been able to recite a column of the matrix as quickly as he recited a row. Luria's (1968) data are sparse but suggest that Shereshevskii was eight times faster at reciting rows than at reciting, say, the third column in a matrix. Thus, the claim that he used imagery to remember matrices is suspect.

It was also claimed that Shereshevskii created stories using strong visual images to remember abstract information, such as mathematical formulas. In one example, he described a complex formula as an old man with a cane walking by his house in the woods. Apparently, Shereshevskii was able to recall this formula 15 years later.

Lastly, Shereshevskii used the method of loci to remember lists of words. In this mnemonic technique one mentally places images in familiar locations and then retraces their "footsteps" to retrieve the items. He was very successful at using this technique to recall word lists but did not use it for digits.

Shereshevskii was able to learn many different types of information, including word lists, matrices of digits, and lists of nonsense words. It is evident that Shereshevskii's skill was not specific to a particular domain.

VP. VP was a memorist who gave exhibitions in which he played seven simultaneous games of chess while blindfolded. Hunt and Love (1972) tested VP on several different tasks ranging from recall of unusual stories to the digit span task. VP demonstrated greater recall on all the tasks than did the control subjects. His exceptional memory performance was based on verbal encoding of most material to be remembered. VP was fluent in four languages and had a reading knowledge of most European languages. VP's skill was versatile because he had a large database from which he could make associations with the material to be memorized.

TE. TE developed exceptional memory performance around the age of 15 when he read a book that described different mnemonic techniques. One technique that TE used was called the "figure-alphabet." In this phonetically based system, each digit is represented by a consonant sound or sounds (e.g., 3 = m, 4 = r, 5 = p or b). The vowels A, E, I, O, and U are used to help form words. A sequence of digits can be encoded as words. For example, the sequence "3495" can be encoded as the word "marble."

Gordon, Valentine, and Wilding (1984; Wilding & Valentine, 1985) conducted several experiments of TE's abilities. Their experiments indicate that TE's memory skills were not specific to just digits, but that he also displayed exceptional memory performance for stories and faces. TE used a repertoire of various mnemonics to achieve high levels of performance. TE was given many of the same tasks that Hunt and Love (1972) gave to VP. TE's performance on most of the tasks was either equal to or greater than that of VP.

Professor Aitken. One of the most interesting memorists to be studied was described by Hunter (1977). This versatile professor of mathematics was also an excellent violinist and mental calculator. Unlike the memorist TE, Aitken's extraordinary memory was not due to the use of mnemonics. Aitken coded information into memory by looking for meaningful or rhythmic patterns in the material he was studying. Aitken's memory span was 15 digits when the digits were presented visually at a rate of two digits per second. For auditory presentation, Aitken preferred that the digits be read at a rate of about five digits per second with a pause between each grouping. He mentioned that there was a rhythmic pattern when the digits were presented in this manner.

Aitken's search for meaningful or rhythmic patterns also included word lists. Hunter (1977) reported that Aitken was able to repeat a word list 28 years after it was given to him. He also wrote out the word list to show the rhythmic pattern in the words to Hunter. Aitken had a very good memory that was not task specific. He had many interests such as music that may have helped him to find meaningful, rhythmic patterns in the material that he studied. His interests, which he applied to many facets of his life, were not limited to one type of task.

Conclusions

We have examined the specificity, or lack thereof, of the memory skill of several memorists. We showed that Rajan Mahadevan's memory skill was specific to digits. Research on some other memorists (specifically, Inaudi, Diamandi, Finkelstein, SF and DD, JC, and Bubbles P.) also suggests that their memory skills were quite specific. In contrast, research on the memorists Rückle, Shereshevskii, VP, TE, and Aitken suggests that their skills were quite generalizable. One is tempted to speculate that memorists such as Rückle, Shereshevskii, and Aitken have naturally powerful memories, whereas those showing specific skills do not. The other possibility is that Aitken and others who show generalizable memory skill have simply developed a set of techniques to allow them to memorize a wide range of materials. Unfortunately, the data necessary to determine which of the two possibilities is correct do not exist.

We also provided evidence for the durability of Rajan's skill. As we demonstrated, Rajan's skill is quite durable. Insofar as we can determine, evidence does not exist for any of the other memorists that could distinguish between maintenance of memory skill and durability of memory skill. Thus, when we speculate about the general durability of memory skills, we are forced to draw on our experience with Rajan. With that caveat, we expect memory skill typically to be as specific and durable as other skills.

References

Bartlett, F. C. (1932). *Remembering: A study in experimental and social psychology*. London: Cambridge University Press.

Battig, W. F., & Montague, W. E. (1969). Category norms for verbal items in 56 categories: A replication and extension of the Connecticut category norms. *Journal of Experimental Psychology Monograph, 80* (3, Pt. 2).

Binet, A. (1894), *Psychologie des grandes calculateurs et jouers d'échecs*. Paris: Librarie Hachette.

Bousfield, W. A. (1953). The occurrence of clustering in the recall of randomly arranged associates. *Journal of General Psychology, 49*, 229-240.

Brown, E., & Deffenbacher, K. (1975). Forgotten mnemonists. *Journal of the History of the Behavioral Sciences, 11*, 342-349.

Brown, E., & Deffenbacher, K. (1988). Superior memory performance and mnemonic encoding. In L. K. Obler & D. Fein (Eds.), *The exceptional brain* (pp. 191-211). New York: Guilford.

Ceci, S., DiSimone, M. D., & Johnson, S. (1993). Memory in context: A case study of "Bubbles P.," a gifted but uneven memorizer. In D. Herrman, H. Weingartner, A. Searlman, & C. McEvoy (Eds.), *Memory improvement: Implications for memory theory* (pp. 169-186). New York: Springer-Verlag.

Chase, W. G., & Ericsson, K. A. (1981). Skilled memory. In J. R. Anderson (Ed.), *Cognitive skills and their acquisition* (pp. 141-180). Hillsdale, NJ: Lawrence Erlbaum.

Chase, W. G., & Ericsson, K. A. (1982). Skill and working memory. In G. H. Bower (Ed.), *The psychology of learning and motivation* (Vol. 16, pp. 1-58). New York: Academic Press

Ebbinghaus, H. (1964). *Memory: A contribution to experimental psychology* (H. Ruger & C. E. Bussenius, Trans.). New York: Dover. (Original work published 1885)

Ericsson, K. A. (1985). Memory skill. *Canadian Journal of Psychology, 39*, 188-231.

Ericsson, K. A. (1988). Analysis of memory performance in terms of memory skill. In R. J. Sternberg (Ed.), *Advances in the psychology of human intelligence* (Vol. 4, pp. 137-179). Hillsdale, NJ: Lawrence Erlbaum.

Ericsson, K. A., & Chase, W. G. (1982). Exceptional memory. *American Scientist, 70*, 607-615.

Ericsson, K. A., Chase, W. G., & Faloon, S. (1980). Acquisition of a memory skill, *Science, 208*, 1181-1182.

Ericsson. K. A., & Faivre, I. A. (1988). What's exceptional about exceptional abilities? In L. K. Obler & D. Fein (Eds.), *The exceptional brain* (pp. 436-473). New York: Guilford.

Ericsson, K. A., & Polson, P. G. (1988). A cognitive analysis of exceptional memory for restaurant orders. In M. Chi, R. Glaser, & M. Farr (Eds.), *The nature of expertise* (pp. 23-70). Hillsdale, NJ: Lawrence Erlbaum.

Gillund, G. & Shiffrin, R. M. (1984). A retrieval model for both recognition and recall. *Psychological Review, 91,* 1-67.

Gordon, P., Valentine, E., & Wilding, J. (1984). One man's memory: A study of a mnemonist. *British Journal of Psychology, 75,* 1-14.

Hanson, J. (1980, November). Numbers whiz tests limits of memory. *Report: A Publication for Faculty and Staff of the University of Minnesota,* pp. 6-7.

Hegge, T. (1918-1919). Beiträge zur analyse der Gedächtnistätigkeit, Über ungewöhnliche und illustrierende und lokalisierende Einprägung. *Zeitschrift für Psychologie, 84,* 349-352.

Horn, J. C. (1981, February). Memory II. *Psychology Today,* pp. 21, 80-81.

Hunt, E., & Love, T. (1972). How good can memory be? In A. W. Melton & E. Martin (Eds.), *Coding processes in human memory* (pp. 237-260). Washington, DC: John Wiley.

Hunter, I.M.L. (1977). An exceptional memory. *British Journal of Psychology, 68,* 155-164.

Kucera, H., & Francis, W. N. (1967). *Computational analysis of present-day American English.* Providence, RI: Brown University Press.

Luria, A. R. (1968). *The mind of a mnemonist.* New York: Basic Books.

Müller, G. (1911). Zur Analyse der Gedächtnistätigkeit und des Vorstellungsverlaufes, 1. *Zeitschrift für Psychologie,* Erganzungsband 5, pp. 1-567.

Osterrieth, P. A. (1944). Le test du copie d'une figure complexe. *Archives of Psychology Chicago, 30,* 206-356.

Pelligrino, J. W. (1971). A general measure of organization in free recall for variable unit size and internal sequential consistency. *Behavioral Research Methods and Instrumentation, 3,* 241-246.

Rey, A. (1942). L'examen psychologique dans les cas d'encephalopathie traumatique. *Archives of Psychology, 28,* 286-340.

Rice, G. E. (1980). On cultural schemata. *American Ethnologist, 7,* 152-171.

Roenker, D. L., Thompson, C. P., & Brown, S. C. (1971). Comparison of measures for the estimation of clustering in free recall. *Psychological Bulletin, 76,* 45-48.

Sandor, B. (1932). Die Gedächtnistätigkeit und Arbeitsweise von Rechenkünstlern. *Charakter, 1,* 47-50.

Shanks, D., & Wrench, J. W., Jr. (1962). Computation of pi to 100,000 decimals. *Mathematics of Computation, 16,* 76-99.

Strong, E. K., Jr. (1912). The effect of length of series upon recognition memory. *Psychological Review, 19,* 447-462.

Susukita, T. (1933). Untersuchung eines ausserordentlichen Gedächtnisses in Japan, 1. *Tohoku Psychologia Folia, 1,* 111-134.

Susukita, T. (1934). Untersuchung eines ausserordentlichen Gedächtnisses in Japan, 2. *Tohoku Psychologia Folia, 2,* 15-42.

Thompson, C. P., Cowan, T. M., & Frieman, J. (1993). *Memory search by a memorist.* Hillsdale, NJ: Lawrence Erlbaum.

Thompson, C. P., Cowan, T. M., Frieman, J., Mahadevan, R. S., Vogl, R. J., & Frieman, J. (1991). Rajan: A study of a memorist. *Journal of Memory and Language, 30,* 702-724.

Thompson, C. P., & Roenker, D. L. (1971). Learning to cluster. *Journal of Experimental Psychology, 91,* 136-139.

Tulving, E. (1962). Subjective organization in the free recall of "unrelated" words. *Psychological Review, 69,* 344-354.

Weinland, J. (1948). The memory of Salo Finkelstein. *Journal of General Psychology, 39,* 243-257.

Wilding, J., & Valentine, E. (1985). One man's memory for prose, faces, and names. *British Journal of Psychology, 76,* 215-219.

Author Index

Subject Index

About the Authors and Editors

Andrew L. Betz received his B.A. magna cum laude from Bowling Green State University and his M.A. and Ph.D. from Ohio State University. His research interests include the study of autobiographical memory, the effects of mental representations on social inference, and the study of social influences on memory.

Lyle E. Bourne, Jr., received his bachelor's degree at Brown University in 1953 and his Ph.D. in psychology from the University of Wisconsin in 1956. Currently, he is Professor of Psychology at the University of Colorado, Boulder. He was elected to membership in the Society of Experimental Psychologists in 1972 and received a Research Scientist Award from the National Institute of Health for the period 1971-1976. His scholarly interests reside largely in the area of human learning, memory, and cognitive processes. He is the author of over 100 journal articles, a dozen book chapters, and six books. He has been a member of the American Psychological Association since 1957, serving on its Council of Representatives, Board of Scientific Affairs, Publication Committee, and Council of Editors. He is past President of the Division of Experimental Psychology and currently acting President of the Federation of Behavioral, Psychological, and Cognitive Sciences.

Deborah M. Clawson is Assistant Professor of Psychology at the Catholic University of America in Washington, D.C. She received her B.A. in psychology and in computer science at Cornell University in 1985 and her M.A. (1992) and Ph.D. (1994) in psychology at the University of Colorado, Boulder. Prior to graduate school she was a computer systems analyst and education program manager for the U.S. Air Force. Her research is in the area of human learning and memory, focusing on the durability and specificity of skilled performance. She has explored these

353

issues in the domains of Stroop task performance, Morse code reception, and computer command production.

Robert J. Crutcher received his bachelor's degree from the University of California, Berkeley, in 1974 and his Ph.D. from the University of Colorado, Boulder, in 1992. He joined the faculty at the University of Illinois at Chicago in 1992 and is currently Assistant Professor in the Psychology Department. His research interests include human memory and learning, the development of cognitive skill and expertise, long-term retention of knowledge and skill, second language acquisition, and the use of verbal report methodologies in studying cognitive processes. He is also very interested in the use of cognitive research in improving human memory and cognition, especially in instructional settings.

Addie Dutta received her Ph.D. from Purdue University in 1993 and is now Assistant Professor of Psychology at Rice University. Her research interests include most aspects of human information processing, with a focus on skill acquisition and response selection. She is co-author of the text *Skill Acquisition and Human Performance* (with R. W. Proctor).

K. Anders Ericsson is FSCW/Conradi Eminent Scholar and Professor of Psychology at Florida State University. In 1976 he received his Ph.D. in psychology from the University of Stockholm, Sweden, followed by a postdoctoral fellowship at Carnegie-Mellon University. In 1980 he moved to the University of Colorado, Boulder, where he remained until 1992. His research with Herbert Simon on verbal reports of thinking is summarized in a book *Protocol Analysis: Verbal Reports as Data*, revised in 1993. With Bill Chase he developed the theory of skilled memory based on detailed analyses of acquired exceptional memory performance. Currently he studies the cognitive structure of expert performance in domains such as music, chess, and sports, and how expert performers acquire their superior performance by extended deliberate practice. In 1991 he published an edited book with Jacqui Smith, *Toward a General Theory of Expertise.*

David W. Fendrich received his Ph.D. from the University of Colorado in 1989. He is currently Assistant Professor at Widener University. His research interests include implicit memory, procedural memory, and the retention of skills.

Antoinette T. Gesi received her bachelor's degree magna cum laude from the University of Colorado, Boulder, in 1988. She is currently at the University of California, Santa Cruz, in the doctoral program in experimental psychology, where she received her master of science degree in 1991. She is co-author of four articles and two chapters in professional journals and books. Her research interests include memory and cognitive processes. Her current research involves reading comprehension in second language learning.

Alice F. Healy received her bachelor's degree from Vassar College in 1968 and her Ph.D. from the Rockefeller University in 1973. She was Assistant and then Associate Professor at Yale University from 1973 to 1981. She joined the faculty of the University of Colorado, Boulder, in 1981 as Associate Professor and was promoted to Professor in 1984. She is currently Chair Elect of the Psychology Division of the AAAS and President of the Rocky Mountain Psychological Association. She also served as Editor of *Memory & Cognition.* She is currently Principal Investigator of a contract from the Army Research Institute. She has published over 80 articles and chapters in professional journals and books, is co-author of *Cognitive Processes,* and is co-editor of *Essays in Honor of William K. Estes.* Her research interests include memory and cognitive processes, especially long-term retention, psycholinguistics, reading, and short-term memory.

Cheri L. King received her master of science degree in 1989 and her Ph.D. in general experimental psychology from Colorado State University in 1992. She is currently conducting postdoctoral research at the Institute of Cognitive Science and the Department of Psychology at the University of Colorado, Boulder. Her research activities in cognitive psychology have focused on categorization; the specificity and maintenance of skills; and spatial, temporal, and item memory. She is also involved in the development of interactive multimedia courseware for use in teaching and research in psychology.

Steen F. Larsen received his B.A. from the University of Copenhagen. He received his M.A. from the University of Aarhus, as well as his Gold Medal (equivalent to the Ph.D.) in psychology and psycholinguistics in 1972. He has been a Fulbright Visiting Scholar, residing at Emory University in 1984. He is currently Docent (Senior Associate Professor) and Deputy Chair at the Institute of Psychology, University of Aarhus. His research interests focus on memory in naturalistic and applied settings, including autobiographical memory, memory for mass media events, and "flashbulb" memory. These interests also extend more broadly to the study of literary fiction, schizophrenia, depression, and aging.

William R. Marmie is a graduate student who received his master's degree from the University of Colorado in 1993. He is currently working on his Ph.D. His interests include comparative psychology and cognitive psychology. He began his career working on the behavior of captive-raised rattlesnakes, and his general interest in herpetology resulted in a week-long lizard chase in Texas in 1991 that uncovered a new lizard hybrid. In cognitive psychology, his work on everyday memory for common objects resulted in the insight that intentional study plays a larger role in memory for the details of everyday objects than was previously thought. He is the sole author of an article in press describing a classroom demonstration for an introductory cognitive psychology course. He is a student member of the American Psychological Association and the Society for Mathematical Psychology.

Danielle S. McNamara received her bachelor's degree in linguistics at the University of Kansas in 1982, a master's degree in clinical psychology at the Wichita State University in 1989, and a Ph.D. in cognitive psychology from the University of Colorado in 1992. Prior to graduate school in psychology, she taught English as a second language for 5 years. She is currently funded by the McDonnell Foundation Fellowship Program to work with Dr. Walter Kintsch as a postdoctoral Research Associate at the University of Colorado. Her research centers primarily on the topics of memory, learning, and text comprehension. She investigates these issues within various domains, including multiplication skill acquisition, foreign vocabulary learning, learning from instructional texts, and expertise in computer languages.

Janet D. Proctor earned her Ph.D. in experimental psychology at the University of Texas, Arlington. She is an Assistant Professor in the Department of Psychological Sciences at Purdue University. Her research interests include pattern recognition and attention, with a particular focus on the effects of experience on the nature and quality of processing.

Robert W. Proctor received his Ph.D. from the University of Texas, Arlington, in 1975 and is now Professor of Psychology at Purdue University. He is currently editor of *Behavior Research Methods, Instruments, and Computers,* and he served as associate editor of *Memory & Cognition* 1986-1993. He is co-author of the text *Human Factors in Simple and Complex Systems* (with T. Van Zandt) and co-editor of the book *Stimulus-Response Compatibility: An Integrated Perspective* (with T. G. Reeve).

Timothy C. Rickard is currently Research Fellow at the Cognitive Neuroscience Section of the National Institutes of Health. He received a B.S. in mechanical engineering and an M.S. in applied statistics at the University of Alabama and a Ph.D. in cognitive psychology from the University of Colorado. His research interests are in the general areas of mathematical cognition, skill acquisition, and memory. He has published in several leading psychological journals and book series, including the *Journal of Experimental Psychology: Learning, Memory, and Cognition, Cognitive Brain Research,* and *The Psychology of Learning and Motivation.*

Vivian I. Schneider received her bachelor's degree from Metropolitan State College of Denver in 1972. She received her M.A. (1988) and her Ph.D. (1991) in psychology from the University of Colorado. She is currently a postdoctoral Research Associate at the University of Colorado, working with Dr. Alice Healy and Dr. Lyle Bourne Jr. on second language acquisition. Previous work has included the study of some of the processes involved in reading and memory and skill acquisition.

Grant P. Sinclair received his bachelor's degree in psychology from the University of Colorado, Boulder, in 1983, and his master's degree and Ph.D. from the University of Colorado, Boulder, in 1986 and 1991, respectively. He has conducted research in a variety of areas including text comprehension and memory, the size of the unit of perception in reading, and the acquisition and long-term retention of trained skills. He is currently a postdoctoral Research Associate at the University of Colorado and is investigating the effects of gender and peace agreements on responses by subjects to varying levels and conditions of international conflict.

John J. Skowronski is currently Associate Professor of Psychology at the Ohio State University, and he resides at the Newark Campus. His M.A. and Ph.D. are from the University of Iowa. His research specialty is social cognition. In addition to his research into autobiographical memory and event dating, his recent work includes the study of spontaneous social inferences using an implicit memory paradigm, differences in social information processing and impression formation between mild depressives and nondepressives, and the possible memory and impression differences produced by implicit versus explicit social information processing.

Charles P. Thompson received his B.S. from Wisconsin State College, Eau Claire, in 1958 and his Ph.D. from the University of Wisconsin in 1962. He began his professional career at the University of Wyoming, where he learned to appreciate mountains and trout fishing. In 1965, he moved to his current position as Professor of Psychology at Kansas State University. His research specialty is memory, with recent emphasis on autobiographical memory, voice identification, and extraordinary memory.

Rodney J. Vogl is a graduate student in cognitive psychology at Kansas State University. He received his B.S. from the University of Iowa in 1988 and his M.S. from Kansas State University in 1994. His research interests currently include autobiographical memory, the generation effect, source confusion, and extraordinary memory.

William T. Wittman is a Lieutenant Colonel in the United States Air Force where he has worked as a Behavioral Scientist since 1980. His initial assignments included providing psychological counseling to Air Force basic trainees and working organizational psychology issues, specifically performance evaluation of officers and enlisted personnel. In 1989 he completed a doctoral program in cognitive psychology at the University of Colorado, Boulder. His dissertation research explored long-term retention of spatial information. This was followed by a teaching assignment at the United States Air Force Academy, where he continued his study of long-term memory. In 1993 he was assigned to his current position in the Air Force's Armstrong Laboratory, where he is involved in research addressing human factors in the design and performance of aircraft systems.